THE PRACTICE AND THEORY OF SCHOOL IMPROVEMENT

This volume is part of a set of four. These volumes together form the *International Handbook of Educational Change,* which was originally published in 1998 as volume 5 in the Springer International Handbooks of Education series (formerly known as Kluwer International Handbooks of Education series), and edited by Andy Hargreaves, Ann Lieberman, Michael Fullan and David Hopkins.

The Table of Contents of the entire *International Handbook of Educational Change* has been printed at the end of this volume.

The Practice and Theory of School Improvement

International Handbook of Educational Change

Edited by:

David Hopkins

Department for Education and Skills, London, U.K.

 Springer

A C.I.P. Catalogue record for this book is available from the Library of Congress.

The Roots of Educational Change: ISBN-10 1-4020-3289-7
Extending Educational Change: ISBN-10 1-4020-3291-9
Fundamental Change: ISBN-10 1-4020-3292-7
The Practice and Theory of School Improvement: ISBN-10 1-4020-3290-0
Set: ISBN-10 1-4020-3423-7
The Roots of Educational Change: ISBN-13 978-1-4020-3289-9
Extending Educational Change: ISBN-13 978-1-4020-3291-2
Fundamental Change: ISBN-13 978-1-4020-3292-9
The Practice and Theory of School Improvement: ISBN-13 978-1-4020-3290-5
Set: ISBN-13 978-1-4020-3423-7
Springer Dordrecht, Berlin, Heidelberg, New York

The volumes can be purchased separately and as a set.

Published by Springer,
P.O. Box 17, 3300 AA Dordrecht, The Netherlands.

springeronline.com

Printed in the Netherlands.

Table of Contents

ANDY HARGREAVES, ANN LIEBERMAN, MICHAEL FULLAN AND DAVID HOPKINS
International Handbook of Educational Change - Introduction   vii

Introduction: Tensions in and Prospects for School Improvement   1

I. Towards a Theory of School Development

PER DALIN
Developing the Twenty-First Century School: A Challenge to
   Reformers   25

KAREN SEASHORE LOUIS
Reconnecting Knowledge Utilization and School Improvement:
   Two Steps Forward, One Step Back   40

JAAP SCHEERENS
The School Effectiveness Knowledge Base as a Guide for School
   Improvement   62

II. The Contemporary Context of School Improvement

ROLF LANDER AND MATS EKHOLM
School Evaluation and Improvement: A Scandinavian View   85

PETER CUTTANCE
Quality Assurance Reviews as a Catalyst for School Improvement in
   Australia   101

BETTY LOU WHITFORD AND KEN JONES
Assessment and Accountability in Kentucky: How High Stakes Affects
   Teaching and Learning   129

III. Tensions and Contrasts in School Improvement Strategies

MIKE WALLACE
Innovations in Planning for School Improvement: Problems and
   Potential   147

GARY MCCULLOCH
Curriculum Reform, Educational Change, and School Improvement   169

BRUCE JOYCE AND EMILY CALHOUN
The Conduct of Inquiry on Teaching: The Search for Models more
   Effective than the Recitation   182

JOHN SMYTH
Three Rival Versions and a Critique of Teacher Staff Development   208

JENNIFER NIAS
Why Teachers Need their Colleagues: A Developmental Perspective   223

IV The Effectiveness of School Improvement Strategies

DAVID REYNOLDS
"World Class" School Improvement: An Analysis of the Implications
   of Recent International School Effectiveness and School
   Improvement Research for Improvement Practice   241

EMILY CALHOUN AND BRUCE JOYCE
"Inside-Out" and "Outside-In": Learning from Past and Present
   School Improvement Paradigms   252

ROBERT SLAVIN
Sands, Bricks, and Seeds: School Change Strategies and Readiness for
   Reform   265

SAM STRINGFIELD, MARY ANN MILLSAP, AND REBECCA HERMAN
Using "Promising Programs" to Improve Educational Processes and
   Student Outcomes   280

International Handbook of Educational Change - Table of Contents   305

International Handbook of Educational Change - Introduction

ANDY HARGREAVES

Department of Teacher Education, Curriculum and Instruction Lynch School of Education, Boston College, MA, U.S.A.

ANN LIEBERMAN

Carnegie Foundation for the Advancement of Teaching, Stanford, CA, U.S.A.

MICHAEL FULLAN

Ontario Institute for Studies in Education, University of Toronto, Canada

DAVID HOPKINS

Department for Education and Skills, London, U.K.

This set of four volumes on *Educational Change* brings together evidence and insights on educational change issues from leading writers and researchers in the field from across the world. Many of these writers, whose chapters have been specially written for these books, have been investigating, helping initiate and implementing educational change, for most or all of their lengthy careers. Others are working on the cutting edge of theory and practice in educational change, taking the field in new or even more challenging directions. And some are more skeptical about the literature of educational change and the assumptions on which it rests. They help us to approach projects of understanding or initiating educational change more deeply, reflectively and realistically.

Educational change and reform have rarely had so much prominence within public policy, in so many different places. Educational change is ubiquitous. It figures large in Presidential and Prime Ministerial speeches. It is at or near the top of many National policy agendas. Everywhere, educational change is not only a policy priority but also major public news. Yet action to bring about educational change usually exceeds people's understanding of how to do so effectively.

The sheer number and range of changes which schools are now confronting is staggering.

Educators have always had to engage with educational changes of one sort or another. But other than in the last three decades or so, these changes were infrequent and episodic and they never really affected or even addressed the core of how teachers taught (Cuban, 1984). The changes were in things like how subjects were organized, how grade levels were clustered together into different school types, or how groups of students were divided between different schools or integrated within them according to ability, gender or race. Thus when educational

D. Hopkins (ed.), The Practice and Theory of School Improvement, vii-xi.
© 2005 *Springer. Printed in the Netherlands.*

historians chastise contemporary change advocates for ignoring the existence of educational change in the past and for exaggerating current crises and change demands "as a marketing device to promote the new possibilities of education in a new century, designed to appeal to consumers of different kinds who are grown weary of the old familiar product" (McCulloch, 1997), they are only partially right. While educational change has always been with us in some sense or other (as also, of course, has educational continuity), many of the changes are very different now, in both their substance and their form.

Since the 1960s, educational change has became a familiar part of teachers' work, and has more directly addressed issues of what teachers teach and how they should teach it. Following the launch of Sputnik and the emergence of post-war egalitarian ideals, public education has been treated as a crucible of technological and economic advancement and as a creator of greater social justice. In the 1960s and 70s, teachers in many countries had to deal with the rhetoric and sometimes the reality of curriculum innovation in mathematics, science and the humanities. They saw students stay in school longer, the ability ranges of their classes grow wider and the walls of their classrooms come down and then go up again just a few years later. Successive waves of different approaches to reading or mathematical learning swept through their classrooms, each one washing away the marks left by its predecessors.

It was in these times of educational expansion and optimism that educational change really began in earnest - as also did the study of it. From the late 1960s and early 1970s, researchers like Matt Miles, Per Dalin, Lou Smith, Neil Gross, Lawrence Stenhouse and Seymour Sarason studied the growing phenomenon of educational innovation - whether in the shape of large-scale curriculum projects and packages, or in the form of newly-created innovative schools. They showed how and why large-scale curriculum innovations rarely progressed beyond the phase of having their packages purchased or "adopted" to the point where they were implemented fully and faithfully, and could bring about real changes in classroom practice. At the same time, they also revealed how the promise of exceptional innovative schools usually faded over time as their staffs grew older, their charismatic leaders left, and the system withdrew permission for them to break the rules.

As the limitations of large-scale curriculum innovations became apparent, educators began to treat the individual school as the centre or focal point of educational change efforts. School-based curriculum development, and school-based staff development initiatives proliferated in many places, instead of development being imposed or initiated from faraway.

Research on what made teachers effective in their classrooms also expanded to address what made schools effective or ineffective as a whole, and as lists of effective schools characteristics were discovered (such as creating a safe and orderly environment for learning, or setting and checking homework regularly), these were sometimes then used as administrative blueprints to try and make particular schools become more effective over time. Many districts or other administrative authorities initiated "effective schools" projects on this basis. Some schools and districts supplemented and sometimes supplanted this science of school effectiveness with a more loosely defined and humanistically interpreted art of school improvement - the process of how to help schools and their staffs become more effective through setting clear goals, creating staff involvement, measuring progress over time and so forth.

Ironically, this approach to school improvement was then translated back into a rational science by many educational systems. It was treated as a process of planned or managed change that schools could be moved through step-by-step, stage-by-stage, guided by the school's improvement team that its region or district mandated it to have.

When these various school-centred changes and improvements didn't work well enough or fast enough (and sometimes even when they did), impatient educational administrators (and American urban school superintendents with an average job tenure of less than two years can be very impatient indeed), imposed their own reform requirements instead. So too did ideologically driven politicians, whose agendas of educational reform have often been shaped by the desire to create public indignation (which they promise their measures will then answer), or by the private idiosyncrasies of their own educational pasts, (which their reforms are meant to cherish or purge).

This quarter century or more of educational change processes and initiatives that have been meant to alter learning and teaching in our schools, has left us with a mixed legacy. On the one hand, studies of what works and what doesn't across all the different change strategies have created a truly powerful knowledge base about the processes, practices and consequences of educational change. During this period, research studies have shown, for example, how educational change moves through distinctive stages of initiation, implementation and institutionalization; how people who encounter changes go through successive "stages of concern" about how those changes will affect them; and how people respond very differently to educational change initiatives depending on what point they have reached in their own lives and careers.

Some of the research findings on educational change have even been accorded the status of generalizable rules or `lessons' of change. These include the maxims that practice changes before beliefs, that successful change is a product of both pressure and support, that evolutionary planning works better than linear planning and so forth (these `lessons' have been synthesized especially effectively by Michael Fullan, 1991, 1993).

So extensive is the current knowledge base of educational change that it has come to constitute a field of study in its own right - drawing on and transcending the disciplines of sociology, psychology, history and philosophy, as well as the fields of curriculum and educational administration. In a way, educational change has now really come of age - but while this is a significant academic achievement, it is also where the problems of the field - the second part of its legacy - also begin.

Our experience of educational change today is stretching far beyond our experience, knowledge and investigations of it in times gone by. While the existing knowledge-base of educational change is impressive, it is no longer really sufficient to address the unique change problems and challenges that educators confront today.

Contemporary patterns of educational change present educators with changes that are multiple, complex and sometimes contradictory. And the change demands with which educators have to deal, seem to follow one another at an increasingly frenetic speed. A typical primary or elementary school these days may be considering a new reading program, developing cooperative learning strategies, thinking about how to implement new computers, designing a better parent newsletter, and trialling portfolio assessments all at the same time. The portfolio assessments favoured by the region or the district may have to be reconciled with imposed standardized test requirements by the nation or the state. A push to develop a more integrated curriculum and to recognize children's multiple intelligences may be reversed by a newly elected government's commitments to more conventionally defined learning standards within existing academic subjects.

All this can make teachers and administrators feel that the systems in which they are working aren't just complex but downright chaotic. This chaos is partly inherent in societies and organizations where information circulates and decisions are made with increasing speed. It is also the result of educational policy constantly being shaped and altered by different and competing interest groups in an ideological battle for the minds of the young. And sometimes it even results from a kind of *manufactured uncertainty* that more than a few governments wilfully create to arouse panic, to set pretexts for their policy interventions and to keep educators and everyone else off-balance.

Few of the existing theories and strategies of educational change equip educators to cope effectively with these complex, chaotic and contradictory environments

- Rational theories of planned change that move through predictable stages of implementation or 'growth' are poorly suited to schools where unexpected twists and turns are the norm rather than the exception in the ways they operate.
- The conventional academic and behavioural outcomes that defined the core of what an effective school should produce in the past are outdated in an age where many people now clamour for schools to develop higher-order thinking skills, problem-solving capacities, and the habits of collaboration and teamwork. Complex as the world of education is, people expect more and more from it, and the effective schools of the past cannot deliver what many expect of schools today.
- Theories and models that helped educators know how (and how not) to implement single curriculum innovations are of little use to schools where innovations are multiple and priorities compete.

While we have learned a lot about how to improve individual schools or small clusters of schools with additional resources, exceptional leaders, the ability to attract or shed particular kinds of staff members, and discretion to break the rules; we are only just beginning to understand the challenges of scaling reform up from small samples of improving schools, to entire school systems. The existing knowledge base of school improvement has shown us how to create islands of improvement, but has been less helpful in assisting people to make archipelagoes from islands, and still less in showing them how to build entire continents of change.

It is time, therefore, to reflect at some length about what we already know and have learned about educational change and to explore how the field can and should be pushed further, to help educators understand and deal effectively with the immensely complex change problems that are customary today. Each of the four volumes on *Educational Change* addresses these fundamental issues in its own distinctive way.

REFERENCES

Cuban, L. (1984). *How teachers taught: Constancy and change in American classrooms, 1890-1980.* New York: Longman.

Fullan, M. (1991). *The new meaning of educational change.* New York: Teachers College Press.

Fullan, M. (1993). *Change forces.* London: Falmer Press.

McCulloch, G. (1997). Marketing the millennium: Education for the twenty-first century. In A. Hargreaves, & R. Evans (Eds.), *Beyond educational reform.* Buckingham: Open University Press.

Introduction

Tensions in and Prospects for School Improvement

DAVID HOPKINS[1]

Department for Education and Skills, London, U.K.

The purpose of this volume of the International Handbook is to review current theories of school development, the evolution of school improvement as a strategy of educational change over the past 30 years, and to critique current theories of development and strategies for growth from a variety of different national contexts. In this introductory chapter the editor outlines the historical development and definitions of school improvement as a strategy for educational change, surveys school improvement practice, assesses the differential impact of school improvement strategies and their links to student achievement and provides an overview of the volume.

Those of us who spend much of our professional lives labouring in that part of the Educational Change vineyard known as "school improvement" have recently been celebrating. For decades now we have been the poor relations of the field, tolerated, talked to at parties, but not really regarded as being a main player. But as Western societies have in recent years grappled with the challenges of economic growth and social dislocation, our particular contribution to educational change has increasingly been recognised as important. As societies continue to set educational goals that are, on current performance, beyond the capacity of the system to deliver, those whose work focuses on strategies for enhancing student learning through school and classroom intervention are taken more seriously. The phrase "school improvement" is now an established part of the educational lexicon; it features in governmental policy, university professors become expert in it, educational conferences focus on it, and even schools are becoming familiar with the rhetoric surrounding it.

The emergence of school improvement from the shadows is to many of us however a mixed blessing. As with any new idea, much is expected of it, particularly from politicians desperately seeking for simple solutions to complex problems. School improvement's time in the sun will be short lived unless it can persuade its new found friends that it is not a "quick fix" response to educational change, and that the challenge of enhancing student achievement requires a purposeful and strategic response. Many of the educational initiatives that have been recently spawned under the school improvement umbrella are simply tinkering at the edges. Governments whose policies emphasise accountability and managerial change, fail to realise that if teachers knew how to teach more effectively they would have changed by themselves decades ago. Blaming teachers and delegating financial

D. Hopkins (ed.), The Practice and Theory of School Improvement, 1-21.
© 2005 *Springer. Printed in the Netherlands.*

responsibility have little positive impact on classroom practice. Similarly, Heads or Principals that restrict their influence to bureaucratic intervention and ignore the 'learning level' should not be surprised when student achievement scores fail to rise. Successful school improvement projects, such as Robert Slavin's "Success For All" literacy programme for elementary age students, involve not simply the introduction of a well designed curriculum and instructional programme, but also a virtual redesign of the school to focus on student learning (Slavin et al., 1996).

At the same time as pressure on schools and school systems have increased, so too has the context of schooling changed dramatically. In most Western educational systems there has been a move from a somewhat paternalistic approach to education to a situation where schools are not only encouraged, but are increasingly required, to take responsibility for their own development. The emphasis on self improvement has increased in the past decade with the trend in most Western countries of decentralising the responsibility for the implementation of educational reform, whilst at the same time decreasing the level of support to schools from external agencies. Alongside this increase in political pressure for institutional renewal, there has been a steady realisation that traditional strategies for educational change are not working. In recent years it has become starkly apparent that as strategies for educational reform, neither centralisation nor decentralisation work and that a better way must be found (Fullan & Miles, 1992).

It is against this background that contemporary approaches to school improvement need to be examined. In exploring the tensions in and prospects for school improvement, this volume of the International Handbook of Educational Change harnesses the perspectives of – in section one, theory and research; in section two, contemporary national policy contexts; in section three, a range of school improvement strategies; and in section four, contemporary research and evaluations of school improvement approaches – to help chart a way forward. The purpose of this editorial introduction is to:

- provide a robust and accessible definition of school improvement
- describe the three sources of school improvement theory and practice
- survey contemporary school improvement practice
- locate the contents of this volume within this context and raise a series of key issues for school improvement as we move into a new century.

DEFINING SCHOOL IMPROVEMENT

There are two senses in which the phrase *school improvement* is generally used. The first is the common sense meaning which relates to general efforts to make schools better places for pupils and students to learn. This is a sensible interpretation of the phrase and its most common usage. In this volume of the International Handbook however, I am principally concerned with a second more technical or specific way in which the phrase is used. In this sense school improvement is a distinct approach to educational change that enhances student outcomes *as well as* strengthening the school's capacity for managing change. School improvement is about raising student achievement through focusing on the teaching – learning process and the conditions which support it. It is about strategies for improving the schools capacity for providing quality education in times of change. It is not about blindly accepting the edicts of a centralised policies, and striving to implement these directives uncritically. But even this more specific definition is open to differing interpretations (see Hopkins et al., 1994, Chapter 1).

Roland Barth (1990) in his book *Improving Schools from Within*, distinguishes between two different approaches to school improvement that rest on sets of very different assumptions. He describes the dominant approach as being predicated on a set of assumptions that has led to an approach to school reform that is based on a proliferation of 'lists'. There are lists of the characteristics of the 'effective' school, teacher, and pupil, lists of minimum competencies, lists of regulations, performance indicators and so on. What is dangerous and self defeating about this view of the world is the mind set that informs it. Inherent in the approach is a set of assumptions about people, how they feel, how they should behave and about how organisations work. It is an approach that encourages someone to do something to someone else: it is about control rather than growth. The argument is less against lists than the values that inform them. Lists can be helpful when they are used to inform action; but even then, they need to be negotiated and subject to the teacher's (or school's) judgement.

Barth then argues for basing school reform on the skills, aspirations and energy of those closest to the school: teachers, senior management, governors and parents. He argues that a such a 'community of learners' approach school improvement from a radically different set of assumptions than those of the list makers. These assumptions are (Barth, 1990, p. 45 *my italics*):

- Schools have the capacity to improve themselves, if the *conditions* are right. A major responsibility of those outside the school is to help provide these conditions for those inside.
- When the need and purpose is there, when the conditions are right, adults and students alike learn and each energises and contributes to the learning of the other.
- What needs to be improved about schools is their *culture*, the quality of interpersonal relationships, and the nature and quality of learning experiences.
- School improvement is an effort to determine and provide, from without and within, conditions under which the adults and youngsters who inhabit schools will promote and sustain learning among themselves.

These assumptions neatly capture the essence of the approach to school improvement taken in this volume of the International Handbook. Barth's assumptions lead to some liberating ways of thinking about change. Schools, and those who live out their daily lives within them, are no longer the "victims" of change, but can take more control of the process. By using the opportunity of external change as a stimulus, and by taking advantage of external support and the evidence of good practice and research, they can subject the specificities of change to their own professional scrutiny and judgement in the pursuit of enhanced learning for their students. As I hope will become clear in the pages that follow, these by and large are the values that are embodied in the approach to school improvement taken by the contributors to this volume of the International Handbook.

SOURCES OF SCHOOL IMPROVEMENT

The aspiration to establish the appropriate contexts in which to enhance learning is as old as civilisation itself. Constraints of both space and scholarship however preclude such a discussion here. Ironically, it is also surprising to realise, as Fullan (1991, p. 5) has also pointed out, how short is the history of serious investigation into the change process and improvement in schools. I will therefore confine myself to some comments on what I see to be the three main contributors to current approaches to school improvement. As brief as such a discussion will be, I believe that it is necessary in order to fully understand the tensions in and prospects for contemporary school improvement. The three sources of contemporary school improvement reflect innovations and strategies that focus on:

- curriculum and instruction
- organisation development
- decentralisation of decision making.

The tensions inherent in contemporary school improvement is that advocates of each of these domains regard them as being sufficient in themselves, which they patently are not. The prospect for school improvement is the synergy created by their integration. This is the theme that will be pursued in various guises throughout the remainder of this introductory chapter.

Curriculum and Instruction

Many date the beginning of the modern period of educational reform back to the successful launch of Sputnik in the old USSR in October 1957. This signal achievement shattered the complacency of the American dream and heralded an unprecedented expenditure on education. This investment led to the "decade of curriculum reform" where from the mid 1960's onwards the major focus of innovation was on the *adoption of curriculum materials*. On both sides of the Atlantic the curriculum reform movement was intended to have a major impact on student achievement through the production and dissemination of exemplary curriculum materials.

Although the materials were often of high quality – being produced by teams of designers, academics and psychologists – in the main, they failed to have an impact on teaching. The reason in hindsight is obvious; teachers were not included in the production process and the staff development that accompanied the new curricula was often perfunctory and rudimentary. Teachers, of course, got their own back. The imaginative educational archaeologist will to this day find partly rifled packs of curriculum materials among the cobwebs at the back of stock rooms and store cupboards. Teachers took what they thought was of use from the materials and integrated them into their own teaching. The curriculum as an innovation, however, was consequently subverted.

In Britain, the materials emanating from the Schools' Council in the late 60's (see Stenhouse, 1980, for a comprehensive account of these projects) experienced a similar fate. Although the Schools' Council curriculum projects involved teachers and some had attendant in-service schemes, they were still conceived within a 'top-down' or 'centre periphery' model of educational change. Few of these projects paid anything more than lip-service to the essential connection between teaching style and curriculum development (Hopkins, 1987a).

Three conclusions can be drawn from this brief analysis. The first is that to many, the principal agent for educational reform is the curriculum. This is still the dominant orthodoxy in many educational systems. Second, the failure of the curriculum reform movement to positively affect levels of student achievement is usually attributed to a failure in implementation. It became increasingly apparent that 'top-down' models of change did not work, that teachers required inservice training to acquire new knowledge and skills, and that implementation does not occur spontaneously as a result of legislative fiat. The third conclusion that was not entirely apparent at the time, is that a curriculum however good cannot impact directly on student learning. To affect learning, the curriculum as artefact has to be mediated through a process of instruction. As a number of the contributions to this volume will demonstrate, it is the ways in which teachers teach – create powerful contexts for learning – that lead to enhanced levels of student achievement.

Organisation Development

The second source of influence on contemporary school improvement practice is *organisation development* (OD). One can trace the development of organisation development back to the social psychological writings and practice of Kurt Lewin (1946) with his emphasis on the influence of the organisation on the behaviour of its members, and the popularisation of 'action research' as *the* research methodology for social action and emancipation (Hopkins 1994). In the sixties, it was Matthew Miles (1967) who among others advocated the adaptation of OD techniques to schools. Later, Miles' (1975) seminal paper on 'organisational health', and the publication of OD in Schools by Schmuck and Miles (1971) provided the first mature expression of the impact of OD in education. A decade later, in a 'State of the Art' paper, Fullan et al. (1980) concluded that OD in schools had 'diffused to a larger extent than we and others had realised'.

Of the various OD strategies described in the research literature survey or data feedback is "the only treatment associated with substantial improvement" (Bowers 1973, p. 21). As Bowers (1973, p. 45) notes, "where the survey feedback is employed with skill and experience, it becomes a sophisticated tool for using the data as a springboard to development." When used in the educational context, most OD advocates suggested the use of a survey feedback, problem solving and collective decision making design. This approach aids goal clarification by giving information on what the staff of a school perceive as goals; its design improves information flow and communication, encourages adaptation, and creates a climate for consensual decision making; finally, the follow-through phase presents a model for problem solving that can be internalised and used as a resource in the future.

An example of a well developed approach to institutional self renewal based on OD techniques is found in the work of Richard Schmuck and Philip Runkel (1985). Schmuck (1984, p. 29) views the capacity for problem solving in a school to be constituted of a series of meta-skills – systematic diagnosis, searching for information and resources, mobilising collaborative action, 'synergy', and the staff's ability to evaluate effectiveness of the previous meta-skills. It is on such approaches to OD in schools that much of the process emphasis in school improvement interventions is based.

Three conclusions can also be drawn from this brief analysis. First, OD approaches emphasise the importance of a school's organisational health. Second and consequently, a major emphasis in many school improvement interventions is based on an approach that attempts to humanise the organisational context within which teachers and students live. Third, and possibly under emphasised at the time, was the empirical support given to the effectiveness of intervention strategies that diagnosed the internal conditions of the organisation as a precursor to development.

Decentralisation of Decision Making

The third source of influence concerns the amount of development expected of schools in most Western countries that has increased exponentially over the past decade or two. This increase in expectations has been accompanied on an international scale by fundamental changes in the ways schools are managed and governed. Most developed countries now face the contradictory pressures of centralisation and decentralisation i.e. increased government control over policy and direction versus more responsibility for implementation, resource management and evaluation at a local level. This tension has made the task of implementing school change both complex and challenging. The task of balancing centrally derived change and locally developed improvement has proved in practice most difficult.

A report by the Organisation for Economic Co-operation and Development (OECD) on decentralisation and school improvement outlined three principle reasons for such difficulties (OECD, 1989, p. 2):

- The decentralisation of decision making as part of school improvement establishes new roles and responsibilities for senior education officials at the centre and for school leaders, teachers and parents at the school level. As new roles are assumed, tensions inevitably develop. Approaches need to be put in place to respond to these tensions.
- Shifts of responsibility to the school raise the possibility that some functions, formerly carried out at the centre, will not be effectively performed. Central authorities need to ensure, through guidance and support for pre-service, in service and community based programmes, that those new roles have developed the capacity to meet their new responsibilities. External support for schools, re-orientated to meet specific school defined needs, must also be sustained (even if the services are no longer provided by central authorities).
- The management of change, whether at the centre or at the school level, requires a strategy which considers change as a dynamic and evolutionary process. Following from a clear vision of the expected results of change, the strategy should anticipate tensions and difficulties but also allow for adaptations and adjustments as the change proceeds.

This last point raises the important issue of selecting strategies for school change which allow for *adaptation and adjustment* within the change process. This implies that strategies for school improvement should be flexible enough to suit different school development and change needs. However, as a number of contributors to this volume emphasise, many school improvement interventions fail to recognise, or respond to, differential school development needs.

The three conclusions to be drawn from this brief analysis are: the general response to the increase in the amount of change expected of schools is a widespread policy of decentralisation; second and consequently, the self renewing school and the strategies for achieving it, has become a major focus of school improvement efforts; and third, a failure to recognise that simply changing bureaucratic procedures or holding people more accountable *does not by itself* improve the quality of education for students.

Although it may be helpful conceptually and strategically to think of these three sources of school improvement as distinct, they need to coalesce in order to impact on student learning. Unfortunately, as we shall see in later chapters, many school improvement policies and practices tend to emphasise one at the expense of the others. This myopia stands in contrast to the research base, and the evidence of effective school improvement strategies developed in the mid eighties and early nineties. It is to these perspectives that we turn in the following section.

Contemporary Perspectives on School Improvement

At the level of strategy and research, rather than policy and practice, attempts were made during the eighties and early nineties by individuals and groups to generate synergy between the three sources of school improvement noted above. A major impetus to the development of school improvement as a strategic response to the challenge of educational change was given by the OECD through its Centre for Educational research and development (CERI), who between 1982 and 1986 sponsored an International School Improvement Project (ISIP). ISIP built on previous OECD/CERI initiatives such as The Creativity of the School (Nisbet 1973) and the INSET (Hopkins, 1986) projects. At a time when the educational system as a whole faced not only retrenchment but also pressure for change, a project that focused on school improvement – at change at the meso level, at strategies for strengthening the school's capacity for problem solving, at making the school more reflexive to change, as well as enhancing the teaching/learning process – was seen as both important and necessary.

ISIP proposed a very different way of thinking about change than the ubiquitous 'top-down' approach. When the school is regarded as the 'centre' of change, then strategies for change need to take this new perspective into account. Although there is no space to discuss the knowledge that emanated from ISIP in detail (van Velzen, 1985; Hopkins, 1987b, 1990), a few of the perspectives adopted by the project are worth commenting on. School Improvement for example, was defined in the ISIP as (van Velzen et al., 1985, p. 48):

- a systematic, sustained effort aimed at change in learning conditions and other related internal conditions in one or more schools, with the ultimate aim of accomplishing educational goals more effectively.

School improvement as an approach to educational change according to ISIP therefore rested on a number of assumptions (Hopkins et al., 1994, p. 69):

- *the school as the centre of change.* This means that external reforms need to be sensitive to the situation in individual schools, rather than assuming that all schools are the same. It also implies that school improvement efforts need to adopt a 'classroom-exceeding' perspective, without ignoring the classroom.
- *a systematic approach to change.* School improvement is a carefully planned and managed process that takes place over a period of several years.
- *a key focus for change are the 'internal conditions' of schools.* These include not only the teaching-learning activities used in the school, but also the schools' procedures, role allocation and resource use that support the teaching learning process.
- *accomplishing educational goals more effectively.* Educational goals reflect the particular mission of a school, and represent what the school itself regards as desirable. This suggests a broader definition of outcome than student scores on achievement tests, even though for some schools these may be pre-eminent. Schools also serve the more general developmental needs of students, the professional development of teachers and the needs of its community.
- *a multi-level perspective.* Although the school is the centre of change it does not act alone. The school is embedded in an educational system that has to work collaboratively, or symbiotically, if the highest degrees of quality are to be achieved. This means that the roles of teachers, heads, governors, parents,

support people (advisers, higher education, consultants etc.), and local authorities should be defined, harnessed and committed to the process of school improvement.

- *integrative implementation strategies.* This implies a linkage between 'top-down' and 'bottom-up'; remembering of course that both approaches can apply at a number of different levels in the system. Ideally 'top-down' provides – policy aims, an overall strategy and operational plans; this is complemented by a 'bottom-up' response involving – diagnosis, priority goal setting and implementation. The former provides the framework, resources and a menu of alternatives; the latter, energy and school based implementation.
- *the drive towards institutionalisation.* Change is only successful when it has become part of the natural behaviour of teachers in the school. Implementation by itself is not enough.

It is this philosophy and approach that underpinned the International School Improvement Project and laid the basis for further thinking and action. Many research studies occurred at around this time which further illuminated the school improvement approach to educational change within these basic parameters. The Rand study (Berman & McLaughlin, 1978) for example which was carried out in the mid seventies, has recently been reanalysed (McLaughlin, 1990). The DESSI study carried out in the early eighties (*e.g.* Crandall et al., 1982, 1986) was a similarly large scale attempt to understand the process of innovation. Karen Seashore Louis and Matthew Miles' (1990) study on Improving the Urban High School, and Miles' together with Michael Huberman's (1984) report on school improvement efforts in twelve American schools in their book *Innovation up Close*, provide more fine grained analyses of the process.

Other examples of this more organic approach are found in the various school improvement networks that are based on a particular philosophy, or set of principles. They are a sort of school improvement 'club' where the rules of admission define a generalised approach to development work in schools. The Comer School Development Programme (Comer et al., 1991); the Coalition of Essential Schools based at Brown University which has evolved on the basis of the ideas of Theodore Sizer (1989); and the League of Professional Schools at the University of Georgia led by Carl Glickman (1990), are all fine examples of this approach to school improvement. The 'Learning Consortium' in Toronto (Fullan et al., 1989), and the 'Improving the Quality of Education for All' (IQEA) project in England, are other well developed examples of this type (Hopkins et al., 1994, 1996).

Although all of these studies have increased knowledge about school improvement in general, evaluations of specific approaches to school improvement are still in short supply. This strategic dimension is however highly visible in Bruce Joyce's review of a series of individual approaches, which he describes as being 'doors' which can open or unlock the process of school improvement. Joyce concludes that each approach emphasises different aspects of school culture at the outset – in other words, they provide a range of ways of 'getting into' school improvement. Each door opens a passageway into the culture of the school. His review reveals five major emphases (Joyce, 1991, p. 59):

1. *Collegiality*: the developing of collaborative and professional relations within a school staff and between their surrounding communities.
2. *Research*: where a school staff studies research findings about, for example, effective school and teaching practices, or the process of change.
3. *Action Research*: teachers collecting and analysing information and data about their classrooms and schools, and their students' progress.
4. *Curriculum Initiatives*: the introduction of changes within subject areas or, as in the case of the computer, across curriculum areas.
5. *Teaching Strategies*: when teachers discuss, observe and acquire a range of teaching skills and strategies.

Joyce argues that all these emphases can eventually change the culture of the school substantially. If we look carefully at each door to school improvement, we can discover where each is likely to lead, how the passageways are connected, what proponents of any one approach can borrow from the others, and the costs and benefits of opening any one (or any combination) first. He maintains that single approaches are unlikely to be as powerful an agent for school improvement as a synthesis. The implicit assumption made by Joyce, is that behind the door are a series of interconnecting pathways that lead inexorably to school improvement.

Unfortunately this is not always so. Because of their singular nature, most school improvement strategies fail to a greater or lesser degree to effect the culture of the school. They tend to focus on individual changes, and individual teachers and classrooms, rather than how these changes can fit in with and adapt the organisation and ethos of the school. As a consequence when the door is opened it only leads into a cul-de-sac. This partially accounts for the uneven effect of most of our educational reforms. To continue in this vein for a moment, it seems logical that if the problems of educational change are to be overcome, some way needs to be found of integrating organisational and curriculum change within a coherent strategy. The doors to school improvement need to be opened simultaneously or consecutively and the pathways behind them linked together.

During the past ten years a number of school improvement strategies have been developed in order to do just this. Most of them, in line with the political pressures for decentralisation, have focused on some form of planning at the school level. Development planning, as this approach is commonly called (school growth plans is another popular term for similar activities), provides a generic and paradigmatic illustration of a school improvement strategy, combining as it does selected curriculum change with modifications to the school's management arrangements or organisation. It is a strategy that is becoming increasingly widespread in British schools for example, as teachers and school leaders struggle to take control of the process of change. The book *The Empowered School* (Hargreaves & Hopkins, 1991) that was based on a governmental project on school development plans (Hargreaves et al., 1989) was highly influential.

School development planning is but one example of a contemporary *genre* of organic approaches to school improvement. The 'Self-Managing School' approach, developed in the mid eighties by Brian Caldwell and Jim Spinks (1988) in Tasmania, Australia as a response to a policy for devolved management and budgets for schools, has also been widely disseminated, adapted and emulated in many other school systems, particularly in Canada and the UK. Other examples include, the 'School Growth Plan' approach developed in Toronto, Canada (Stoll & Fink, 1992); the IMTEC approach to institutional development developed in Norway (Dalin et al., 1993), and certain approaches to 'Restructuring' in the United States of America (e.g. Elmore, 1990; Murphy, 1991), are also taking a more fundamental approach to educational reform by transforming the organisation of the school in the quest for enhanced student achievement.

There have also been a number of 'meta-analyses' of the research literature and current best practice that assisted the development of the school improvement movement, if one can deign it so, during this period. The two editions of Michael Fullan's The Meaning of Educational Change (Fullan, 1982, 1991) have influenced a generation of researchers and practitioners; similarly Bruce Joyce and colleagues' (1984) The Structure of School Improvement. Other book length syntheses of research and practice include our *School Improvement in an Era of Change* (Hopkins et al., 1994), Stoll and Fink's (1996) *Changing Our Schools*, and Reynolds and colleagues' (1996) *Making Good Schools*.

This accumulated experience and reflective knowledge has moved school improvement to a position where some reasonably robust guidelines for action have been established. It is appropriate to conclude this review of contemporary school improvement practice by a brief summary. In general, it appears that effective school improvement initiatives tended to:

- focus on specific outcomes which can be related to student learning, rather than succumbing to external pressure to identify non-specific goals such as 'improve exam results';
- draw on theory, research into practice, and the teachers' own experiences in formulating strategies, so that the rationale for the required changes is established in the minds of those expected to bring them about;
- recognise the importance of staff development, since it is unlikely that developments in student learning will occur without developments in teachers' practice;
- provide for monitoring the impact of policy and strategy on teacher practice and student learning early and regularly, rather than rely on 'post-hoc' evaluations;
- 'pull all relevant levers' by emphasising the instructional behaviour of teachers as well as school level processes;
- pay careful attention to the consistency of implementation.

Overview of the Volume

It is against this background that this volume of the International Handbook was conceptualised and contributions solicited. The volume was planned with the recent history of school improvement in mind. The purpose was to locate school improvement within a theoretical and practical framework, to illustrate the challenges facing school improvement strategies from a policy context, to demonstrate the evolution of a range of school improvement strategies in recent times, and through reports of recent research to challenge the assumptions underlying contemporary school improvement approaches. These concerns are reflected in the four major sections of the book.

Section One – Towards a Theory of School Development to reprise what we know about school improvement and to locate it within a practical and theoretical framework. One of the more unfortunate aspects of recent efforts at educational change is the tendency to "pretend to not know what is known" (Joyce Carol Oates, quoted in Glickman, 1991, p. 4). The contributions to this section are an attempt not to fall into this particular trap. Traditionally, the school improvement movement has channelled its energies into devising and developing strategies for educational change. However, as the chapter by Dalin illustrates, such strategies have largely been of a "top-down" or "bottom-up" variety. They have either been externally driven with an emphasis upon structural change and development, or internally generated with an emphasis upon the process of change.

"Top-down" or "bottom-up" improvement strategies tend to premised on uniformity rather than diversity. They are not sufficiently fine tuned enough to address different types of school development, school cultures or school contexts. This point is further reinforced in the chapters by Seashore Louis and Scheerens who both illustrate the limitations of existing models for bringing about sustained development and improvement in schools. They argue forcefully that if school improvement is to become more effective, then its strategies need to be better integrated with and informed by the relevant theoretical and research literatures.

Section Two – The Contemporary Context of School Improvement is an attempt to capture something of the contemporary context of the international policy context, within which school improvement operates. Space obviously precludes detailed international policy analysis, so three examples that represent a range of recent policy initiatives are included. The description of the Kentucky Reform Act in the USA by Whitford and Jones contrasts sharply with the educational change context in Scandinavia as described by Lander and Ekholm. In this respect Kentucky and Scandinavia represent something like the ends of a continuum. The recent history of educational reform in New South Wales, Australia as described by Cuttance presents a middle way, typical of a number of other Western educational systems. The issues raised by these three accounts reflect the tensions in school improvement policies internationally.

Section Three – Tensions and Contrasts in School Improvement Strategies contains a series of discussions on a variety of school improvement strategies. Historically school improvement has been largely centred on the notion of strategies, and the literature on school improvement has been preoccupied with establishing and refining generic strategies for improving schools. This approach is reflected in Joyce's (1991) representation of the range of school improvement strategies as a series of 'doors'. In order to reflect this tradition, this section contains a series of discussions around individual approaches. The chapters by Wallace on planning, McCulloch on curriculum reform, Joyce and Calhoun on instructional strategies, Smyth on staff development for teachers, and Nias on teacher collaboration represent a fair range of individual school improvement approaches.

What is significant about these contributions is that they not only survey their respective fields, but in all cases subject them to rigorous analysis. All argue for a re-interpretation of what is necessary if these strategies are to result in more effective schooling. Whilst these individual contributions hint at limitations in the various approaches to school improvement, when taken together they suggest a more fundamental critique. Put simply, conventional approaches do not adequately address the more pressing and critical issue of differentiating school improvement strategies to match individual school development needs. As is seen in the following section, failure of both externally and internally driven models of improvement have been their relative inability to delineate particular strategies, or groups of strategies for particular types of school.

Section Four – The Effectiveness of School Improvement Strategies builds on this critique of contemporary school improvement with a series of 'state of the art' reflections and research analyses. Reynolds' synthesis of the school effectiveness and school improvement traditions represents a secure foundation for future work. Calhoun and Joyce, by labelling the research and development, and the site-based models of improvement the "inside out" and "outside in " paradigms of school reform, point to another creative tension in the field. They suggest that in terms of school improvement both paradigms made essentially the same mistake, in so far as "they believed that they had a sure fire strategy, that they were unlikely to fail and thus, didn't conduct school improvement as an inquiry making modifications as they went." Slavin and Stringfield strike a complementary chord in their chapters as they both underline the need for carefully selected instructional strategies which are designed to meet the particular development needs of schools. Yet, within the field of school improvement, at present, it is clear that few such differentiated strategies exist. These four chapters present therefore not only a valuable review of current practice they also point a way forward for school improvement practice, research and theory.

In taking the argument a stage further one raises an issue which has only recently been acknowledged in the literature. This is that much school improvement work assumes that all schools are identical i.e. that a strategy such as development planning will work as well in one school as another. Yet it is evident from the research on school effectiveness that schools are differentially effective. This would suggest that schools at different levels of effectiveness require different school improvement strategies. This is not well trodden territory. It would seem important, however, to recognise that different types of school require different strategies for development. In other words, that strategies for school development need to fit the "growth state", or particular culture of the school. It is issues such as these that are addressed in the final section of this chapter.

KEY ISSUES FOR SCHOOL IMPROVEMENT[2]

Besides offering an up-to-date review of the field of school improvement, the following chapters also demonstrate the limitations of school improvement efforts in practice. Their collective critique highlights five main problems with current school improvement interventions:

- a failure to embed school improvement initiatives within a contextual and diagnostic analysis of the school;
- a lack of focus upon the level of the classroom and the primacy of instruction;
- a neglect to consider differences between schools and the need for more accurately targeted programmes focused upon the particular growth states of schools;
- the continuing need to understand the complex dynamic between structure and culture in school reform;
- the necessity to focus not just on how innovations impact on schools, but how such innovations can move up to scale and impact on many schools and systems.

In concluding I will comment briefly on each of these issues.

Context specific school improvement. School improvement accounts have been notable for a 'one size fits all' orientation, in which implementation of programme characteristics is assumed to be the same, or similar, independent of any 'presenting characteristics' of schools themselves. Whilst 'context specific' school improvement strategies have been outlined that respect and respond to factors such as the differential socio-economic status of school catchment areas (Stringfield & Teddlie, 1990) and to levels of school effectiveness (Hopkins 1996), it is clear to us that there are a large range of further contextual factors in addition that will influence the likely progress and choice of improvement efforts.

Our own present list of powerful contextual factors would include: *Socio-economic Status of Catchment Area*; (Undoubtedly the nature of the social class distribution, and the closely linked educational levels, that exist in the neighbourhood(s) of schools have effects). *Age Levels of Staff*: (the presence of a group of persons over fifty is often seen as a problem for a school wishing to improve); *Relational Variables:* (the extent to which cliques and groups exist that represent both relational and ideological groupings, which can fragment whole school responses to organisational change); *Open-Ness of Historic Leadership Style* (the extent to which collegiality, ownership and laterality have been historically employed as techniques in the last decade); *(the Local Education Authority* or *School District* (the extent to which schools are facilitated in being 'data rich' by having value-added data which is made available to schools); and *the Local Market Situation of the School* (the extent to which local competition exists between schools or a school inhabits a monopoly position).

The missing instructional level. Most initiatives are poorly conceptualised in the precise ways in which they might impact upon the learning or classroom level, which in all the most recent evidence is the educational factor with the greatest impact upon pupil outcomes (Reynolds et al, 1994). Whilst many schools are pulling the 'levers' of curriculum and organisation, the precise ways in which these changes impact upon learning is unclear and usually unaddressed. There are some signs that the more rapidly improving schools are aware that 'the learning level' may have changed less than the other levels 'above' it in the school. Any school which is aware of the need to modify this level is aware that the 'technology' of a knowledge base about effective instructional practices is missing in the United Kingdom (Joyce & Weil, 1996; Calhoun & Hopkins, 1997). Surrogates such as 'appraisal' schemes which allow teachers to concentrate on further development of their 'best', self selected areas of practice are rarely a potent mechanism of change.

This is not the place to speculate on the type of instructional strategies that characterise excellent schooling. We are convinced however that powerful learning does not occur by accident. It is usually the product of an effective learning situation created by a skilful teacher (Hopkins, 1997). Such learning and teaching engagements are commonplace in schools that have an ethos characterised by high expectations, collaboration and innovativeness. Schools that are designed and organised to support powerful teaching and learning are on the evidence of this research unfortunately only too rare. Our experience suggests that there are relatively few 'excellent' schools that appear able to conceptualise exactly what they should be doing to effectively implement changes at the instructional level.

Differential "growth states" and strategies. There are two complex issues at stake here. The first is to do with the 'growth state' or 'performance level' of the school; the second is related to the strategy necessary to move the school from one level to another. Space precludes a sufficiently detailed discussion that would allow the disentangling of the two constructs, although we have attempted this task elsewhere (Hopkins, 1996, Hopkins & Harris, 1997).

Research by the American Quality Foundation (1992) suggests that different management strategies are required at different phases of the performance development cycle in organisations. The message here is that there are few universal quality management strategies that are applicable across all stages of an organisation's development. As we have already seen, much current school improvement practice assumes that all strategies are equally effective, and for all schools, irrespective of their effectiveness or stage in the performance cycle. The vital message is that organisations need to change their quality management strategies as they progress through their performance development cycle. The strategies which are effective for improving performance at one stage of the cycle are not necessarily effective at other stages of the cycle. This suggests that, firstly, we should begin to adapt our strategies for school development according to the "growth state" of the individual school. And, secondly, that we need to know more about how different school improvement strategies affect different schools.

The research base on the effects of school development strategies is unfortunately very weak. We can assume however that the same strategy will not move an ineffective school directly to effectiveness. In beginning this discussion it may be helpful, initially at least, to consider three different growth state and three related school improvement strategies. One could label these strategies Type I, Type II, and Type III.

Type 1 strategies are those that assist failing schools become moderately effective. They need to involve a high level of external support. Failing schools cannot improve themselves. These strategies have to involve a clear and direct focus on a limited number of basic curriculum and organisational issues in order to build the confidence and competence to continue.

Type 11 strategies are those that assist moderately effective schools become effective. These schools need to refine their developmental priorities and focus on specific teaching and learning issues and build the capacity within the school to support this work. These strategies usually involve a certain level of external support, but it is theoretically possible for schools in this category to 'improve' by themselves.

Type 111 strategies are those that assist effective schools remain so. In these instances external support although often welcomed is not necessary as the school searches out and creates its own support networks. Exposure to new ideas and practices, collaboration through consortia or 'pairing' type arrangements seem to be common in these situations.

As work in this area progresses it will hopefully be possible to describe more specifically these *types* of school improvement interventions and strategies. Even at present it is feasible to classify *types* on criteria such as: range and number of priorities addressed; focus *i.e.* curriculum, instruction, school organisation; research knowledge / school generated knowledge; external directives / internal purpose; level of capacity building, and so on. Such a classification, when complete, would allow us to move a step closer to a full conceptualisation of school improvement by linking "type" of strategy to various stages of school development and growth.

The dynamic between structure and culture in school reform. Throughout the remaining chapters in this Handbook there are many references to the term 'school culture.' This is problematic because there is a great deal of confusion about what the word actually means and what the concept looks like in practice. The common view that the culture of the school is best thought of as the procedures, norms, expectations and values of its members does not take us very far. Nor do the popular phrases that describe the culture of the school as 'the way we get things done around here' or 'what keeps the herd moving west' (Deal & Kennedy, 1983, p. 4), advance our understanding in a profound way. At best they provide a cosy image that every one is comfortable with; more often they act as a cover for the sloppy thinking of which we are all at times guilty. Slogans such as this provide an excuse for not engaging in the difficult and painful conceptual work that is required to gain some clarity on this important concept (Hargreaves, 1995).

We have found it helpful in our own work to heed the sociologists distinction between *structure* and *culture*. Ignoring this important distinction is, in our opinion, one of the main reasons for the confusion that reigns in the discussions of culture and its impact on schools. Structure and culture are of course interdependent, and the relationship between them is dialectical. Structure influences culture, but it works the other way around too. Structures are often regarded as the more basic and profound, in that they generate cultures which not only allow the structures to 'work', but also justify or legitimate the structures. On the other hand, changes in culture *i.e.* value systems and beliefs, can change underlying structures. The two go hand in hand and are mutually reinforcing. At a practical level however, it is often easier to change structures than cultures. But if one changes structures too radically, without paying attention to the underlying culture, then one may get the appearance of change (change in structure), but not the reality of change (change in culture). Similarly it is difficult to sustain changes in culture, perhaps inspired by a charismatic leader, without some concomitant change in structure to support their ideas about curriculum or instructional innovation (see Hargreaves 1994). In terms of school improvement we need to direct equal attention to both structure and culture, and to be alert to the effect one has on the other.

Getting to Scale

This is another complex problem for the new generation of school improvers to confront. The real question is not simply how can we improve schools, but more how can we create capacity for school improvement at all levels of the system? The problems of "getting to scale" are substantial and are only beginning to be recognised (Elmore, 1996). Again this is a theme that is raised by the contributors to Section Four of the Handbook. One of these, Sam Stringfield (1996) has suggested a series of initial hypotheses regarding successfully "getting to scale" at three different levels.

PROGRAMME LEVEL

P1: To be successfully scaled up, a program/design must have clearly stated goals.

P2: The program/design should make a clear presentation of the "Technology" that will be employed to achieve the changes.

P3: The program/design should provide a reasonable depth of evidence that it has, in at least some environments, been able to produce the claimed goals and objectives.

P4: The program/design should provide a full statement of resources needed to achieve strong implementation.

P5:   Technical Assistance on the particulars of the design/program must be available and regularly accessed.

P6:   Programs/Designs should facilitate cross-site visitations among schools.

P7:   To have credibility and to uphold minimum implementation standards, Programs/Designs should build in triennial implementation checks by representatives of the designer.

P8:   Programs should commit a percentage of their ongoing research and development funding to studying sites where their designs did not produce desired results.

P9:   The program/design should provide mechanisms for communication among schools and teachers participating in the reform.

SCHOOL LEVEL

S1:   The school must have clear goals, well matched to the goals of the program/design the school chooses.

S2:   The school must have strong leadership.

S3:   The school must have a facilitator and/or a leadership team to guide the effort.

S4:   The school must engage in an honest self assessment.

S5:   The school should consider multiple options.

S6:   The school's facilitator should conduct a secret ballot on whether to adopt a program/design, and on which program/design to adopt.

DISTRICT LEVEL

D1:   Clear observable goals that are compatible with the reform design.

D2:   The district must provide a reasonably stable environment for reform.

D3:   The district must commit to a clear understanding between itself and the restructuring school.

It is on such an iterative approach to theory building, that develops hypotheses on the basis of research evidence and good practice and subjects them to further testing and refinement, that the future of school improvement lies.

This list of issues confronting the next generation of school improvement researchers is still in a rather primitive state. However, four concluding comments are worth making at this stage about effective school improvement strategies. The first is that school improvement strategies are not homogeneous, but holistic and eclectic. The second is that effective strategies have both a direct and a nurturant focus. At one and the same time they are directed at the achievement of pupils, the structure/organisation of the school and the intangible "culture of the school". Third, effective strategies represent a combination of external and internal approaches, the particular blend of strategies being modified to fit the 'context specificity' of the individual school. Fourth, and the previous comments notwithstanding, there is increasing evidence of a bi-polarity in school improvement interventions. To put it starkly, it is only school improvement strategies that embody a direct curriculum and instructional focus that have any chance of positively impacting on student achievement. It is as simple and as complex as that.

CODA

Even though such discussion is at this stage speculative, the issues raised in this chapter have the potential to give us a better grasp of the dynamics of the process of school improvement. There are a number of issues arising from this discussion which will impinge upon future research policy making and practice.

Firstly in research terms there needs to be more evaluative work conducted into the relative effect of different development strategies upon schools with different growth rates. This will mean, among other things, taking seriously the school's 'internal conditions' or 'capacity for development', as well differentiating between different strategies for school development.

On an international scale there is much potential for cross cultural research into differential school development strategies. Yet, little empirical evidence exists which has considered the nature and impact of different developmental strategies in various countries, or contexts. International surveys have listed the various improvement projects and approaches within developing countries, but there has been little comparative analysis of the transferability or effectiveness of such programmes in different contexts.

In policy terms, it would seem that governments would benefit from moving away from development approaches which do not acknowledge the differences between schools. Instead, their energies at both central and local level should be channelled into identifying differential school capacities for development. Central and local government should be promoting strategies which enable schools to move forward from where they are, rather than apply strategies which remind them where they should be.

Finally, schools and those assisting them, need to focus their improvement efforts on creating powerful contexts for student learning. What are needed are powerful and integrative curriculum and instructional strategies that directly address the range of student learning goals and outcomes. It is through linking more precise specifications of teaching practice to curriculum content that progress in student learning and achievement is made. Strategies for school improvement that focus solely on whole school processes without much substantive content, or have addressed single curriculum innovations or isolated teaching practices, rather than whole school developments are 'doomed to tinkering'. In short, we need to see school improvement whole; and when we do this we begin to meet the real challenge of educational reform.

ENDNOTES

[1] I am very grateful to my colleague Alma Harris for assistance in the preparation of this editorial introduction.

[2] Some of the issues raised in this section of the chapter are also discussed and further elaborated on in our paper "Moving On and Moving Up: Confronting the Complexities of Improvement" (Hopkins et al., in press).

REFERENCES

American Quality Foundation. (1992). *The international quality study: Best practices report*. Cleveland, Ohio: American Quality Foundation and Ernst & Young.

Barth, R. (1990). *Improving schools from within*. San Francisco: Jossey Bass.

Berman, P. & McLaughlin. M. (1978). Implementation of educational innovation. *Educational Forum*, **40**(3) 345–370.

Bowers, D. (1973). Organisation techniques and their results in 23 organisations: The Michigan I.C.C. study. *Journal of Applied Behavioural Science*, **9**, 21–43.

Caldwell, B. & Spinks, J. (1988). *The self managing school*. Lewes, Sussex: Falmer Press

Comer, J. (1988, November). Educating poor minority children. *Scientific American*, 42–48.

Crandall, D. et al. (1982). *People policies and practice: Examining the chain of school improvement* (Vols 1–10). Andover, M.A: The Network.

Crandall, D. et al. (1986). Strategic planning issues that bear on the Success of School Improvement Efforts. *Educational Administration Quarterly*, **22** (2), 21–53.

Dalin, P., & Rust, V. (1983). *Can schools learn*. Windsor: NFER-Nelson.

Deal, T. & Kennedy, A. (1983). Culture and School Performance. *Educational Leadership*, **40**(5), 14–15.

Elmore, R. (1990). *Restructuring schools*. Oakland, California: Jossey-Bass.

Elmore, R. (1996). Getting to scale with good educational practice. *Harvard Educational Review*, **66**(1), 1–26.

Fullan, M. (1982). *The meaning of educational change*. New York: Teachers College Press.

Fullan, M. (1991). *The new meaning of educational change*. London: Cassell

Fullan, M. et al. (1990, May). Linking classroom and school improvement. *Educational Leadership*, **47**(8), 13–19

Fullan, M. et al. (1980). Organization development in schools: The state of the art. *Review of Educational Research*, **50**(1), 121–183

Fullan, M. & Miles, M. (1992). Getting reform right: What works and what doesn't. *Phi Delta Kappan*, **73**(10), 745–52.

Glickman, C. (1990). Pushing school reforms to a new edge: The seven ironies of school empowerment. *Phi Delta Kappan*, 68–75

Glickman, C. (1991, May). Pretending not to know what we know. *Educational Leadership*, 4–10.

Hargreaves, A. (1994). *Changing teachers, changing times*. London: Cassell.

Hargreaves, D. H. (1995). School culture, school effectiveness and school improvement. *School Effectiveness and School Improvement*, **6**(1), 23–46

Hargreaves, D. H. et al. (1989). *Planning for school development*. London: DES

Hargreaves, D. H., & Hopkins, D. (1991). *The empowered school*. London: Cassell.

Hopkins, D. H. (Ed.). (1986). *Inservice training and educational development*. London: Croom Helm.

Hopkins, D. (1987a). *Knowledge information skills and the curriculum*. London: British Library

Hopkins, D. (1987b). *Improving the quality of schooling*. Lewes, Sussex: Falmer Press

Hopkins, D. (1990). 'The international school improvement project and effective schooling: towards a synthesis'. *School Organisation*, **10**(2&3), 179–194.

Hopkins, D. (1994). Institutional self evaluation and renewal. In T. Husen & N. Postlethwaite (Eds.), *The international encyclopaedia of education*. New York: Pergamon Press.

Hopkins, D. (1996). Towards a theory for school improvement. In J. Gray, D. Reynolds, & C. Fitz-Gibbon (Eds.), *Merging traditions: The future of research on school effectiveness and school improvement*. London: Cassell.

Hopkins, D. (1997). *"Powerful learning, powerful teaching and powerful schools" – An inaugural lecture*. Nottingham: Centre for Teacher and School Development, University of Nottingham.

Hopkins, D., Ainscow, M., & West, M. (1994). *School improvement in an era of change.* London: Cassell.

Hopkins, D., West, M., & Ainscow, M. (1996). *Improving the quality of education for all.* London: David Fulton Publishers.

Hopkins, D., & Harris, A. (1997). Understanding the school's capacity for development. *School Leadership and Management*, **17**(3).

Hopkins, D., Reynolds, D., & Farrell, S. (in press). Moving on and moving up: Confronting the complexities of improvement. To be published in *Educational Research and Evaluation*.

Huberman, M., & Miles, M. (1984). *Innovation up close.* New York: Plenum

Joyce, B. (1991). The doors to school improvement. *Educational Leadership*, **48**(8), 59–62.

Joyce, B. et al. (1984). *The structure of school improvement.* New York: Longman.

Joyce, B., & Weil, M. (1996). *Models of teaching* (5th Edition). Englewood Cliffs, NJ: Prentice- Hall.

Joyce B., Calhoun, E., & Hopkins, D. (1997). *Models of learning – tools for teaching.* Buckingham: Open University Press.

Lewin, K. (1946). Action research and minority problems. *Journal of Social Issues*, **2**, 34–46.

Louis K. S., & Miles, M. B. (1990). *Improving the urban high school: What works and why.* New York: Teachers College Press.

McLaughlin, M. (1990). The Rand change agent study revisited: Macro perspectives, micro realities. *Educational Researcher*, **19**, 11–16

Miles, M. B. (1975). 'Planned change and organisational health'. In J. V. Baldrige & T. Deal (Eds.), *Managing change in educational organisations.* Berkeley: McCutchen.

Murphy, J. (1991). *Restructuring schools: Capturing and assessing the phenomena.* New York: Teachers College Press.

Nisbet, J. (Ed). (1973). The creativity of the school. Paris: OECD.

OECD. (1989). *Decentralisation and school improvement.* Paris: OECD-CERI

Reynolds, D., Creemers, B. P. M., Stringfield, S., Teddlie, C., Schaffer, E., & Nesselrodt, P. (1994). *Advances in school effectiveness research and practice.* Oxford: Pergamon Press.

Reynolds, D., Creemers, B., Hopkins, D., Stoll, L., & Bollen, R. (1996). Making Good Schools. London : Routledge.

Schmuck, R. (1984). 'The place of organisation of development in schools'. In D. Hopkins & M. Wideen (Eds.), *Alternative perspectives in school improvement.* London: Falmer.

Schmuck, R., & Miles, M. (Eds.). (1971). *Organizational development in schools.* La Jolla, California: University Associates.

Schmuck, R., & Runkel, P. (1985). *The handbook of organization in schools.* Palo Alto, California: Mayfield.

Sizer, T. (1989). Diverse practice, shared ideas: The essential school. In H. Walberg & J. Lane (Eds.), *Organizing for Learning: Towards the twenty-first century.* Reston, Virginia: NASSP.

Slavin, R., Madden, N., Dolan, L., & Wasik, B. (1996). *Every school, every child – success for all.* Thousand Oaks, California: Corwin Press.

Stenhouse, L. (1980). *An introduction to curriculum research and development in action.* London: Heinemann Educational Books.

Stoll, L., & Fink, D. (1992). Effecting school change: The Halton approach. *School Effectiveness and Improvement*, **3**(1), 19–41.

Stoll, L., & Fink, D. (1996). *Changing our schools.* Buckingham: Open University Press.

Stringfield, S., & Teddlie, C. (1991). Observers as predictors of school's effectiveness status. *The Elementary School Journal*, **91**(4), 357–76.

Stringfield, S. (1996). *"Scaling Up" reforms that can benefit students placed at risk.* Paper presented at the meeting of the American Educational Research Association, New York City, April 10, 1996.

Van Velzen W. et al. (1985). *Making school improvement work.* Leuven, Belgium: ACCO.

I: Towards a Theory of School Development

Developing the Twenty-First Century School:
A Challenge to Reformers

PER DALIN

The International Learning Cooperative, Norway

In this chapter Per Dalin reviews three decades of research on and involvement in educational innovation. He traces the evolution of innovation strategies and describes the range of challenges currently facing educational reformers. These challenges – the societal paradigm shift, changing local contexts, the expansion of children's learning needs – place great demands on the school improvement strategies employed by educational reformers. Basing his analysis and advice on best contemporary research and practice, Dalin outlines strategies that will assist educational reformers to more effectively develop the twenty-first century school.

My first study of educational innovations in Norway in 1967 convinced me that knowledge about the process of innovation is central to our ability to improve the learning conditions of students. I studied a very successful interdisciplinary course in primary schools and found that after five years of successful pilot experiences, no other school in the local community had adapted the approach. The early adapters were schools many hundred miles away! We formulated the slogan: *"Innovators have everything to gain and nothing to loose, while followers have everything to loose and nothing to gain."* This was the time in Scandinavia when the government heavily subsidised innovators. The innovators, who got very favourable conditions, were exposed to the media and earned fortunes on new learning materials. We concluded that both elements of personal incentives, as well as characteristics of the school culture, could help to explain the lack of dissemination. My interests in educational innovations led me to studies of educational reforms in all parts of the world, and I have probably more questions now than 30 years ago.

How is it possible for a teacher with more than 70 children in the classroom, in the middle of the jungle of Sri Lanka, to perform wonderful project instruction, authentic learning for the children, without any external support and with only the very minimum of local materials?

In Indonesia, the Teacher Training Institution for Secondary Education (IKIP) in Yogyakarta, performed a comprehensive internal and external school review with full and competent participation by nearly all actors. Why was it relatively simple to import this innovation in spite of their tradition of central inspection?

In Germany, most states are moving towards more decentralised decision-making, in some cases towards more school autonomy, and in most cases with great difficulties. The tradition of "Schulaufsicht", or school inspection, a hierarchical control tradition, penetrates the system. What can explain the rigidity of German educational bureaucracy? Is it cultural, structural or political?

D. Hopkins (ed.), The Practice and Theory of School Improvement, 25-39.
© 2005 *Springer. Printed in the Netherlands.*

In Norway a radical curriculum reform of secondary education reduces the main options for students from 110 to only 13 in the first years of upper secondary education. The Ministry does *"everything right"* according to many recent advises in the reform literature. However, the reform process is getting into major trouble at school level. How is it possible that Norway, with more resources per student than almost any country gets into severe implementation problems?

In Ethiopia, the reform of primary education has been under tight control by the Ministry of Education, but with relatively small resources at hand. This very centralised reform seems to have succeeded reaching its main objectives, and there seems to be much less teacher opposition than in Norway. A relatively hierarchical system seems to be able to develop favourable conditions for comprehensive school reforms. What does it mean?

In Colombia the famous rural school reform project Escuela Nueva, that started with the collaboration of a university professor and a teacher has spread to thousands of schools, in the first ten years without any central support. What are the lessons to be learned about *"bottom-up"* versus *"top-down"* strategies?

In the USA one innovation strategy after the other has been introduced, like reform waves, over the past 40 years. Few have penetrated the system, or influenced the system in a deep sense. At the same time several alarming status reports tell us about severe problems in American schools.

The paradoxes and irony of school reforms are many, at least if one takes on an international perspective. Do we really know what effective reform strategies are? Or do we know what they are under given political, structural, cultural, organisational and individual conditions?

In the sixties and seventies we thought we had some answers to practical reform strategies, for example to move from a planning perspective towards an implementation perspective (*"Implementation dominates outcomes"*, McLaughlin, 1990) or investing in management training. They proved piecemeal.

During the eighties a more comprehensive approach to school reform characterised most countries, often combining a strong state involvement with an attempt to decentralise decision-making. The lesson from the eighties is that restructuring is more a dream than a reality, and the efforts during the nineties show that the field is really wide open. (Fullan & Stiegelbauer, 1991).

SCHOOL REFORM OR STATUS QUO?

Increasingly I am battered with the reform intentions themselves, or with the content of the reforms. I was already getting worried in the seventies, working with the school reform projects funded by the World Bank. There was a narrow emphasis on educational achievements (as measured by relatively simple tests). There was little concern for what knowledge could best help these children getting out of their poverty and meeting an uncertain (surely demanding) future.

What did they learn in school? To be able to repeat what the teacher said, to learn that there is always *one* right answer, to be obedient and to stop questioning?

Indonesian educators knew that this type of traditional instruction imported from (the worst of) western school systems would be a disservice to Indonesia. They therefore introduced *student active learning* as a principle for education. They are still working on it.

Are *we* much better off with our focus on school effectiveness? In particular if we measure it up against standardised test results? Over the past years the dependent variables in school effectiveness research have been more complex and comprehensive. The tests attempt to grasp broader and deeper learning goals. However, we are measuring effectiveness based on yesterday's definition of success.

YESTERDAY AND TOMORROW

The unique challenge and opportunity the school has got is that it is (or ought to be) the future laboratory of our society. What goes on there should not only prepare students for *today*, but for their lives in a fundamental new society. At present, the school mainly prepares for yesterday.

A typical scenario is the following: In the seventies both teachers and parents (and others) recognised a problem. Some less successful local efforts were made to solve it. A commission was established to study the problem and to come up with recommendations. A political, bureaucratic and professional discussion followed and a compromising strategy was found (This process usually takes at least five years from when the problem is identified by teachers). Then followed an implementation process (that normally takes at least ten years before it touches all schools). Meanwhile the program was attacked, other priorities were pressing to get a piece of the action, the program slowed down and watered down. They had probably still got the problem before evaluating the effects of the program. In the nineties we may be lucky enough to contribute to the solution of a problem that schools felt so strongly about in the seventies.

Schools are similar to other organisations in many ways, including the responsibility to solve today's problems. That, however, can be done much more effectively and efficiently than it is being done at present. (This paper is not concerned about that process.)

What we are concerned about is how schools can master a reform process that deals with the unique mission of schools in our societies, namely to prepare students for an uncertain and challenging future.

Only to concentrate on *effectiveness*, in a sense of meeting today's (or yesterday's) problems more successfully, is shortcutting the very mission of schools and the life opportunities of our students.

THE PARADIGM SHIFT

This paper argues that the challenges our students face in their adult lives in the twenty-first century, will be markedly different from the challenges of today's societies. Our schools are totally unprepared to help their students face the realities of the twenty-first century (Dalin & Rust, 1996). I also argue that we need to review our knowledge base about school improvement to assess what is relevant as a guide for long range projects that prepare students for the twenty-first century.

Unlike many researchers, we do not attempt to present future scenarios and make predictions of a very concrete nature. Looking at the predictions, we are not tempted to continue on the same path.

We argue that the world is presently undergoing a major paradigm shift. Those of us who followed the amazing fall of communism in the fall of 1989, are not only aware of the major changes in the world and in our lives, but our entire mental orientation has changed. As a European who has lived and experienced a divided world since the end of the World War II, I can now think of Europe (and other parts of the world) as one. There are no longer *"those countries behind the iron curtain"*, that we really knew little about and were little concerned about as long as they didn't hurt us.

This is an example of a paradigm shift, a change in mental cognition that helps us to understand the world in a different way than before. We believe that the world is not only undergoing major political changes, but that *the Ten Revolutions* that are occurring (among other things), will have remarkable influence on the lives of our students. The Ten Revolutions are (Dalin & Rust, 1996, pp. 31–32):

The Knowledge and Information Revolution. Fundamental questions about the pluralistic society are being raised which may contribute to a set of global values.

The Population Revolution. Also called a population explosion, population growth is covering the whole planet at exceptional speed.

The Globalising and Localising Revolution. A new world political picture is being formed, resulting in new alliances, a globalisation of trade, and major population movements accompanied by ethnic and political crises that are transforming and changing cultures.

The Social Relationships Revolution. Minority groups and women are taking on new roles, creating new ways of living in a multicultural and pluralistic society.

The Economic Revolution. Economic growth is reaching new countries at faster speed, creating new competition, development toward a global economy featuring enormous multinational companies and new goods and services.

The Technological Revolution. New perspectives and possibilities, as well as new products and services promise to solve an expanding array of problems and also create unanticipated problems.

The Ecological Revolution. A whole new meaning for life on earth and boundaries for our future development are being created.

The Aesthetics Revolution. A complex artistic transformation is renewing people's lives.

The Political Revolution. Fundamental questions about democracy and minority rights are being raised.

The Values Revolution. Fundamental questions about the pluralistic society are being raised which may contribute to a set of global values.

These Ten Revolutions are part of a larger process of change. Other forces are at work, but these ten are fundamental and of special importance for the future of education and schooling. It must be understood that these revolutions are inter-lined and constitute an integrated phenomenon. Even though they must be seen as a complex whole, it is conceptually necessary to treat them as individual revolutions. It is crucial, however, to understand that these forces function in combination and that the synergy effect of various revolutions will have significant consequences that cannot be anticipated.

THE LOCAL FORCES

Macro forces have individually and in combination, major and sometimes surprising influence on our daily lives:

Our workplace is undergoing rapid changes, unemployment seems to become a larger challenge, and only those societies with a major capacity for renewal are able to compete. Faced with global competition, supported by free accessible information and technologies, our traditional workplaces will constantly need to renew themselves (Der Speigel, 1993)

Our local environment, at least in major cities, is undergoing rapid change, becoming much more of a multicultural melting pot, full of conflict potential as well as of opportunities, and constantly faced with social changes. Young people are faced with the adult world in a very real sense at a very early age.

Our religious institutions undergo challenges, as they are faced with alternatives both within their own religions as well as from other religions and ideologies. Young people are growing up in a pluralistic society, they *"start without luggage"* and often with a very unclear value base. They increasingly meet new value-challenges, like the balance between economic growth and challenges to the environment. They must find a common platform of values and norms in an increasingly complex environment.

Our media has grown to a remarkable institution in our societies within a generation. It often sets the agenda, greatly influencing politics, values and norms. As more and more (often destructive) information is available via films, video, television and computer networks, the free flow of information is becoming one of the most problematic issues in modern societies (Postman, 1987).

Our homes are undergoing dramatic changes as well. As the media and the peer group and local environment get an increasingly more important role in the formation of values and norms, the role of the adults in the family becomes more vulnerable. Parallel to this development the social capital seems to erode in our societies (Hurrelmann & Engel, 1989).

These major forces changes the role of schooling in our societies and indeed what schools will be able to accomplish. The traditional contract between homes and schools is undergoing change (Coleman & Hoffer 1987), our students are living in a global village, and creativity and the ability to live with the unfinished seems to be attitudes and skills that are needed.

LEARNING NEEDS OF CHILDREN AND YOUTH

Students are faced with an ever increasingly complex world in which they need to define their lives. Never have the challenges been greater, never the opportunities wider. What are their learning needs for facing an uncertain future?

We argue that schools should not prepare for a given future, but first and foremost to help students *prepare for the unknown*. With this perspective, some learning needs become more important than others:

Basic knowledge and skills: To include mastery in their mother's language, basic numerical competence, the ability to deal with a second language and the ability to understand the natural and social sciences. Maybe more important is learning how to solve problems and to communicate.

Knowledge and understanding: School culture is built on the misconception that understanding is synonymous with knowing. In school we learn to describe a phenomenon, and we learn to explain it. Understanding is more than knowing. It has to do with putting knowledge into practice. We understand something first when it has meaning, when it leads into practical use, when it leads to insight (Max-Neef, 1992). Students need to get real responsibility, also to develop their independence. At the same time they need to experience closeness and belonging and to experience adult role models.

Consumer and producer skills: All of us are daily in a consumer role, and one skill we need today (and even more in the future) is the ability to critically play this role. However, the role of *producer* will be a critical and attractive role in the next century. The producer group consists not just of those who produce goods and services but also those who are engaged in the production of ideas, new insights, art, politics, research, free time outlets, etc. What we need is people who have learned how to use their creativity, who have learned how to *creatively* solve problems, and who have training in choosing values *actively*. One characteristic of the people *"who has got it"* in the next century is that they play active producer roles.

WHAT IS A GOOD SCHOOL?

We argue that schools cannot deal with such a comprehensive future learning agenda on their own, in particular because the media, the workplace and the peer group have such major influences on the attitudes and behaviour of the students. Therefore, the organisational structure of schools will have to include those other actors, and the challenge is to use the many opportunities in the local environment, the work place and the media to help students fulfil their learning needs.

Of course, traditional schooling will take place. There will be subjects taught, projects developed, etc. Students, however, will have choices and ability to meet the requirements in many different ways (not only through ordinary class work).

There will be time for personal growth and social development. Learning is taking place much more in a workshop setting than in a classroom. The school is full of activities, it is a meeting point for people of all ages, its members have a role in decision-making and take responsibility for implementation.

The role of students have to change dramatically by bringing them into the school development work, both at the classroom level as well as at the school level. They need to experience the change process, learn the skills of solving problems, of communication in groups, of leadership and membership. It is by practising change process in the *"school laboratory"* that they can gain the security and strength to face an uncertain future (for more details see Dalin & Rust, 1996).

CHALLENGES TO SCHOOLS

Although many schools are working on parts of this agenda, we do not know of any example of schools taking on the entire reform agenda preparing students for the twenty-first century. Our argument is that if schools do not face up to the future challenges, they will increasingly be seen as obsolete, loose their public support and funding and (at most) fulfil a much more modest mission. Here are some of the challenges to schools:

- To connect essentials of today's curriculum, with the curriculum preparing students for the twenty-first century.
- To define and develop the future curriculum.
- To move from a traditional reproduction process in the classroom towards creativity and production in multiple environments?
- To move from fixed images of the future to work with the unfinished.
- To dramatically reduce much of the activities of today, define and develop the new school organisation providing space for both student and teacher initiatives.
- To prepare staff and other human resources for new roles and a new curriculum, drawing on human resources from all segments of society, using the best available approaches to staff development.
- To work politically in the local community (as well as nationwide) to build alliances for the Twenty-First Century School.

We could continue this list, only to illustrate that if schools (in particular individual schools on their own) should wish to embark on the future agenda, they would most likely be overburdened (knowing what we know about the daily challenges of schools). What then are our options?

WHAT DO WE KNOW ABOUT THE CHANGE PROCESS?

We assume that the Twenty-First Century School looks different in Ethiopia than in Norway, or should we not? It is reasonable to assume that the lives of today's Ethiopian and Norwegian first grade students will differ markedly in year 2030, although not necessarily in the same way and to the same degree as today.

We assume for a moment that developing the Twenty-First Century School has become a challenge in several countries across the globe. The reformers are however faced with major political, professional and popular opposition.

How can we draw on the reform literature to assist the reformers in our case? Do we have a knowledge base from school improvement research that could guide us through the planning and implementation of the Twenty-First Century School Project? I shall try to use my knowledge base in giving advice, later we shall see if the advice has a base in research! It may be useful for the reader of this document, before further reading, to consider what advice one would give to this project.

REAL NEEDS?

Many innovations have failed because they didn't reflect real needs felt by students and teachers (Dalin, 1978). I have argued strongly in the past that innovations have to reflect real needs, or at least that the effects of the innovation on classroom practices should be convincing.

The Twenty-First Century School is faced with a similar problem as many environmentalists argue for very unpopular changes today, in order to save the environment in the next century. It may mean higher taxes, more expensive fuel, changes in communication and transport patterns, major changes in production, etc., changes that do not seem necessary today. They do not reflect real needs. There are many reasons why the reformers might fail to get support (hopefully they will succeed before it is too late).

In a democracy, changes in social systems cannot be mandated. They need popular support. So far most innovations in education have been technical improvements that have improved the means, and not the objectives of education (Tangerud & Wallin, 1983). Our reform proposal is challenging the very nature of schooling and sets out to realise a totally new vision. How would one *get started* with such a radical idea?

What can we, from our research base, tell the policy maker who is convinced that schools need dramatic changes in the sense we are talking about? What would we tell a union leader? A headmaster? A teacher? A student?

ADVICE TO THE BOTTOM

Any one of the persons mentioned above, may well be a change agent, but our advice would probably be different depending on who we were talking to? Here is some general advice I would give to change agents at the bottom of the hierarchy, built on what we have learned from the very few radical reforms in the past:

- Work with parents and other partners to build alliances strong enough to convince key persons (grassroots movements, Escuela Nueva, etc.) (Dalin et al., 1994).
- The future is already here. In segments of society, build support and get help from multicultural groups, advanced firms who seek creative talents, environmentalists who are concerned with the ecology and others who work with future relevant issues.
- Involve students actively in the development of the reform. Students intuitively understand the urgency and the needs, and can be used as human resources in many of the curriculum areas (information technologies, ecology, etc.).
- Help the involved teachers to work in settings with human resources from the local community and industry, to make the task challenging and interesting and to use it as a part of Staff Development.
- When you are ready, ask for permission by your authority (Superintendent, regional administration, National Department of Education, etc.) to test the comprehensive reform in a five plus five year test with in-build and ongoing evaluation. The project would build on voluntary participation.
- Get the funding from whatever constituency agree to support the future agenda. For pilot projects this is often easier than one thinks!

What do we know from innovation research about the creation of ideas, the process of getting popular support, getting an entry and a project idea adopted by the policy makers? Fairly little, I think, although there has been some research on the creation of new settings in the USA (Sarason, 1972; Huberman & Miles 1984). Most research on change has looked at the implementation process, taking the innovation for granted. In particular there is little research on political ideas that run against the popular opinion at a given time.

ADVICE TO THE TOP

What would I tell the policy maker at the top, who is convinced that schools today do not make a sufficiently good job preparing for the twenty-first century?

The policy maker needs to build alliances and base his platform on popular support. He is, however, vulnerable because what he decides usually has implications for the system as a whole. He therefore faces different kinds of entry problems:

Before political support can be counted on, he would probably need to have backing by the research community, at least for legitimisation purposes (a case for a future research project?). He would need support by the country's future-oriented industry (what talents are they looking for?) and an agreement with the unions.

Who should lead this development program? In the new balance between central and decentralised responsibility that has occurred over the past 15 years, a clear trend has developed towards increased school autonomy (Von Reichard, 1992). Since our case is a reform that challenges the very basis of present day schooling, has a high political and economic significance and probably costs considerable development resources, my advice would be to lead the activity from the centre and give large room for individual school developments.

- Should it be mandatory for all schools? In the first ten year period I believe such a giant project needs to work with schools who are interested, a core group of staff at all levels need to be developed, materials developed and tested, and evaluations and research done. My advice would be to provide generous incentives and invite those who are interested and secure a solid institutional base (support and competence).
- Build in a review process agreement, by setting some fairly precise short term goals to be assessed. They would influence the further development of the program. All parties should work to learn from the first period, and thereby gradually clarify the vision.

GENERAL IMPLEMENTATION ADVICE

This is (again) a case where the expert are the learners. No one can be expert on year 2020 in 1996! Support to the implementation process cannot be sought in some expert group. It will be necessary to build a project based on knowledge learned from the daily work with students, colleagues, external resource persons and others. My advice, both at the bottom as well as at the top, would be:

- Develop a project organisation that reflects a future learning organisation in terms of evolutionary planning, on-going developmental oriented evaluation, staff development, team work and visionary leadership (Senge, 1990).
- Be concerned about giving all actors real, challenging and responsible roles. This also includes real (not only symbolic) participation of students, simply because they represent a resource. Besides, it is all being done for them and they are the ones taking the real chance(!).
- Teachers will be faced with a very demanding and challenging job situation. Be sure that there is enough time and room for discussions, collaboration, team work, peer support and peer reviews. It is by creating a group with a joint mission, with an open dialogue, that trust is developed to enable creative problem solving.
- Build additional security and professional quality by a school based in-service training program, where not only external experts are used, but where teachers from several twenty-first century schools can learn from each other's practice.
- Take teachers' (and other actors') concerns serious. *Problems are our friends*, they send a signal that things can be improved. Create norms of conflict resolution and general norms of interaction (Schmuck & Runkel, 1985).
- Take external pressures and demands seriously, but always analyse these forces

(as with internal forces) in relation to your mission and objectives. Real innovations imply mutual adaptation and development. Be sure it means development and not a watered down reform.

● Keep the project as a holistic concept, but break it down in digestible pieces to avoid overload of single actors and of the organisation. Overload is probably the most serious challenge of this reform.

IS THIS ADVICE BASED ON SCHOOL IMPROVEMENT RESEARCH?

I am partly basing my general orientation on a conflict paradigm (e.g. Paulston, 1976). This is however, mainly in the first mobilisation phase. As alliances are build and support secured, I see this reform in the light of evolutionary theories (Persons, 1950), mainly based on a contingency orientation.

First, I discover that my advice is much more based on research on organisations, than on school improvement research. Behind my advice are several research findings about schools as organisations (e.g. Lortie, 1975; Louis & Miles, 1990). At a more basic level I draw on more general theories of organisations and apply them to my knowledge about schools (e.g. Mintzberg, 1991; Senge, 1990; Gomez & Zimmermann, 1992).

The advice to keep the project as a separate development project is simply to minimise the danger of overload, watering down and conflicts. This could be the result if one should try to develop and implement the project in a normal school setting. Accepting the advice of a separate project, you are on the other hand, left with the transfer challenge from the pilot project to the ordinary system.

This is the traditional problem associated with the Research Development and Diffusion (RD & D) model of change, a problem that many developers in the seventies found hard to resolve (Dalin, 1973). There are, however, many techniques, mainly based on a change perspective rather than a product perspective that can be applied.

The values and norms behind the proposals on how to manage the project is drawn partly from organisational theory and practice (e.g. Weisbord, 1978; Schmuck & Runkel, 1985; Dalin & Rolff, 1993). Although the findings are probably not directly applicable to this project, I have also drawn on Effective School Research in terms of leadership factors (e.g. Sammons, Willman, & Mortimore, 1995).

The advice concerning implementation is drawing on Fullan and Stieglbauer (1991), the notions about a learning organisation from Senge (1990), several aspects of leadership based on Louis and Miles (1990) and Huberman and Miles (1984). As far as the system discussion is concerned, I have used work by Malik (1981) and the ad hoc form from Mintzberg (1991).

Although I am drawing on the research base, much of my advice is based on my practical experience and my beliefs. I simply belief for example, that there is a connection between how we organise a learning organisation and what students actually learn.

I am, of course, also drawing on my own research, to include an understanding of an innovation as a creative development process taking consideration of both external and internal needs. I am also building on the Real Needs Model of change, where ownership, professional mastery and leadership play a central role (Dalin, in press).

WOULD IT WORK WORLD WIDE?

Finally, in our visit to consultancy for the Twenty-First Century School, would the advice be relevant worldwide, or would it need adaptation dependent of the culture we work in? The popular answer is: *Yes, of course.* The notion is that the national (and local) culture makes a difference. The issue here is whether the most important variables are *structural* or *cultural*, and how they influence each other.

In recent years, interest in culture has risen markedly. A very important contribution to our understanding of which cultural factors can play a role in processes of change worldwide, has been made by Geert Hofstede in a study entitled "Cultures and Organizations" (1991). He has studied characteristics of national cultures by studying a (relatively speaking) uniform company culture (IBM) in 40 countries. He found that four factors were important for whether a given culture was willing to participate in the process of change:

Acceptance of power differences, or the extent to which a culture accepts the fact that power is unevenly distributed in an organisation (and in a society).

Degree of individuality, or whether it is expected that the individual or the individual school should take matters into their own hands or whether the group/company/society has (collective) responsibility.

Degree of masculinity, or the extent to which the predominant features of the culture are concerned about money, prestige, a career, and things (masculine) as opposed to being concerned about other human beings, the quality of life, expressing emotion, etc. (feminine).

The tendency to shy away from uncertainty by preparing for a safe career, creating a safety net of rules, monitoring conduct, and making sure that the rules are followed.

These findings may well spawn further questions. Is it, for example, reasonable that a typical individualistic culture will to any great extent rest content with the traditional school in which the individual teacher is mostly working for himself? Or can it be that a typically masculine culture, that also accepts immense power differences, will be more content with a hierarchical school organisation? Could it be that a culture which is largely security oriented will be cautious when it comes to major change in the schools? (Dalin, in press)

Our project, the Twenty-First Century School, can be characterised by Hofstede's four variables, because:

- The project needs to work with expertise at all levels, and it demands a horizontal organisation (low acceptance of power differences).
- The project demands co-operation among all actors to succeed (collective norms).
- The project probably will be seen as representing more feminine values than masculine values.
- People involved in the project need a high degree of tolerance for uncertainties.

In a country where the cultural tendencies differ from the characteristics of our project, we would need to consider alternative strategies. The most serious concern would be tolerance for uncertainties. It cannot be avoided. The experience shows however, that within a given culture (also within a given sub culture as the school system that is largely status quo oriented) there would be volunteers that react differently to the average teacher.

This means that it would be possible to develop the project in a pilot version. However, it would be hard to disseminate (in spite of success). Lack of dissemination is often the story of alternative schools that becomes islands in the great school landscape, and as we have discussed above, the lesson from projects developed according to the traditional RD & D model.

The differences *within* a culture are just as important as the differences *between* cultures. Focusing on national cultures can easily stigmatise and create superficial models. Nevertheless, Hofstede's work helps us to focus and understand more of the cultural variable in school improvement.

The other question is what part of the cultural variable is really a structural phenomena, based on years of tradition, but not necessarily a cultural trait. Indonesia, as we mentioned earlier, has learned traditional bureaucratic administration from the Dutch Colonial Administration, and it really functions as a barrier to meaningful change. Observing Indonesian educators in other settings show that they are not bureaucratic at all. The Yogyakarta experiment proved that when they were given a chance to function outside the traditional structure, they functioned extremely well!

After nine years as a consultant to reforms in German education, I have left the popular assumption that the Germans are rigid and bureaucratic. It is true that the school system functions that way (the connection goes all the way back to the Prussic administration). In development environments, however, the German partners work as creatively as any. It is when they have to consider the structure, as it interacts with the institutionalisation process, that they need to reserve themselves.

What is to be changed will largely determine *how* it should take place. Knowing which enormous challenges that are facing our educational system in the coming century, it is essential that we clarify which strategies are likely to be successful. We are faced not only with purely technological changes, nor merely changes in attitude and behaviour, nor structural changes, nor changes in norms and values. *What we are faced with is the changing of the entire school system's role in society, its adaptability, its relationship to users and society alike, as well as internal changes in roles, content and methods.* The focus is on an entirely new educational delivery system. What I mean is that the school system, like every other public institution, will have to make fundamental changes before it can master its new role in the society of the future, in close partnership with the media, industry, the church, the home, the health care system, and the local community.

THE ROLE OF SCHOOL IMPROVEMENT RESEARCH

I am convinced that the public sector in general, and the school sector in particular, needs to re-address itself facing an increasingly open future agenda. It is clearly necessary to build a change capacity into the system and the institutions. Thus, the school system preparing today's students for the future, also needs to reform its content and methods.

School Improvement Research can become a very valuable support in the coming years, helping pioneers to succeed. At a deep process level much of the research base that exists is valid in many settings. The challenge will be to reflect and learn alongside future oriented projects, and be able to act as a useful partner in development.

REFERENCES

Coleman, J. S., & Hoffer, T. (1987). *Public and private high schools: the impact of communities.* New York: Basic Books.

Dalin, P. (1978). *Limits to educational change.* London: McMillan.

Dalin, P. (1994). *How schools improve: An international report.* London: Cassell.

Dalin, P. (in press). *School improvement, theory & practice: An international handbook.* London: Cassell.

Dalin, P., & Rolff, H. G. (1993). *Changing the school culture.* London: Cassell.

Dalin, P., & Rust, V. D. (1983). *Can schools learn?.* London: NFER-Nelson.

Dalin, P., Dollar, B., Rust, V. D., Van der Bosch, L., Kershaw, N., & Skrindo, M. (1983). *Learning from work and community experience.* Windsor: NFER-Nelson Publishing.

Dalin, P., & Rust, V. D. (1996). *Towards schooling for the twenty-first Century.* London: Cassell.

Der Spiegel . (1993). Interview with Jürgen Mittelstraß, 18 October.

Fullan, M. G., & Stiegelbauer, S. (1991). *The new meaning of educational change.* New York: Teachers College Press, Colombia University.

Gomez, P., & Zimmermann, T. (1992). *Unternehmensorganisation. Profile, dynamik, methodik.* Frankfurt/New York: Campus Verlag.

Hofstede, G. (1991). *Cultures and organizations. software of the mind.* London: McGraw-Hill Co.

Huberman, M. (1983). Recipes for busy kitchens. *Knowledge; Creation, Diffusion, Utilization,* **4,** 478–570.

Huberman, M. A., & Miles, M. B. (1984). *Innovation up close: How schools improvement works.* New York: Plenum Press.

Hurrelman, K., & Engel, V. (1989). *The social world of adolescence, international perspectives.* Berlin/New York: Walter de Gruyter.

Lortie, D. C. (1975). *Schoolteacher. A sociological study.* Chicago: University of Chicago Press.

Louis, K. S., & Miles, M. B. (1990). *Improving the urban high school: What works and why.* New York: Teachers College Press, Colombia University.

Malik, F. (1981). Management Systeme, *Die orientierung,* **78.** Bern: Schweizerische Volksbank.

Max-Neef, M. A. (1992). *From the outside looking in: Experiences in 'barefoot economics'*. London: Atlantic Highlands.

McLaughlin, M. (1990). The Rand change agent study revisited: Macro realities. *Educational Researcher,* **19**(9), 11–16.

Mintzberg, H. (1991). The effective organisation: Forces and forms. *Sloan Management Review,* **54**. Winter.

Paulston, R. G. (1976). *Conflicting theories of social and educational change: A typological review.* University Center for International Studies, University of Pittsburg.

Persons, S. (red.) (1950). *Evolutionary thought in America.* New Haven: Yale University Press.

Postman, N. (1987). *Will the new technologies of communication weaken or destroy what is most worth preserving in education and culture?* IMTEC Schoolyear 2020 MAP no. 362.

Sammons, P., Willman, J., & Mortimore, P. (1995). *Key characteristics of effective schools: A review of school effectiveness research.* London: OFSTED.

Sarason, S. (1972). *The creation of settings and the future societies.* San Francisco: Jossey-Bass.

Sarason, S. (1982). *The culture of the school and the problem of change.* Boston: Allyn & Bacon.

Schmuck, R. A., & Runkel, P. J. (1985). *The handbook of organization development in schools* (Vol. 35, 3rd edition). Palo Alto, CA: Mayfield.

Senge, P. M. (1990). *The fifth dicipline, the art & practice of the learning organization.* New York: Doubleday Currency.

Tangerud, H., & Wallin, E. (1983). *Values and contextual factors in school improvement.* Paris: CERI, OECD.

von Reichard, C. (1992). Kommunales management im internationalen Vergleich, *Der Städtetag,* 12 January.

Weisbord, M. (1978). The wizard of O. D., *OD Practitioner,* **10**(2), 1–7.

Reconnecting Knowledge Utilization and School Improvement: Two Steps Forward, One Step Back[1]

KAREN SEASHORE LOUIS
University of Minnesota

Concerned about the lack of attention currently being given to dissemination and knowledge utilization in school reform, Karen Seashore Louis' main purpose in this chapter is to 'reconnect' knowledge utilization and school improvement. In addressing her theme, she reviews the current "state of the art" in knowledge utilization theory, and discusses how it is connected both to school effectiveness and improvement research. In the second section of the chapter some new perspectives, that have the potential for altering the way in which we understand knowledge utilization, are considered. In concluding, Seashore Louis outlines an emerging model that reconnects knowledge utilization and school improvement theory, as well as identifying implications for practice.

Theories of knowledge utilization and educational improvement have been closely linked since Havelock's (1969) classic literature review. This connection is also apparent in practice. On the one hand, school improvement depends on the implementation of new ideas about school organization and instruction; on the other, the refinement of theories about how schools use knowledge depends on having schools that serve as natural loci of experimentation and change. In recent years, however, explicit attention to dissemination and knowledge utilization have dropped from the agenda of most scholars interested in school reform. The purpose of this paper is to review emerging theories that may help to reconnect research on knowledge utilization with research on educational improvement. The analysis presented below assumes that the reader is familiar with the broad outlines of both school improvement and school effectiveness research (for example, Creemers, forthcoming; Fullan & Stiegelbauer, 1991), but less familiar with research traditions related to knowledge utilization.

In the first section of this paper I briefly review the current "state of the art" in knowledge utilization theory, and discuss how it is connected both to school effectiveness and improvement research streams. I then go on to look at some of the challenges to traditional theories of knowledge use that have been posed by postmodernists. Finally, I will briefly discuss why both the dominant and the challenging paradigms are not adequate to explain observed phenomena relating to dissemination and knowledge utilization in education.

In the second section of the paper I examine some new perspectives that have the potential for altering the way in which we analyze and interpret the observed phenomena discussed in the first section. In reviewing new ideas that can contribute to our understanding of knowledge utilization, it is critical that we maintain the

40

D. Hopkins (ed.), The Practice and Theory of School Improvement, 40-61.
© 2005 *Springer. Printed in the Netherlands.*

thoroughly interdisciplinary base of this field. Various writers approach the problem of putting knowledge to work with different lenses, and major reviews of the field (Rogers, 1982; Glaser, 1976) demonstrate that high quality research and ideas come from many disciplines. This paper cannot, of course, range as broadly as these book-length synthetic reviews, and since my objective is primarily to stimulate thinking about theory, I will confine myself to a few viewpoints from political, historical, organizational, and cognitive learning theory. In each case, I will briefly illustrate how the knowledge utilization perspective is reflected in current school improvement or school reform issues. I then turn to some elements of an intersection between knowledge utilization theories and school improvement theories that may drive us forward to a synthetic model of D&U that represents a paradigm shift rather than a paradigm revolution (Kuhn, 1970). Some suggestions about practical implications will also be made.

STATE OF THE ART

A recent issue of *Knowledge and Policy*, which emerged from a 1993 conference in Haifa on the topic of dissemination and utilization (D&U) in education, contains very timely reviews of both the "state of the art" in more traditional theory (Huberman, 1994), and a postmodernist critique of that perspective (Watkins, 1994). Because these are both thoughtful essays, I will review some of the main features of their arguments rather than to reinvent them. In addition, I will suggest some of the implications of traditional and postmodernist theories for school effectiveness and school improvement research.

Traditional D&U Theory Renewed

Huberman's review of the 'state of the art' begins with the common assumption that there is a "gap" between research knowledge and practitioner knowledge that cannot be bridged without calculated interventions. Early efforts to do so have long been viewed as hyper-rational due to their assumptions that (1) the flow of knowledge should be largely one-way, from the research community to the practice community; and (2) that more sophisticated forms of knowledge packaging and communication strategies would reduce, if not eliminate, the "gap" between what was known and what people did.

However, this body of research was never as simplistic as latter-day critics contend. As Havelock (1969) notes, scholarly work led to the conclusion that there was no simple, direct line between knowledge production and utilization. Early on, for example, there was attention to systemic and organizational barriers to and facilitators of knowledge utilization (as, for example, in the long line of work that started in the 1940s at Teachers College, which emphasized organizational and community factors in the spread of educational innovations, or the network analysis used to study the spread of medical and educational innovations (Mort,

1963; Coleman, Katz, & Menzel, 1966; Carlson, 1965)). While these and other studies operated within a positivist frame, in that they studied the spread of identifiable, research-based innovations within a defined population of practitioners, they foreshadow many of the more recent themes that look at situated or contextually specific reasons for learning and knowing.

Huberman (op cit.) notes the many challenges to a rational model of knowledge use but chooses to review the subtleties of the existing paradigm as it has emerged in the 1980s and early 1990s. He argues that five factors, at least in education, have demonstrated strong empirical relationships with knowledge utilization. These include: (1) the context of research, including characteristics of the knowledge base and the motivation of the researcher to disseminate to practitioners; (2) the user's context, including factors ranging from perceived needs to the perception of the value of the research information; (3) linkage mechanisms – a major focus of Huberman's own research – such as the 'sustained interactivity' between researchers and practitioners during the production and utilization phases; (4) the impacts of context and linkages on the resources, including attention, time, and acceptability of the research; and (5) the amount of effort expended creating an appropriate environment for use, which includes both the amount and quality of dissemination effort, the "useability" of the knowledge, and the quality of planning and execution in the "using site."

Huberman focuses on the role of reciprocally influential relationships in the process of knowledge utilization, but his perspective is consistent with the main lines of D&U research which emphasize the dispersion of knowledge to multiple sites of practice. This perspective can be seen in D&U efforts in a number of contexts, particularly those that emerge from the school effectiveness research tradition. For example, beginning in the late 1970s in the U.S., there were a number of efforts by regional educational laboratories and individual entrepreneurs to develop research-to-practice models that translated the results of the "effective schools" and "effective teaching" research into training and support programs for local schools. Similar experiments involving collaboration between schools, trainers and researchers, have been conducted in the Netherlands. Recent policy analyses in the U.S. and the Netherlands also point to the possibility of taking solid research findings related to effective schools and "translating" them into programs that can be adopted/adapted by schools (Datta, 1994; Overlegscommissie Verkennings, 1996). Policy makers in most countries believe that, with proper sticks and carrots, schools can be encouraged (or required) to become better consumers of "good research results." Popular documents, funded by a variety of agencies and teacher associations, (U.S. Department of Education, 1990; Fullan & Hargreaves, 1991) are intended to pave the way toward a better understanding of the connection between research knowledge and good school practice. Individual researchers who believe that they have found a key to improved student performance may also "package" their ideas with materials, models and training/support, as in Slavin's "Success for All" or Levin's "Accelerated Schools."

While Huberman's review is centered in this tradition, he makes a bridge to alternative perspectives in an important regard: he ties his own research findings regarding the importance of mutual influence to the notion of *social constructivism*. Huberman notes that researchers and practitioners may have a reciprocal influence on each other, and suggests that the need for sustained interactivity to promote research/knowledge utilization is consistent with some elements of the contemporary constructivist approach to teaching. The latter asserts that teachers' practitioner knowledge is constructed, largely by individuals, through both reflective practice (Schön, 1983) and through more disciplined inquiry, such as action research (Carr & Kemmis, 1986).[2] This perspective is more consistent with emerging ideas about D&U that are associated with school improvement research: an emphasis on the uniqueness of schools, on the importance of local development activity, and on the centrality of school culture and leadership to improvement (and even effectiveness) (Lagerweij & Haak, 1994; Newmann & Wehlege, 1995).

Challenges from Postmodernist Thinking[3]

Postmodern theory provides a sharp critique of the renewed conceptual framework presented in Huberman's review. Watkins (1994) succinctly summarizes a variety of different perspectives within the broad postmodernist frame. He begins where Huberman leaves off, with the observation that teachers construct knowledge as they go about their work, particularly when they engage in professional discussions around their own practice. Like many postmodernists, he then goes on to equate daily efforts to solve classroom problems with research – research that is highly contextualized because it is grounded in many years of "experience, training, problem solving, reflection and the struggle to make sense . . ." (p. 56). The school's process may appear nonlinear and random to outsiders, but a constructivist perspective accepts that (1) all knowledge is "local" (Geertz, 1983); (2) all knowledge is contested and partial, and there is no clear way to differentiate whether one knowledge claim is better than another; and (3) all knowledge is political, and influenced by the interests of those who develop and/or use it.

Watkins' discussion is grounded in philosophical debates about the nature of knowledge, which range at one extreme from a positivist argument for the objectivity of some forms of knowledge (e.g., scientific knowledge) to interpretivism, which argues that all knowledge is socially or individually constructed, and that the dominance of some ideas (ideologies) is largely a result of the power that groups may exert in promoting their perspectives. While Watkins distinguishes his own view, "critical realism" from extreme interpretivism (he acknowledges objective realities, but argues that we cannot perceive them directly or fully), but argues that:

> If [knowledge] meets scientific criteria, if it is generalizable, objective and theoretical, it is necessarily disembodied from its cognitive and social matrix, and no longer constitutes valid knowledge . . . it is intrinsically meaningless in other contexts. (p. 65)

Since it is obvious that people communicate with others every day, and that these communications have a clear impact on behavior (e.g., utilization), the apparent dilemma of observations of use and the theoretical impossibility of use can be resolved in two ways. The critical perspective espoused by Watkins, on the one hand, emphasizes the hegemony of particular groups who are able to make their interpretations of facts and information prevail. To avoid being a knowledge oppressor, the research community must, at minimum, give up control over the production of knowledge by creating learning communities with others, and at maximum eliminate any distinction between researcher and user (p. 69).

On the other hand, a "non critical theory" approach might differentiate between *knowledge* and *information*: Information can be easily transferred, but until it is interpreted, either by the individual or the group, it does not become useable knowledge (Louis, 1994). This position is consistent with a long line of mainstream sociological research that emphasizes the importance of socially constructed frames of reference that make learning at both the individual and group level possible – a position that predates the current wave of postmodernist thinking by several decades (Berger & Luckmann, 1966). It does not, however, demand adherence to Watkins' assumption that "knowledge is . . . not disseminateable per se . . . [but] will need to be reconstructed in any use setting" (p. 72).

Just as traditional views of knowledge utilization are alive and well in public policy arenas, so are modified postmodernist perspectives. A paper recently commissioned by the U.S. Office of Education (Campbell, 1995) suggests that teachers and other educational practitioners will only "buy" our scholarly research if they contribute to it in meaningful ways. The paper goes on to propose a variety of techniques that could be used to involve practitioners in the process of research, and of testing and developing practices based on scholarly knowledge. Permeating the paper is the assumption that knowledge produced "outside" the practitioner's own system is legitimately viewed as invalid, or "non-knowledge." Some forms of action research also adopt a similar position, arguing that teacher creation of knowledge within their own classrooms is the preferred strategy for creating renewed educational settings. The notion that local invention is the most effective response to variable local conditions is part of the policy thrust toward deconcentration and decentralization occuring in several countries. The "charter schools movement" in the U.S., for example, is promoted as an antidote to centrally managed effectiveness programs that "don't work." Proponents of charter schools, which are typically new schools founded by groups of teachers and parents, assume that improving educational performance requires invention at the lowest level, not the diffusion of centrally developed and approved ideas.[4] This assumption has been adopted as a public policy option in Sweden, where the National Board of Education was disbanded, the national curriculum simplified, and funding for education decentralized to municipalities (most of whom pass it through to individual schools).

A Critique

The so-called debate between "objectivist modernists" and "constructivist post-modernists" is, in my view, useful but limited. The debates are based in competing assumptions about science and the nature of knowledge, in which both modernists and postmodernists fail to fully reflect the conditions of inquiry or practice that are related to the development and utilization of knowledge in schools. In fact, there are also some similarities between the two. Both focus on the nature of knowledge and the relationship between knowledge production and knowledge utilization. Both assume, for the most part – even though the postmodernist perspective is critical of this situation – that formal knowledge is currently produced by researchers, and knowledge utilization, whether formal or informal, takes place in the work of practice. In other words, as Huberman posits, there is "a gap." In fact, as both acknowledge, the picture is more complex. However, neither has built a theoretical base that incorporates the complexity that they acknowledge.

Postmodernism appears to be more flawed than the revisionist versions of traditional theory. Most basic scientists have long ago given up the straw man of radical empiricism, which claims that "research knowledge" is entirely objective and capable of "trust tests" in a cross-cultural, value-free context (Duening, 1991). Similarly, it is hard to imagine even the most anti-research practitioners accepting the contention that the only knowledge that exists to guide what they do in their classroom is their own interpreted experience. Furthermore, some observational empirical evidence suggests that, although there is a gap between what researchers think they know and how users and practitioners of various sorts behave, there is also considerable activity around knowledge utilization that does not obviously involve dark efforts to impose ideas on a passive audience.

One thing is clear: even if postmodern philosophy is correct, it has not damaged "science" at all.[5] In a number of disciplines, for example, scholars are eagerly sought out for the potential commercial value of their ideas (Blumenthal, Causino, Campbell, & Louis, 1995). Rather than bemoaning lack of utilization, the research community debates where to draw the line between science and development of valuable ideas. The value of a scholar's "sticky knowledge" – Von Hippel's (1994) term for the insights from research that are not published, but can be communicated – is also apparent in education, where the work of some researchers leads them to be in high demand among the practitioner community (for example, U.S. researchers who have developed cooperative learning, or the university-based scholars who have new strategies for reading instruction). There is also clear evidence that people in normal positions and regularized circumstances seek and use knowledge that they believe to be, if not "objective" in the philosophical sense, at least useful, comprehensible and applicable. This knowledge is not always purveyed by social scientists and educational developers, but the fact that some of "our knowledge" is not viewed as "useable" (Lindblom & Cohen, 1979) does not obviate observations of knowledge use in educational practice.

If we see many examples of educators looking for or using externally generated knowledge as if it had real meaning, then postmodernism's argument that all knowledge that is local must be flawed. Similarly, if we see that most knowledge from the outside is viewed as suspect – or at least imperfect – until other additions have been made to it, then the modernist/positivist view is also problematic. Although the revisions to traditional theory suggested by Huberman attempt to address the problematic and contingent nature of knowledge, and to suggest ways in which dissemination activities may take account of this, his discussion does not address the other issues raised by postmodernists, namely that all knowledge is local, contested, and political.

In addition, there is an emerging body of theory and research that suggests a middle ground for dissemination scholars between the modernist extremes articulated by Popper (1972), on the one hand, and Geertz's (1983) more recent postmodernist work on the other. Furthermore, these middle ground positions are helpful in thinking about the problem of D&U and efforts to reform education than either of the more extreme positions. Some of these will be reviewed below.

NEW PERSPECTIVES

The new perspectives on dissemination and knowledge utilization that will be described briefly below can be viewed like layers on an onion of the problem of knowledge and practice. While it is clear that philosophers and most Western individuals – accept Descartes's dictum of "I think, therefore I am," which encapsulates the individual and psychological perspective on knowledge use, there has been a long recognition that thinking and subsequent knowing is constrained by context. Scholars have recently begun to examine these layers at a number of different levels: societal, organizational, and cognitive. Each of these will be briefly examined below, and the relationship of theoretical ideas to the problem of school improvement will be suggested.

Societal

At the societal level, two problems emerge from the current theoretical debates. The first has to do with the notion of research inquiry as hegemonic, while the second poses a fundamental problem of how knowledge becomes socially constructed/institutionalized if it is, by definition, local. Both of these issues are clearly related to current debates about how to reform schools, although they do not intersect neatly with the theoretical and practical perspectives of school effectiveness and school improvement scholars.

Political Perspectives

The notion that knowledge use is constrained by political contexts is not new. In the late 1980s, when evaluation research was well established on the policy scene, observers began to notice that publicly funded research was often used primarily because it "fits" a set of partisan purposes that were formed prior to the availability of the results. Legislative staff members did not read research to find out how their elected bosses should vote; instead they often combed research to find results that would fit the Congressperson's preferred stance. Thus, for example, even the most rigorous multimillion dollar educational evaluations relating to supplementary educational services for less advantaged children in the U.S. were ignored or embraced depending on personal perspectives.

Weiss and Bucuvalas (1980) were among the first to propose that knowledge produced through more-or-less rigorous inquiry needs to pass two types of tests before it is used: there is a *truth test*, which helps the individual or group looking at the information to decide whether it is a reasonable approximation of "reality," but there is also a *utility test*, by which the same groups determine whether or not it can be applied given a set of constraints, which could range from financial to potential negative consequences not considered in the research. Thus, for example, educational researchers in the U.S. wonder why policy makers continue to advocate for large schools and large districts when cumulative research evidence suggests strongly that size is negatively related to student achievement (Wahlberg, 1991; Lee & Smith, 1994). Yet, local school boards and superintendents can present compelling evidence to support bigger institutions that range from obvious (cost savings) to symbolic (large schools are more likely to have comprehensive programs, which increases public support for education).[6] The research may be true, but does not yet pass the utility test.

Weiss views knowledge as value laden, but, unlike the critical theorists, her perspective does not emphasize hegemony and explicit power interests, but the chaotic nature of knowledge and social cognition that make both dissemination and knowledge utilization uncertain activities. Research ideas can pop up and rejuvenate public discourse long after their initial proponents have forgotten them (Weiss & Bucuvalas, 1980). Knowledge that at least partially passes a truth test may creep into the public consciousness through the accretion of small decisions, producing a slow but nonlinear movement towards consistency. Thus, for example, the "small school" research is now beginning to shape U.S. public debates in a different form, through current efforts to create "charter schools" and alternative learning environments for special populations.

A recent analysis by Vickers (1994) compares Weiss's theory of semi-ordered chaos and the hegemonic, critical perspective in two cases where "outside" knowledge was incorporated into Australian educational policy. In one instance, she shows that in the school-to-work transition policies used knowledge produced by the Organization for Economic Cooperation and Development (OECD) in ways that are consistent with the "knowledge creep" process, gradually producing a new social consensus. In a second, a single policy maker used OECD knowledge to justify a decision already reached rather than to engender a public discussion. In both cases there was a "paradigm shift" in policy, but in one the process of utilization was decentralized and focused on changing meanings among a broad set of actors, while in the other it represented legitimation for a policy arrived at among a small group. As Vickers points out, both of these cases support Weiss's basic assumptions that the meaning of knowledge use is not simple, and that, while "knowledge is power," that power can take on different forms, not all of which involve imposing one world-view upon another.

These contrasting political perspectives on knowledge utilization are clearly related to problems of school improvement today. On the one hand, in many countries we observe devolution or decentralization policies that place the responsibility for knowledge utilization and change more clearly in the hands of schools, where teachers and school leaders struggle together to create better learning conditions for students. The assumption that localized processes of knowledge utilization can contribute to educational improvement is a distinct "paradigm shift" that has occurred on an international basis, propounded by an increasing consensus among teacher associations, politicians and parents in countries as diverse in educational tradition as Sweden, the Netherlands and the U.S. On the other hand, political actors continue, even in these settings, to make decisions that involve centralized, hegemonic decisions that are intended to shock parts of the system into change – for example, efforts to introduce new standards-based reforms in both the U.S. and the Netherlands, and to argue for more central control over some "high stakes" examination system in Sweden. The fact that these are international trends, often involving the borrowing of language and ideas between countries, suggests a strong currency for an international flow of political perspective about educational reform. Ideas about effective schools and effective teaching have also been widely diffused through international research networks, and later, within countries, have been influential in affecting policy discourse.

Historical Perspectives

The problem of determining how, under the constructivists/local knowledge assumptions, technologies become used over a wide area is addressed in a creative study by Turnbull (1994). Turnbull begins with a basic assumption of constructivism and postmodernism, namely that all knowledge is local. However, he points out that the localness of knowledge refers to its *production*, and not to its *distribution and/or use* by others. Turnbull points out that modern science is not the only example of knowledge produced at one site being broadly shared. He goes on to explore the processes by which this occurred in historical situations: The Anasazi Indians of the American Southwest, the Incas of Central and South America, the Micronesian navigators, and the stonemasons who were responsible for the building of the medieval cathedrals.[7] His analysis of the strategies that were used by earlier cultures to transmit theories and "useable knowledge" across groups that were loosely connected and, in some cases, did not even share a base of common language, is instructive for our current understanding of how knowledge becomes widely shared and acted on.

For example, the European cathedrals were built over many years by illiterate craftsmen who shared no measurement systems, geometries or other tools that we would normally think of as essential to the creation of a complex, coherent building. Coherence was also achieved in spite of many major design changes. This was done through the use of transferable templates, which permitted a single design to be reproduced as often as necessary. This illustrates a basic principal of knowledge dissemination and utilization: theory, to become widely shared, demands "templates of practice." His analysis of historical systems also suggests that the boundaries of the movement of knowledge are affected by power: at some boundary, the "owners" of the knowledge, whether they are stonemasons or priests, lose their communication or network influence, and the knowledge system that they represent becomes culture bound. However, it is not only formal power but the utility of the knowledge across sites that accounts for its spread.

Turnbull's analysis focuses on the implications of communications technology for the hegemony of ideas in modern science. I interpret his data from another perspective: *although all knowledge may be local, local knowledge can be shared under conditions where there are both limited and elaborate infrastructures and communication vehicles.* Furthermore, the analysis demonstrates rather compellingly that human beings can exercise limited control over difficult environments only when they share such knowledge beyond the localized groups.

Although Turnbull's historical analysis may seem remote from the issues of educational improvement, I would argue that it is pertinent to adjudicating the traditional and postmodernist perspectives on the role of practitioner in the development of educational knowledge. A romantic view of school practice argues that teachers, as artists, must invent, reflect and study in their own settings. Unlike artists, however, many constructivist perspectives on practice do not carry the artistic analogy further: the teacher, unlike the artist, does not have a concrete artifact of their developmental work. However, we increasingly see ideas about practice spreading through networks of teachers with a communication infrastructure (journals, professional meetings and books) that is very limited. This is particularly evident in the networks of innovative schools that have been initiated in both the U.S. and other countries, where there is an explicit effort to ensure that the development and flow of knowledge is controlled by teachers and not scholars.[8] The flow of ideas across organizational and even cultural boundaries suggests that even when teachers create their own knowledge, there is a strong desire to share and spread under largely non-hegemonic conditions.

Organizational

Two recent developments in organizational studies seem to have profound implications for D&U and school reform. Each also contributes to the debate between the modernists and postmodernists. The first builds on the work of institutional sociologists of the 1950s and early 60s, but takes a more radical stance in terms of the degree to which external influences condition internal stabilities in organizations, and thus affect the knowledge that will or will not be used. This school of thought, which emerged in the early 80s, is referred to as the "new institutional-ism" (Powell & DiMaggio, 1991). A second line of work, which is more recent, examines organizations as systems that learn. This perspective is consistent with traditional open-systems theory as it applies to organizations (Scott, 1981; Katz & Kahn, 1966), but pays more attention to the mechanisms that foster or inhibit the ability of organizations to take advantage of knowledge that is generated locally or from outside.

The "New Institutionalism"

The new institutionalism in organizational theory begins with the assumption that the patterned regularity of organizational behavior, which is particularly notice-able within sectors or industries, is a major social phenomenon that requires explanation. The assumption that repetitive social relations are "facts" that can-not be reduced to individual explanations is as old as the field of sociology itself. What is "new" about the current perspectives, however, is the emphasis placed on explaining lack of variation in organizational patterns – for example, why do all modernized countries have a higher education system that is increasingly similar both in terms of types of institutions, length of study, and the names of courses of study? Why are school classrooms remarkably similar whether one is in California or Illinois?

The answer, according to institutional theory, is that the emergence of an organizational field, or a collection of organizations in the same line of business, becomes both an opportunity to influence the environment and also a normative environment. This has tremendous implications for dissemination and utilization of knowledge, because:

> . . . in the long run, organization's actors making rational decisions construct around themselves an environment that constrains their ability to change in later years. *Early adopters of organizational innovations are commonly driven by a desire to improve performance. But . . . as an innovation spreads [within the field] a threshold is reached beyond which adoption provides legitimacy rather than improves performance . . . .* Thus organizations may try to change constantly; but after a certain point in the structuration of an organizational field, the aggregate effective of individual [organizational] change is to lessen the extent of diversity within the field. (DiMaggio & Powell, 1991, p. 65) (Italics added).

The spread of the community college system throughout the United States after its initial "invention" in California is an example of this. Particularly striking is its institutionalization as a system that contains both academic and vocational programs and the similarity of programs between units that avowedly respond to local needs (Brint & Karabel, 1989).

The similar nature of individual organizations within an institutionalized field is maintained not by rational choices, but by the dominance of the norms and symbols that come to exemplify "the best of what we do." Through their participation in symbolic rituals, organizational action reinforces the order of the institution and its relationship to society (Friedland & Alford, 1991, p. 250). To give just a small example, the use of bells in U.S. high schools to signify the end of classes has little practical significance. Yet, in many schools, efforts to eliminate the use of bells raised intense passion among constituents: bells are an important symbol of the orderliness of schooling, as contrasted with the chaos of adolescence. But resistance to change is not a consequence of individual concerns, but of environmental pressures from the organizational field, and, especially in the case of public sector organizations, from other constituencies who reinforce the norms and symbols. These may range from the general public (who expect bells) to the government and accrediting associations/inspectorates.

In spite of the rigidities introduced into an institutionalized organizational field, change and knowledge utilization do, of course, occur. However, reforms often occur in a mimetic fashion, and become quickly institutionalized (DiMaggio & Powell, 1991). The "middle school movement" in the U.S. is an example of the diffusion of institutional change based on a mixture of scholarly research, information about practices in other schools, and "local knowledge" of what will work given district customs and constraints. What the institutional perspective points to, however, is the increasing similarity in features of schools that are deemed necessary in order to qualify as "a real middle school." The initial period of reform was more localized and chaotic, with many efforts to invent new solutions to the problem of creating more academic engagement among early adolescents. In the past few years, on the other hand, key structural elements, such as teacher teams, interdisciplinary curriculum, and co-operative pedagogical styles, have become widely shared and legitimated, *although the research base supporting their value is still rather slim.* Having these changed structures and practice becomes prima facie evidence that the school has reformed, even in the absence of data about student academic success.

To summarize, the institutional perspective picks up the postmodernist themes of hegemony of particular ideas and forms of knowledge, but argues that these are largely created within the organizational field (often in response to external pressure) and are self-sustaining. Rather than emphasizing the "localness" of knowledge construction and use, they point to empirical evidence suggesting the impossibility of local change in the absence of similar pressures and needs to change throughout the field. Furthermore, they point to the mimetic nature of organizations within an institutionalized field as a determinant of what knowledge will be used. Traditional D&U concerns with communication, packaging of knowledge, etc., are relatively unimportant in this perspective, as are postmodernist concerns about "whose knowledge is it?" Educational reform within the broad organizational field is not dependent on the availability of specific externally developed models complete with training and support, although these may support change in individual schools. More important to determining whether there will be broadly based reform is the intersection between pressures for change from outside, local development activities, and the rapid spread of workable ideas between adopting units.

Organizational Learning

If the new institutionalism examines the environment for dissemination and knowledge utilization activities that affect whether information will spread within an organizational field, the organizational learning model moves into the interior of the school, looking at features that affect the adaptability of individual units.

Organizational learning begins with a social constructivist perspective: knowledge is not useable at the local site until it has been "socially processed" through some collective discussion and agreement on its validity and applicability (Louis, 1994). Organizations that are more effective in using knowledge have certain characteristics – for example, they have denser internal communication networks, and more individuals serve in boundary spanning roles where they legitimately bring in new ideas from the outside (Senge, 1990; Daft & Huber, 1987). Conversely, organizations that don't learn – even from information that they request – are characterized by internal boundaries, competition, excessive individual entrepreneurship and lack of continuity in personnel (Corwin & Louis, 1984).

Three features of school culture and practice – memory, knowledge base and development, and information distribution and interpretation – can also have a big impact on teachers' ability to sustain an openness to learning (Kruse & Louis, 1994):

Shared memory consists of collective understandings that are developed in an organization over time. The shared memories held within a school will influence its capacity to learn (Louis & Miles, 1990). Positive shared memories from previous learning situations create an openness to future learning; conversely, memories based on bad experiences act as barriers to new learning efforts. Without an adequate base of common understandings from which to draw, teachers can be reticent to begin new learning activities (Louis, 1994).

Individual learning is usually defined by the notions of acquisition, storage and retrieval. Organizational learning adds an additional step because *collective knowledge* must be created through discussion so that all (or most) members of the school share it. Schools cannot learn until there is explicit or implicit agreement about what they know – about their students, about teaching and learning, and about how to change. As schools work to create a shared knowledge base, they draw from three sources:

- *Individual knowledge*: Teachers possess knowledge about the curriculum and their own instructional methods, but do not always have a common language or the skills to engage in serious conversations about their practice. Structures such as teaching teams or peer coaching relationships have often fallen short of their promise to increase conversation (Hargreaves, 1994; Kruse & Louis,

1996). Thus, to create a dynamic learning environment in school, we usually need more than individual knowledge.

- *Knowledge they create*: Teachers generate knowledge when they systematically examine their practice (Carr & Kemmis, 1986), and practitioner-driven research and other means of self-appraisal can be more effective stimuli for change than external mandates (Fullan, 1993). Self-appraisal is not easy, however, and requires support for mutual learning, such as shared planning periods, regular faculty meetings devoted to discussion, and informal communication (Louis, Marks & Kruse, 1994).

- *Knowledge sought from others*: When schools embark on reform they may be given or seek solutions to problems from other schools or "experts." If this externally provided information is discussed sufficiently, it can become shared knowledge. But as with self-appraisal, the ability to seek and to absorb information varies between schools (Louis, 1994).

An information base is not enough. Teachers must also *interpret and distribute* information before it becomes knowledge that is applicable across classrooms. Joint efforts to interpret information must provide a foundation for challenging existing beliefs about the school, or previous views of teaching and learning remain unchanged (Louis, Kruse & Raywid, 1996). Genuinely understanding an innovation or the basis on which it rests is necessary if teachers are to make the new information applicable in the classroom.

The organizational learning perspective is critical when we consider the relationship of D&U and improvement theories in education. It suggests that the possibility for reaching a school with new knowledge is not dependent on where the knowledge comes from or the linkage mechanism, but on characteristics of the school and its ability to process information. While "sustained interaction" with a researcher might enhance utilization, it cannot produce it in the absence of the structures and culture that encourage the development of a shared knowledge base that will guide collective action. In this respect, Huberman's (1994) focus on school characteristics as a factor mediating knowledge use intersects clearly with emerging ideas about school development and improvement.

Cognitive Learning Theory

At the most micro-level, new advances in cognitive theory suggest many directions for theories about dissemination and knowledge utilization. Many of these are consistent with postmodernist perspectives, but they assume that individuals not only create their own knowledge, but also incorporate knowledge from outside. Since few postmodernists attend to cognitive psychology, assumptions about individual learning are not well reflected in their work. The new traditionalists, such as Huberman, however, have made considerable progress in thinking about ways that emergent findings related to how both children and adults learn, should affect how we think about dissemination and knowledge utilization (Huberman & Broderick, 1995).

Huberman and Broderick argue that "the most hopeful new avenue of inquiry in the D&U literature emerges when dissemination takes place . . . through . . . sustained interactions between researchers and practitioners" (pp. 3–4), a point that is central to the renewed traditional theory. They go on, however, to explore the cognitive and structural conditions under which sustained interaction may result in increased meaning on the part of both. Central to their argument is the idea of socially shared cognition that has begun to dominate the field of cognitive development (Brown, 1994). This perspective assumes that individuals learn best when they interact with peers and relate new ideas to an existing core of shared knowledge, and when peers challenge individually held assumptions and provide incentives to rethink their previous ideas. However, this learning-through-interaction works best when the learners have reached a minimal level of understanding of the content, and the challenges are not too great.[9] This perspective differs from organizational learning theory discussed above in that it draws on Vygotsky (1986), who argues that interpersonal processes must be translated into intra personal processes before learning can be said to have occurred. Thus, their emphasis is largely on the way in which individual researchers and practitioners enter into relationships that cause them, as individuals, to change their assumptions and even their behaviors.

The notion that thinking is "irreducibly a social practice" implies that dissemination and utilization are best thought of as a process of reflection, in which people with different, but overlapping, knowledge and culture meet to consider their common concerns (Huberman & Broderick, 1995, p. 21). Researchers (or others who operate at the edge of applicable knowledge) point to dissemination as a factor in obtaining greater clarity about their own work, just as young students obtain greater mastery of concepts when they are obliged to teach them to others.

Because researchers and practitioners in education share some assumptions, but have divergent experiences on most dimensions, "opportunities for cognitive discrepancy are good; they are fed by attempts to reconcile the conflicting versions of what those issues now mean" (Huberman & Broderick, 1995, p. 30). In other words, if there were no sustained interaction, both would be likely to be startled by the response of the other, but fail to give it serious consideration as they moved on to other pressing issues and social partners. By creating some shared meanings and language through discussion of cognitively dissonant ideas, a new reality is created that did not previously exist:

> Thus, cognitive shifts are not activated 'within the person' or 'within the setting' but rather within the mediating activity itself, dynamically and dialectically – a bit like Leontiev's concept of a continuously shifting 'construction zone' or Schön's notion of 'reflecting in practice' and Dewey's idea of 'knowing in action.' (p. 31)

While retaining the notion of the valid-yet-different perspectives of research knowledge and practice knowledge, Huberman and Broderick argue that it is at the intersection between the two (or between any two sets of "local knowledge" for that matter) that cognitive progress is made at the individual level.

PARADIGM SHIFT OR PARADIGM REVOLUTION?

The purpose of the above review of recent research in a number of disciplines is to point to two issues: first, there is a proliferation of research and theory bearing on the intersection of knowledge dissemination and utilization and school improvement, and second, much of this research already incorporates elements of a postmodernist position, although none of the new approaches discussed, with the exception of Turnbull, is consciously postmodernist. The convergence taking place around the key elements of postmodernist views of knowledge will be considered first, and then the implications for school improvement practice:

- *All knowledge is local.* The above discussions assume that local knowledge is a key feature of the landscape of change, but most would agree that there is important knowledge that is not local. Knowledge created elsewhere must, according to all theories, be compatible with existing belief structures, diffuse rapidly throughout the organization field so that it becomes legitimized, have utility in local sites, and be "processed" in ways that make it fit with local preferences. The "new institutionalism" adds another wrinkle to this: knowledge that is widely diffused is itself institutionalized so that it can be easily legitimated and shared within the "field" of organizations, sites or other members of the culture. Although a great deal of important knowledge may come from outside the organization, the above theories also suggest that this information is always combined with local knowledge.
- *All knowledge is contested and partial.* This feature of postmodernism is supported by most of the new theoretical advances. At the cognitive learning level, for example, the contesting of knowledge is central to the learning process. The "new institutionalism" (at a very different level) argues that it is the incontestability of many features of an organizational field that make it difficult to change: only where there are chaotic events that cause either insiders or outsiders to question the knowledge will change/knowledge utilization occur. The contested nature of knowledge is a key element of political theory, and the primary element that lead both Weiss and Vickers to conclude that there are many ways of using knowledge, depending on the degree to which it is "solid" – e.g., meets truth and utility tests. In the organizational learning model, it is the debate and discussion around contested or partial knowledge that leads to a new consensus about how to solve problems or modus operandi, a perspective that is consistent with emergent cognitive learning theory.
- *All knowledge is political.* Insofar as the newer theories address power, there is a tendency to follow Macauley's assumption that "knowledge is power" and that the creation of knowledge creates powerful settings (including constraints).

None of the perspectives reviewed here adopt, however, the critical postmodernist perspective, in which the power associated with knowledge is viewed as an instrument of oppression. Cognitive learning psychologists, for example, do not find that children who temporarily have knowledge that others lack use this power to dominate. Turnbull, who applies a postmodernist frame, assumes that knowledge becomes less powerful as one moves from the center to the edges of the social group. Nevertheless, political contexts are critical to understanding knowledge use, as is demonstrated by the analysis of knowledge utilization among policy makers, and the "new institutionalists" observations that knowledge use is constrained as the organizational field becomes defined both by internal norms/patterns and external expectations/regulation.

While all of the perspectives reviewed are consistent with some of the basic tenets of postmodernist views of knowledge, they also assume that knowledge has some realist qualities, and that it can be used by individuals who have not created it. The use process is complex and difficult to predict: there will be no production function D&U models emerging from this set of scholars. But messy cannot be equated with impossible. In fact, we may draw some lessons from Bordieu and Waquant (1992) in this regard:

> Awareness of the limits of objectivist objectivation made me discover that there exists, within the social world, and particularly within the academic world, a whole nexus of institutions whose effect is to render acceptable the gap between the objective truth of the world and the lived truth of what we are and what we do in it. . . . It is this double truth, objective and subjective, which constitutes the whole truth of the social world. (pp. 254–5)

Postmodernist theory has taken us two steps forward, demanding that we examine a wide variety of assumptions that we make about the nature of knowledge and its effects on ourselves and our settings. However, we must also take one step back and realize that the most profound of these insights are compatible with revised versions of existing theories, particularly if we broaden where we look for research to inform dissemination practice. In addition, as I have argued throughout this paper, the modifications to theories about knowledge and knowledge utilization are compatible with what we know about educational improvement and the directions of educational reform policies in a variety of settings.

SOME IMPLICATIONS FOR PRACTICE

"But is there any there, there" – the bitter query of the disillusioned postmodernist? If we think of "there" as D&U applications in pursuit of educational change, there are many implications of the layered approach to D&U theory proposed in this paper. In particular, I would argue that there is a self-conscious need to reintegrate our understanding of the nature of three arenas of knowledge: research results related to educational goal achievement (school effectiveness, broadly conceived), educational change processes (school improvement, broadly conceived), and the knowledge use strategies that can be pursued both inside and outside schools to improve student learning and development. None of these are inconsistent with Huberman's reformulation of traditional dissemination theory, but suggest an expanded context for thinking about D&U. In particular, we need to draw upon the research about political, historical and organizational contexts affecting knowledge use to enrich the micro-level perspectives that are emphasized in Huberman's formulation. While it is beyond the scope of this paper to suggest a model for D&U and school development that fully incorporates these theories, a few examples can demonstrate the practical connections:

- *Research knowledge generated in universities or research institutes is only one source of knowing, and its use must be negotiated during a dissemination process. This fluid relationship-and even co-dependence – between research and practice must be acknowledged, and researchers must be prepared to be open to involvement in the development process at the user level.* If this is true for "gold standard" science (Datta, 1994), it is particularly true for social science and educational research, which is less likely to be "gold standard." Much of the best practice in education is not generated by scholars in laboratories, but by teachers and school leaders in actual settings. On the other hand, the spread of new ideas in education is frequently aided by research, which may codify and extend practice-based knowledge as well as making independent contributions to it. In many cases, researchers may not be as well equipped to engage in field-based development over long periods of time (they have students and new research projects to carry out), but the others may fulfill this function *if* they have a deep understanding of the emerging nature of the negotiated knowledge.
- There has been a trend in many countries to involve practitioners in setting some educational research agendas (for example, serving on peer review panels), and even as co-participants in carrying out research. This is thought to make research more grounded and, hence, useable. However, *involving "users" in research will not necessarily make the research more useable – except at a particular site or among those who have been directly involved.* While it may be good for researchers to become more connected to practice settings and vice-versa, the power of site or place when it comes to change is infinite. Thus, extensive involvement of practitioners as researchers should occur for its own direct benefits, and not because it improves the possibility of dissemination and utilization.
- The main barriers to knowledge use in education are not at the level of individual resistance, but lie in the *rigidities induced in institutionalized organizational fields, organizational designs that do not foster learning, and political agendas that are not consistent with the information.* Changing these inter-organizational rigidities in the short run may be extremely difficult. The motto under these circumstances is not to engage in Sisyphysian efforts, but to "try again another day" because contextual circumstances change for reasons that have nothing to do with research or educational policy.[10]
- The barriers to knowledge utilization are often to be found in organizational

design. This suggests that *redesigning the school should be part of any effort to engage in "sustained interactivity"* around research utilization. The emphasis on developing school capacities for self management that is emerging in many countries should be shaped around those capacities that augment not only the ability to manage budgets and personnel policies, but also that attends to the creating of schools that can learn from knowledge that is generated inside and outside the school.[11] This objective will require policies, and direct training and support to schools that have previously not engaged in these efforts.

- *Some forms of useful educational knowledge will spread with minimal dissemination effort* – due to organizational field compatibility or because the field develops an infrastructure to assess and legitimate the type of knowledge. We do not always need elaborate infrastructures or sustained interactivity to ensure the incorporation of new ideas in practice. On the other hand, *other knowledge that is equally important may require systematic policy interventions and organizational support before it becomes integrated into practical thinking.* Assessing what will catch on naturally, and what will not is, at least at this point, not easily predictable, which makes the job of D&U practitioners difficult.

- *Utilization and impact can only be assessed over the long haul.* Short run efforts to foster major utilization are likely to appear shallow and hegemonic to practitioners, and to fail to disrupt the interorganizational rigidities of the field. Policy makers and disappointed researchers are likely to view these efforts as "failures" and to pronounce schools as impossible to change. Thus, research-based efforts to create school reform must be based on an extended time-line.

- Creating sustained interactivity is not a solution to the D&U problem but, if it becomes a norm, it may well increase the scholarly impact because it *enlarges the organizational field.* We should not limit the idea of sustained interactivity to the relationship between a "knowledge producer/researcher" and "knowledge consumers/practitioners" but focus also on formal and informal networks for transmitting knowledge between units. These networks, to be successful, must involve "practice templates" that combine research knowledge and practice knowledge.

These are only a few suggestions. The main point of this paper has been to argue that we do not need to throw away our theories about school reform processes and D&U, but to merge and enlarge them. The fact that enlarged perspectives have reasonable practical implications is only one of many criteria that need to be applied to determine whether the analysis presented above is valid.

ENDNOTES

[1]   The preparation of this paper was supported in part by the University of Oslo, and the Center for the Organization and Restructuring of Schools at the University of Wisconsin. None of the sponsoring agencies is responsible for the ideas presented herein.
[2]   Huberman also correctly notes that the constructivist teaching models, which emphasize the need

for knowledge from "the outside," whether it is generated by research or through teacher inquiry, to be filtered through an interpretive individual lens, do not meet the tests of contemporary postmodernist theory, which fundamentally contests the empiricist assumptions underlying both Huberman and constructivist teaching stances.

3   Andy Hargreaves recently noted that one may whole-heartedly agree that we live in a postmodern era, defined by a radical shift in the nature of economies, employment and social relations, and disagree with many of the propositions put forward by self-style postmodern thinkers (personal communication). This point should be borne in mind in reading this entire essay.

4   It is important to distinguish between the U.S. "charter schools movement" which emphasizes the creation of new, alternative educational settings that have specific, measureable learning objectives, and the "voucher movement," which advocates a market model of parental choice. Although both give increased flexibility to parents, the underlying assumptions about how educational will improve (quasi-regulated market versus professional knowledge creation and accountability within new schools) are entirely different.

5   Datta (1994) argues that educational research knowledge has certain "fuzzy" properties that make it more disputable, but shows that reaching consensus in harder disciplines, such as medical research, is also extremely difficult.

6   The tendency of policy makers to ignore research on the negative effects of large schools is not confined to the U.S. National policy in the Netherlands has supported mergers between smaller schools, creating some of the largest – and adminisratively incoherent – secondary schools in Europe.

7   In doing so, Turnbull confronts two assumptions: first, that "prescientific" societies did not have authoritative knowledge or shared paradigms; and second, that modern scientific knowledge is "different" and more disseminateable because it is more universal and value free.

8   Similar results could have been located in the strong Teacher Center movement in England, which has now been largely de-funded.

9   While Huberman and Broderick do not note this, it also assumes that the group has certain characteristics: that there is a shared 'culture' at some level, and that there is a level of familiarity that permits communication of challenges in ways that are not excessively threatening.

10   A particularly interesting example is the Netherlands, where 70% of the schools operate under public funding but private auspices. Only a few years ago it would have been politically impossible for the government to make strong recommendations related to curriculum or teaching methods within the quasi-private sector. Today, the Inspectorate and the government are increasingly putting pressure on schools to, for example, adopt research validated reading instruction rather than older models that are commonly used.

11   Bryk, Camburn and Louis (1996) have shown a strong relationship between the development of professional communities in Chicago elementary schools and knowledge utilization or oganizational learning. Marks and Louis (1996) also show strong relationships between school structure (increasing teacher influence over school policy) and learning capacities.

REFERENCES

Berger, P., & Luckmann, T. (1966). *The social construction of reality*. New York: Doubleday.

Blumenthal, D., Causino, N., Campbell, E., & Louis, K. S. (1996, February 8). Relationships between academic institutions and industry in the life sciences B: An industry survey. *New England Journal of Medicine*, **334**(6), 368–373.

Bordieu, P., & Wacquant, L. (1992). *An invitation to reflexive sociology*. Chicago: University of Chicago Press.

Brint, S., & Karabel, J. (1989). *The diverted dream: Community colleges and the promise of educational opportunity in America, 1900–1985*. New York: Oxford University Press.

Brown, A. (1994). The advancement of learning. *Educational Researcher*, **7**(8), 4–12.

Bryk, A., Camburn, E., & Louis, K. S. (1995). *Promoting school improvement through professional communities: An analysis of Chicago elementary schools*. Paper presented at the annual meeting of the American Educational Research Association, New York.

Campbell, P. (1994). *Whose knowledge is it?: Involving teachers in the generating and using of information on educational innovations*. Washington, D.C.: USOE/OERI.

Carlson, R. (1965). *The adoption of education innovations*. Eugene: Oregon Press.

Carr, W., & Kemmis, S. (1986). *Becoming critical: Education, knowledge and action research*. London: Falmer.

Coleman, J., Katz, E., & Menzel, H. (1966). *The diffusion of medical innovations*. Indianapolis, Indiana: Bobbs-Merrill.

Corwin, R. G., & Louis, K. S. (1982). Organizational barriers to knowledge use. *Administrative Science Quarterly*, **27**.

Daft, R., & Huber, G. (1987). How organizations learn. In N. DiTomaso & S. Bacharach (Eds.), *Research in the sociology of organizations* (Vol. 5). Greenwish, CT: JAI.

Datta, L. (1994). *A matter of consensus*. Washington, D.C.: U.S.D.E., O.E.R.I.

DiMaggio, P., & Powell, W. (1991). The iron cage revisited: Institutional isomorphism and collective rationality in organizational fields. In Powell, W & DiMaggio, P. (Eds), *The new institutionalism in organizational analysis*. Chicago: University of Chicago Press.

Duening, T. (1991). *Rorty's liberal ironist: A model for information age undergraduate education*. Dissertation: University of Minnesota.

Friedland, R., & Alford, R. (1991). Bringing society back in: Symbols, practices and institutional contradictions. In W. Powell & P. DiMaggio (Eds), *The new institutionalism in organizational analysis*. Chicago: University of Chicago Press.

Fullan, M. (1993). *Change forces*. London: Cassell.

Fullan, M., & Hargreaves, A. (1991). *What's worth fighting for?: Working together for your school*. Ottawa: Ontario Public School Teachers' Federation.

Fullan, M., & Stiegelbauer, S. (1991). *The new meaning of educational change*. New York: Teachers College Press.

Geertz, C. (1983). *Local knowledge: Further essays in interpretive anthropology*. New York: Basic Books.

Glaser, E., et al. (1976). *Putting knowledge to use: A distillation of the literature regarding knowledge transfer and change*. Los Angeles: Human Interaction Research Institute.

Hargreaves, D. (1994). The new professionalism: The synthesis of professional and institutional development. *Teaching and Teacher Education*, **10**(4) 423–438.

Havelock, R. (1969). *Planning for innovation through the dissemination and utilization of knowledge*. Ann Arbor, MI: CRUSK, Institute for Social Research, University of Michigan.

Huberman, M. (1994). Research utilization: The state of the art. *Knowledge and Policy*, **7**(4), 13–33.

Huberman, M., & Broderick, M. (1995). *Research utilization: An exploration into new territories*. Prepublication manuscript.

Katz, R., & Kahn, R. (1966). *The social psychology of organizations*. New York: Wiley.

Kruse, S., & Louis, K. S. (1994). *Organizational learning in schools: A framework for analysis*. Paper presented at the annual meetings of the American Educational Research Association, New Orleans.

Kuhn, T. (1970). *The structure of scientific revolutions* (2nd ed.). Chicago: University of Chicago Press.

Lagerweij, N., & Haak, E. (1994). *Eerst goed kijke*.

Lee, V., & Smith, J. (1994). *Effects of restructured teacher worklife on gains in achievement and engagement for early secondary school students*. Paper presented at the annual meeting of the American Educational Research Association, New Orleans.

Lindblom C., & Cohen, D. (1979). *Usable knowledge: Social science and social problem-solving*. New Haven: Yale University Press.

Little J. (1993). Teachers' professional development in a climate of educational reform. *Educational Evaluation and Policy Analysis*, **15**(2), 129–151.

Louis, K. S. (1994). Beyond managed change: Rethinking how schools improve. *School Effectiveness and School Improvement*, **5**, 1–22.

Louis, K. S., Kruse, S., & Raywid, M. (1996). Putting teachers at the center of reform: Learning schools and professional communities. *NASSP Bulletin*, **80**, 9–22.

Louis, K. S., Marks, M., & Kruse, S. D. (1994). *Teachers' professional community in restructuring schools*. Paper presented at the annual meeting of the American Educational Research Association, New Orleans.

Louis, K. S., & Miles, M. (1990). *Reforming the urban high school: What works and why*. New York: Teachers College Press.

Marks, H., & Louis, K. S. (1996). *Teacher empowerment and school organizational capacity*. Paper presented at the annual meeting of the American Educational Research Association, New York, April.

Mort, P. R. (1963). Studies in educational innovation from the Institute of Administrative Research: An overview. In M. B. Miles (Ed.), *Innovation in education* (pp. 317–328). New York: Teachers College Press.

Newmann, F., & Wehlege, G. (1995). *Effective school restructuring*. Madison, WI: Center for Educational Research, University of Wisconsin.

Overlegscommissie Verkennings. (1996). Amsterdam: KNAW

Popper, K. (1972). *Objective knowledge: An evolutionary approach*. Oxford: Clarendon Press.

Powell, W., & DiMaggio, P. (Eds). (1991). *The new institutionalism in organizational analysis*. Chicago: University of Chicago Press.

Rogers, E. (1982). *The diffusion of innovations*. New York: The Free Press.

Schön, D. (1983). *The reflective practitioner: How professionals think in action*. New York: Basic Books.

Scott, W. R. (1981). *Organizations: Rational, natural, and open systems*. Englewood Cliffs, N.J.: Prentice Hall.

Senge, P. (1990). *The fifth dimension: The art and practice of the learning organization*. New York: Doubleday.

Turnbull, D. (1994). Local knowledge and comparative scientific traditions. *Knowledge and Policy*, **8**, 29–54.

U.S. Department of Education. (1990). *What works*. Washington, D.C.: author.

Vickers, M. (1994). Cross-national exchange, the OECD and Australian education policy. *Knowledge and Policy*, 7, 24–47.

Von Hippel, E. (1994). "Sticky Information" and the locus of problem solving: Implications for innovation. *Management Science*, 40(4), 429–437.

Vygotsky, L. S. (1986). *Thought and language*. Cambridge, MA: MIT Press.

Wahlberg, H. (1989). District size and learning. *Education and Urban Society*, **21**, 154–163.

Watkins, J. (1994). A postmodern critical theory of research use. *Knowledge and Policy*, 7(4), 55–77.

Weiss, C., & Buculvalas, M. (1980). *Social science research and decision making*. New York: Columbia University Press.

Weiss, C. (1980). Knowledge creep and decision accretion. *Knowledge*, **1**, 381–404.

The School Effectiveness Knowledge Base as a Guide for School Improvement

JAAP SCHEERENS

University of Twente, Netherlands

In this chapter Jaap Scheerens outlines a conceptual map of the conditions for effective school-ing. He does this by examining the ' modes', 'mechanisms' and 'levers'of schooling. Modes are the various malleable dimensions of schooling. Mechanisms are theory embedded principles that could explain why certain factors work in education. Levers are the operational action implications of mechanisms. In the second part of the chapter he assesses the knowledge base of school effectiveness research by establishing to what extent empirical research covers the conceptual map, by examining the formal structure of integrated models and by evaluating the results of empirical research. In the last section of the chapter Scheerens draws out the implica-tions for school improvement. He further discusses the concepts of educational leadership and evaluation-oriented school policy as being the most promising levers for school improvement, particularly within the school management mode.

There are some strikingly successful examples in which the relationship between school effectiveness research findings and school improvement appears to take the simple form of using the research results as recipes for improvement programmes (e.g. Houtveen & Osinga, 1995). Despite these findings the relationship between effectiveness research and improvement-oriented action is generally considered as less straightforward (Reynolds, Hopkins, & Stoll, 1993).

One main reason for this latter position is the fact that a lot still needs to be done in the realm of making sense of the research knowledge on school effective-ness, in order to obtain a clear picture on its usefulness for school improvement. The main focus of this contribution will be a critical assessment of this knowledge base, examining basic mechanisms, rather than recipes, for their improvement-oriented potential.

THE CONCEPTUAL MAP OF SCHOOL EFFECTIVENESS: CRITERIA AND MODES

School effectiveness is a causal concept. The basic orientation refers to the extent to which education output or outcomes are influenced by malleable conditions. These conditions may be financial or material "inputs" or more complete activi-ties and processes in areas like school management, the curriculum and teaching.

In practically all types of educational effectiveness research, ranging from stud-ies on "education productive functions" to case-studies of unusually high (or low)

62

D. Hopkins (ed.), The Practice and Theory of School Improvement, 62-84.
© 2005 *Springer. Printed in the Netherlands.*

performing schools, achievement in basic subjects like reading, arithmetic, mathematics and mother tongue, are used as the effect or outcome variables. In order to assess the "added value" of schooling these effects need to be adjusted by taking into account prior achievement and other relevant background variables of pupils, like intelligence and socio-economic status. Main traditions in educational effectiveness research (cf. Scheerens, 1992) focus on different types of antecedent conditions of adjusted effects. Economic-oriented research on educational production functions has concentrated on resource-related input variables like per pupil expenditure and class size. Instructional effectiveness has focused on classroom management and teaching strategies, while school effectiveness research has a strong bias towards school level organizational and managerial conditions, including "structural" as well as "cultural" factors. In more recent integrated studies these three types of malleable conditions are all taken into account (cf. Creemers, 1994).

Despite the wider scope of such integrated studies empirical, school effectiveness research is still focused at a sub-set of possible effect criteria and a sub-set of possible malleable antecedent conditions. A broader look at both key-elements of the school effectiveness definition is needed as part of the aim to assess the relevance of current effectiveness research for school improvement. This will be done by referring to alternative criteria of organizational effectiveness and by considering a more extensive set of antecedent conditions, to be labelled as "modes of schooling".

Criteria

Drawing upon the organizational effectiveness literature, Scheerens (1992) distinguishes five alternative effectiveness criteria, each embedded in a particular type of administration or organizational theory.

The criterion that is consistent with the choice of effect variables in empirical school effectiveness research is the *productivity* criterion. Its background is economic rationality. In operational terms the productivity criterion means that the output of an organization's primary (or "production") process is taken as the effect criterion.

The orientation in organizational science, known as organic systems theory, views the organization as being in constant open exchange with the environment. In order to survive, the organization should adapt to external circumstances. According to this view *adaptability* is the main criterion to judge whether an organization is to be seen as effective or not.

Adaptability can be manifested by choosing the "right" objectives, by acquiring vital resources and by satisfying external constituencies and clients.

Involvement and satisfaction of the members of the organization is a criterion that originates from the human relations school of organizational thought.

The ideal of the organization as a smooth running machine and a harmonious whole, reflected in the image of the bureaucracy emphasises the value of predictability, and *continuity* and "bureaucratic" survival of the organization or department.

The political view on organizational functioning emphasises a particular type of adaptivity, namely the kind of *responsiveness* that strengthens the power of parts of the organization. This is accomplished best by satisfying important external stakeholders.

These various perspectives on organizational effectiveness are summarized in table 1 (cited from Scheerens, 1992).

There are different points of view on how to deal with these multiple effectiveness criteria, Faerman & Quinn, (1985) see these as "competing" values, whereas Scheerens (1992) argues that the criteria can be related to each other according to a means-to-end framework, with "productivity" as the ultimate criterion and the others as "supportive conditions" to this criterion. Cheng (1993) considers alternative effectiveness criteria from a contingency perspective. This implies that he sees the relevance of a particular criterion as dependent on characteristics of the situation in which the organization finds itself at a given time. Relevant situational dimensions that he recognizes are: the degree to which goals are clear and consensual, the importance of powerful constituencies, and the degree to which relevant environmental contingencies are changing (ibid, p. 11).

These are two important implications of this exposure on alternative criteria of educational effectiveness for school improvement: first of all that each of these criteria can be used as a target for school improvement oriented action. Secondly, and an implication of the final point, there is the realization that the bulk of school effectiveness research is only relevant to the degree that school improvement is outcome oriented. A "holistic" approach to school improvement might want to address all criteria at the same time, perhaps (as in Scheerens', 1992 perspective) as mutually supportive, rather than competing conditions.

Table 1: Organizational effectiveness models

theoretical background	effectiveness criterium	level at which the effectiveness question is asked	main areas of attention
(business) economic rationality	productivity	organization	output and its determinants
organic system theory	adaptability	organization	acquiring essential inputs
human relations approach	involvement	individual members of the organization	motivation
bureaucratic theory; system members theory; social psychological homeostatic theories	continuity	organization + individual	formal structure
political theory on how organizations work	responsiveness to external stakeholders	subgroups and individuals	independence power

Modes of schooling, as points of impact for attaining effectiveness

In the previous section it was established that the overall concept of school effectiveness can be differentiated according to normative criteria related to various schools of thought in organizational science.

When, according to a very general framework, the concept of school effectiveness is divided into a domain of *effects* and a domain of *causes, or means,* we will now turn to a further differentiation of the cause/means domain. In doing so the question that is dealt with concerns the *distinction of all possible features of the functioning of schools that are malleable in order to reach the effects that are aimed for*. Such a broad perspective is needed to obtain as complete a picture as possible on elements and aspects of schooling and school functioning that are potentially useable in improving effectiveness.

According to well-known distinctions in organizational science (e.g. Mintzberg, 1979; De Leeuw, 1986) the following categories ought to be used as a core framework:

- goals
- the structure of positions and sub-units ("Aufbau")
- the structure of procedures ("Ablauf")
- culture
- the organization's environment
- the organization's primary process

Table 2 below gives a further elaboration of these main categories. Since the sub-categories refer to aspects of school organizational functioning that are fairly well-known, they will not be described in detail (for a more extensive treatment see Scheerens & Bosker, 1997). The two sub-categories in the cultural domain refer to measures that can be used to shape the organization's culture in a way that is supposed to be effectiveness enhancing. Direct measures refer to attempts to deal directly with cultural aspects, whereas indirect measures are thought of as cultural implications of structural innovations.

Modes, as distinguished in table 2 above, that have received relatively little attention in empirical school effectiveness research are:

- setting goals in terms of various effectiveness criteria
- division of tasks and positions
- grouping of teachers and students
- personnel management
- financial & administrative management
- indirect measures to change culture
- buffering

Again, as with respect to criteria of organizational effectiveness, the exposition on "modes" indicates that the set of conditions that empirical school effectiveness research has concentrated on, is by no means exhaustive. The "white spots" listed

Table 2: Modes of schooling

Goals
- goals in terms of various effectiveness criteria
- priorities in goal specifications (cognitive – non-cognitive)
- aspirations in terms of attainment level and distribution of attainment
- goal coordination

Aufbau (position structure)
- management structure
- support structure
- division of tasks and positions
- grouping of teachers and students

Ablauf (structure of procedures)
- general management
- production management   planning

- marketing management   coordinating
- personnel management (among which hrm, hrd)   }   controlling
- financial & administrative management   assessing
- cooperation

Culture
- indirect measures
- direct measures

Environment
- routine exchange (influx of resources, delivery of products)
- buffering
- active manipulation

Primary process
- curricular choices
- curriculum alignment
- curriculum in terms of prestructuring instructional process
- pupil selection
- levels of individualization and differentiation
- instructional arrangements in terms of teaching strategies and classroom organization

above are as many additional possibilities for both future effectiveness oriented research and school improvement programs.

Theoretical redirection: mechanisms and leves of school effectiveness

The school effectiveness research literature has been criticized for its lack of theory. Scheerens (1996) made an attempt to relate various more established economic and organization theories to the findings of school effectiveness research. He considers synoptic planning and bureaucratic organization, retroactive planning and the learning organization as its structural pendant, public choice theory, contingency theory and chaos theory.

From each of these theories he extracts a basic mechanism or principle that is seen as explanatory to established findings in organizational (and school) effectiveness.

Mechanisms

These mechanisms or "theory embedded principles" are considered as generally applicable explanatory principles that may be used in making clear "why" "what works" in educational organizations. "Levers" are very much implied in these principles. Nevertheless, the term is thought to have additional meaning because the "levers" refer to directly operational measures to realize the action potential implied in the levers. So, for instance, the cybernetic principle (evaluation/feedback/correctisation) is seen as a mechanism, whereas the application of a school self-evaluation system is taken as an associated "lever".

Theoretical redirection of in-school effectiveness thinking can be paraphrased as using available theory to deduct levers that, applied to a particular mode of schooling may explain why a particular factor (or set of factors) is expected to increase the chance of the attainment of a particular effectiveness criterion.

Since a "recipe-orientation" of gearing school improvement to the findings of school effectiveness research has already been put aside as less relevant, mechanisms and levers may be particularly useful as general orientations for school improvement activities.

Synoptic planning and bureaucratic structuring

The ideal of "synoptic" planning is to conceptualize a broad spectrum of long term goals and possible means to attain these goals. Scientific knowledge about instrumental relationships is thought to play an important role in the selection of alternatives. Campbell's (1969) notion of "reforms as experiments" combines a rational planning approach to social (e.g. educational) innovation with the scientific approach of (quasi-) experimentation.

The main characteristics of synoptic planning as a prescriptive principal conducive to effective (in the sense of productive) organizational functioning, as applied to education, are:

- "proactive" statement of goals, careful deduction of concrete goals, operational objectives and assessment instruments;
- decomposition of subject-matter, creating sequences in a way that intermediate and ultimate objectives are approached systematically;
- alignment of teaching methods (design of didactical situations) to subject-matter segments;
- monitoring of the learning progress of students, preferably by means of objective tests.

As stated before, given the orientation towards the primary process, inherent in economic rationality, the synoptic planning approach in education applies most of all to curriculum planning, design of textbooks, instructional design and preparation of (series of) lessons.

When the ideal of rational planning is extended to organizational structuring, related principles about "controlled arrangements" are applied to the division of work, the formation of units and the way supervision is given shape. "Mechanistic structure", "scientific management" and "machine bureaucracy" are the organizational-structural pendants of rational planning (cf. Morgan, 1986, ch. 2). The basic ideas go back to Max Weber, who stated the principles of bureaucracy as "a form of organization that emphasizes precision, speed, clarity, regularity, reliability, and efficiency achieved through the creation of a fixed division of tasks, hierarchical supervision, and detailed rules and regulations". Although Mintzberg's conception of the professional bureaucracy, applicable to schools and universities, is often treated as the complete antithesis of classical bureaucracy, it should be underlined that the basic notion of standardization and predictability of work-processes, be it with a considerable band-width of individual leeway, is retained.

Alignment of individual and organizational rationality

A central assumption in the synoptic planning and bureaucracy interpretation of the rationality paradigm is that organizations act as integrated purposeful units. Individual efforts are expected to be jointly directed at the attainment of organizational goals. In the so called political image of organizations (Morgan, 1986, ch. 6) this assumption is rejected, emphasizing that "organizational goals may be rational for some people's interests, but not for others" (ibid, p. 195). The fact that educational organizations consist of relatively autonomous professionals, and loosely coupled sub-systems is seen as a general condition stimulating political behaviour of the members of the organization.

In public choice theory the lack of effective control from democratically elected bodies over public sector organizations marks these organizations as being particularly prone to inefficient behaviour, essentially caused by the leeway that is given to managers and officers to pursue their own goals besides serving their organization's primary mission (see Scheerens, 1992, ch. 2).

Public choice theory provides the diagnosis of instances of organizational ineffectiveness, such as goal displacement, over-production of services, purposefully counter-productive behaviour, "make work" (i.e. officials creating work for each other), hidden agendas and time and energy consuming schisms between sub-units. When discretional leeway of subordinate units goes together with unclear technology this too adds to the overall nourishing ground for inefficient organizational functioning; see Cohen, March and Olsen's famous garbage can model of organizational decision-making (Cohen, March, & Olsen, 1972). Not only government departments but also universities are usually mentioned as examples of types of organizations where these phenomena are likely to occur. Market mechanisms and "choice" are seen as the remedy against these sources of organizational mal-functioning.

Notes of criticism that have been made with respect to the propagation of choice are that parents' choices of schools are based on other than performance criteria (Riley, 1990, p. 558), that "choice" might stimulate inequalities in education (Hirsch, 1994) and that completely autonomous primary and secondary schools create problems in offering a common educational level for further education (Leune, 1994).

The alleged superiority of private over public schools is the most supportive piece of empirical effectiveness research for the claims of public choice theory, although the significance of the results in question is much debated (Scheerens, 1992). At the macro level there is no evidence whatsoever that national educational systems with more autonomy of schools perform better in the area of basic competencies (Meuret & Scheerens, 1995).

Retroactive planning and the learning organization

A less demanding type of planning than synoptic planning is the practice of using evaluative information on organizational functioning as a basis for corrective or improvement-oriented action. In that case planning is likely to have a more "step by step", incremental orientation, and "goals" or expectations get the function of standards for interpreting evaluative information. The discrepancy between actual achievement and expectations creates the dynamics that could eventually lead to more effectiveness.

In cybernetics the cycle of assessment, feedback and corrective action is one of the central principles.

Evaluation – feedback – corrective action and learning cycles comprise of four phases:

- measurement and assessment of performance;
- evaluative interpretation based on "given" or newly created norms;
- communication or feedback of this information to units that have the capacity to take corrective action;
- actual and sustained use (learning) of this information to improve organizational performance.

In the concept of the learning organization procedural and structural conditions thought to be conducive of this type of cycles are of central importance. Examples are: the encouragement of openness and reflectivity, recognition of the importance of exploring different viewpoints and avoiding the defensive attitudes against bureaucratic accountability procedures (Morgan, 1986, p. 90).

From a theoretical point of view the cybernetic principle of evaluation – feedback – action is very powerful as an explanatory mechanism of organizational effectiveness. It should be noted that evaluation and feedback also have a place in synoptic planning *and* in the perspective from public choice theory. In the former case evaluations are most likely to be used for *control* purposes, while in the latter case there would be an emphasis on positive and negative *incentives* associated with review and evaluations. From the organizational image of the learning organization, adaptive and learning implications of evaluations are highlightened.

It can be concluded that in depth empirical study on school-based evaluations and pupil monitoring, both with respect to the evaluation procedures and the impact on school-organizational functioning deserves a high place on the agenda of theory-driven school effectiveness research.

Contingency theory

"Contingency" is described as a "thing dependent on an uncertain event" and "contingent" as "true only under certain conditions" (Concise Oxford Dictionary). In organizational science "contingency theory", also referred to as the "situational approach" or contingency approach (Kieser & Kubicek, 1977), is taken as the perspective from which the optimal structure of an organization is seen as dependent on a number of "other" factors or conditions (De Leeuw, 1982, p. 172). These other factors are mostly referred to as "contingency factors" (Mintzberg, 1979). Contingency factors are a rather heterogeneous set of conditions, both internal and external to the organization: age and size of the organization, the complexity of the organization's environment and the technology of the organization's primary process.

Some well-known general hypotheses about effective combinations of contingency factors and structural configurations are:

- "the older the organization, the more formalized its behaviour";
- "the larger the organization, the more elaborate its structure, that is, the more specialized its tasks, the more differentiated its units, and the more developed its administrative components";
- "the more sophisticated the technical system, the more elaborated the administrative structure, specifically the larger and more professional the support staff, the greater the selective decentralization (to that staff), and the greater the use of liaison devices (to coordinate the work of that staff)";
- "the more dynamic the environment, the more organic the structure" (Mintzberg, 1979, ch. 12).

When the question is raised whether relevant substantive hypotheses can be deduced from contingency theory to further research into contextual effectiveness, the most promising areas appear to be:

- hypotheses concerning changes in the technology of the primary process of learning and instruction, e.g. the contrast between very structured approaches and educational practices inspired by constructivism (Scheerens, 1994);

- hypotheses concerning increased environmental uncertainty for educational organizations, here international comparisons with respect to different degrees and patterns of functional and territorial decentralization could be mentioned as an example (cf. Meuret & Scheerens, 1995)

In making up the balance, contingency theory appears to have more "in it" than has currently been used in educational effectiveness research. In this way it offers certain possibilities to improve the theoretical basis on educational effectiveness that research could become driven by specific hypothesis deduced from theory.

Chaos theory

"Chaos theory" or dynamical systems theory is concerned with "the exploration of patterns emerging from apparently random events within a physical or social system" (Griffith, Hart, & Blair, 1991).

One of the basic principles of chaos theory is that "small causes may have large effects" and that relatively minor variations in entrance conditions may have enormous consequences when interrelationships between phenomena develop over time. In some mathematical functions there may be linear growth for a particular range of values of a critical parameter, but when this range of values is exceeded chaotic patterns may appear. Examples are the constraint growth function and Kaldor's macro-economic model (Van Lidt de Jeude & Brouwer, 1992, pp. 14–15).

New patterns of sub-systems that may emerge in a seemingly chaotic environment are sometimes interpreted in terms like synergism, self-organization or autopoiesis. Autopoiesis points at the tendency of self-reproduction of systems and organism. Synergism is to do with the evolvement of new macro-level structures when micro-level sub-systems interact in a complex way. It should be noted that the construct of self-organization inspired by chaos theory is more extensive than the principle of double loop learning in Morgan's characterization of the learning organization, as discussed in an earlier section. Chaos theoretical conceptions of self-organization include *positive* feedback cycles, next to negative feedback (emphasized in cybernetics) and developments that do not confirm to the phenomenon of homeostasis.

Mechanisms and levers

Mechanisms have been described as general explanatory principles. In order to emphasize the action potential that is more or less inherent in these mechanisms the term "levers" is coined. A lever characterizes a particular type of action orientation (see the example given earlier of the cybernetic principle as a mechanism and school self-evaluation as a lever). Table 3 connects levers to mechanisms.

The most straightforward mechanisms are the ones in the two upper rows of table 3. Both levers require structured action and instrumentation. They differ, however, by a proactive versus retroactive orientation. The retroactive orientation

Table 3: Theories, mechanisms and levers of effective schooling

theory	mechanism	lever
synoptic planning machine bureaucracy	proactive planning and control	programming/monitoring, structuring
retroactive planning learning organization	cybernetic principle	evaluation and feedback
public choice theory	market mechanism	choice, competition
contingency theory	fit	organizational design
chaos theory	self organization	laissez-faire serendipity

in "evaluation-based school improvement" is also more modest in the comprehensiveness and time-horizon of taking action. Retroactive planning is more in line with piece-meal engineering and incrementalism.

Creating market-mechanisms is probably a lever that is more relevant at the above school level (district, region, country) than it is a likely measure that individual schools can take. Nevertheless a school may enlarge opportunities for parent involvement and consumer review, as it may use improved performance to compete with other schools.

The same type of reasoning applies to the lever of organizational design to make the school organization responsive to basic contingencies, like change in educational technology, increased complexity of the environment. Some of the contingencies will not be school specific. Others, like a dramatic change in school size, are, and are therefore amenable by specific actions, to adapt to such contingency factors. The congruence thesis from contingency theory is even more amenable to internal control of the school. This thesis calls for fitting arrangements between internal design parameters like the style of leadership and the autonomy of sub-units.

"Levers" with respect to the enhancement of self organization are creating a low degree of formalization, horizontal decentralization and a playful, dynamic interaction vis à vis external developments. The problem with this organizational image is the degree to which it corresponds to the reality of schools in most countries, assuming that this reality is still rather formalized, predictable and situated in relatively stable environments.

So far the mechanisms have been associated with levers that are of a structural nature. The question arises to what extent cultural aspects should be seen as independent from these mechanisms and are to be seen as an area of "leverage" in itself. This question will be addressed in the following sub-section, after having globally described the cultural dimension.

The leverage of culture

Organizational culture is a mode of school functioning rather than a mechanism. Culture, in the sense of shared meanings, collective norms, and views on interaction and collaboration, is of great importance in providing the "normative glue" that holds the organization together.

In the literature (Maslowski, 1995) three aspects of organizational culture are usually distinguished:

a) The *substance or direction* of a culture. In the school effectiveness research literature substantive dimensions that have been emphasized are: an achievement-oriented ethos, and a safe orderly climate.

b) The *homogeneity* of the culture, that is the degree to which the organizational culture is shared among the members of the organizations. This aspect of organizational culture is of particular relevance to educational organizations, which have been described as "loosely coupled", "professional bureaucracies" and even "organized anarchies". Although there are some important general factors like common training and a relatively stable tool base of skills inherent in the concept of the professional bureaucracy, enstrengthening consistency of practice and the cohesion among teachers is usually seen as an important factor of increasing school effectiveness.

c) The strength of the culture, i.e. the degree to which cultural elements more or less coercively influence the attitudes and behaviours of the members of the organization. The strength of the organization's culture could best be seen as a relative phenomenon. Given the supposedly loosely coupled nature of most schools some degree of strengthening the culture will generally be seen as conducive to increased effectiveness.

It is a matter of debate whether operational measures (levers in our terminology) can be discerned that directly influence organizational culture. Most of the structural mechanisms and levers that were discussed in previous sections clearly have cultural implications. For example, synoptic planning and bureaucracy call for unity of purpose and harmonious cooperation. The choice perspective encompasses value conflicts between individual and organizational goals and the metaphor of the learning organization implies openness to new developments and participative planning. So, one could take the position that culture is to be changed indirectly, through structural modifications. Schein (1985) distinguishes several other indirect mechanisms to change organizational culture, apart from structural (re)design and common procedures: the design of buildings and interial decoration; stories and myths about the organizations, and formal agreements on principles.

But apart from these Schein also mentions five "direct mechanisms":

1) Priorities set by the organization's leader(s).
2) The leader's reaction to critical events.
3) The enactment of desired behaviour.
4) The setting of norms and standards for delivering rewards and providing status.
5) Criteria with respect to hiring and firing.

In the light of the previous discussion these direct mechanisms distinguished by Schein rather enforce the earlier impression that "culture follows structure".

A preliminary question, with regards to some of these points, is the question which arrangements exist for activities like priority setting, being explicit on desired behaviour, student and criteria setting. The question to which degree they exist and what their substantive direction is, seems to me a question of structure rather than culture.

Although several analysts of this issue (Hargreaves, 1995; Cheng, 1993) leave the matter open (i.e. do not take a stance on the issue of structure shaping culture or vice versa) a final, rather down to earth argument for the primary of structure would be that structure appears to be more directly (and therefore more easily) malleable than culture. Nevertheless the cultural dimension, even if it is seen as a "by-product" of particular structural arrangements should be seen as a very important "booster" of school improvement.

THE EMPIRICAL KNOWLEDGE BASE ON SCHOOL EFFECTIVENESS

In literature reviews there appears to be a considerable consensus on the factors that are seen as effectiveness enhancing conditions at school and classroom level. The summary tables cited from Scheerens and Bosker (1996), combines seminal reviews by Sammons, Hillman and Mortimore (1995), Levine & Lezotte (1990), and Cotton (1995) provide an adequate representation of this growing consensus.

Coverage of the modes of schooling

When comparing these summaries with the modes of schooling that were distinguished in the previous section, most of them appear to be represented. "Finance" being the main exception, while "curriculum" is less pronounced than was perhaps to be expected. In both overviews "structural" factors (like monitoring, parent involvement, educational leadership) and "cultural" factors (expectations, achievement orientation, cohesion) are about evenly represented. The overall assessment of the coverage of the school effectiveness knowledge base of the main aspects of school functioning is that this coverage is sufficiently comprehensive.

Empirical basis

It is not easy to assess the exact empirical basis of the list of factors summarized in tables 3 and 4. Most reviews do not state the statistical significance nor the size of the effects of the various factors in terms of association with adjusted achievement results. There are, as yet, hardly any meta-analyses which have been specifically focused on school management and organization variables. A recent exception is the meta-analysis constructed by Witziers, Bosker & Scheerens (see Scheerens &

Table 4: Effectiveness enhancing conditions of schooling in three review studies (italics in the column of the Cotton study refers to sub-categories).

Levine & Lezotte, 1990	Sammons, Hillman & Mortimore, 1995	Cotton, 1995
Productive climate and culture	Shared vision and goals A learning environment Positive reinforcement	Planning and learning goals Curriculum planning and development
Focus on central learning skills	Concentration on teaching and learning	Planning and learning goals *school wide emphasis on learning*
Appropriate monitoring	Monitoring progress	Assessment (district, school, classroom level)
Practice-oriented staff development	A learning organization	*professional development* collegial learning
Outstanding leadership	Professional leadership	School management and organization Leadership and school improvement Leadership and planning
Salient parent involvement	Home school partnership	Parent community involvement
Effective instructional arrangements	Purposeful teaching	Classroom management and organization Instruction
High expectations	High expectations Pupil rights and responsibilities	Teacher student interactions Distinct-school interactions Equity Special programs

Bosker, 1997). In more comprehensive meta-analyses, such as those by Fraser et al. (1987) and Wang, Haertel and Walberg (1993), such variables are represented by far less empirical studies than the variables that concern instructional conditions. What these meta-analyses indicate is that instructional conditions generally have larger effects than school level conditions (see also Hill, Rowe, & Holmes-Smith, 1995). From the meta-analysis reported in Scheerens & Bosker it appears that school organizational key-factors have a negligible impact. A comprehensive overview of various sources (qualitative reviews, exemplary studies, international composition studies and meta-analyses) is presented in table 5 cited from Scheerens and Bosker, 1996.

The stronger impact of instructional factors as compared to school organization and management factors is also shown by Hill, Rowe & Holmes-Smith (1995).

A first conclusion that should be drawn from this assessment of the school effectiveness knowledge base is that a fully specified causal model of "value added" educational output does not exist. In other words, there is no conclusive knowledge on the exact instrumental impact of hypothetical school and classroom characteristic on achievement. In this respect one must come to a similar conclusion as did Monk (1992) in his analysis of research on "education production functions". Although one finds such statements occasionally in the literature (Levin,

Table 5: Review of the evidence from qualitative reviews, international studies and research syntheses

	qualitative reviews	international analyses	research syntheses
resource input variables			
pupil teacher ratio		−.03	.02
teacher training		.00	−.03
teacher experience			.04
teachers' salaries			−.07[1]
expenditure per pupil			.20[2]
School organizational factors			
productive climate culture	+		
achievement press for basic subjects	+	.02	.14
educational leadership	+	.04	.05
monitoring/evaluation	+	.00	.15
cooperation/consensus	+	−.02	.02
parental involvement	+	.08	.13
staff development<Tc+			
high expectations	+	.20	
orderly climate	+	.04	.11
Instructional conditions			
opportunity to learn	+	.15	.09
time on task/homework	+	.00/−.01 (n.s.)	.19/.06
structured teaching	+	−.01 (n.s.)	.11 (n.s.)
aspects of structured teaching:			
– cooperative learning			.27
– feedback			.48
– reinforcement			.58
differentiation/adaptive instruction			.22

Numbers refer to correlations, the size of which might be interpreted as: 0.10 small; 0.30 medium; 0.50 large.
+: positive influence; n.s.: statistically not significant.
[1] Having assumed a standard deviation of $ 5000 for teacher salary.
[2] Assuming a standard deviation of $ 100 for PPE.

1988), there is insufficient evidence for assertions like: "a 10% increment in time on task will lead to a 2% increase in adjusted achievement on average".

The second conclusion is that we know more about the impact of instructional conditions operating at classroom level than about the impact of organizational and management factors at the school level. Furthermore, the relatively few empirical studies that have investigated this in a comparative way indicate that the impact of instructional conditions in stronger than the impact of organizational conditions (Scheerens, Vermeulen, & Pelgrum, 1989; Hill, Rowe, & Holmes-Smith, 1995; Wang, Haertel, & Walberg, 1993).

In the third place, despite its plausibility at face level, there is as yet inconclusive evidence for the hypothesis that higher level conditions facilitate lower level conditions in producing higher outcomes.

The knowledge on educational leadership, in the sense of the school head providing guidance and support to optimize curricular choices, stimulate effective teaching and the use of records on the progress of pupils is, as yet, inconclusive.

It has been noted repeatedly that the effectiveness of this type of leadership is dependent on educational cultures, as they vary between countries (Witziers, 1995). A problem in obtaining an overall assessment of the effectiveness enhancing value of educational (or instructional) leadership is the fact that it is defined quite differently across studies (Witziers, 1995; Hendriks, 1996).

Despite these limitations with respect to the "hard evidence" on hypothetical school effectiveness models there are two perspectives from which a slightly more favourable appraisal may result.

The fact that many reviewers have cited the factors summarized in table 4 as plausible conditions in stimulating educational effectiveness should be taken more seriously than talking in a pejorative sense of a "parrot circuit" of reviewers citing each other. Also the fact that numerous designers of school improvement projects have already taken these factors as a source of inspiration underlines that "they appear to make sense" among relevant groups of educational theorists, researchers and practitioners. In this it should also be considered that it is very difficult and expensive to carry out a technically unflawed school effectiveness study, and that the better, more sophisticated studies have shown the more promising results (Scheerens, 1995).

The second perspective that leads to a somewhat more favourable assessment is that the hypothetical factors "fit" in several more established social scientific theories (see the exposition in the section on "mechanisms" and Scheerens, 1996).

Proactive and retroactive planning can be seen as the general principles behind most of the "structural" factors. Culture and climate as a general aspect of organization functioning is the common denominator of the rest of the factors summarized in tables 3 and 4.

CONCLUSION: IMPLICATIONS FOR SCHOOL IMPROVEMENT AND IMPROVEMENT-ORIENTED SCHOOL MANAGEMENT

Also considering the inconclusive evidence on the factors that "work" in schooling, the implications of the school effectiveness knowledge base for improvement-oriented school management, should be seen in terms of general orientation rather than precise "recipes".

At a time where governmental policies of decentralization in the financial and administrative domain put a certain premium on administrative school management, school effectiveness thinking provides a counterbalance by emphasizing educational leadership.

The modes of schooling (apart from management itself) that have received most emphasis in school effectiveness research are instruction and culture. Some authors who define educational leadership, say more about structural conditions surrounding the instructional process, whereas others are more focused on cultural aspects. Irwin (1986, p. 126) belongs to the former category in mentioning the following aspects of educational leadership:

The school leader:

- functions as an initiator and co-ordinator of the improvement of the instructional programme;
- states a clear mission of the school;
- has a task-oriented attitude;
- establishes clear objectives;
- supports innovation strategies;
- stimulates effective instruction;
- is quite visible in the organization;
- sees to it that pupils' progress is monitored regularly;
- delegates routine-tasks to others;
- regularly observes both the work of teachers and pupils.

Leithwood and Montgomery (1982, p. 334) mention the following more cultural aspects of educational leadership:

- stimulation of an achievement-oriented school policy that should not be detrimental to pupils' well-being;
- commitment to all types of educational decisions in the school;
- stimulating co-operative relationship between teacher, in order to realize a joint commitment to the achievement-oriented school mission;
- advertising the central mission of the school and obtaining of support of external stakeholders.

In more recent views on educational leadership, inspired by the concept of the learning organization motivating staff by providing incentives and creating consensus on goals are emphasized. Mitchell and Tucker's concepts of transactional leadership and transformational leadership (Mitchell & Tucker, 1992) form a case in point. Staff development and the "human resource" factor are further underlined in these approaches. These newer perspectives do not create a sharp break with the longer existing conceptualizations of educational leadership, but emphasize the cultural and the staffing mode of schooling.

Some hypothetical school effectiveness enhancing factors fall in line with the mechanism of synoptic planning and bureaucratic structuring (clear goal statements, orderly climate, frequent monitoring). This general principle of organizational functioning is also close to the principles of structured, direct instruction. Stringfield (1995) uses the metaphor of "high reliability organizations" in a further conceptualization of this general principle and also provides a very interesting successful example (the Barclay/Calvert programme).

The synoptic planning and bureaucratic structuring principle is currently challenged in pedagogical views inspired by constructivism, where self-oriented discovery learning in "rich" learning environments is emphasized. Perhaps the general paradigm of contingency theory can be applied here, in assuming that planning and structuring will work better in certain situations (for instance at primary school level, in schools with a high proportion of children with lower socioeconomic status) whereas a less structured approach might work better in other situations (for instance in the academic streams of upper secondary education).

The cybernetic principle of monitoring and feedback highlights one factor of the hypothetical school effectiveness enhancing factors, namely evaluation and the use of evaluations for improvement purposes. The cybernetic principles can be seen as one of the corner stones of the concept of the learning organization. School self-evaluation is therefore seen as one of the most promising levers for school improvement. It can be linked with learning in various levels of the school, the pupils level, but the teachers level as well.

The alignment of individual and organizational rationality, which is seen as the elementary principle of public choice theory, emphasizes the importance of obtaining consensus on a particular mission of the organization. From the perspective of school effectiveness thinking the substance of this mission is achievement orientation. However, the means to ensure alignment propagated by public choice theory, namely competition between schools is much debated.

Images like "High reliability organizations" (Stringfield, 1995), "Schools as output-driven organizations" (Coleman, 1993) and "The evaluative school" (Scheerens & Bosker, 1997) may provide help in targeting school effectiveness to the basic mechanisms that are laid base in the theoretical redirection of school effectiveness research and analyses, discussed in the earlier sections.

In summary, the message from school effectiveness thinking, as far as improvement-oriented school management is concerned, focuses on three main principles: clear structuring, enhancing of organizational learning by means of evaluation and feedback, and obtaining consensus and cohesion with respect to basic goals and values. As was stated repeatedly the messages that we can draw from the school effectiveness literature are general orientations rather than very precise recommendations.

REFERENCES

Argyris, C. (1982). *Reasoning, learning and action*. San Francisco: Jossey-Bass Publishers.

Bosker, R.J., & Scheerens, J. (1994). Alternative models of school effectiveness put to the test. In R. J. Bosker, B. P. M. Creemers, & J. Scheerens (Eds.), *Conceptual and methodological advances in educational effectiveness research* (pp. 159–180). Special issue of the *International Journal of Educational Research*, **21**(2).

Bosker, R. J., & Witziers, B. (1995). A meta-analytical approach regarding school effectiveness: The true size of school effects and the effect size and educational leadership. Paper presented at the ECER Congress, Bath, England.

Campbell, D. T. (1969). Reforms as experiments. *American Psychologist*, **24**(4).

Cheng, Y. C. (1993). *Conceptualization and measurement of school effectiveness: An organizational perspective*. Paper presented at AERA annual meeting, Atlanta, Georgia.

Chubb, J. E., & Moe, T. M. (1990). *Politics, markets and American schools*. Washington, D.C.: Brookings Institute.

Cohen, M. D., March, J. G., & Olsen, J. P. (1972). A garbage can model of organizational choice. *Administrative Quarterly*, **17**, 1–25.

Coleman, J. S. (1993). *The design of schools as output-driven organizations*. Internal paper, University of Chicago.

Cotton, K. (1995). *Effective schooling practices: A research synthesis*. School Improvement Research Series. Northwest Regional Educational Laboratory.

Creemers, B. P. M. (1994). *The effective classroom*. London: Cassell.

Dror, Y. (1968). *Public policy-making reexamined*. Chandler, Scranton, Pennsylvania.

Faerman, S. R., & Quinn, R. E. (1985). Effectiveness: The perspective from organization theory. *Review of Higher Education*, **9**, 83–100.

Fowler, H. W., & Fowler, F. G. (1964). *Concise oxford dictionary of current English* (5th Edition). Oxford: Clarendon Press.

Fraser, B. J., Walberg, H. J., Welch, W. W., & Hattie, J. A. (1987). *Syntheses of educational productivity research*. Special issue of the *International Journal of Educational Research*, **11**(2).

Gresov, C. (1989). Exploring fit and misfit with multiple contingencies. *Administrative Science Quarterly*, **34**, 431–453.

Griffith, D. E., Hart, A. W., & Blair, B. G. (1991). Still another approach to administrate: Chaos theory. *Educational Administration Quarterly*, **17**, 430–451.

Hargreaves, D. (1995). School culture, school effectiveness and school improvement. *School Effectiveness and School Improvement*, **6**, 23–46.

Hendriks, M. (1996). *Analysis of school self-evaluation and effective schools' instruments*. Enschede: OCTO, University of Twente (in Dutch).

Hill, P. W., Rowe, K. J., & Holmes-Smith, P. (1995). *Factors affecting students' educational progress: multilevel modelling of educational effectiveness*. Paper presented at the International Congress for School Effectiveness and School Improvement, Leeuwarden, the Netherlands, January 1995.

Hirsch, D. (1994). *School: A matter of choice*. Paris: OECD/CERI.

Hofman, W. H. A. (1995). Cross-level relationships within effective schools. *School Effectiveness and School Improvement*, **6**, 146–174.

Hofman, R., Hoeben, W., & Guldemond, H. (1995). Denominatie en effectiviteit van schoolbesturen [Denomination and the effectiveness of school boards]. *Tijdschrift voor Onderwijsresearch*, **20**(1), 63–78.

Houtveen, A. A. M., & Osinga, N. (1995). *A case of school effectiveness: The Dutch national improvement project*. Paper presented at the ICSEI Conference, Leeuwarden, the Netherlands.

Irwin, C.C. (1986). What research tells the principal about educational leadership. *Scientica Paedagogica Experimentalis*, *23*, 124–137.

Kieser, A., & Kubicek, H. (1977). *Organisation*. Berlin: De Gruyter Lehrbuch.

Leeuw, A. C. J. de (1982). *Organisaties: management, analyse, ontwerp en verandering*. Een systeemvisie. Assen: Van Gorcum.

Leithwood, K. A., & Montgomery, D. J. (1982). The role of the elementary school principal in program improvement. *Review of Educational Research*, **52**, 309–399.

Leune, J. M. G. (1994). Onderwijskwaliteit en de autonomie van scholen. In B. P. M. Creemers (Ed.), *Deregulering en de Kwaliteit van het Onderwijs*. Groningen: RION.

Levin, H. H. (1988). Cost-effectiveness and educational policy. *Educational Evaluation and Policy Analysis*, **10**, 51–69.

Levine, D. K., & Lezotte, L. W. (1990). *Unusually effective schools: A review and analysis of research and practice*. Madison, Wis.: National Center for Effective Schools Research and Development.

Maslowski, R. (1995). *Organisatiecultuur systematisch benaderd*. Enschede: Universiteit Twente.

Meuret, D., & Scheerens, J. (1995). *An international comparison of functional and territorial decentralization of public educational systems*. Paper presented at AERA 1995, San Francisco.

Mintzberg, H. (1979). *The structuring of organizations*. Englewood Cliffs, NJ: Prentice-Hall.

Mitchell, D. E., & Tucker, Sh. (1992). Leadership as a way of thinking. *Educational Leadership*, **49**(5), 30–35.

Monk, D. H. (1992). *Microeconomics of school productions*. Paper for the Economics of Education Section of the International Encyclopaedia of Education. Oxford: Pergamon Press.

Morgan, G. (1986). *Images of Organization*. Beverly Hills, CA: Sage.

Reynolds, D., Hopkins, D., & Stoll, L. (1993). Linking school effectiveness knowledge and school improvement practices: Towards a synergy. *School Effectiveness and School Improvement*, **4**, 34–58.

Riley, D. D. (1990). Should market forces control educational decision making? *American Political Science Review*, **84**, 554–558.

Rist, R. C., & Joyce, M. K. (1995). Qualitative research and implementation evaluation: a path to organizational learning. In T. E. Barone (Ed.), *The uses of educational research* (pp. 127–136). Special issue of the *International Journal of Educational Research*, **23**(2).

Sammons, P., Hillman, J., & Mortimore, P. (1995). *Key characteristics of effective schools: A review of school effectiveness research.* London: OFSTED.

Scheerens, J. (1992). *Effective schooling: Research, theory and practice.* London: Cassell.

Scheerens, J. (1993). Basic school effectiveness research: items for a research agenda. *School Effectiveness and School Improvement*, **4**(1), 17–36.

Scheerens, J. (1994). The school-level context of instructional effectiveness: a comparison between school effectiveness and restructuring models. *Tijdschrift voor Onderwijsresearch*, **19**(1), 26–38.

Scheerens, J. (1995). *School effectiveness as a research discipline.* Paper presented at the ICSEI Congress, Leeuwarden, the Netherlands, January 1995.

Scheerens, J. (1996). Theoretically embedded principles of effective schooling. *School Effectiveness and School Improvement* (in press).

Scheerens, J., & Bosker, R. J. (1997). *The foundations of Educational Effectiveness.* Oxford: Elsevier Science Ltd.

Scheerens, J., & Creemers, B. P. M. (1995). School effectiveness in the Netherlands; research, policy and practice. In B. P. M. Creemers & N. Osinga (Eds.), *Country reports ICSEI 1995* [pp. 81–106]. Leeuwarden: Gemeenschappelijk Centrum voor Onderwijsbegeleiding.

Scheerens, J., Vermeulen, C. J. A. J., & Pelgrum, W. J. (1989). Generalizability of school and instructional effectiveness indicators across nations. In B. P. M. Creemers & J. Scheerens (Eds.), *Developments in school effectiveness research.* Special issue of the *International Journal of Educational Research*, **13**(7).

Schein, E. H. (1985). *Organizational culture and leadership: A dynamic view.* San Francisco: Jossey Bass.

Simon, H. A. (1964). *Administrative behavior.* New York: Macmillan.

Stringfield, S. (1995). Attempting to enhance students' learning through innovative programs: the case for schools evolving into high reliability organizations. *School Effectiveness and School Improvement*, **6**(1), 67–96.

Stringfield, S. C., & Slavin, R. E. (1992). A hierarchical longitudinal model for elementary school effects. In B. P. M. Creemers & G. J. Reezigt (Eds.), *Evaluation of effectiveness.* ICO-Publication 2.

Van Lidt de Jeude, J., & Brouwer, T. (1992). Kleine oorzaken, grote gevolgen: een inleiding op de chaostheorie. In C. van Dijkum & D. de Tombe (Eds.), *Gamma chaos: Onzekerheden en Orde in de Menswetenschappen.* Bloemendaal: Aramith.

Wang, M. C., Haertel, G. D., & Walberg, H. J. (1993). Toward a knowledge base for school learning. Naam tijdschrift **63**(3), 249–294.

II: The Contemporary Context of School Improvement

School Evaluation and Improvement: A Scandinavian View

ROLF LANDER
Göteborg University, Sweden

MATS EKHOLM
University of Karlstad, Sweden

Rolf Lander's and Mats Ekholm's account of school improvement in Scandinavia is centrally concerned with the implications of a national policy that links together evaluation and development. Using an established framework for integrating evaluation and school improvement, Lander and Ekholm use a series of case studies to explore the impact of such national policies on educational development. Despite national differences, the style of educational reform employed in Scandinavia is generally less invasive than that of many other Western Educational Systems. In common with other systems however Lander and Ekholm argue on the basis of their data that too great an emphasis on goal based accountability results in a reduction of professional commitment and autonomy. Following their review of research and analysis of Scandinavian policy initiatives, Lander and Ekholm conclude that policy makers' view of evaluation is more as a means of gathering information and achieving control, rather than as a tool for school improvement. Schools in Scandinavia that are striving to use evaluation as a means of school improvement are on the basis of this evidence likely to have their efforts negated by the predominant 'evaluation as management' orthodoxy.

School improvement plays a considerable part in the interwoven nets of causes and development that constitute educational change. In Scandinavia – Denmark, Norway and Sweden – from which our examples are taken, a process of change started during the seventies, but the learning about change has been slow. At the political and administrative levels there has been a shift of focus, from trying to directly influence individual teachers or groups of teachers, to influencing schools, and thereby indirectly their teaching staff. This change in strategy by no means implies that teachers have ceased to be the main targets of policy. They are still the targets, for example, of the national assessment systems in Sweden and Norway that guide student attainment.

It was also recognised in the seventies that use could be made of evaluation to stimulate school improvement, but not until the nineties did this become an important idea. This was largely due to the increasing interest in more efficient and productive schools. In different forms 'management by objectives'attracted most interest at the political level during this period, especially in Sweden and Norway, where today it is the 'official' philosophy behind both local and national government.

D. Hopkins (ed.), The Practice and Theory of School Improvement, 85-100.

We regard school improvement as a process of deliberate change in structures, rules, norms, conceptions, habits and working patterns, which immediately, or over a longer period, help students to improve their learning and development according to the requirements of school and society. The national curricula in Scandinavia place a strong emphasis on the fostering of democratic values and on social development, in addition to the acquisition of subject knowledge.

Evaluation in the Scandinavian context is an over-arching concept which embraces both single evaluation studies of discrete areas, for example of assessment and indicator systems, and monitoring of work done by students or teachers. We mean by evaluation the judging of the worth and rationality of some purposeful activity grounded in simple or complex or complex investigations. The objects of evaluation are very often the students, but we focus here on the relationship between evaluation demands, methods and results involving adults in the educational system, including those who are stakeholders. It is this relationship that makes evaluation a tool for school improvement. We also include the concept of quality assurance in evaluation; we exclude however examinations and the testing of students.

We have learned from Holly and Hopkins (1988) to distinguish between evaluation of, evaluation for and evaluation as school improvement (see also Hopkins, 1989). Evaluation *of* school improvement is often of a summative kind, drawing conclusions about the worth, rationality, effects and implications of the area being evaluated. Evaluation *for* school improvement is often intended as formative evaluation, seeking to stimulate and guide those trying to improve schools. Evaluation *as* school improvement can be seen as action research, improvement work and evaluation, where all three are tightly integrated. The distinction between evaluation *as* and evaluation *for* improvement is clear: the latter presupposes a dichotomy between the evaluation and its utilisation, while the former suspends the difference. Evaluation *as* improvement implies that improvers themselves know how to use evaluation in the improvement process. This is not necessarily the case with the other two uses.

Evaluation as a political tool for improving or managing schools and teaching is an idea largely suggested from above, not introduced from below. Governments in Scandinavia have urged schools to engage in evaluation. In parallel with developments in England outlined by Hopkins et al. (1995), we can hypothesise that there has been a change at both local and national levels from focusing on evaluation *of* improvement to evaluation *for* and *as* improvement. We have also recently seen an emerging focus on evaluation as management, that is on making evaluation an integrated part of the management of staff and the organisation of schools. The demands of policy-makers for evaluation *as* school improvement started during the seventies and was, for example, encoded in the Swedish National Curriculum of 1980. Since then Swedish schools, and somewhat later Norwegian schools, have been expected to make working (or development) plans. These working plans combine a school's interpretation of political goals with its own priorities. Schools are thus required to synthesise the results of their own evaluations with municipal and national priorities. We know that the implementation of these working plans has been very slow (see below), but nevertheless the intentions of policy-makers have been longstanding and clear.

Theoretically, evaluation can be used for school improvement in at least two ways:

1) By commissioning external evaluations, or by stimulating or demanding internal self-evaluations, stakeholders can cause schools as systems to open up and offer a better insight into when and where to intervene. Evaluations initiated within schools can have similar effects, and the desire to make the school system more open may indeed be one of the main aims of such an evaluation.

2) Evaluations can be used for learning about the system and its improvement process. In this instance it is often assumed that evaluation initiates the process with an analysis of the system, and is later used to monitor the improvement process and look for results and consequences. In the case of quality assurance, evaluation is used as a finely-tuned feedback mechanism in successive adjustments of working methods.

It is our thesis that to date there are very few examples of the systematic and skilled use of evaluation in school improvement within individual Scandinavian schools, and in particular of evaluation *as* improvement. Despite this, it is interesting to note that policy-makers have kept faith with the tool of evaluation during the twenty or so years it has been in operation. The strategy has, however, changed, and there are indications that its sphere of influence is growing. We would argue that opening up schools to stake-holder influences is the most common and tested way of using evaluation for improvement, and that this use at present overshadows the use of evaluation *of* or *as* improvement, as well as its heuristic function.

Our aim in this chapter is to illuminate how changes in the interpretation of the relationship between school improvement and evaluation has emerged in Scandinavia; primarily in Sweden and to some extent in Norway. We will describe key events in the introduction of these ideas in the two countries, and use what is known about the schools' reactions to them. We begin by offering some background facts about Scandinavian schools and systems of school government.

THE GOVERNANCE OF SCANDINAVIAN SCHOOLS.

In all three countries the organisation of the school system was changed during the fifties, when comprehensive schools were developed. The school systems in all three countries have a simple structure. The children start school at six or seven, and are permitted to leave at sixteen. If a child's family lives in the same neighbourhood during this time, the child often attends the same school for the whole comprehensive school period. The individual pupil-teacher relationship lasts longer in Scandinavian countries than in many others, which means that teachers and parents can also develop long-term relationships. During the first grades children usually meet with only one teacher, even though team-teaching is on the increase. In Denmark one teacher can maintain a relationship with the same children and their families for as long as ten years. In Norway and Sweden the teachers follow their pupils for between three and seven years of their school careers.

School improvement during the fifties and sixties largely focused on efforts to implement and refine the comprehensive systems. During that time there was a strong growth of centralism, particularly in Sweden, less so in Norway and even less so in Denmark. All primary and secondary schools in Norway and Sweden follow central guidelines, while schools in Denmark have enjoyed a greater opportunity to innovate and to develop their own unique profiles. In recent years both the Norwegian and Swedish school systems have moved in the direction of the Danish system, so that now the schools in both of these countries are expected to develop a more distinctive profile of their own. The implementation of working plans mentioned above is one step in that direction.

Parent participation in the running of schools has long been a feature of the Danish system, and has recently been introduced in Sweden and Norway. A quasi-voucher system was introduced by the neo-liberal governments in Denmark and Sweden during the eighties and nineties. In Sweden this system is now severely circumscribed by the present Social-Democratic government. One of the justifications for introducing this system in Sweden – to increase private education – was of less concern to the Danes, who had a relatively high proportion of private schools already. About 10% of Danish pupils between the ages of six and sixteen attend private schools. In Sweden the comparable figure is around 2%, and in Norway even less.

The Scandinavian countries have during the past decades tried to marry central control with decentralisation. Through the adoption of 'management by objectives', central regulation has been abolished, and centralised functions are achieved instead by formulating clearer goals and by evaluation. In Sweden there is a special national authority, the National Agency of Education (NAE), directly under the Ministry, with the main function of making and utilising evaluations. In Norway the state authority has shifted from a national to a regional level, but the regional level is increasingly losing its autonomy and influence. The Ministry plans and implements evaluation measures. In Denmark the Ministry of Education manages the schools' examination systems, which is by far the most important part of the national assessment scheme, but it has also required schools to undertake self-evaluations.

In all three countries the municipalities are the 'owners' of the schools. We refer here to the municipalities as 'kommuns', to emphasise that these historical entities have always been quite powerful, and that with decentralisation they have become even more powerful. This shift in power to kommuns is most marked in Sweden: in Denmark and Norway kommuns have traditionally had a greater say. Each Scandinavian kommun has its own parliament which reflects the local political balance. Traditionally these kommuns have school boards which exercise political control over education, but the nineties has seen a strong tendency (especially in Sweden) to replace them with boards which have a wider responsibility. This means that schools have to compete with other sectors for resources. Nearly 10% of Swedish kommuns have a contractual relationship with their schools, and organise their administration into separate boards for managing and evaluating schools. Kommuns actively use their new right to hire and fire headteachers, thereby highlighting that headteachers are the agents of policy-makers, and not *primus inter pares* in the school.

It is important to note that policy-makers, by insisting on evaluation at all levels, seek to pursue accountability, and thus to influence power relationships within the educational system. In Scandinavia evaluation is often said to be the democratic check on the decentralisation of power to the kommun and the school. Compared to earlier systems, the most novel feature of the new approach is that policy-makers, by using evaluation and pressing schools to self-evaluate, are opening up schools to external scrutiny. The notional monopoly enjoyed by teachers of pedagogic knowledge has been challenged more than ever before. For teachers, evaluation can offer the prospect of more focused professional development and a richer, more equal, partnership with stake-holders. It also, however, threatens the hegemony of their professional judgement in all matters educational. The new tool of evaluation is likely to be first experimented with by administrators at all levels. Politicians will employ administrators, and for evaluation probably new kinds of administrators. Traditionally many administrators are former headteachers, but they often lack knowledge of evaluation methodology. As we have seen in the field of medicine, this may give rise to competition between administrators and education professionals (Granstrom & Lander, 1995).

Both parents and citizens stand to gain from the development of these new power relationships. As schools and the work of teachers become more meaningful to parents, so will parental influence in the running of schools increase. The use of questionnaires to explore the opinions of both parents and students, for example, has been the most prominent feature of the new vogue of evaluation in Scandinavia.

Teacher unions in Sweden and Norway were slow to react to these new policies. In the past decade teacher unions in both countries have accepted the challenge, and have tried to adapt both quality assurance and evaluation to the interests of teachers. They incorporate these concepts in their union programmes, and publish their own literature about them.

In Denmark the national evaluation system is dominated by examinations, in which teachers take an active part. Teachers here seem more comfortable with evaluation demands imposed from above, although there was some nervousness when the concept of quality assurance attracted the interest of policy-makers. One union journal reported a recent report from its own congress – *"Development – not control. Congress legitimises the discussion of quality in schools."*

EVALUATION AS A TOOL FOR SCHOOL IMPROVEMENT.

The following examples – three from Sweden and one from Norway – are of orchestrated state interventions to persuade teachers and schools of the worth of undertaking evaluations, and of linking them to school improvement.

In Sweden, the introduction of a national curriculum for comprehensive schools took two years (1980–82), during which time the schools were instructed to experiment with working plans and to evaluate their own efforts at least once every year. Schools were expected to use evaluation *as* school improvement, with the new curriculum document providing guidance.

A representative, longitudinal study of 35 school management localities (each containing between one and seven schools) showed for 1985 only a limited amount of evaluation having taken place. In 15 of the localities one day in the year had been set aside for evaluation activities of some description; in the other 20 practically nothing except the traditional ways of assessing and rating pupil performance and behaviour had been attempted. There was little evidence of any preparation for the day's activities, so the evaluation undertaken had been of a perfunctory nature. The use of working plans had also made slow progress, but was generally more purposeful. In 1980 there had hardly been any discussion about 'aims' in the schools involved; there was an increase in such discussions however in most of the schools in 1982, but comparatively few of them had been able to translate these discussions into working documents. In 1985 only half the primary schools in the localities had such documents. Localities consisting only of secondary schools had largely failed to develop such plans (Ekholm, Fransson, & Lander, 1987; Ekholm 1987).

Direct state support for the implementation of the national curriculum in 1980 consisted of resources for additional work by teachers, but the true period of implementation had taken place some years before with the introduction of two large-scale programmes. These consisted of compulsory school leadership training, and an in-service programme of training for staff teams from all of the country's comprehensive schools. Both programmes included training in the diagnostic evaluation of schools, and in planning for improvement. The programme for staff teams was largely one of mobilisation. About a third of the school staff (not just teaching staff) were recruited to discuss goals and praxis, and to stimulate similar discussions amongst their colleagues back at school. This support strategy can be characterised as a professional investment model, where governments provide schools with resources such as quality training and then trust them to formulate goals and make improvements.

With the advent of the national curriculum schools could be said to be operating within a very different model, one of goal-based accountability, where governments now formulated policy and left decisions relating to its implementation to other levels of the school system. The training for discussion, diagnosis, planning and evaluation adopted a new aim, to implement given goals by adapting them to local circumstances. The confusion of models may provide one explanation for the partial failure of teachers to use the skills provided – working plans and evaluation. The central authorities assumed that the goal-based accountability model was in place. Staff in schools persisted with the professional investment view of training which allowed them to use the lessons learnt in the programmes for their own school aims. It might be that schools regarded planning and evaluation not as tools providing them with a wide ranging freedom to improve, but as imposed and unnecessary administrative inconveniences. That the failure of schools to evaluate was more apparent than their failure to plan suggests that the art of evaluation is harder to master (see Louis & Van Velzen, 1986).

In 1995 our more recent research (in which we cooperated with Kjell Granstrom) surveyed a nationwide sample of grade 6 teachers. The first question was:

> *How often in your work unit do you evaluate how effective your teaching is, using data (for example knowledge tests, observations, interviews, attitude surveys) to support your discussions? (This includes data collected by other people as well as by yourselves.)*

The second question substituted 'school or the school organisation' for 'work unit'. 921 teachers (a response rate of 80%) answered the questions, in the following way:

Evaluation in my	2–3 times a year or more often	Once a year	Every other year or less often	Total (%)
work unit	46	29	25	100
school	25	45	28	100

To evaluate with support from data derived from an investigation would appear to be more common in the work unit than it is with the whole school. What the figures cannot tell us is how much of the evaluation was about school improvement. We do know, however, that a number of primary school teachers have received training in evaluation. Despite this, the majority of primary schools still only engage in whole-school evaluation on one day a year, at most, hardly an improvement on the situation in 1985.

During the early eighties evaluation was one of the primary functions of the National Board of Education. The Board was also required to prepare and implement national curricula through "rolling reforms", and not to over-concentrate on the implementation of one, politically-determined curriculum at a time. The inspection function of the regional state boards of education was re-interpreted by the government as one of "active supervision", a model which embraced the act of inspection as well as consultation on the basis of any inspection. A challenging test for these ideas occurred between 1984 and 1988, when the National Board was instructed by the Minister to pilot ideas for the future reform of secondary education through developmental work at a local level. The Board did this by creating a huge evaluation programme.

Almost all upper secondary schools in the country took part, the kommuns however were largely inactive. As in 1980 the schools were expected to use projects, planning and evaluation. Ideas for improvement projects came largely from the centre. On the basis of these planning projects, schools bid for resources from the regional state boards of education. The design of the improvement work however was left to the individual school, although the competition for resources enabled the regional boards to select what they regarded as the best projects. The aim of the whole programme was to provide information for the government before the drafting of new national goals. This process has been characterised as a model of gradual development by which improvement methods are decided centrally, but where improvement goals are stimulated, not mandated. For a limited period, Swedish schools were able to experience what was a traditionally Danish form of educational governance.

Responsibility for evaluation was linked to successful bids for resources. Schools reported to the regional boards, which in turn made their own investigations of the improvement process in those schools. These two sets of reports were collated at regional level and presented to the National Board, who as a result received at least 25 reports annually, with a large number of appendices. In addition there were special assignments undertaken in those 20 schools known to have interesting or broadbased improvement projects. Each of these schools were given sufficient funds to enable one of its staff to take on the role of a part-time local evaluator, writing annual reports to both the regional board and the National Board of Education. These schools were also evaluated by ten researchers (of whom Rolf Lander was one), each taking responsibility for a number of schools, as well as reporting to the National Board.

So by paying quite small amounts of money for improvement work, and considerably more for evaluation, the National Board of Education stimulated change at the local level whilst at the same time obtaining information on what was happening nationally. It is no exaggeration to say that this approach placed too great a burden on the evaluation process. The National Board received some important information, but not enough on which to base a new curriculum. An inbuilt lack of coordination in the evaluation process, and an equal lack of experimental design in the programme, left state administrators with an unmanageable task of data interpretation. Schools tended to use their evaluations to justify the extra resources they received, yet were not successful in using the evaluations to support their improvement efforts. No-one had advised them how to proceed. The services offered by the regional boards did not include that of consultancy. Too much energy was taken up by meeting the information requirements of the state.

The Danish experience is that local evaluation within similar state-commissioned projects also experienced severe difficulties in fulfilling both national and local needs (Kruchov, 1993). It is for this reason that researchers are increasingly being used by the state to collate and analyse local implementation and evaluations. Equally depressing is the finding that local project reports are rarely read by other schools, even though they are printed and published by the state (Lander, 1995). What seems to be common to both the Swedish and Danish situations is that evaluation is used *for* improvement within schools, but rarely *as* improvement.

The third attempt by the Swedish government to orchestrate local utilisation of evaluation took place between 1987 and 1994. It involved 101 comprehensive schools, consisting of a representative sample taking part in a project of national assessment (the NU project). The responsibility for test construction was divided amongst different groups of researchers. A large part of the battery of tests was of a constructivist character, and some used 'authentic' test items (cf. Newman & Wehlage, 1993; Taylor, 1994). Researchers were also used to take responsibility for measuring student norms and attitudes, and for organising field visits to each of the 101 schools, in order that the schools' climate, leadership, degree of staff collaboration and other vital organisational features could be described and rated (Ekholm & Karang, 1994). Although some developmental work was going on in Norway and Denmark, nothing as elaborate as this programme existed in other Scandinavian countries.

While the NU project was in full flow, Parliament passed the biggest decentralisation reform in Swedish history. In 1991 the kommuns became the owners of the state schools, as the state all but withdrew its direct control. To balance the new powers given to the kommuns a new agency was created – The National Agency of Education (NAE) – while simultaneously the old agency (The National Board of Education) was closed down, along with its 25 regional boards. This shift in the level of administration was considered vital in order that the Agency could forge a new role at the national level, one predominantly involving evaluation and assessment. The NAE is now represented in the regions by its field staff of about 100 civil servants. They are rarely used as inspectors, nor do they have any authority over kommuns or schools. They are designated 'evaluation generalists', assisting the NAE with evaluations and the provision of information.

Economic writers (e.g. Jacobsson & Sahlin-Andersson, 1995) argue that the new National Agency should be seen as a prototype for a modern centralised agency. The school sector has been the most radically reorganised of all the sectors of Swedish society, in line with the new ideals of decentralisation, of 'management by objectives' and of evaluation. The agency is intended as a 'knowledge organisation', the kommuns and schools as 'learning organisations'.

The function of directly stimulating school improvement has now moved from the national level, to the kommun level. Nevertheless the NAE decided to use the NU tests of 1992 to stimulate improvement efforts within participating secondary schools. By so doing the NAE adopted one of the strategies of the old National Board originally used in 1989, after the first evaluation and assessment trials at the primary level. It is useful to look at the strategies employed by the two national agencies. We here use data derived from a representative meta-evaluation of about a quarter of the participating schools (Lander, Thang, & Torper, 1994).

The initial plan of the National Board was to assess pupils in grades 2, 5 and 8, and to provide rapid feedback, in order that any changes in teaching practices could affect the same students before they graduated to the next level. However, the Board soon realised that it was unable to resource a research staff large enough to process the test results as quickly as the plan required. Another strategy of the National Board was to give private feedback directly to each participating teacher. The rationale behind this approach was an ethical one, that the results attributed to individual teachers should not be made public. A further implication was that the school as an organisation could not respond to improvement data. The feedback to primary teachers in 1989 was thus built on the premise that schools were not in touch with current research on educational change.

The new National Agency however deliberately chose the school as the recipient of feedback, and the school received aggregated data at the school level for each assessment measure. The NAE stressed the model-building potentiality of the NU project for the local level. Taking into account the constructivist nature of many of the tests, this particular form of feedback was far more realistic. The tests themselves, the test process and the feedback could be used to stimulate new or ongoing improvement projects in the schools. The model-building effect of the feedback is important for school improvement. Using our earlier terminology, it represents a goal-based accountability model, where the tests operationalise the goals but where the feedback leaves implementation to the schools. The NU data were also clearly used as evaluation *for* school improvement: only if schools adopted its methods could it eventually become evaluation *as* improvement.

Each school was resourced to enable one of its staff to take responsibility for administering the assessments and the process of data utilisation. The field staff of the NAE was instructed to assist the schools in their vicinity to arrange the feedback. In retrospect it is clear that the training of the field staff was largely inadequate. Their selection and training gave no guarantee that they had the required understanding of constructivist teaching or school improvement. In this respect the NAE, like the National Board before them, were forced to concede that the size of the central resource did not match their ambition to become influential at the local level.

Another puzzling feature of the feedback design was that it gave no explicit role to the kommuns. This was discussed at an early stage with representatives of the National Association of Kommuns, who suggested that the money for local use should be directed through the superintendents' offices. But the NAE were concerned that such an arrangement could contaminate the test process itself. Once the actual process started, however, very few kommuns showed any interest in what was going on in the 101 schools. This is remarkable, particularly when kommuns could have learned a great deal about the processes of assessment and feedback.

One of the likely causes of this lack of interest was that the feedback coincided with one of the busiest phases in the decentralisation of power to the kommun level. These organisational changes absorbed much of the energy which many of the kommuns would have expended on other issues. The result was that the old model, of the national authority maintaining direct contact with schools and ignoring the kommuns, survived.

Some schools managed to use the feedback for their own improvement work – 43% of them took considerable advantage of the data. But 57% either used the data in a limited way (9%), used it only temporarily or superficially (31%), or could not use it at all (17%). The figures of the meta-evaluation derive from fieldworkers' descriptions of local use. In 56% of the cases schools introduced immediate changes. Half of these projects focused directly on the curriculum or pedagogy. The other half featured teacher cooperation, student participation or other aspects of school organisation.

In interviews, 39% of the school leaders said that the feedback of the NU evaluation gave them a means for influencing subject-specific discussions with teachers, and that it thereby compensated for their own lack of expertise in various subjects.

Both teachers and headteachers felt that the instruments and data from the project gave substance and credibility to discussions with colleagues.

In order to try to explain the factors accounting for differences in data utilisation, a teacher questionnaire was used, together with some ranked measures from the qualitative studies. The analysis showed that the *tradition* of improvement work at the school was the most important factor. The initial direction taken by these improvement projects was dictated by this tradition, but there was one common factor – the feeling of teachers that the NU data gave an accurate as well as interesting diagnosis of the school's situation. Both the diagnoses of students' achievements in school subjects and in their social development were deemed to be important.

In those schools with a deeper tradition of improvement work the experience of diagnosis appeared inextricably linked to a constructive debate following the feedback. The quality of the debate related more to data utilisation than to diagnosis, which suggests that the ability of a school to debate constructively facilitates the ability to see diagnostic possibilities in external input. In schools with less of an improvement tradition, but where there was some success in utilising the data, the diagnosis and debate was intertwined with negative feelings about the feedback itself and to negative attitudes about the validity of the NU tests. It would seem that data utilisation in these schools developed through some kind of turmoil, connected to the feedback process. Some members of staff reacted to what they saw as a threat to their pedagogical practice. This turmoil, however, usually resolved itself in a positive way. This occurred because the process of utilisation only affected small numbers of staff in these schools. The teachers who utilised the data seemed able to legitimise their own improvement efforts within the school without involving the rest.

Complementary data on school climate derived from the NAE's rating of schools. Two aspects are of particular interest – the importance paid by school staff to an orderly school environment, and to having high and realistic expectations of pupil achievement. The correlations of improvement tradition with utilisation, and of school climate with utilisation are markedly different – 0.75 and 0.30. Improvement tradition and school climate correlate only moderately (0.30). But school climate operates independently, by supporting utilisation primarily within schools with less of a tradition of improvement. A 'stronger' climate may harness the negative reactions to the feedback as well as the criticisms relating to curriculum validity, using their combined energy in a constructive debate involving those who want to act upon the NU project findings. Thus a higher degree of utilisation is achieved in these schools than in those with a weaker climate.

The Norwegian government also has a high regard for evaluation as a means of improving schools. Unlike other Scandinavian governments it has chosen to instruct and advise individual schools on how local evaluation should be done. This advice and instruction was provided in a 1994 booklet entitled *Underveis*, which was sent to every Norwegian teacher. The booklet uses a quality assurance approach to evaluation, although the concept is not specifically acknowledged in the text. According to Granstrom and Lander (1995b), the booklet claims that evaluation will promote rational planning and teaching. It insists that evaluation be done collaboratively by the staff, and that it should also include parents as stakeholders. Democratic involvement is used as the justification for engaging parents, but there is also the fear that the interests of stakeholders may harm schools if they are based on ignorance and misinformation. Thus school-based evaluation also needs to build legitimacy for the school, "to strengthen the school's position in the community" (Granstrom & Lander, 1995b, p. 5).

There are 49 examples of evaluation questions, and ten case studies of evaluations, in the booklet. Questions require predominantly descriptive (55%) or judgmental (38%) answers, and are largely rhetorical. Very few (7%) seek explanations. For example, *Is bullying a problem at your school?* is asked, rather than *Why is there bullying at your school?* or *What has been done against bullying, and with what effect?* This is in keeping with the booklet's warning against using evaluation to dig too deeply. The advice is: don't be too ambitious and don't collect more material than you can handle.

Comparing what is said in these examples and case studies with the typology of van der Knaap (1995), it can be concluded that Norwegian teachers are intended to learn from feedback and by social learning, but not from cognitive learning. van der Knaap identifies feedback learning with cybernetic single-loop learning. Cognitive learning is more complex, as it implies accommodation of cognitive challenges. Social learning is less about new insights, and more about mutual adjustments in thinking and behaviour achieved through cooperation. Cognitive learning validates using new criteria for the work done, social learning validates using common conceptions: 'now I understand why pupils cannot learn this', as opposed to 'at least we may all agree on why pupils cannot learn this'.

Without anywhere specifying it, the booklet adheres to the kind of learning that is at the heart of quality assurance – social agreements on standards, and feedback to check the result. Another feature of quality assurance is the emphasis on documentation: if the staff doesn't know anything about their school, why has everything to be written down? Three of the ten case studies are about the construction of quality assurance systems. One area is, however, ignored: nothing is said in the booklet about how to formulate goals or construct standards, or how to carry out studies or analysis of errors.

The important issue for us surrounds the social technology implied in quality assurance. Teachers' roles are expected to be changed by its introduction. Partly overt, partly implied, is the intention to stimulate a local process which limits the right of individual teachers to work in isolation, and to involve them in collaborative norm-setting related to teaching and learning. The booklet seeks to give assurance that school-based evaluation is not concerned with judgments about the achievements of individual teachers, and no examples of this usage are given. But neither is the function of the collaborative process in achieving a common standard of acceptable teacher performance discussed. It is, however, clearly stated that the collaborative process is not voluntary: "it is not . . . . up to the individual teacher to decide if s/he wants to take part" (Granstrom & Lander, 1995b, p. 15).

The booklet does not merely encourage more collaborative work amongst teachers: it also seeks to standardise quality. The ministry argues that equality of opportunity in education cannot be measured only with regard to pupils' gender or social background, but that equal rights "must also be independent of which school class the student ends up in".

The booklet cites headteachers, students and parents as part of the process, without going into detail about their roles. Especially important is the headteacher, who is responsible for school-based evaluation taking place. Nothing is said, however, about how any desired standardisation of teaching quality can be achieved. It may be reasonable to believe that some headteachers use teacher appraisal to this end, as part of the process of quality assurance in their schools.

We have thus seen that the Norwegian Ministry of Education adheres to a model of quality assurance in giving advice about school-based evaluation. It is not a fully-fledged model, but it is one that is designed to suit education and the perceived pressing need to change its social technology. The booklet seems to be written not to provoke resistance among teachers, but more to present them with professional challenges. It is the most explicit example in Scandinavian education of what central political authorities expect from evaluation as a tool of school government at the local level.

The Norwegian state also promotes inservice training in school-based evaluation. To organise this, the regional state authority in one of the counties has for several years cooperated with the regional university, which is noted for its expertise in evaluation. Earlier, only schools were invited to the training, but from the academic year 1992–3 kommuns were also invited, with the purpose of bringing them closer to schools. This is a somewhat politically sensitive matter in Norway. In the Ministry's plan for a national evaluation and assessment scheme, school-based evaluation is a part, with no formal connection to other parts of the scheme. It is stressed that the school "owns" its own evaluation. But in *Underveis* this is not made clear: the booklet states that school-based evaluation does not contribute to the report to higher authorities "today". The wording implies this could be changed.

There is also an ongoing evaluation study of whether kommuns and schools in this county are establishing closer relations as a result of the evaluation process in schools (Bredvold, 1995). The first results, two years after the inservice training of 1992–3, showed that cooperation had developed to some extent within about half of the participating kommuns, but that many officials were confused about what school-based evaluation meant both for school improvement and school government. Most kommuns delegated the matter to the schools, and it is unclear how many of them actually reserved a role for themselves in the future development of the process. There is a fear that many schools look upon evaluation as one improvement project among many, one that is finite and not meant for everyday use.

THE RELATIONSHIP BETWEEN SCHOOL EVALUATION AND SCHOOL IMPROVEMENT

The examples from research cited above are not success stories about the use of evaluation for school improvement. Teachers have often reacted with suspicion and resistance to such state initiatives. The NU project largely shows that only schools already engaged in a process of school improvement can make good use of external feedback from an evaluation of their systems. Other research provides an even more negative picture. Case studies of successful schools suggest that school evaluation does not play a leading role in the school improvement process (Vasstrom 1985, Ekholm, 1990; Hameyer, Anderson, van den Akker, & Ekholm, 1995). Schools utilising feedback from the NU project responded to the offer made, but may not have opted for evaluation if they had had to look for external help themselves. In the review of school improvement literature by Louis and Miles (1987) we were struck by the absence of evaluation as a vehicle of change. However, in analysing improvement processes in urban high schools, Louis and Miles (1990) identified aspects of evaluation in the first of the four vital components of the process – evolutionary planning, vision building, resource management and problem-solving.

In Scandinavia today policy-makers often seem to view school improvement as evaluation rather than the other way round, a view which is almost certain to overburden evaluation as a concept. When evaluation is introduced from above, as it is in Scandinavia, it is often also used to satisfy the policy-makers' need to know and to influence. Methods of evaluation are therefore more suited to these needs and less to the needs of schools, who are still struggling with their informal analyses of the internal school improvement process – the process of evaluation *as* school improvement.

In the case of Norway, however, school-based evaluation is redefined. It is no longer the instrument of improvement through the implementation of challenging new ideas derived from cognitive learning. It is rather the tool for a piecemeal refinement of the existing order. Evaluation is clearly subordinated to the need for a changed social technology in schools. That change – to more powerful leadership and staff collaboration – is supposed to produce higher levels of teacher quality. School improvement takes on a partly new *gestalt*, of using what you can in a better way, rather than of transforming and improving yourself.

However, it is clear from the research discussed here, that evaluation and its modest contribution to school improvement may well get lost in the struggle between the social technology of teaching and the running of schools. If evaluation as management becomes too dominant, it is likely that teachers will administer the kiss of death to the whole idea of evaluation *as* improvement.

REFERENCES

Bredvold, R. (1995). *Skolebasert vurdering 1992/93*. Etterundersøkelse. Statens utdanningskontor i Oppland/Høgskolen i Lillehammer. (School-based evaluation 1992/93. Follow-up study)
Ekholm, M. (1987). School reforms and local response: An evaluation of school reviews in 35 school management areas in Sweden 1980–1985. *Compare*, 17(2), 107–118.

Ekholm, M. (1990). *Utvecklingsarbete och elevstod i vidaregående skolor i Norden.* Nordisk Ministerråd, NORD, Köpenhamn (Improvement work and student support in secondary schools in Nordic countries)

Ekholm, M., Fransson, A., & Lander, R. (1987). *Skolreform och lokalt gensvar. Utvärdering av 35 grundskolor genom upprepade l_gesbedomningar 1980–1985.* Publikation från institutionen för pedagogik, Göteborgs universitet 1987: 3. (School reform and local response. Evaluation of 35 comprehensive schools by repeated reviews 1980–1985.)

Ekholm, M., & Kåräng, G. (1994). *School qualities and educational outcomes. Report from a national evaluation programme in Sweden.* Paper presented at the 7th conference of the International Society of School Effectiveness and School Improvement, Melbourne, Australia, 2–6 January.

Granström, K., & Lander, R. (1995a). *Professionalism i skolans utvärdering och uppföljning.* Praxis, No 2. (Professionalism in the evaluation and assessment of schools.)

Granström, K., & Lander, R. (1995b). Underveis – norska statens handbok om skolbaserad evaluering: Accepted *by Norsk Pedagogisk Tidskrift.* (Underveis – the Norwegian state's handbook for school-based evaluation.)

Hameyer, U., Anderson, R., van den Akker, I., & Ekholm, M. (1995). *Portraits of productive schools. Activity based learning in elementary science – sustained improvement in four countries.* SUNY-Press: New York

Holly, P., & Hopkins, D. (1988). Evaluation and school improvement. *Cambridge Journal of Education,* **18**(2), 221 – 245.

Hopkins, D. (1989). *Evaluation for school development.* Milton Keynes: Open University Press.

Hopkins, D., Jackson, D., West, M., & Terrell, I. (1995). *Evaluation: Trinkets for the natives or cultural change.* Paper presented at an International Conference on "Systemic and Individual Consequences of Evaluation" sponsored by the Swedish National Agency for Education, Stockholm, 23–25 October 1995.

Jacobsson, B., & Sahlin-Andersson, K. (1995). *Skolan och det nya verket, Skildringar från styrningens och utvärderingarnas tidevarv.* Stockholm: Nerenius & Sameras Publishers. (Schools and the New Agency. Tales from the age of governing and evaluations)

Kruchov, C. (1993). Skoleudvikling og foroendringsstrategier-kommunen som udviklingsenhet. Nordiska Ministerrådet: *Evaluering av skolor i Norden – tankar och diskussioner.* Nordisk Seminar – och Arbejdsrapporter 1993: 508. (School development and change strategies – the kommun as unit of development)

Lander, R. (1994). *The assessment of school performance: Background report to OECD/CERI – Sweden.* Department of Education and Educational Research, University of Göteborg.

Lander, R. (1995). *Nationell evaluering. Kort beskrivning av de norska, danska och svenska nationella myndigheternas evalueringsmodeller.* Institutionen för pedagogik, Göteborgs universitet. (National evaluation. Short description of the Norwegian, Danish and Swedish national authorities' models of evaluation)

Lander, R. (1996). *Gymnasisterna i Helsingborg 1996. Svar på enkätfrågor om skolan och studierna.* Rapport till gymnasienämnden i Helsingborgs kommun. (Upper secondary students in Helsingborg – responses about their schools and studies. Report to the political board of the secondary education in Helsingborg.)

Lander, R; Thång, P. O., & Torper, U. (Eds.). (1994). *Den nationella utvärderingen av grundskolan 1987 – 1994.* Synpunkter och empiri om intern debatt och lokal användning. Rapport från institutionen för pedagogik, Göteborgs universitet 14. (National evaluation of the grund-school 1987–1994. School internal debates and local use)

Louis, K. S., & Miles, M. B. (1987). 'Research on institutionalization'. In M. B. Miles, M. Ekholm, & R. Vandenberghe (Eds.), *Lasting school improvement: Exploring the process of institutionalization.* OECD-ISIP No. 5, Leuven: ACCO.

Louis, K. S., & Miles, M. B. (1990). *Improving the urban high school: What works and why?* New York: Teachers College Press.

Louis, K. S., & van Velzen, W. G. (1986). *Policies for school improvement: A comparative analysis of four policy issues.* Paper presented at the meeting of the International School Improvement Project, OECD, Toronto, October 19–25.

Newman, F. M. & Wehlage, G. G. (1993). Five standards of authentic instruction. *Educational Leadership,* 50,(7), 8–12.

Taylor, C. (Summer, 1994). Assessment for measurement or standards: The peril and promise of large-scale assessment reform. *American Educational Research Journal,* **31**(2), 231–262.

100   *Lander and Ekholm*

van der Knaap, P. (1995). Policy evaluation and learning: Feedback, enlightenment or argumentation? *Evaluation*, **1**(2).

Vasstrom, U. (Ed.). (1985). *Nordiska skolor i utveckling. Utvecklingsarbete vid 14 grundskolor i Norden.* Nordiska ministerrådet, Köpenhamn, NORD. (Developing Nordic schools. Improvement work in 14 grund schools in Nordic countries.)

Quality Assurance Reviews as a Catalyst for School Improvement in Australia

PETER CUTTANCE

University of Sydney, NSW, Australia

INTRODUCTION

This chapter discusses the foundation and operation of models for school review and their contribution to school improvement. The key elements of the chapter are a review of the literature on variation in student outcomes between schools and within schools (which leads into a discussion of the essentials of school change) the politics of accountability and improvement, frameworks for assuring quality in schooling, and the operationalisation of school reviews in the context of school improvement.

Quality assurance approaches to school review and improvement are now a core element of State and Government school systems in many parts of the world: for example Scotland (McGlynn & Stalker, 1995), England (Barber, Gough, & Johnson, 1995; Ofsted, 1993), Australia (Department of Education, Victoria, 1997) and New Zealand (NZ ERO, 1991).

In order to design a systemic model of school review and improvement it is necessary to address the range and variation in performance and effectiveness in school systems.

- How much of student learning can be attributed to schools, and how much is simply a reflection of the differences in the background characteristics of students?
- How much difference does it make as to which school a student attends?
- How much variation is there in the performance and effectiveness of schools for various subgroups of students in the school population?
- What is the dimensionality of school performance and effectiveness across cognitive, affective and social domains of student outcomes?
- How can information on school performance and effectiveness be used to constructively support schools' efforts to improve opportunities for students?

Although school systems have moved in the direction of developing a performance orientation over the last few years, they are still not driven by a focus on the performances that ultimately matter – those reflected in the achievements of their students. The management of school systems still focuses on the performances of

D. Hopkins (ed.), The Practice and Theory of School Improvement, 101-128.
© 2005 *Springer. Printed in the Netherlands.*

key players in management achieving intermediate 'outputs', with only a secondary consideration of the 'outcomes' of these performances as reflected in student learning.

Further, the systemic programs that are required to consistently support school improvement often fail, due to the instability of the political and bureaucratic environment of school systems. The effectiveness of school support programs is often undermined by changes in the political and bureaucratic environment. Hence, school systems are not consistent over time, in the ways they attempt to support the efforts of individual schools to improve their performance and effectiveness.

A performance orientated system needs to focus on whether appropriate outcomes are being achieved by students. Where high student performance is evident, the system needs to ensure that it is providing the conditions required for continuing high levels of achievement. This means providing opportunities for school staff to keep themselves abreast of the necessary knowledge and skills in curriculum, learning and teaching, etc. Where performance is not as high as it could be and the value added by schools is less than expected, a performance orientation assists in focusing efforts both on the provision of appropriate support and on providing the necessary pressure for schools to improve their performance.

A high performing school system requires a focus on both support and pressure (Fullan, 1993). Pressure comes from the setting of clear expectations and targets for schools and students. It requires the publication of appropriate performance information so that others can assess progress against standards.

Further, pressure comes from rigorous and focussed reviews of the development and performance of individual schools. Such reviews provide support, through working collaboratively with school communities and those accountable for school performance, to identify key matters to be addressed through a program of focussed further development. Once reviews have been conducted, school support networks need to ensure that appropriate resources and expertise are applied to the specific aspects of the work of schools that have been identified for improvement. It is crucial that such support be tailored to the specific improvement needs of each school, in addition to any systemic improvement needs across all schools.

VARIATION IN STUDENT LEARNING ATTRIBUTABLE TO SCHOOLS

There has been little disputation of the findings during the last decade or so that schools have a significant impact on student learning. The research on students who do not attend school or do not receive tuition clearly indicates that they learn less in comparison to those who do attend school.

Reynolds (1992) reported that the percentage of variation in student achievement in Europe and USA that can be attributed to schools is in the range 8–15%. In their benchmark study of Inner London middle schools conducted during the 1980s, Mortimore et al., (1988) found 7% of variation of Year 3 reading test scores and 14% of Year 3 mathematics test scores could be attributed to schools. The variation between schools in Year 3 achievement test scores would have been due to variation in the effectiveness of schools on student learning from the infant years to Year 3 and to variation in the social composition and ability of students between schools. The variation between schools at Year 5 was 17% for mathematics and 19% for reading. The variation in student attainment between schools increased from Year 3 to Year 5 for this cohort of students.

Australian research by Hill (1995) found that the variation in performance between state schools in Victoria is about the same as that found in the above London study, 16–19%. An analysis of the variation in performance between state schools in New South Wales indicated that 11% of the variance in achievement scores in Year 5 (primary) and 19% of the variance at Year 12 (secondary) lies between schools. For secondary schools this reduces to 12% after taking account of the attainments of students at intake.

Approximately half of this variation in NSW in the value added by secondary schools is attributable to differences between types of schools in the system. Once the single-sex and academically selective status of schools is taken into account, the variance in effectiveness between schools accounts for only 7% of the total variation in students' Year 12 achievements. That is, about 40% of the total variation in effectiveness between the 430 secondary schools can be attributed to the small number of single–sex and academically selective schools which together cater for approximately one-fifth of the students in the system.

Most school effectiveness research has concentrated on the differences between schools, with little analysis of other variation, such as that between classrooms within schools. Between classroom effects accounted for up to 45% of the variation in performance in the Second International Mathematics Study (Scheerens, Vermeulen, & Pelgrum, 1989), but a classroom-level of analysis of the contribution of schools has not been included in most school effectiveness studies.

Hill's (1995) study has significantly altered our understanding of the variation within and between schools. The study found that 38–45% of individual student achievement in English and 53–55% in mathematics was attributable to differences between classrooms. Adding school and classroom influence together, Hill found that up to 60% of the variation in achievement between students was attributable to the impact of schools on student learning. These findings were broadly similar for both primary schools and high schools. Analysis of the effectiveness of schools in New South Wales (NSW) indicates that 45% of the variance between students in Year 12 outcomes can be accounted for by prior attainment (measured in Year 6) and student gender. Six percentage points of variance are attributable to differences between types of schools and seven percentage points attributable to variance between schools. Hence, by deduction, up to 42% of the variation in student attainment at Year 12 is attributable to variation within schools.

The analyses also indicated that Year 6 achievement measures explained 60% of the variance in individual achievement at Year 10 and that Year 10 achievement explained 79% of variance in individual achievement at Year 12. Thus, the largest possible effects that can be attributed to the combined differences of school sectors, schools and classrooms and programs within schools is 40% at Year 10 and 21% at Year 12, after taking account of student's achievements at Year 10.

The discussion above relates to the variance in student achievement that lies between schools. Mortimore et al. (1988) investigated the variance in student progress from Years 3 to 5 that lies between schools. The proportion of the variance in student progress between schools was found to be higher than the proportion of the variance in Year 3 achievement scores between schools. The study utilised sequential assessment instruments in both Year 3 and Year 5. Hence, the variation between schools in Year 5 achievement after taking account of student's Year 3 achievements represented the variation in the growth in achievement made by students between Years 3 and 5. It is reasonable to conclude that the schools themselves were the primary source of this variation in the growth made by students and, therefore, that the study found significant differences in the effectiveness of schools. The study found that data on student's background (social class, race, sex) was a poor predictor of the growth in students' learning over the four years of the research. Student background characteristics appeared to have little influence on growth in achievement from Year 3–5 beyond the initial impact of such background characteristics on Year 3 achievement. The variance in student progress attributable to differences between schools was found to be ten times greater than that attributable to student background characteristics for progress from Year 3 to 5 in mathematics learning. Similarly, schools were found to be four times more influential than student social background characteristics for student growth in reading. This finding of the impact of student background does not provide support for a double–jeopardy effect in which students who are disadvantaged in their initial achievements, are disadvantaged again by the further impact of background factors on progress in achievement.

SOME FUNDAMENTALS OF SUCCESSFUL EDUCATIONAL CHANGE

The relationship of school reviews to change in schools is summarised by the following quotation from a paper that was prepared for use by schools in New South Wales:

> . . . [reviews of] the effectiveness of practices and processes for achieving improved student outcomes in school systems . . . contributes to the process through which schools as learning organisations develop a planned approach to constructing their future.

(Cuttance, 1993)

Hopkins (1989) summarised the key elements of successful reviews as a catalyst for school improvement:

- they are based on a systematic review and evaluation process, and are not simply an exercise in reflection;
- their focus is to obtain information about a school's condition, purposes, and achievements;

- they lead to action on aspects of the school's organisation or curriculum;
- they are a group activity that involves participants in a collegial process;
- the process and its outcomes are 'owned' by the school; and
- their purpose is school improvement and development, and their aspiration is to progress towards the goal of a 'problem solving' or 'relatively autonomous' school.

The educational change literature has signalled the importance of the phenomenon of simultaneous top–down and bottom–up pressure and support for effective educational change. As Fullan points out:

> we have known for decades that top–down change doesn't work (you can't mandate what matters) . . . [but] decentralised solutions like site–based management also fail because groups get preoccupied with governance and frequently flounder when left on their own . . . Even when they are successful for short periods they cannot stay successful unless they pay attention to the centre and vice-versa.
>
> (Fullan, 1993, p. 37)

Organisations that effectively manage change, invest in their capacity to reflect, build on team learning, develop shared visions and shared understandings of complex issues. But it is imperative that this involves both looking–outward as well as looking–inward if the school's future is to be the result of coordinated development.

> What is required is a . . . two–way relationship of pressure, support and continuous negotiation. It amounts to simultaneous top–down bottom–up influence.
>
> (Fullan, 1993, p. 38)

> There is a pattern underlying . . . lessons of dynamic change and it concerns one's ability to work with polar opposites: simultaneously pushing for change while allowing self–learning to unfold; being prepared for a journey of uncertainty; seeing problems as sources of creative resolution; having a vision, but not being blinded by it; valuing the individual and the group; incorporating centralising and decentralising forces; being internally cohesive, but externally orientated; and valuing personal change agentry as the route to system change.
>
> What this analysis means is that in the current struggle between state accountability and local autonomy, both are right. Success depends on the extent to which each force can willingly contend with if not embrace the other as necessary for productive educational change.
>
> (Fullan, 1993, p. 40)

The challenge to continuing school development, however, lies not simply in the initiatives of individual teachers. Cuban (1988) categorised innovations into first-order and second–order change. First–order changes are those that improve the effectiveness of that which already exists "without disturbing the basic organisational features, without altering the way that children and adults perform their roles" (1988, p. 342). Second–order changes aim to alter the fundamental relationships of a school, creating new goals, reorganising structures and creating new cultures. In picking up this theme, Fullan argues that the:

> challenge of the 1990s [is] to deal with more second–order changes-changes that affect the culture and structure of schools, restructuring roles and reorganising responsibilities, including those of students and parents. In the past we have worked on the notion that if we just 'fix it' and if all perform their roles better [the run faster syndrome] we will have improved education.
>
> (Fullan, 1991, p. 29)

The processes and structures required to provide effective support and pressure for performance development are different for schools at different stages of their performance development cycle (Cuttance, 1994; Gray, 1993; Gray et al., 1995; Hopkins, 1995). The strategies that schools need to implement, to achieve enhanced performance, range from basic direction setting when at the trailing edge of the performance development cycle to strategies that harness innovation and creative professional practice when at the leading edge of the performance development cycle. Stringfield (1995) has proposed the adoption of practices from 'high reliability' systems for schools. These may be particularly germane to schools in the lower parts of the performance development cycle as they seek to minimise the scope for error in all aspects of the organisation's work. Louis (1994) and Hargreaves (1995) describe contexts in which strategic change management strategies may be effective and other contexts in which other less structured strategies may be the appropriate methodology for enhancing the performance of schools. It is crucial that support and pressure be appropriately variegated if it is to be effective for a system of schools at varying levels of performance. Providers of support services must come to an understanding with schools as to which practices will provide effective support and pressure, given each school's particular stage in developing its performance.

THE POLITICS OF SCHOOL IMPROVEMENT AND ACCOUNTABILITY

The organisational and political structures in which school review and improvement systems are embedded also have a powerful influence on their impact. Research on the development and introduction of accountability systems in Australia has highlighted the threat to their effectiveness posed by the response of school system bureaucracies (Cuttance, forthcoming).

Although school review programs in Australia have achieved many successes in the last decade or so, none of those currently surviving with integrity have a lifespan of more than a few years. The political and bureaucratic response to accountability has, in most cases, been one that has sought to subvert and destabilise programs of school review and system evaluation before or soon after they have developed a capacity to contribute to accountability at the system level (Cuttance, forthcoming).

School system bureaucracies have the power and potential to impede and dismantle school review and improvement systems within a few years of their introduction. Such responses from school system bureaucracies are particularly likely to arise where school review and improvement systems do not have organisational or legislative independence from the school system whose performance they review. The issue of independence has been paramount in the literature on the relationship between Her Majesty's Inspectorate of Schools and Government in England for much of the last century (Cuttance, 1995a; Lawton & Gordon, 1987).

Systems that have ensured their school review programs have independence from the school bureaucracy that they review have been able to provide a much more secure environment for such work to make a continuing and substantial contribution to improving the performance of the school system. New Zealand and the UK are two countries that have been successful in pursuing this latter path. No Australian State has granted its school review system the level of autonomy and authority required for it to be able to report independently and publicly on the school system. Although school systems in Australia are subject to financial and administrative accountability, they are not subject to effective regimes of accountability for the educational outcomes of students.

Review systems established within school system bureaucracies have typically been neutralised by the response of the bureaucracy and have failed to contribute in the long–term to the processes of accountability and improvement for schools and for the systems as a whole. The response of the highly centralised school system bureaucracies in Australia has been first to render the role of accountability at the system–level ineffective, through the formal and informal suppression of public reports on aspects of the school system's performance. Second, the bureaucracies have viewed processes of review and improvement for individual schools as a shift of power from the 'centre' to schools and their communities, and have taken steps to confine the way in which school reviews are able to involve and engage school communities in the accountability process. For example, 'central' authorities have proscribed the domains of school performance and the dimensions of the enabling structures and conditions that reviews could discuss in their public reports. The school review program in NSW was proscribed from publicly reporting on the adequacy of school buildings and facilities, and there was pressure from system administrators to not include explicit data on student achievement in school review reports. The latter was in response to the concern of the bureaucracy that this would inflame the Teachers' Union.

A team of Her Majesty's Inspectors from England visited South Australia to assess aspects of the school review program in that state in 1992. While they were positive in their assessments of certain aspects of the review program, such as the high level of participation by parents, school staff and students, they expressed concern that the program of reviews:

[focussed] exclusively on the structures and processes, rather than the outputs and quality of learning . . . the central issues of teaching and learning were addressed only at the margin despite the fact that the parents interviewed [in the reviews] were frequently anxious to talk about these aspects [of their children's education]. (Ofsted, 1992)

School quality assurance review systems, that have been established with independent authority to publish reports on schools and systemic performance in the UK and NZ, operate within a context of a 'market' system of education. These market systems are characterised by increased access to performance information, local governance and management of schools, and 'parent choice' as a significant controlling mechanism, replacing the former controlling function of the bureaucracy. In such systems, the quality assurance system provides an essential element of the regulatory framework, one that provides public information on quality and recommends action to regulate schools that fail to meet prescribed standards for teaching and learning.

THE FRAMEWORK FOR ASSURING QUALITY IN EDUCATION

The framework for assuring the quality of learning outcomes is governed by the nature of educational services and outputs. Unlike many everyday products, the quality of educational learning outcomes cannot be ascertained prior to the point at which the student is in possession of them. The teaching and curriculum services of schools can be classified as 'experience' services and the learning outcomes of schooling can be classified as 'credence' products.

Experience products and services are those for which quality can only be determined after purchase through experience in their use. *Credence* products are those for which quality attributes cannot be detected at the time of delivery or in an immediate way when they are in use. This may be due to the fact that the qualities, in principal, cannot be detected in normal use or because they are intrinsically inter-related with other features of the environment in which they are used, or cannot be disentangled from the form in which they are embodied. For example, a student's analytical or mathematical skills are embodied in the student in such a way that their effect cannot be distinguished uniquely from the student's abilities, attitudes, motivation, etc.

Quality assurance systems for experience and credence services and outputs cannot focus only on providing knowledge about the quality of the outputs themselves, since that cannot be fully established until a later stage in which they are in use by the consumer, and may not be separable from other conjoint factors impacting on their use. Quality assurance systems for experience outputs must, therefore, also have a significant focus on the processes and systems that are used to deliver the outputs. In schooling, this means that quality assurance processes must focus on the competencies of systems that schools have in place for providing educational services through which students can acquire particular skills and knowledge.

The 'credence' aspect of learning outcomes means that quality assurance frameworks for education often take the form of the accreditation of the processes of schools and of the outputs of individual programs. The content focus of such accreditation processes are benchmarks, established as 'best practice' in relation to organisational competencies required to maintain and improve the delivery of educational programs and the standard of the outputs from those programs.

Quality assurance school reviews focus on the competency of a school to develop and manage the delivery of a prescribed curriculum and the standards of the learning achieved by students, to the extent that the latter can be ascertained, although only after they have been acquired by the student. In contradistinction to many products and services, there is no opportunity for a student to return a defective educational experience in lieu of a refund and an opportunity to purchase the experience from another supplier. Further, the skills and knowledge acquired by a student are intrinsically unobservable prior to their acquisition by students, and even after they are acquired they cannot be observed in a disembodied form that would allow for the determination of their specific qualities. Hence, student's learning experiences and learning outcomes reflect both 'experience' and 'credence' attributes.

The assurance of the development and delivery of a curriculum needs to focus on factors that have been shown to influence the effectiveness of a school's competency in management, teaching and learning. The assurance of learning outcomes requires the assessment of skills and knowledge expressed by students against specified benchmarks and standards *during* the process of learning. As in the provision of many services the quality of the output from schools may vary over time. The achievements of students in one year must be interpreted as a fallible indicator of the likely achievements of subsequent cohorts of students.

Systems of quality assurance can be classified as first, second or third party processes of assurance. First–party quality assurance is established when a producer provides purchasers with a statement of the steps taken to ensure that design standards and specifications are met by a product or service. Such systems are based entirely on whatever the supplier decides to provide as information for consumers, often in the form of sales materials. As a system of accountability, first–party assurance processes lack the essential qualities of transparency and independence.

Second–party quality assurance is provided when the purchaser is able to ascertain for themselves that the producer has met the design standards and specifications for the product or service, usually through a process of inspecting the production and compliance processes first hand. Parent's visits to schools that they are considering choosing can be viewed in this light, however, such visits are rarely of a form that allows the parent to ascertain in any detail the quality of the processes and learning outcomes produced by the school. Further, such visits are not normally designed to provide the parent with access to the information on the school's competencies and capabilities to continue to produce particular learning outcomes for its students. As in industry, an effective and credible second–party assurance process would need to be carried out by an individual or team with the requisite professional and technical competence to make such judgements.

Parent's visits to schools are better viewed as having a similar function to 'customer surveys' in service industries. Such surveys provide an overview of customer satisfaction, but they are not a recognised form of quality assurance for a product or service. Rather, they inform the producer about changes in customer preferences and, hence, about possible shifts in market demand. As a form of accountability, second–party assurance processes are inefficient because they require every purchaser to seek individual assurance that the design standards and specifications are met for the product or service they purchase.

Third–party quality assurance is established when design standards and specifications are verified through a process of assessment by an external independent body. The external body is organisationally and professionally independent of both the producer and the purchaser, hence, third–party quality assurance processes meet the formal standards required for independent and transparent accountability for the quality of a product or service. Such processes are often accompanied by the issuance of a certificate, that is backed by a report providing justification in relation to recognised quality assurance standards for the award of the certificate.

In education, both 'purchasers' (parents) and 'funders' (government, in many cases) require an assurance process that meets third–party quality assurance standards. Such assurance needs to be carried out in accordance with a set of professional and technical standards that are specifically relevant to education.

The central foci of school review and improvement are the learning achievements and associated outcomes for students. The curriculum, learning environment and management structures that schools provide for student learning can be viewed as the enabling structures for learning. The key elements of frameworks for the assurance of quality in schooling are set out in Figure 1. The common elements of these frameworks can be synthesised into the following five dimensions.

- Student achievement and progress: as assessed against specified standards and examinations, performance of students relative to those in schools with similar intakes, achievements of designated subgroups of students, monitoring and assessment of student progress.
- Curriculum: planning and implementation of prescribed curricula, the co-curricular or elective curriculum provided, processes for the assessment of educational outcomes against standards, reporting to parents.
- Learning environment: provision of support for learning, assessments of the extent to which the school meets the learning needs of individual students, adaptation of teaching practices to the needs of individual students and groups, student behaviour and attendance.
- Management: of the human, physical and financial resources of the school.
- Community participation: involvement of parents, meeting community educational needs, links with related agencies.

It is important for quality assurance purposes that school review programs encompass all schools in the system. Otherwise, parents do not have an assurance

England (Ofsted, 1993)

- Achievement of students.
- Quality of teaching.
- Efficiency of the school.
- Pupil's spiritual, moral, social and cultural development.
- Behaviour and discipline.
- Attendance.
- Curricular provision.
- Factors contributing to the findings on the above, including: quality of teaching, assessment, recording and reporting; quality and range of the curriculum, equality of opportunity, provision for pupils with special needs; management and administration of staff, learning resources and accommodation; pupil welfare; and links with parents, agencies and other related institutions.

New Zealand (NZ Education Review Office, 1991)

- Student achievement: standards of achievement, progress of learners, identification and analysis of underachievement, achievement of predetermined learning objectives in all National Curriculum requirements for all students, achievement of Maori students, achievement of other activities and essential skills related to the National Curriculum.
- Learning and teaching: compliance with National Curriculum Guidelines, effectiveness of teaching practices, student/student and student/teacher relationships, planning of teaching programs, adaptation of teaching practices for minority students, classroom and school environment, staffing and resources.
- Assessment and evaluation: monitoring student progress and performance, identification of needs of students, use of assessment & evaluation in teaching, student contribution to learning context, identification of needs of minority students, reporting to families on student achievement & progress.
- Leadership and management: development and achievement of charter goals and policies, educational leadership, quality control systems, communication with the school community, effectiveness of the relationship between governance and management, minority participation in governance and management, employment practices, maintenance of buildings.
- Community participation: consultation with and reporting to community groups, involvement of parents in student learning, response to educational needs of the community, processes for feedback from community groups.

Victoria (Victorian Department of Education, 1997)

- Student achievement: achievement in relation to the levels set out in specified curriculum and standards frameworks and in external examinations, relative performance of the school in relation to other schools serving similar students, achievement of designated subgroups of students within the school and post-school destinations of students.
- Curriculum and teaching: time allocated to specified Key Learning Areas, student participation in elective programs and external examinations, parent assessments of the school's curriculum provision.
- Learning environment: student accident data, parent assessments of the quality of the learning environment, student attendance.
- Management: staff assessment of the management of the school and the quality of their work lives, professional development of staff, sick leave and absence of staff.
- Resources: management and utilisation of resources to achieve the school's Charter goals and priorities.
- Charter Goals and Priorities: progress towards the achievement of the outcomes specified in the school's Charter.

Figure 1: Key content elements of quality assurance in state school systems

that relates to each of the schools that they may wish to consider choosing from. Further, ensuring that all schools are covered by the program provides the necessary pressure to simultaneously push out the envelope of the leading edge of performance and raise the trailing edge of the system. Approaches to quality assurance that target only the schools considered to be performing below some predetermined level simply leads to the establishment of a subsystem that focuses on ineffective schools. This is also likely to lead to quality assurance processes taking on the much more limited role of inspection – the postproduction process that is designed to detect outputs that fail to meet design standards.

Effective review systems integrate knowledge of educational change processes and school improvement processes. Their quality assurance function needs to be linked to the knowledge base of factors that are associated with effective schools. The challenge of educational change in schools can be supported through the school review process by identifying 'incremental' (i.e. first–order) and 'fundamental' (i.e. second–order) change (Cooney, 1994; Cuttance, 1994).

Principles for the Conduct of School Reviews

The educational change literature indicates a number of key factors that can be incorporated into systemic programs of school quality assurance reviews to ensure they also provide support in a way that assists schools in their development. A high level of participation by all stakeholder groups in the school community provides a framework for school ownership of the outcomes of the review and provides support through the suggested future directions encapsulated in recommendations for further development. School reviews can provide elements of both pressure and support for school improvement. Pressure is provided through assessment against best practice benchmarks derived from factors identified as important for the effectiveness of schools, including the analysis of student achievements against systemwide standards.

Quality assurance review programs in Australia have enunciated specific principles designed to encapsulate the imperatives from the educational change and school effectiveness literatures. For example, the program in NSW was developed within a framework of the following eight key principles.

1. School reviews support schools in evaluating and assessing their practices and outcomes to improve student learning.
2. School reviews contribute to the evaluation and assessment of services and programs which support schools.
3. School reviews strengthen accountability for the quality of education in individual schools.
4. School reviews are undertaken through the participation of school staff, students, parents and the review team. Reviews provide opportunities for input from all those interested in the school's performance and development.

5. School reviews are planned and conducted to take account of the context of each school.
6. School review teams have the knowledge and skills necessary to ensure reviews are of direct benefit to schools.
7. School review team members are bound by ethical and professional standards.
8. School review teams use methods which are consistent with established best practices in school review and evaluation. (NSW DSE, 1995)

The reviews of schools in NSW were based on a philosophy that the assurance of quality required a challenging and structured analysis of the key issues for the further development and performance of schools. This process of analysis was built on a basis of trust, collaboration and participation that aimed to cement ownership of the further development of the school in the school community. The analysis of learning outcomes along with the rigour of the review methodology, was designed to ensure that the reviews tackled the core issues for the school's further development.

The discussion, in a previous section, delineated a framework for assuring quality in schools based jointly on an assessment of competencies and capabilities to develop and deliver a curriculum and the standard of the learning outcomes of students. The remaining two sections of this chapter provide illustrations of the types of assessments that are being implemented by the Department of Education in Victoria through school self–assessment and independent verification of these aspects of schooling.

REVIEWS OF SCHOOL PERFORMANCE AND EFFECTIVENESS

Over the last decade, many school systems have embarked on strategies of regular school review as a means of providing both support for school improvement, and as a central element of quality assurance for schools. As indicated in an earlier section, recent attempts to develop accountability systems based on school reviews in Australia have been disbanded because they created too great a challenge to school system bureaucracies (Cuttance et al., forthcoming). South Australia developed a system of school reviews that reviewed all schools over the period 1979–93. NSW developed a system of school reviews that reviewed about half of all schools during the period 1992–96. The latter system was disbanded in favour of the publication of school test and examination results as an initiative of the incoming Labour Government in 1996. Victoria, has more recently introduced a system of school reviews and public reports that are conducted by independent educational reviewers. The output of these independent reviews is provided as information from a quasi third–party quality assurance process to inform parents of the quality and standards of individual schools.

The quality assurance school review system in Victoria requires schools to undertake a self–assessment that presents data for the quality assurance panel to utilise in its evaluation and assessment of the performance, competencies and capacities of the school. The Victorian system operationalises first– and second–order change by identifying priorities and focus areas for further improvement. These priorities and focus areas are subsequently incorporated into the school's triennial Charter.[1]

Assuring the Management and Delivery of the Curriculum

School review systems have developed a number of different approaches to the assurance of the quality of the development and delivery of curriculum. State school systems in Australia, UK and NZ are presently based on a philosophy that government has the role of describing and prescribing a curriculum that is to be taught in all schools. This function of the State in defining the knowledge base and set of skills that are to be provided to all students is sanctioned through social control mechanisms that derive their authority from legislation, Ministerial Orders, accreditation processes, review systems and government funded teacher training schemes, etc. These control mechanisms extend well beyond the prescription of curriculum content to the training and professional development of teachers, accreditation of non-government schools, public examinations and credentials, quality assurance systems and student attendance and time requirements for each phase of schooling.

This situation of State control of knowledge and learning is in marked contrast to the regime in the USA, where State authorities have more circumscribed powers in relation to the definition and control of the curriculum and assessment. In the USA, authority in relation to the curriculum is a shared remit with a broader basis of governance, emanating from the Constitution and the role of the judiciary.

The benchmarks that various systems have developed are critical to operationalising quality assurance frameworks. They provide the basis for educational audits in schools. In school reviews in Victoria the data from these audits provides an essential input to the evaluation of each school's development and achievements. Consideration of this audit information focuses on the development of recommendations for priorities and focus areas for improvement to be incorporated in the school's next triennial Charter.

The Victorian Department of Education has developed benchmarks in a number of areas for school auditing purposes. The figures below illustrate examples of these benchmarks and the analysis of selected aspects of school effectiveness and performance.

The time allocated to each Key Learning Area (KLA), in Years 7–10 varies from school to school because most schools manage their curriculum in these years within a 'core + electives' structure. There is no prescribed time requirement for each KLA. Figure 2 shows the time allocation to the eight KLAs in one high school. Statewide averages are provided for schools to utilise in comparing their curriculum time allocations, but variation is accepted, particularly as it relates to

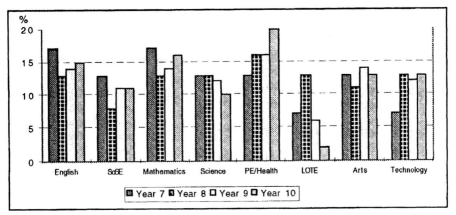

SoSE: Studies of Society and the Environment. PE/Health: Physical Education/Health.
LOTE: Languages other than English.

Figure 2: Curriculum time allocations by Key Learning Area

the Charter objectives of individual schools in meeting the needs and requirements of different groups of students. In Years 11 and 12 the time requirements
are specified by the courses that students study for end of school examinations.

The survey of parents provides information on a number of dimensions of the
quality of schooling as perceived by parents: Teaching Quality, Academic Rigour,
Student Reporting, and General Environment. Figure 3 shows that, in the school
from which these data are drawn, parent assessments have improved on all five
items on the 'teaching quality' scale between 1995 to 1996. Over 80% of parents
were in agreement with each of the items on this scale in 1996.

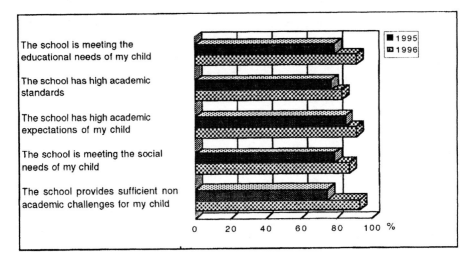

Figure 3: Parent assessments of educational quality

The school review program in NSW developed a series of benchmarks to assess a number of aspects of teaching and learning in schools in that state. The data from the reviews of schools in terms 2 and 3 1995 are presented in Figure 4 (Cuttance, 1995b).

The information in Figure 4 provides an indication of how data can be aggregated across schools to provide a basis for formulating priorities for systemic support for schools. From Figure 4 it is clear that the aspects of the learning environment that are least evidently meeting the benchmarks are those that relate to student learning practices: student risk taking in their learning, student's taking responsibility for their learning, collaboration between students and teachers, student involvement and engagement, student participation in the evaluation of teaching and learning practice, and student reflection.

Assuring Student Learning Outcomes

The learning outcomes of schooling can be described in terms of the cognitive and affective outcomes that students acquire as a result of their schooling. In addition, a

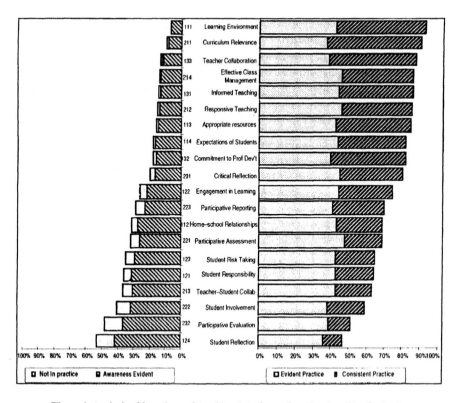

Figure 4: Analysis of learning and teaching data from educational audits of schools

number of social outcomes derive from schooling's socialisation and social control functions. Because these latter outcomes relate to schools as institutions, measures of them are normally described at the level of the school. The broad set of outcomes from schooling can be described by the following.

- Cognitive outcomes – curriculum–based knowledge and skills.
  - The acquisition of propositional knowledge, knowledge application, higher–order problem solving skills and the development of the capacity to construct knowledge from constituent elements and contexts. Aspects of language and mathematics are assumed by most school systems to be an essential focus of such skills, but the wider curriculum includes elements of science, social and human systems, technology, the arts, and health.
- Affective outcomes – the development of personal and social skills and self–knowledge.
  - The development of student attitudes, values, self–worth, communication skills, leadership skills, collaborative skills, etc.
- Social outcomes – relating to the role of schooling as a socialising, selection and control function in society.
  - Attendance, suspension and expulsion, behaviour in the classroom and other parts of the school, retention rates, post–school destinations, community participation, all reflect aspects of this function of schooling.

There is a substantial research literature on the appropriate use of information on student learning outcomes in school review and improvement. The literature on the assessment of school performance focuses on three types of analysis of student learning outcomes data.

- The level of achievement of students in relation to externally established standards (standards–based performance).
- The relative change over time in cohort differences in student achievement and the differences in achievement among groups of students (cohort–based and equity–based analyses of school performance).
- The progress made over time by students attending a particular school (the value–added by the school).

Examples of the ways in which the information in schools has been collated to provide the input to quality assurance assessments of these dimensions are indicated by the following presentations taken from the self–assessment reports prepared by schools in Victoria for individual external school review audits. The self–assessment reports prepared by schools at the end of their triennial Charter period provide the basis for verification and discussion by the school review panel, which consists of an external independent educational reviewer, the President of the School Council, the Principal of the school and one or two other members of the school's management team.

Cognitive outcomes

Student achievements expressed through teacher–assessments, portfolios of student work, tests and examinations have been used as the primary measures of cognitive learning outcomes. In research on the effectiveness of primary schools, the cognitive outcomes used to measure school performance have most often focussed on the core curriculum areas of literacy and numeracy.

In secondary schooling, UK research and school review/inspection processes have focussed on various overall measures of student outcomes in public examinations (for example, the number of passes in the range A–C at GCSE level). Because most school systems in the USA have few measures of student outcomes that provide a comprehensive overview of student attainment across the curriculum, most cognate research and school evaluation processes have utilised data from either purpose specific testing or systemwide testing of students in particular content domains.

A significant feature of the measures of student attainment employed in school effectiveness research and school evaluation in the USA is that they are often not formally aligned with the curriculum that schools are teaching, whereas the external examinations that are used as the measures of student achievement in many other systems are formally aligned with the taught curriculum in schools.

Figures 5–7 show a range of ways in which the performance of schools is analysed using public examination and teacher assessment data in the review process for government schools in Victoria.

These analyses form the core of the cognitive outcomes data presented by each school in its self–assessment report. The school's self–assessment provides the information base for the work of the independent reviewer. Schools contextualise their self–assessment by presenting additional information that relates to their circumstances. In particular, schools present information about their specific curriculum programs and achievements that reflect their areas of strength.

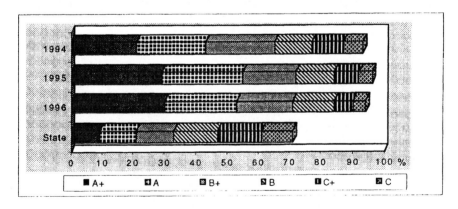

Figure 5: Distribution of grades overall in Year 12 examinations

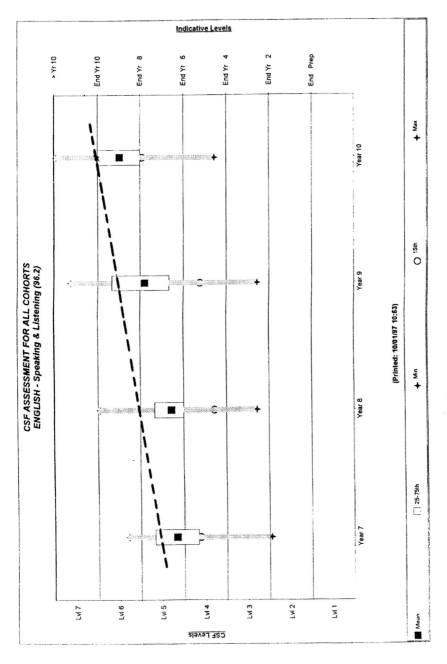

Figure 6

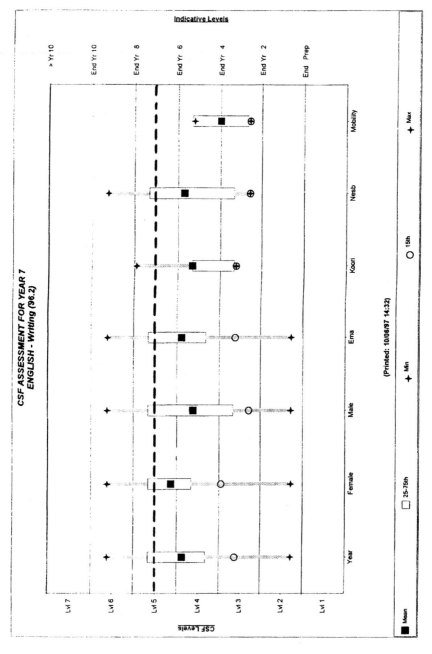

Figure 7

Figure 5 shows the data on the overall distribution of grades across courses for students in the Year 12 examination for one school from 1994–96, and for the examination statewide. The figure indicates that the proportion of students in this school gaining a grade of 'C' or higher has steadily increased each year, even though it started from a high base level in 1994. Over 90% of the grades achieved in this school are 'C' or better, compared to 70% statewide. Further, the percentage of student grades of 'A+' has increased from about 20% in 1994 to 30% in 1996, compared to a statewide distribution of 10% in each year. The information provided by such analyses has to be interpreted in the context of other information about individual schools. For example, the high level of performance of students in this school is partially due to the fact that it has an academically selective intake.

Figure 6 shows an application of a standards–based performance assessment in a school. The distribution of achievements for students in the school is displayed for one curriculum dimension (English – Speaking & Listening) for each of the year–cohorts in Years 7–10 in the school. The 'standard' (indicated by the broken line) indicates the level of student achievement described by the standard in each of the Years 7–10. This analysis indicates that the achievements of the students in all cohorts are below standard by half a year or more, with the Year 9 cohort below standard by the largest amount. The distribution of student achievements in Year 9 is also wider than for other years.

Figure 7 shows an equity–based analysis of school performance. The distribution of student achievements is shown for different subgroups of students in Year 7 in one dimension of curriculum outcomes (English – Writing). Similar analyses are routinely generated for each cohort and for other curriculum dimensions. In this figure, it is clear that the achievement levels of all groups are substantially below the Year 7 'standard' (represented by the horizontal broken line). Further, there is a marked difference in the performance of male and female students, with the level of achievement for Year 7 males being on average about one year below that of girls in this school. The achievements of students from disadvantaged backgrounds (represented in the figure as 'Ema'), Koori (Aboriginal) students, those from Non-English speaking backgrounds (Nesb), and students who have arrived at the school since the commencement of the year (Mobility) all have lower average levels of achievement than female students as a group. Males and Nesb students have a considerably wider distribution of achievement than the other groups. The circles on the whiskers of each plot indicate the fifteenth percentile of the distribution for each group. In this figure, the fifteenth percentile of the Male and Nesb distributions of achievement for this Year 7 cohort equate to a level of achievement below the standard for Year 3, ie. such students are achieving at a level that is four years below the standard for their stage of schooling.

Figure 8 shows an analysis of the achievement of students in the school for the curriculum dimension of Mathematical Methods in Year 12. The information does not formally describe the value added by the school, but provides similar information by presenting the performance of the school in the context of the achievement of students in other schools serving similar populations. In this case, schools are classified into 'like' groups on the basis of two characteristics of their intakes:

School No.:
Subject: **MA08**
"Like" School Grouping 1: 5
"Like" School Grouping 2: 14

Secondary College
Mathematical Methods
Low proportions of LOTE speakers at home/
Medium proportions of EMA or Austudy recipients

Nil or low proportions of LOTE speakers at home/
Medium proportions of EMA or Austudy recipients

1996

	No. students	Maximum	Mean + STD	Mean	Mean - STD	Minimum
School Result	49	39	30.94	25.51	20.08	15
State Result	8327	50	35.64	28.62	21.60	4
Best Group 1 "Like" School result	8	48	40.17	31.00	21.83	19
Average Group 1 "Like" School result	937	48	32.99	26.53	20.06	9
Best Group 2 "Like" School result	25	42	39.24	33.25	27.26	23
Average Group 2 "Like" School result	2222	47	34.30	27.96	21.61	8

Figure 8

(1) the proportions of students from socially and economically disadvantaged backgrounds, and (2) the proportion of students from families where English is not the main language. This provides a basis on which to make an assessment of the achievements of students in the school against that for other schools with similar intakes. It is expected that at a later stage of the development of this review framework, schools will also be classified into like groups on the basis of the prior educational achievements of students.

The mean level of achievement of students in Mathematical Methods is 0.44 of a standard deviation below that for the statewide mean and 0.39 of a standard deviation below that of students in 'like–group 2' schools. In this particular case, the distribution of achievement for the school should be interpreted in the context of the relatively low participation rate of only 46% of students taking mathematics in Year 12, compared to 80% statewide. Hence, the relatively weak profile of achievement in mathematics in this school is compounded by a low participation rate. An additional piece of information is provided by the fact that the highest score was only 39 (out of a possible of 50), hence, there is evidence that even the most able students may not be reaching their potential in this school.

Affective and social outcomes

A range of research instruments could be utilised to assess school performance in terms of affective student outcomes, although no school review system has formally incorporated these into their quality assurance reviews. This may be due in part to the fact that most of the instruments available have not been formally aligned with the outcomes that schools teach towards. Further, there is the problem that out-of-school experiences contribute significantly to affective development during the years of schooling.

Most school review systems have, however, incorporated some aspects of social outcomes. In the Victorian reviews these focus on student behaviour, attendance, retention and post-school destinations. Figure 9 provides information on an aspect of student behaviour from a primary school. The graph shows a fairly typical pattern of boys being responsible for all but a few incidences of disruptive behaviour in primary schools.

In Victoria, secondary school reviews also assess the outcomes of schooling for students by analysing student's post-school destinations. Figure 10 shows that a much lower proportion of students completing their secondary education in this school are entering university, compared to the statewide benchmark. This is offset to some extent by a higher proportion gaining direct entry into employment, but there is also a higher proportion of students unemployed, which represents the largest proportion of the 'other' classification. The school from which these data were drawn is the same school as that shown in Figure 8, which indicated a problem with mathematics achievement. By bringing a number of pieces of data together as depicted in the examples shown above it is possible to build up an analysis of the priority areas for improvement in each school.

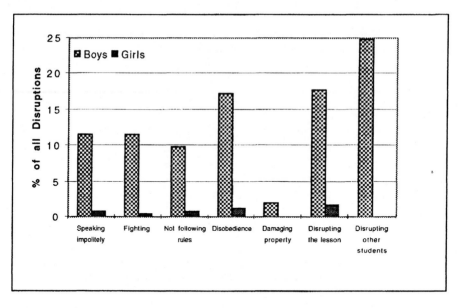

Figure 9: Classroom disruptions by type and gender

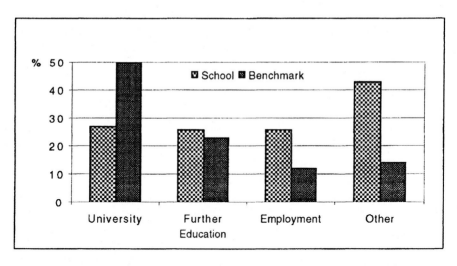

Figure 10: Year 12 post-school destinations of students for one high school

DISCUSSION AND CONCLUSIONS

Recent research on the impact of schools on student learning leads to the conclusion that 8–19% of the variation in student learning outcomes lies between schools, with a further amount of up to 55% of the variation in individual learning outcomes between classrooms within schools. In total, approximately 60% of the variation in the performance of students lies either between schools or between classrooms, with the remaining 40% being due to either variation associated with students themselves or to random influences in school systems.

After taking account of the differences between types of schools, probably less than 10% of the variance in the value–added to student outcomes lies between schools in Australian state school systems. A considerably larger proportion of the variance lies between classrooms and programs within schools. The evidence also indicates that there is substantial variation in the impact that schools and classrooms have on the progress that students make over time. The implications of these findings are that school review and improvement efforts should focus on within school differences in effectiveness more than on the differences in effectiveness between schools.

The modest level of correlation in the effectiveness of schools across a range of cognitive and non-cognitive outcomes for students means that schools that are effective in one domain may be more or less effective in another domain. There may, of course, also be schools that are equally effective or ineffective across a number of domains of student learning outcomes. Hence, improvement efforts need to ensure that they target the particular student outcomes that are most in need of further development in individual schools.

Although school review systems in Australia have been successful in enhancing the environment for effective school development by providing the basis for a strategic evaluation of school performance, they have been hampered by the reluctance of school system bureaucracies to tackle the hard issues of improving performance and by the politics of self-interest within their host bureaucracies. These school review programs have been grounded in research on evaluation and school change and improvement and their existence has resulted in a change in the expectations of what can be achieved through the contribution of such quality assurance systems. However, they have been found to be insufficiently robust to withstand organisational pressures within their host bureaucracies, and from external political pressures, once they reached the stage of maturity where their contribution to accountability was perceived to be a threat to these institutions. The lesson to be learned from this is that accountability and quality assurance systems require the 'protection' of formal independence if they are to have a constructive and enduring impact on the improvement and performance of schools. Developments over the last decade have revealed a significant element of naivety, due to a misplaced belief that host bureaucracies and political organisations had sufficient structural integrity to allow review systems to effectively contribute to system–level accountability.

The conclusions that must be drawn from studies of the response of school system bureaucracies in Australia to programs of accountability, school review and improvement strongly support the establishment of accountability and review systems that are organisationally independent of the school system. Such systems require the backing of legislative authority to report publicly on the performance of individual schools.

An independent organisation empowered to report publicly on the performance of individual schools and school systems is an essential element in the more decentralised systems of government now emerging in Australia. In particular, such a system of performance accountability is fundamental to the regulation of school systems in the context of government which views its primary role as the funding and regulation of schooling, with the provision of schooling being devolved to schools operating with management autonomy and local governance structures.

Effective school development requires both pressure for change and support for the process of change. Constructive change is more likely to emerge when external pressures focus the school's attention on a significant area for further development. The change process itself is enhanced by support in the form of knowledge, skills and process facilitation. The optimal mix of strategies to exert pressure and support will vary according to the level of performance of the school, which among other things will also reflect a specific capacity or potential to successfully implement change strategies to achieve directed change. Change strategies need to address both incremental improvement in some areas and fundamental development of other areas if they are to sustain the impact of development. Fundamental development requires schools to address major challenges to change their structure and culture.

The nature of educational services and learning outcomes is such that it is not possible to fully assess the quality of the outcomes achieved by individual students. Further, it may not be feasible to change unsatisfactory learning outcomes once they have been produced. Hence, the assurance of quality in schooling must focus also on the processes and systems that are responsible for the delivery of the services and experiences that students engage in as part of their learning.

Third–party independent quality assurance processes provide more effective assurance than processes that rely on the school system to provide its own assurance. Australian experience indicates that processes of assurance that are not independent of the school system are likely to be corrupted by political processes within school system bureaucracies.

Assuring the quality and improvement of schools requires a focus on the development and delivery of curriculum and the evaluation of learning outcomes against agreed standards. The common elements of systems for the review and improvement of schools are those that focus on: student achievement and progress, curriculum provision and implementation, the learning environment, school management, and community participation.

Effective school review and improvement systems encompass all schools and do not focus only on schools that are identified as underperforming. Focussing on the full set of schools exerts pressure to improve the overall performance of the school system, provides pressure for schools that might otherwise fall into the category of 'ineffective' and provides support to the schools that lack the competencies and capability to improve entirely on the basis of their own resources. School reviews can provide direct support to school improvement by identifying aspects of the school's operation and performance that require major development, in addition to aspects of the school's operation that would benefit from smaller scale improvement efforts. Major areas of school development may require substantial changes to the culture and structure of individual schools.

The assessment of school effectiveness requires the analyses of the cognitive, affective and social outcomes of schooling for students. The assessment of the effectiveness of schools in terms of these outcomes should be considered in the context of change over time, the impact for designated groups of students, achievements in relation to externally established standards and the relative progress that students have made while attending a particular school. Many of the analyses undertaken in school reviews do not themselves directly indicate the effectiveness of a school, but provide information that fits together with other information as part of an evaluation of the mosaic of effectiveness and improvement.

School review programs that encompass a wide range of strategic analyses as discussed in this chapter should nevertheless be viewed as only partially addressing the range of issues that need to be covered by a comprehensive quality assurance system for schools. For example, there are significant lacunae in the measurement of student learning. The most common measures of learning outcomes are weak in their ability to represent learning in the affective domain. Further, the measures of cognitive learning in common use are limited in their ability to represent student skills in most aspects of the construction of knowledge.

Another deficit in current systems is their restricted capacity to assure the quality of the processes of schooling. The processes of schooling must be a central element in assuring quality given the necessary focus on the provision of an educative environment and learning as the outcome of schooling.

Focussing quality assurance systems exclusively on testing student outcomes as they exit the system is manifestly inadequate. It incorporates failure as a feature of the system because it offers no chance to remediate cases where students have failed to gain the appropriate learning outcomes.

ENDNOTES

[1] The Charter in Victorian schools "contains the school's statement of purpose and educational values, consistent with Department of Education policies and reflecting local community needs. It defines in terms of measurable achievements, the school's educational goals and priority tasks for improvement over a three-year period." (Department of Education, Victoria, 1997, p.9)

REFERENCES

Barber, M., Gough, G., & Johnson, M. (1995). *Promoting successful schooling: The development of a school improvement index and the use of pupil and parent surveys*. A Report to the Association of London Authorities. Keele University: Staffordshire.

Cooney, J. (1993). *Generating recommendations to support sustainable school development*. Unpublished paper. Sydney: New South Wales Department of School Education, Quality Assurance Directorate.

Cuban, L. (1988). A fundamental puzzle of school reform. *Phi Delta Kappan, 70*, 341–344

Cuttance, P. (1993). *The Development of quality assurance reviews in the NSW public school system:*

what works? Paper published by the Quality Assurance Directorate, New South Wales Department of School Education. Sydney: Australia.

Cuttance, P. (1994). *Quality systems for the performance development cycle of schools.* Paper prepared for the International Congress for School Effectiveness and Improvement, Melbourne.

Cuttance, P. (1995a). Quality assurance and quality management in education systems. In C. W. Evers and J. D. Chapman, (Eds.), *Educational administration: An Australian perspective* (pp. 296–316). Sydney: Allen & Unwin.

Cuttance, P. (1995b). *Strengthening equity, improvement and performance in government schools.* Paper prepared for the International School Effectiveness and Improvement Centre Conference Learning from Each Other, October 6–7, Institute of Education, University of London.

Cuttance, P. (forthcoming). The politics of accountability in Australian education. In R. Macpherson, J. Cibilka, D. Monk, & K. Wong (Eds.), *The Politics of accountability: Educative and international perspectives.* 1998 Politics of Education Yearbook. Thousand Oaks, CA: Corwin Press

Department of Education, Victoria. (1997). *An accountability framework.* Melbourne: Office of Review.

Fullan, M. (1991). *The new meaning of educational change.* London: Cassell.

Fullan, M. (1993). *Change forces: Probing the depths of educational reform.* The Falmer Press: London.

Gray, J. (1993). *The statistics of school improvement: establishing the agenda.* Paper presented to the ESRC Seminar Series on School Effectiveness and School Improvement, Sheffield.

Gray, J., Jesson, D., Goldstein, H., Hedger, K., & Rasbach, J. (1995). A multi–level analysis of school improvement: changes in schools' performance over time. *School Effectiveness and School Improvement,* **6,** 97–114.

Hargreaves, D. (1995). School culture, school effectiveness and school improvement. *School Effectiveness and School Improvement,* **6,** 23–46.

Hill, P. (1995). *School effectiveness and improvement: Present realities and future possibilities.* Inaugural Professorial Lecture. University of Melbourne: Melbourne.

Hopkins, D. (1989). *A teachers' guide to evaluation in schools.* Milton Keynes: Open University Press.

Hopkins, D. (1995). *Towards effective school improvement.* Paper presented at the eight annual International Congress for School Effectiveness and Improvement, Leeuwarden, The Netherlands.

Lawton, D., &Gordon, P. (1987). *HMI,* London: Routledge & Kegan Paul.

Louis, K. (1994). Beyond 'managed change: Rethinking how schools improve. *School Effectiveness and School Improvement,* **5,** 2–24.

McGlynn, A., & Stalker, H. (1995). Recent developments in the Scottish process of school inspection. *Cambridge Journal of Education,* **25**(1), 13–21.

Mortimore, P., Sammons, P., Ecob, R., Stoll, L., & Lewis D. (1988). *School matters: The junior years.* Salisbury: Open Books.

NSW DSE. (1995). *Quality assurance school reviews: Principles and processes.* Sydney: New South Wales Department of School Education.

NZ Education Review Office. (1991). *Review methodology: Schools.* Wellington: Education Review Office.

Ofsted. (1992). *Aspects of school review in South Australia.* A report from Her Majesty's Chief inspector of Schools. London: HMSO.

Ofsted. (1993). *Framework for the inspection of schools.* London: Office for Standards in Education.

Reynolds, D. (1992). School effectiveness and school improvement: An updated review of the British literature. In D. Reynolds & P. Cuttance (Eds.), *School Effectiveness: Research, policy and practice.* London: Cassell.

Scheerens, J., Vermeulen, C., & Pelgrum, W. (1989). Generalisability of instructional and school effectiveness indicators across nations. *International Journal of Educational Research,* **13,** 789–799.

Stringfield, S. (1995). Attempting to enhance students' learning through innovative programs: the case for schools evolving into high reliability organisations. *School Effectiveness and School Improvement,* **6,** 67–96.

Assessment and Accountability in Kentucky: How High Stakes Affects Teaching and Learning

BETTY LOU WHITFORD

KEN JONES
University of Louisville, Kentucky, USA

In their analysis of 'assessment and accountability in Kentucky' Betty Lou Whitford and Ken Jones describe one of the better known and contentious large scale approaches to educational reform. The 1990 Kentucky Education Reform Act (KERA) is one of the most pervasive and radical policies for systemic educational change ever enacted. At the basis of KERA is a performance-based approach to assessment that forms the basis of an accountability system intended to compel teachers to elicit higher levels of student learning. As Whitford and Jones point out, what is really being tested in Kentucky is the effectiveness of a change strategy predicated on student performance assessment and high stakes accountability. Using a blend of description and analysis, Whitford and Jones, outline the main components of KERA and assess its impact on curriculum, teaching and learning. They paint a picture full of ambivalence and compromise, where there is ambivalence over whether it is the school or the student that is being assessed, and where learning and achievement are fundamentally confused. Although 'high stakes' has focused attention on important questions related to teaching and learning, Whitford and Jones conclude that "accountability that reduces school quality to a numeric formula is over-simplified and ill-suited to evaluating many important aspects of schooling"

The Kentucky Education Reform Act, widely known as KERA, was enacted in 1990 as a result of a law suit filed by 66 of the state's 176 school districts on the basis of inequities in the financing of public schools. The suit was dramatically resolved by a state Supreme Court decision in June, 1989 which went far beyond issues of financing to declare as unconstitutional over 700 laws related to public schooling (Luhr, 1990). In effect, the Court gave the state legislature license to create, within about a year, an entirely new system of common schools (Kannapel, 1991).

As pointed out in an Appalachian Educational Laboratory report (1996), KERA was conceived as a statewide, systemic approach to school reform. That is, its various components were intended to address many interconnected facets of schooling in order to bring about high levels of achievement from all students. The components include an appointed, rather than elected, education commissioner, an ungraded primary program replacing grades K-3, school-based decision-making councils, a new financing formula, preschools, technology, extended school services, regional service centers, family resource and youth services centers in

D. Hopkins (ed.), The Practice and Theory of School Improvement, 129-144.

schools with economically disadvantaged students, and a new approach to assessment and accountability. Of particular interest in this chapter are the changes KERA mandated in these latter two – assessment and accountability.

There is no doubt that fundamental education change has been needed in Kentucky concerning issues of excellence as well as equity. For many years, the state's schools have ranked near the bottom of the 50 states on many measures of effectiveness. As KERA was being drafted, Kentucky ranked 50th in the percentage of adults with high school diplomas, 49th in the percentage of college graduates, and 1st in adult illiteracy and teenage pregnancy (Holland, 1995). During the 1988–89 school year, Kentucky ranked 41st in the nation in per pupil expenditure, 40th in teacher salaries, and 48th in local government support for public schools (NEA, 1989). These conditions have deep historical roots since education had never been a priority in the state. Though it became the 15th state in 1792, Kentucky did not provide tax support for schools until 1904 (Kannapel, 1991).

The central and clearly stated belief underlying the new law is that all students can learn at high levels (Kentucky Department of Education, 1992). This view of the school's mission is a dramatic shift from the factory model of teaching, testing, arraying students across the A-B-C-D-F grading scale, and moving on to the next section of curriculum. Rather, schools are now to ensure learning, not just teach.

Ensuring learning means emphasizing new approaches, including problem-solving, reasoning, and communication in real-life situations. These approaches in turn require an assessment system designed to go beyond traditional standardized testing which does little to address such higher-order thinking skills. Thus, to evaluate the degree of progress toward the goal of success for all students, KERA mandated the development of a new testing system that would be "primarily performance based."

Generally speaking, performance assessment focuses on what students can do with their knowledge in realistic situations. According to Herman, Aschbacher, and Winters (1994), "it requires students to actively accomplish complex and significant tasks, while bringing to bear prior knowledge, recent learning, and relevant skills to solve realistic or authentic problems" (p. 2).

Responding to KERA, the Kentucky Department of Education, in conjunction with its testing contractor, Advanced Systems in Measurement and Evaluation, developed a performance assessment system called the Kentucky Instructional Results Information System (KIRIS). Further, this performance-based approach to assessment would form the basis of a "carrot-and-stick" accountability system intended to compel teachers to embrace the use performance assessment and compatible strategies and materials, in order to enable all students to learn at high levels. Substantial financial rewards would be provided for schools the state determines are making significant progress toward this goal while sanctions, including dismissal of tenured personnel, could be imposed on schools not making adequate progress.

This link between student performance assessment and high stakes accountability for schools is the dominant change strategy being tested in Kentucky. To date, what effects on curriculum, teaching, and learning can be seen in the state? To develop our response to this question, we must first describe the state's approaches to assessment and accountability in some detail.

INTRODUCING NEW STATE TESTING: KIRIS

Both highly innovative and controversial is the change in state testing since 1990. KIRIS was created as the chief means of "driving" changes in curriculum and instruction toward an emphasis on higher order thinking and performance assessment – demonstrations of what students know and can do with their knowledge. Aimed at setting and having schools achieve new "world-class" standards with students, KIRIS coupled performance assessment with a high-stakes system for holding schools accountable for improvement in student scores.

An examination of how KIRIS was initially designed and how it has since been modified reveals key stances policy makers have taken regarding how education reform would proceed in Kentucky. The initial stances on six elements of improving schooling-student outcomes, assessment, local control of curriculum, accountability, expected rate of school improvement, and incentives – are briefly described below. How they have evolved and with what effects is addressed in the next sections of the chapter. The initial state stances were:

Outcomes:	The state should broadly define what students should know and be able to do.
Assessment:	The state should assess student achievement of the outcomes with a performance-based test that sets high standards for all students.
Local control of curriculum:	Individual schools should develop or select their own curriculum related to the outcomes. The state should provide support rather than monitoring.
Accountability:	School improvement should be measured by a state-devised "accountability index," a formula which determines a single numerical score for each school, based largely on the aggregated results of student testing.[1]
Expected rate of improvement:	Schools should improve their scores in two-year cycles from a "baseline" to a state-prescribed target or "threshold" score. Schools should be compared only to themselves, not to other schools.
Incentives:	Every two years, schools should be rewarded for meeting their thresholds or sanctioned for not. Rewards mean financial

bonuses for teachers; sanctions include state takeover and dismissal of tenured personnel.

The new test initially included three performance assessment components: group problem-solving tasks called "performance events," writing and mathematics portfolios, and open-response questions. Without any piloting or phasing in, this new assessment system for school accountability was launched during the 1991–92 school year. Teachers, even those most supportive of the reforms, struggled with trying to help their students respond to the assessment formats that they themselves were only just learning. At the same time, the state department of education – the primary source of information about the nature of the reforms and how they were to be implemented – was being reorganized.

Given these dramatic changes, many educators, parents, and other citizens were largely uninformed or ill-informed about the shift in the testing approach, much less the details of how schools were now to be held accountable. Teachers commonly reacted to the large, vague, and threatening set of changes imposed by KIRIS with fear, anger, and anxiety. As the 5-year AEL study (1996) of 21 schools in Kentucky has determined, teachers' attention has focused much more on the threat of sanctions than the prospect of rewards, creating a highly stressful climate in many schools.

Inevitably, with KIRIS as with other controversial KERA reforms such as school councils and the primary program, implementation problems emerged and rules and procedures changed along the way. State officials began to talk about "building the airplane as we're flying it" to explain the resulting confusion. Many teachers began to feel that the new system was so unpredictable that it should perhaps crash.

CHANGES AFFECTING KIRIS: 1991–1996

At best, the evolution of KIRIS in the ensuing five years reveals how initial plans, especially those developed in a complex, systemic reform effort, need revision when tested in the real world. At worst, the story is a powerful lesson about how such a high-stakes accountability system can distort and undermine original assumptions and visions for effective curriculum, instruction, and assessment practices (e.g., Gardner, 1985; Darling-Hammond & Snyder, 1992; Darling-Hammond, Snyder, Ancess, Einbender, Goodwin, & Macdonald, 1993; Wiggins, 1993; Kohn, 1993). This story is the focus of the next section of the chapter and is organized around how the six stances previously described unfolded.

OUTCOMES

The state-defined outcomes originally focused on six "learning goals." These stated that students should be able to:

1. Use basic communication and mathematics skills for purposes and situations they will encounter throughout their lives;
2. Apply core concepts and principles from mathematics, the sciences, the arts, the humanities, social studies, practical living studies, and vocational studies to situations they will encounter throughout their lives;
3. Become self-sufficient individuals;
4. Become responsible members of a family, work group, or community;
5. Think and solve problems in school situations and in a variety of situations they will encounter in life;
6. Connect and integrate experiences and new knowledge from all subject matter fields with what they have previously learned and build on past learning experiences to acquire new information through various media sources.

These six goals were then elaborated into 75 "valued outcomes" which were meant to serve as the basis of KIRIS. After KIRIS testing was developed and implemented in the first two-year cycle, the "valued outcomes" came under intense scrutiny from various public factions. To make them more acceptable, the State Board of Education decided that Goals 3 and 4 and corresponding outcomes – concerning self sufficiency and responsible group membership – were not "academic" enough and would not be assessed. Many others were rephrased, and the remaining 57 outcomes were re-christened "academic expectations."

It also became clear that the broadly-stated outcomes did little to reveal what content would be tested. Indeed, the state had deliberately left unstated what exactly would be tested in order to honor the local role for curriculum development given by the statute. Not surprisingly, a high-stakes assessment addressing content knowledge created increasing demands for a more precise state document that would identify not only what content would be tested – content standards – but also how well students would be expected to demonstrate command of that content-performance standards. By June, 1996, the state responded with a draft of content standards in a document titled *Core Content for KIRIS Assessment.*

ASSESSMENT

As noted, KERA specified that the new assessment system should be "primarily performance-based." Work on creating such an assessment proceeded before much attention was given to defining content beyond the broadly-stated outcomes. Prior to the development of the new state curriculum framework, a battery of state committees with strong teacher representation began the process of composing test items in various formats: multiple-choice (later dropped), performance events, and open-response-questions requiring short, on-demand written responses, given and scored under controlled circumstances. Guidelines for a writing portfolio, and later a mathematics portfolio, were constructed with specific scoring criteria. Both portfolios were to contain a student's best work rather than show progress over time.

As the system has evolved, certain effects have become visible. Given the high stakes involved, scoring reliability has become an overriding consideration. Open-response questions have clearly become the most reliable of the formats. Performance events, which were largely untried, have proven to be quite difficult to score reliably. Portfolios have yet to achieve a level of scoring reliability deemed acceptable for a high-stakes system, although there is evidence that the writing portfolio in particular has had a significant impact in that more children are writing more often (AEL, 1996).

Open response questions, the most reliable format to score, have been given the greatest weight in the accountability index. As a result, they have become a primary focus for most schools. Professional development activities across the state have focused on this format; and checklists for students to follow in answering these questions have become a standard fixture in classrooms.

Over the course of KIRIS testing, the increasing pressure for higher reliability and tighter alignment with a specified body of content, brought on by the high-stakes purpose of the state testing, has translated into a shift away from "open-endedness" and performance in the assessments. The logic is clear. The more open and performance-based an assessment is, the more variety in responses; the more variety there is, the more judgment is involved in scoring. The more judgment involved, the lower the reliability. Hence, less open-endedness and less performance.

At this point, multiple choice items have been reintroduced, performance events discontinued, and the mathematics portfolio removed from the accountability index, while efforts are made to improve its scoring reliability. According to some teachers, the open response items themselves appear to be more centered on "correct" answers, making them less and less "open."

LOCAL CONTROL OF CURRICULUM

The KERA mandate for school-based decision-making councils (SBDM) was intended to change the balance of power between schools, their district authorities, and the state. An often heard rationale was that those closest to the work should be empowered to make decisions about the best way to conduct that work. In particular, one of the most important functions given to councils was the right to determine the school's curriculum. In 1994, the state Supreme Court upheld this right.

By making schools as a whole accountable for student performance with KIRIS, the state created a need for school councils to overcome the common history of isolated teacher decision-making and to articulate a school-wide approach to curriculum. Many state education leaders hoped that councils would be a powerful vehicle to focus school-wide instruction on the state outcomes and on performance-based assessment.

However, school councils were not mandated for immediate implementation and are only now required for most schools. Those councils that have been in operation for a few years appear to be only beginning to address matters of curriculum. For the most part, they are enacting policies intended to ensure that the school teaches the content and format of KIRIS. With the recent state publication of the *Core Content for KIRIS Assessment*, it appears likely that councils will decide that this document should form the basis of school curricula. There are already added calls for the state to prescribe what *level* of understanding will be required with that content. State-defined performance standards for the core content may logically be the next development. State-sponsored units of study have already been developed, and there is every reason to believe that the supply and the demand for such units will only increase.

A further constraint to local curriculum development has been added by the growing state and district requirement for each school to have an improvement plan, called the School Transformation Plan (STP). Required of schools that do not meet their target scores and for any school applying for state grant funds, this plan focuses curriculum and instruction tightly on the KIRIS assessment. Virtually all schools are developing STPs.

Thus, there is a rebound effect. Pressure generated by the state test for high-stakes accountability has led school-based educators to pressure the state to be more explicit about content that will be tested. This in turn constrains local school decision making about curriculum. This dialectic works to increase the state control of local curriculum.

ACCOUNTABILITY

Kentucky's accountability system is noted for translating student performance assessment results into school scores to determine a school's degree of improvement. Essentially, school quality is judged by how well students do on the state test.

KERA required that the state department of education create an accountability index that would indicate student success rate. The state department, in cooperation with its testing contractor, developed a formula that aggregates the scores of students on the various components of KIRIS. Each year, a school receives a numerical score figured to the tenth of a decimal place.

It is important to note that KIRIS is designed to provide information for *school* accountability, not *student* accountability. This is primarily because there are not enough test items in any given subject area to assess individuals. (Despite this, individual scores on portfolios and open response items are sent to parents.) State officials and the testing contractor argue that open-response questions are valid at the school level because of matrix sampling, a technique that aggregates a larger number of subject-specific questions from multiple test forms. The lack of student validity means that the testing program also lacks student accountability, another source of frustration among teachers and administrators trying to convince students to take the test seriously when there is nothing at stake for them as individuals.

Perhaps the most significant controversy arises from the fact that, in determining whether or not a school is making progress, different cohorts of students are tested each year. This results in a circumstance where schools are judged – and rewarded or sanctioned – not by the improvement that individual students show over time, but by how one group in the school performs compared with another. This practice is particularly problematic in small schools where differences in cohorts of fourth graders, for example, are likely to be greater than in large schools, thus affecting test scores more dramatically.

EXPECTED RATE OF IMPROVEMENT

Setting the formula for establishing school threshold scores – how much a school is expected to improve in each two-year cycle – was an especially thorny problem. The outcomes were new, the assessments were new, the accountability system was new. Thus, there were no empirical data to suggest what might be reasonable to expect in terms of improvement. As a result, the formula had to be based on something other than empirical evidence.

State education leaders decided, based on the "all students can learn at high levels" premise, that in twenty years, schools must register a score of at least proficient, defined numerically as 100 out of 140 possible points. By that time, the argument went, all students would have experienced a KERA-based school system from beginning to end.

This reasoning then led to the following method for determining a school threshold, the score each school must meet or exceed every two years to be rewarded and avoid sanctions. Since there are 10 two-year cycles in a 20-year span, in each cycle, schools must gain one-tenth of the difference between its first baseline score and the target of 100. Thus, if a school originally scored 30 in 1992, its baseline was 30 and its target for 1994 was 37 (i.e., 70 remaining to get to 100, divided by 10 cycles, yields an expected growth of 7). The score a school actually receives in each cycle becomes the basis for the baseline for the next cycle. Each school is expected to reach or exceed its target during each two-year cycle.

To say that teachers and school administrators feel that this is an arbitrary expectation is an enormous understatement. The concept of a constant rate of growth, cycle after cycle, towards total "proficiency" in 20 years has not been well accepted, to say the least. Along with the testing of different cohorts, this approach to determining target scores accounts for much of the lack of credibility in the system among many educators.

Some state officials are now discussing alternative ways to construct the accountability index. For example, with five years of testing experience, it is now possible to establish a school trend line to determine improvement goals more grounded in data over time. It would also be possible to use a longitudinal design to follow the same cohort of students in a given school, thus allowing for a "value added" approach to school accountability.

INCENTIVES

The use of external rewards and sanctions is basic to KERA. Many in the state legislature and the public apparently believe that rewards and sanctions will work to improve schools in one of two ways. Teachers will teach better knowing they can receive a cash bonus (which can exceed $2000 per teacher) for higher student test scores. Or, teachers will teach better knowing that if student performance does not improve, they will be sanctioned in various ways. Schools not meeting their target scores receive "assistance" in the form of a state mandated improvement plan and the services of a "distinguished educator." For the first time in 1996, nine schools were declared "in crisis" for insufficient improvement in test scores. In these cases, the "distinguished educators" have assumed control of the schools. Significantly, five of these schools were "in rewards" two years ago because they had exceeded their target scores. Several of the schools are small, with 120–200 students.

In such a context, schools are intensely involved in the pursuit of higher test scores. Everywhere, teachers are using KIRIS-style open response questions in their classrooms. Some are targeting small groups of students for extra practice on the test formats in efforts to gain greater leverage on the school's score. Test-taking strategies such as restating the question, always giving at least three examples, and writing longer rather than shorter responses have become commonly viewed as ways to increase scores. There is also considerable push to "align curriculum" by concentrating on covering the *Core Content for KIRIS Assessment*.

DISCUSSION

Based on these developments, what are the effects of linking performance assessment with a high stakes approach to accountability? It is not yet possible to determine if KIRIS has improved student learning. Differences in a school's score could be attributable to many factors other than changes in student learning, e.g., better test taking skill, school size, whether the content tested (which changes) has actually been taught, the degree to which teachers have changed their practice, changes in cohorts tested. However, logic indicates several expected consequences related to the teacher-student relationship and the instructional effects of KIRIS.

TEACHER-STUDENT RELATIONSHIP

Many consider the quality of the teacher-student interaction to be the heart of the matter concerning how well students learn. A good deal of theory, research, and documented practice suggest that thinking and learning are enhanced in constructivist classrooms where teachers know their students well and have the expertise to diversify instruction to meet varying student needs, include student interests and appropriate student choice in curricular decisions, promote social interaction and collaboration, and foster problem-solving and inquiry (Dewey, 1916, 1938; Vygotsky, 1978; Wigginton, 1985; Gardner, 1985; Darling-Hammond et al., 1993). In order to develop such learning environments, teachers must have the professional knowledge and power to make decisions and judgments regarding curriculum and instruction for particular groups of students (Lieberman & Miller, 1990; McLaughlin, 1992; Little, 1993).

Yet, as we have argued, Kentucky's accountability system has undermined such decision making at the school level, a condition the KERA-mandated school councils were meant to nurture. Instead of giving local schools and teachers a greater say in curriculum, the accountability system is inexorably driving the creation of a de facto state curriculum. While many educators do not trust the tests, given the high stakes, they will continue to pressure the state to be more and more precise about what will be tested.

While some welcome the development of such standardization, others recognize that the more the curriculum is specified *and* defined externally, the more the role of the teacher becomes that of the technician, expected to put into play decisions made by others outside the school. This is true whether the external source is the state, a textbook company, or a standardized test (Eisner, 1986). In each case, professional judgment is curtailed. Teachers are to deliver knowledge and skills determined by others, not decide what is best for individual students. This inhibits the need for productive teacher-student relationships by creating a model that is counter-productive to constructivist learning. How can we expect students to be problem-solvers, thinkers, and decision makers when we do not expect the same from teachers?

Teacher-student relationships have been compromised in another way because of the accountability system. By making teachers, not students, accountable for student test results, teachers are assumed to be fully in control of their students' learning. This posture further assumes that the solutions to bringing about higher quality for all students are known; they only have to be implemented, not invented. This view, in turn, promotes relationships based on control and manipulation rather than joint learning endeavors among teachers and between teachers and students.

Hence, there is another trickle-down effect. As teachers are subjected to rewards and sanctions, so do they treat their students. Great pressure is put on students to do well on the KIRIS test. Many schools have developed systems of external rewards for students who take the test seriously. It has become the norm rather than the exception that students, just like their teachers, resent the test, treating it as an unwelcome but required ordeal. How ironic and unfortunate that a form of assessment meant to engage students in more meaningful work is so dreaded.

INSTRUCTIONAL EFFECTS OF KIRIS

Given the linkage to a high-stakes accountability system, a second effect is that the emerging state curriculum will increasingly stress learning that can be measured reliably and validly. What can be measured reliably and validly becomes what is important to know. It will literally become "what counts" in determining whether or not a school is performing as the state thinks it should. While perhaps not the direction intended when state officials expressed the point of view that assessment should drive curriculum, this "measurement orientation" is nonetheless becoming the reality, as psychometric concerns increasingly restrict assessments to what can be easily measured and scored, rather than more open-ended demonstrations of what students can do with their knowledge. Some in fact argue that KIRIS has essentially evolved into a system that is *not* "primarily performance based" as KERA mandated.

As the test relies more on items with higher scoring reliability, it is less likely that KIRIS will "drive" teaching and learning toward constructivist classrooms. The mandated portfolios have been considered powerful levers for instructional change, yet even with them, it is common practice for teachers to simply "add-on" portfolio prompts, without significantly changing routine classroom practice, by declaring "portfolio days" or giving prompts as homework. Such an adding-on strategy is much easier and more commonplace with the short, relatively unobtrusive open-response items. With the possible exception of the writing portfolio, there is little evidence to suggest that teachers have incorporated the principles of performance assessment into their on-going practice (KIER, 1995). Thus, while the accountability system has gotten their attention, there is little evidence to show that it has substantially altered either classroom practice or the relationships between and among students and teachers toward a more constructivist environment. A recent study of KIRIS suggests that there is a good chance the test score gains observed to date are the result of students getting better at taking the test rather than actually demonstrating improved learning. (Hambleton et al., 1995).[2]

Some argue that the reliability and validity issues are merely technical problems that can be resolved in time. Others acknowledge that there are problems, but they do not support abandoning the high stakes approach to accountability while these technical issues are addressed. For example, The Prichard Committee for Academic Excellence, a highly visible and influential citizen's advocacy group that has consistently been pro-KERA, issued a report with this statement: "We believe delay awaiting technical advances would seriously impair the opportunity to fully evaluate the advantages of improving educational quality based upon an incentive program" (1995, p. 12).

However, it is doubtful that these issues can be resolved with better psychometric techniques alone. A more fundamental problem is that using performance assessment as the primary basis for high stakes accountability compromises the very nature of performance assessment. As Stiggins (1997) argues, performance assessment, based as it is on context and judgment, is well suited for improving student learning in the classroom, but not so well-suited for producing scores to be used in external evaluations of schools.

Performance assessments that improve learning are focused on individual children as they demonstrate what they are learning through their writing, reading, speaking, facility with numbers, group skills, individual initiative and so on.

The assessment is of a single child's work, assumed to be a demonstration of what he or she knows and is able to do. It often involves the learner in self-assessment, and it is done to help the child, the teacher, and parents understand what a child is doing and what the child might do to improve. Such assessments are not intended to be aggregated since they are directed toward individuals.

Because the emphasis is on the quality of unique, student-generated responses, performance assessment depends upon the exercise of professional judgment, both in design of tasks and evaluation of student responses. As Wiggins (1993) comments, "Higher-order assessment will. . .almost always be judgment based" (pp. 10–11). And according to Stiggins, "Professional judgment guides almost every aspect. . .of every performance assessment" (1997, p. 187). As a child's work is evaluated against a set of explicit criteria, often called rubrics, the evaluator – most often a teacher or coach – is making a judgment. Judgments by their very nature vary depending on who is judging. An office worker's performance might be judged differently by different bosses; doctors might make different recommendations based on the same diagnostic evidence; and, what a student might do to improve performance might vary across teachers.

For example, a teacher might listen to a child read and make suggestions about what the child should read next. The recommendation might be based on interest expressed by the child and also skills the child needs to develop. Teachers who are experts in children's literature will know some books to recommend, but the specific recommendation might vary by teacher. Further, the particular judgments and recommendations are responsive to specific learning contexts and dependent on knowing individual students and their experiences well. They are not necessarily generalizable for all students. What is important is that individual teachers need to be informed and capable enough to make wise professional judgments in behalf of their students.

To use performance assessment to improve learning, Wiggins (1993) argues that a number of principles must be followed: assessment must flow from the immediate curriculum; students must know what the standards for performance are; and feedback must be immediate and specific. A state system devoted to aggregating student results in order to produce an annual accountability score for schools does little to address such principles. Thus, the Kentucky linkage of high-stakes accountability to performance assessment seems to be an ill-fated marriage. As policy makers have emphasized accountability, the performance-oriented nature of KIRIS has receded. The likely reason is that the two approaches – high stakes accountability and performance assessment – are not compatible as practiced in Kentucky.

ALTERNATIVE APPROACHES

At present, Kentucky's accountability approach is undermining the very changes in teaching and learning that it was intended to promote, thereby calling into question the use of performance assessment for high stakes accountability. These conditions require that the state take some corrective action – either by improving the current system, or, as we propose, replacing what is an arbitrary, punitive, control-oriented system with one that is more collaborative, professional, and improvement oriented.

At present, Kentucky policy makers are choosing high-stakes accountability over performance assessment. While some education leaders privately acknowledge that the high stakes system has unintended, dysfunctional consequences, they believe that the political environment will not permit backing away it. Thus, there is talk about ways to make the current system better, by such means as factoring college entrance test scores into the accountability index or developing other quantitative measures.

Improving the existing system is one approach. We believe, however, that the current accountability approach is fundamentally flawed and that school reform will not progress without major changes in it. Accountability that reduces school quality to a numeric formula is over-simplified and ill-suited to evaluating many important aspects of schooling.

We agree that schools should be accountable, in fact, more accountable that they are with KIRIS. Specifically, what schools are asked to account for should be broadened beyond student outcome measures to include professional practices and equity issues such as opportunities to learn. A school quality review process, including school self-evaluations and periodic site visits, is an appropriate means for developing and reporting such components of a school's practice. Efforts in this regard, based to some extent on the British Inspectorate model, are being tried in various places in the United States, including southern Maine, New York, Rhode Island, Illinois, and Oregon. Also, the National Study for School Evaluation (Fitzpatrick, 1996) is currently enlisting school accreditation agencies to develop new indicators of school quality beyond simply counting inputs or aggregating outcomes.

Moving to such an accountability model would necessitate de-emphasizing high-stakes, since no school visitation would reveal realities or foster improvement if it were perceived as a police action. Indeed, this model depends upon the repositioning of the state away from bureaucratic control toward providing support, an intended direction for the state department of education just after KERA was enacted (Adams-Rodgers, 1994). The posture that many reform strategies describe for teachers and administrators-facilitation and shared leadership – should be adopted by the government itself since mandates and coercion will undermine school quality review processes just as they undermine performance assessment. As McLaughlin (1990) and others have argued, "You can't mandate what matters."

A longer range strategy needed to support additional improvement is the shift away from bureaucratic control to professional accountability – that which guides and improves responsible practice (Darling-Hammond & Snyder, 1992). For both student learning and professional practice to improve, bureaucratic control and teacher compliance are not enough. Rather, educators must be supported for working together to continuously invent new approaches to ensuring learning for all students. For this to occur, policy makers and education leaders must inspire commitment, not just compliance.

Inspiring commitment rather than compliance means that teacher preparation and continuing professional development must also improve. There is some evidence that school-university collaboration can improve teacher preparation (e.g., Whitford, Ruscoe, & Fickel, forthcoming) and teacher networks can provide much needed assistance for improving professional practice (Lieberman & Grolnick, 1996). Other forms of on-going professional support are needed as well, that are explicitly designed to address the goal of ensuring learning for all students (Little, 1993). In Kentucky, steps in that direction may have started with the state's commitment to implement the recommendations of the National Commission on Teaching and America's Future (1996) which include strong support for professional practice.

As such support increases in the state, professional accountability must also increase. Such an approach would include honoring the principals of performance-based assessment, reflection and self-improvement, and the informed use of professional judgment to decide on matters of curriculum and instruction to best suit the learning needs of individual students.

If the purpose of accountability is to improve teaching and learning, then the methods of accountability must suit that purpose. In Kentucky, this means that the school accountability index, together with the rewards and sanctions, should give way to a more inclusive and collaborative accountability system that would include qualitative as well as quantitative information. In effect, it means that *high-stakes* accountability must be transformed into *high-resolution* accountability, where the level of detail provided matches the degree of complexity inherent in schools and the learning of individual children.

High stakes in Kentucky has served to focus attention on important questions about teaching and learning. But it has not and cannot supply the answers to those questions. Those must come from the responses of teaching professionals, released from the narrow constraints of a high-stakes testing system. It may be that Kentucky is poised to enter the next stage of educational reform in the United States, in which the emphasis is placed on teacher professionalism. That depends in large part on whether or not those who hold power over schools are able to move from a controlling role into a collaborative one.

ENDNOTES

[1]   "Noncognitive" factors-attendance, retention, dropout rates, and transition to post-secondary life
      – are also factored into the formula but about 80% of the score comes from student test scores.
[2]   Data from a current study of Kentucky elementary schools is indicating that more constructivist
      or learner-centered practices are present in classrooms where *Different Ways of Knowing* (DWOK)
      has been used the longest. KIRIS scores are also rising in these schools (Hargen, 1996). DWOK is
      a comprehensive ungraded, constructivist, thematic elementary curriculum with built-in perform-
      ance assessments and substantial professional development and support developed by the Galef
      Institute in Los Angeles, California. Yet because different cohorts of students are being assessed
      each year, it is not known what accounts for the improved scores.

REFERENCES

Adams-Rodgers, L. C. (1994). *The role of the Kentucky Department of Education in facilitating systemic change and school-based decision-making: A case study.* Unpublished doctoral dissertation, University of Louisville.

Appalachia Educational Laboratory. (February, 1996). Five years of reform in rural Kentucky, *Notes from the field: Educational reform in rural Kentucky,* 5 (1). Charleston, WV: Appalachia Educational Laboratory.

Darling-Hammond, L., & Snyder, J. (1992). Reframing accountability: Creating learner-centered schools. In A. Lieberman (Ed.), *The changing contexts of teaching: Ninety-first yearbook of the National Society for the Study of Education* (pp. 11–36). Chicago, IL: University of Chicago Press.

Darling-Hammond, L., Snyder, J., Ancess, J., Einbender, L., Goodwin, A. L., & Macdonald, M. B. (1993). *Creating learner-centered accountability.* New York: National Center for Restructuring Education, Schools, and Teaching.

Dewey, J. (1916). *Democracy and education.* New York, NY: Macmillan.

Dewey, J. (1938). *Experience and education.* New York, NY: Macmillan.

Eisner, E. (1986). *The educational imagination.* New York, NY: Macmillan.

Fitzpatrick, K. A. (1996, October). *Indicators of schools of quality.* Presentation at the Conference on Assessment, Association for Supervision and Curriculum Development, Dallas.

Gardner, H. (1985). *Frames of mind: The theory of multiple intelligences.* New York, NY: Basic Books.

Hambleton, R., Jaeger, R., Koretz, D., Linn, R., Millman, J., & Phillips, S. (1995). *Review of the measurement quality of the Kentucky Instructional Results Information System 1991–1994.* Frankfort, KY: Office of Educational Accountability.

Hargen, L. (1996). Executive Director, Galef Institute/Kentucky Collaborative for Elementary Learning. Louisville, KY. *Personal communication.*

Herman, J. L., Aschbacker, P. R., & Winters. L. (1994). *A practical guide to alternative assessment.* Alexandria, Va: Association for Supervision and Curriculum Development.

Holland, H. (1995, October 15). The truth about KERA. Louisville, KY: *The Courier-Journal,* p. D1, 4.

Kannapel, P. J. (1991). *Education reform in Kentucky: Expert theory, folk theory, and the Kentucky Education Reform Act of 1990.* Unpublished thesis. Lexington, Kentucky: University of Kentucky, Department of Anthropology.

Kentucky Department of Education. (1992). *Transformations: Kentucky's curriculum framework* (Vol. 1), p. ii.

Kentucky Institute for Education Research. (August, 1995). *The implementation of performance assessment in Kentucky classrooms.* Frankfort, KY: Kentucky Institute for Education Research.

Kohn, A. (1993). *Punished by rewards: The trouble with gold starts, incentive plans, A's, praise, and other bribes.* Boston: Houghton Mifflin.

Lieberman, A., & Grolnick, M. (1996). Networks and reform in American education. *Teachers College Record,* 98(1), 7–45.

Lieberman, A., & Miller, L. (June, 1990). Restructuring schools: What matters and what works. *Phi Delta Kappan,* 759–764.

Little, J. W. (1993). Teachers' professional development in a climate of educational reform. *Educational Evaluation and Policy Analysis,* 15, 129–151.

Luhr, G. (1990, June). Kentucky's new day – The long awaited education reforms may be Kentucky's most promising hope for the future. *Kentucky Living,* pp. 21–25.

McLaughlin, M. (1990). The Rand Change Agent Study revisited: Macro perspectives, micro realities. *Educational Researcher,* 19(9), 11–16.

McLaughlin, M. (1992). *What matters most in teachers' workplace context?* (pp. 92–139). Stanford, CA: Center for Research on the Context of Secondary Teaching, Stanford University.

National Commission on Teaching and America's Future. (1996). *What matters most: Teaching for America's future.* New York: National Commission on Teaching and America's Future.

National Education Association (NEA). (1989). *Rankings of the states, 1989.* Washington, D.C.: NEA.

The Prichard Committee for Academic Excellence. (1995). *Keepin' on: Five years down the road to better schools.* Reports of the Task Force on Improving Kentucky Schools and the Task Force on Restructuring Time and Learning. Lexington, KY: The Prichard Committee for Academic Excellence.

Stiggins, R. J. (1997). *Student-centered classroom assessment* (2nd ed.). Engelwood Cliffs, N.J.: Merrill-Prentice-Hall.

Vygotsky, L. S. (1978). *Mind in society: The development of higher psychological processes.* Cambridge, MA: Harvard University Press.

Whitford, B. L., Ruscoe, G. C., Fickel, L. (Forthcoming). Knitting it all together: Collaborative teacher education in southern Maine. In L. Darling-Hammond (as yet untitled). New York: Teachers College Press.

Wiggins, G. (1993). *Assessing student performance: Exploring the purpose and limits of testing.* San Francisco: Jossey Bass.

Wigginton, E. (1985). *Sometimes a shining moment: The Foxfire experience.* New York: Doubleday.

III: Tensions and Contrasts in School Improvement Strategies

Innovations in Planning for School Improvement: Problems and Potential

MIKE WALLACE

Cardiff School of Education, University of Wales

Mike Wallace's purposes in this chapter are twofold: to examine the key factors influencing the design and implementation of school self evaluation and school development planning through a seletive historical account focusing on major initiatives originating outside schools; and to argue that these kinds of innovation embody intrinsic contradictions that are incapable of resolution, yet must be addressed by initiators if they are to maximise the potential for promoting school improvement rather than contributing to the problems that inhibit it. The chapter is divided into six sections. First, concepts framing the analysis are outlined. Second, major forms taken by school self evaluation and its implementation are summarised. Third, the origin and design of school development planning are explored, with reference to the lessons learned from experience with school self evaluation. Fourth, early implementation of this innovation is examined. Fifth, development planning is located within the broader frame of planning for change in a rapidly evolving context significantly affecting implementation. Finally, three contradictions emerging from the account are highlighted and the need is suggested for a more sophisticated way of thinking about innovations in planning for school improvement.

Paradoxically perhaps, a constant feature of our professional lives as teachers, politicians, government officials, trainers and researchers these days is change: not only in the pressures on us and in our day to day work, but also in our understanding of the nature of the change process. Experience of changing, attempting to influence others' practice, or researching change efforts affects our perceptions about educational change which, in turn, impact on our actions as educators, change agents, and commentators. One common reason why an innovation (a planned change in practice) may produce implementation problems and fail to realise the potential envisaged by its advocates is that their limited understanding of what changing practice entails for users leads to poor design or an inadequate implementation strategy. Where the innovation is evaluated and lessons are learned, our revised understanding of the change process should enable us to do better next time.

The increasing pace and complexity of educational change in recent years, however, gives rise to another danger: we may unwittingly base tomorrow's improved intervention on yesterday's comprehension of change, progressively outmoded as the political and administrative context of schooling shifts in ways that alter the process and content of educational change experienced by school staff (faculty). It may take time before our grasp of the changing nature of change

D. Hopkins (ed.), The Practice and Theory of School Improvement, 147-168.

has caught up; meanwhile implementation of our intervention brings new problems limiting its ability to make much difference.

Both these explanations of the fate of change efforts feature in the story told in this chapter. It concerns the evolution of the managerial innovations of school self evaluation (also known as school based review) and its successor, school development planning, both of which have been championed by external agents for the good of schools in England and Wales. The aims of their initiators included stimulating and helping practitioners at school level to develop their capacity to identify areas for improvement and plan a coherent and feasible strategy for implementing improvement efforts. In other words, if implemented successfully, these managerial innovations held out the promise of a means to the end of creating a co-ordinated approach to managing other innovations and, as such, a strategy contributing to school improvement.

But did they promise more than they could deliver? While these managerial innovations were being introduced, the advent of the British central government's recent educational reform programme led to an expanding range of changes in the national and local policy and administrative context surrounding schools. I will explore whether policy makers and other change agents may have been uninformed about the nature of change or well informed by an understanding of change which, nevertheless, lagged progressively behind the times.

CHANGE IN PERSPECTIVE

Fullan (1993) has pointed to the importance of understanding how users of an innovation struggle to make sense of it, drawing on their past experience and the shared beliefs and values of their professional culture. Changing practices is easier than changing culture which, however, is often necessary if users are to enter into the spirit of an innovation and implement it fully rather than merely going through the motions. There is likely to be mutual adaptation (Berman & McLaughlin, 1978), the innovation as implemented varying to some extent from initiators' original vision. Both school self evaluation and school development planning were innovations for groups at different levels of the British education system, each of whom had to make some meaning from them. We may distinguish three levels in this system and some of their key players most closely connected with the innovations at hand (see Table I). They interacted in complex ways, some attempting to influence the practice of others at the same or a different system level.

Bolam (1975) suggested that any innovation spanning different system levels may be analysed according to who acts as change agent and user and the form that this planned change in practice takes at each level. Local education authority (LEA) or district officials were both users of changes in practice following from central government initiatives and change agents where they were responsible for introducing related innovations into schools. Not only were school self evaluation and school development planning innovations for staff at this level, but they were

Table 1: Levels and Key Groups in the Education System of England and Wales

System level	Key groups connected with innovations in planning for school improvement
national	• education ministers from the political party forming central government • civil servants who work for ministers • Her Majesty's Inspectors (HMI) responsible for inspection schools and advising ministers • development project leaders – from higher education institutions • independent researchers – also from higher education institutions
local	• local government councillors • local education authority officials, especially advisers and inspectors responsible for managerial and other LEA innovations for schools, for inspection and in-service training
school	• headteachers (principals) responsible for school management including introducing external innovations • other staff, especially teachers • governors (school board members) responsible for overseeing the work of the school

also something of a novelty for LEA officials centrally involved in devising the form these innovations were to take in their locality.

The design of the innovations at each level for users who were at the same or another level reflected change agents' explicit or implicit assumptions, including those covering the nature of planning, needs of users, kinds of action for improvement which should emerge from planning, and the environment into which they were to be integrated. Similarly, implementation strategies related to assumptions such as how the change process works, the alternative 'policy instruments' (McDonnell & Elmore, 1991) like mandates or incentives available, provision of resources and preparatory training, and skills and attitudes of users.

A significant assumption underpinning the advocated planning process was the degree of rationality attributed to it: the idea that a logical and cyclic procedure of identifying goals and organising activities to achieve them should be employed. Wise (1983, p. 113) has suggested that efforts in the United States to introduce comprehensive logical planning procedures into education institutions rested on an overly rational view of management, amounting to an attempt at the hyper-rationalisation of education which was bound to fail:

> . . . much of the collective efforts of policy makers, researchers, and administrators is aimed at making school reality conform to the rational model. We then bemoan the fact that the schools fail to conform to the model. It may just be that we need a new paradigm.

I will consider how far the design of the innovations for managing planning for school improvement was hyper-rational, and so limited in potential for managing change in school contexts, and whether the design of planning innovations might better embrace an emerging paradigm reflecting the changing nature of change in a context of multiple reform that depicts schools as 'non-rational' organisations (Patterson, Purkey, & Parker, 1986).

Analysis of the implementation of school self evaluation and school development planning will draw on some of the implementation factors and themes identified in mainly North American research focusing on particular innovations or improvement efforts, based on the summary by Fullan (1993). Of course, innovations are neither developed nor implemented in a vacuum. It has long been recognised that the policy context surrounding an innovation is a significant factor influencing its course. The artificiality of focusing on single innovations has been questioned, since they rarely come conveniently in ones (Bolam, 1982a; Fullan, Anderson, & Newton, 1986). School staff are likely to face multiple innovations together with unplanned changes, such as demographic shifts in population, which are likely to interact with the innovation at hand – especially managerial innovations intended as a framework for stimulating and managing other innovations.

Exploratory research into the management of multiple innovations in English schools (Wallace, 1991a) and the part played by interaction between diverse policies in the implementation of a single innovation (Wallace, 1996) suggests, first, that headteachers take the lead in the managerial task of juggling with a continually evolving profile of innovations, whether originating inside or outside the school, each at different stages along the road from adoption, through implementation, to institutionalisation or abandonment, alongside other changes and the rest of ongoing work.

Second, a characteristic of individual innovations affecting this juggling act is the extent of their interrelatedness with other innovations in the profile, whether or not by design. An integral part of school development planning is planning the implementation of other innovations, and planning may also be affected by other managerial innovations such as local management of schools or LMS (site based management) and arrangements for staff development and appraisal, so implementation issues connected with them may also affect the content and the process of the managerial innovation through which their implementation is to be orchestrated.

Third, where the policies that impinge on an innovation evolve, as happens frequently during a reform period, they affect its design and implementation. Even a long institutionalised innovation may suddenly be subject to new implementation requirements. The factors and themes in Table 2 are based on Fullan's list, supplemented by findings from my work on multiple innovations and policy interaction.

Recent research (Wallace & McMahon, 1994) suggests a simple conceptualisation summarising the influence of environmental factors on the form that planning for school improvement takes in different circumstances. A critical feature of the context of planning innovations affecting their fitness for purpose is the ever changing balance between turbulence and stability in the internal and external environment of the institution where they are to be implemented. Turbulence refers to changes in information and practice relating to the internal environment of an organisation, and to changes in information about pressures coming from the

Table 2: Factors and Themes Affecting Implementation
(adapted from Fullan 1991l; Wallace 1991a, 1996)

Characteristics of the innovation:

o   need – how far users of an innovation perceive a need for it relative to other competing needs;
o   clarity – about the goals of an innovation and the strategy for its implementation. The more complex the innovation, the less clarity users are likely to experience during early implementation. There is also a danger of false clarity when a change is interpreted in an oversimplified way;
o   complexity – the difficulty and extent of change in practice required of users of an innovation. One form of complexity is a major innovation which contains a set of sub-innovations or is designed to manage other innovations;
o   quality – for an innovation to succeed it must be implementable, yet many inadequately thought through and resourced innovations are adopted on the grounds of political expediency or where a need is perceived but there is insufficient preparation time;
o   practicality – the extent to which potential users of an innovation perceive it to offer concrete possibilities for action that are feasible within their context;
o   interrelatedness between one innovation and others – how far whether by design or default the innovation at hand is linked to other innovations;
o   degree of compulsion – many external innovations for schools are either fully compulsory or constitute an 'offer you dare not refuse' because they are technically optional but carry desired resources. A compulsory innovation results in some form of compliance, so competing with other innovations.

School, local and national characteristics:

o   part played by groups at school, local and national levels in design, adoption and implementation of the innovation (see Table I)

Implementation themes:

o   vision building – leaders have a vision of what the institution should become (addressing the content of an innovation) and how to achieve the desired state (addressing the implementation process). It is important that support for this vision is gained from those in the organisation involved in implementation;
o   evolutionary planning – plans for implementation are adapted opportunistically as the process proceeds;
o   initiative taking and empowerment – leaders share power within the institution and encourage others to take initiatives within the vision;
o   staff development and resource assistance – provision of preparatory and ongoing training and other resources needed for users to learn new practices;
o   monitoring/problem coping – formative evaluation of implementation provides feedback to users about ideas and practices that do or do not work. Problems with implementation are to be expected and routine strategies help users to cope effectively;
o   restructuring – the development of management structures and roles that facilitate implementation of innovations.

external environment. Conversely, stability means the continuance of existing practice within the organisation, uninfluenced by internal changes or changes in external demands.

Schools are organisations where there may be turbulence in some areas, as where several innovations are simultaneously imposed from outside, while others remain stable, as in the day to day arrangements for teaching of classes. Innovations for managing planning for school improvement may create turbulence as they add to staff workloads during early implementation or stimulate other changes, or contribute to stabilising the internal school environment if they live up to their promise of helping staff to prioritise and coordinate their improvement efforts.

SCHOOL SELF EVALUATION

Several strands of development contributed to emergence of the notion of school self evaluation in this country (Hopkins, 1985; Clift, Nuttall, & McCormick, 1987) which included increasing attention to schools as a whole, rather than individual teachers. During the early 1970s, school staff had enjoyed unusually high control over the curriculum compared with their counterparts in other western countries. The education system amounted to 'a national service, locally administered', with school and LEA staff being left by politicians to get on with the job. The 1973 world oil crisis changed all that. Mounting concern among politicians and the wider public over education standards led to increasing pressure on school and LEA staff to ensure that teachers were more accountable to LEAs and to central government. Ministers published documents setting out a view of the curriculum and encouraging school staff to review theirs.

Teachers were also encouraged through several nationwide curriculum development projects funded by the Schools Council, a national funding agency with strong representation of teaching staff, to investigate their work as a route to improvement. A small minority of school staff initiated their own approach to evaluating their practice. At the same time, dissatisfaction with the limited impact of traditional off-site in-service training courses led to initiatives spearheaded by LEAs and central government agencies to promote in-service training focusing on identified needs of the school as a whole, so establishing a link between individual professional development and school wide development (Bolam, 1982b).

Major school self evaluation initiatives were launched sporadically in several LEAs (Nuttall, 1981). The earliest consisted of questions about practice that school staff were expected to answer in reviewing their work, agreeing areas for improvement and implementing improvement efforts (e.g. ILEA, 1977). Representatives of local teachers and heads were generally consulted about the design. LEA staff appear to have made variable but cautious assumptions about how far to make inroads into what had been exclusively the domain of teaching staff. At the light touch extreme was the voluntary Solihull Education Committee (1980, p. 1) initiative, documentation for which included an introductory statement inviting mutual adaptation:

It is not intended to impose the evaluation techniques suggested within this book on any school, but rather it is hoped that the guide will assist those schools interested in evaluating their performance by providing a framework on which to base group and staff in-service training. This framework may be modified or extended to suit the intentions and interests of the individual school.

In other LEAs a mandate was used, confined to a very occasional report which must be presented to governors (where an LEA representative would be present), or linked with school inspection by LEA officials every few years. Here LEA staff were change agents directly targeting headteachers as principal users and, through them, other staff (as depicted in Table 3).

Research into these schemes (Clift et al., 1987; Hopkins, 1989; Cuttance, 1994) revealed that they had limited impact for connected reasons relating to their status as innovations. The findings suggested, first, that school self evaluation was an unwelcome and threatening exercise where teaching staff believed that schooling should be left to the professionals, especially where reporting to outsiders was involved. The values underpinning school self evaluation were inimical to this professional culture. Consequently there was limited perception of a need for the innovation.

Second, there was lack of clarity at LEA and school levels over two potentially conflicting purposes: to promote internal school wide development, which would entail acknowledgement of strengths and frankness in revealing weaknesses; and to increase external accountability, where admitting weaknesses could be perceived by school staff as inviting retribution, leading to many weaknesses identified being those (like provision of facilities) which were LEA responsibilities, and to avoidance of issues at the heart of schooling, like teaching styles and their impact on pupil learning. Implementation strategies did not solve the problem. Mandates ensured minimal compliance but not commitment; invitation to participate in voluntary schemes was not much of an incentive, resulting in many school staff declining the offer or abandoning implementation later on.

Third, LEA initiators appear to have made false assumptions about ease of implementation, underestimating the complexity of school self evaluation for novice users, since little guidance was provided on the process. Collecting data on present practice, identifying and agreeing areas for improvement and implementing changes turned out to require skills that many school staff did not have; staff were often overly ambitious in undertaking extensive efforts that then dragged on – all review and no action for improvement; and the initiative took an inordinate amount of time that competed with other priorities. The quality and practicality

Table 3: One LEA's School Self Evaluation Scheme as an Innovation

Change Agent	Innovation	User
LEA officials	designing and implementing questionnaire and accountability procedure	LEA officials
LEA officials	procedure for completion of questionnaire and presentation of four yearly report to governors and including an LEA official	Headteachers, other staff
Headteachers	approach to procedure for completion and presentation of questionnaire	Other staff

of the schemes was therefore low, and the absence of related staff development and resource assistance in the form of preparatory training and facilitation in school did nothing to help implementation along.

Fourth, the balance between environmental stability and turbulence, while variable, was weighted towards stability in most schools. Strong professional control over schooling meant that most innovations connected with teaching and management were either initiated in school or optional, so headteachers could keep the turbulence brought by changes within bounds. Many staff lacked experience of implementing substantial planned changes, including managing redeployment of resources. It seems that the associated lack of skill in managing change at school level may have been mirrored by lack of skill amongst LEA officials in managing change to be implemented by users in schools.

A rather different approach to school self evaluation was influenced by research knowledge of educational change, and proved to have greater potential. The Schools Council supported researchers from higher education, at the vanguard of the movement to focus in-service training more firmly on the school as a whole, in developing a process approach to school self evaluation – Guidelines for Review and Internal Development in Schools (GRIDS) – and trialling it extensively in schools (McMahon, Bolam, Abbott, & Holly, 1984a, 1984b). External accountability did not figure: the aim was restricted to promoting internal school wide development through participation of all teaching staff. The design adopted a rational approach to managing the review and development process based on a cycle of sequential stages (each divided into steps):

- getting started – including considering resources and appointing a school co-ordinator;
- initial review – based on an anonymous questionnaire for all teaching staff from which areas meriting further review would be identified;
- specific review(s) – each tackled by a team led by a co-ordinator, leading to recommendations to include in-service training, to be agreed by all staff;
- action for development – implementing and monitoring action to achieve agreed targets and associated in-service training;
- assessing and adopting GRIDS – a one-off stage where staff would review the GRIDS procedures and decide how to institutionalise those they valued.

The project operated through LEAs, officials being asked to support school staff who volunteered to participate. As with other voluntary LEA schemes, GRIDS made most impact on schools whose headteachers and other staff already shared a culture valuing the emphasis built into the innovation on collaboration and school wide improvement. The singularity of purpose appealed to those who valued internal development, but did not satisfy the requirements of promoting external accountability which were to overtake schools in the coming years. The scheme was modified to take into account mounting pressure from central government policies for other constituencies, primarily governors and parents, to have a say; but it did not become a mandatory component of LEA policy. The introduction of school development planning put paid to many earlier school self evaluation initiatives, although elements of the earlier innovation were sometimes incorporated in its successor.

TRANSITION TO SCHOOL DEVELOPMENT PLANNING

It is notable that, during this period extending into the late 1980s, a strategic attempt was made in the Inner London Education Authority (ILEA) to review its education service – an exercise in external accountability. One committee of enquiry reviewed the quality of secondary schooling while another dealt with primary (elementary) schools. The secondary schools review, chaired by David Hargreaves, recommended a planned approach to school development where staff should be required to identify priorities for improvement (ILEA, 1984). The primary schools report amplified the idea in a recommendation arising from committee members' observation of plans initiated in schools (ILEA, 1985, par. 3.94):

> . . .every school should have a plan for development, taking account of the policies of the Authority, the needs of the children, the capabilities of the staff, and the known views of the parents. The plan should have an action sheet attached to it, showing what the responsibilities of members of staff will be and setting target dates. The plan should also show what, if any, outside assistance or special resources will be needed and indicate time scales; it should also show by what means the effects of the plan are to be assessed.

Such a document could constitute a valuable source of information for LEA inspections, serving the interests of external accountability.

Hargreaves, later the ILEA Chief Inspector, developed an innovation in which he overhauled school self review requirements, combining internal improvement efforts with external evaluation and so bringing internal development and external accountability together in the same scheme. External inspections fed into the review undertaken by school staff as part of development planning. Staff in schools causing most concern to inspectors were supported by an 'Inspectors Based in Schools' team with the diagnosis of weaknesses and remedial action. External accountability featured, strongly, inspection reports on individual schools and an annual overview by the Chief Inspector of provision in the LEA being published (Hargreaves, 1990). The design of this innovation went some way towards meeting the interest of central government ministers in combining greater external accountability with supporting school staff in raising educational standards. Ironically, ministers replaced the ILEA with smaller LEAs before the scheme could be fully implemented or evaluated.

During the late 1980s officials in a few other LEAs had experimented with initiatives to promote planning for school improvement. In the London Borough of Enfield (1985), for example, school staff were encouraged to draw up a plan for institutional development focusing on the curriculum. Such local developments became subsumed in LEA responses to the launch of a massive central government reform agenda in 1988. The reforms triggered an urgent sense of need amongst LEA officials for an initiative which would enable school staff to manage the implementation of multiple innovations. First, the Education Reform Act of that year had spawned a set of major, concurrent, interrelated and mandatory innovations for school staff and governors encompassing the curriculum, its assessment, creation of conditions promoting competition between neighbouring institutions, and management. This recipe for turbulence very quickly featured in the innovation profile of every school.

Second, one mandatory managerial innovation, the LMS initiative, entailed creating an annual plan for the school budget; another, arrangements for central government contribution to funding of LEA provision of in-service training to support reform, required LEA officials to submit an annual plan indicating how staff development needs at school level had been identified. Both initiatives were based on the financial year (April to March).

Third, central government ministers held LEAs responsible for the implementation of central government innovations in schools within their jurisdiction. The central government grant enabling LEA officials to fulfil this duty to support implementation in schools was conditional on LEAs ensuring that school staff had a 'National Curriculum development plan' covering the phasing in of this innovation, subject by subject, over several academic years (September to August).

Small wonder that LEA officials were attracted to the idea of a single overarching planning innovation which would meet school and LEA needs at the same time! Their thinking was affected by advice documents emanating from central government (DES, 1989, 1991; Hargreaves, Hopkins, & Leask, 1990), the outcome of a national development project sponsored by ministers and directed by Hargreaves and Hopkins (1991). This advice was based on information gathered from 40 schools and 14 LEAs between April 1989 and the summer of the following year. The first document was published in December 1989 and sent to all schools. A national survey of governing bodies conducted in the spring of 1990 (Keys & Fernandes, 1990) found that 60% of headteachers who had elected to be governors had used it and, of these, 90% had found it useful. Hargreaves and Hopkins were therefore very significant change agents promoting a particular approach to development planning (Table 4), whose advice reached every LEA and school in the country and influenced the form that LEA development planning initiatives were to take.

In this document, development planning was advocated as a key to integrating plans for external demands for change with self evaluation (DES, 1989, p. 4):

> The distinctive feature of a development plan is that it brings together, in an overall plan, national and LEA policies and initiatives, the school's aims and values, its existing achievements and its needs for development. By co-ordinating aspects of planning which are otherwise separate, the school acquires a shared sense of direction and is able to control and manage the tasks of development and change. Priorities for development are planned in detail for one year and are supported by action plans or working documents

Table 4: Development Planning as an Innovation

Change agent	Innovation	User
Central government ministers and civil servants	bidding procedure for in-service training grant and ensuring schools have a National Curriculum development plan	LEA officials
LEA officials	design and implementation of school development planning procedure and document submission to LEA	Headteachers, other staff (to a varying extent governors)
Headteachers	approach to development planning procedure and completion and submission of documents	other staff (to a varying extent governors)
Development project leaders, with backing of central government ministers and civil servants	advice documents for LEAs and schools on development planning procedure and documentation	LEA officials, headteachers and other staff
Latterly, HMI	requirement that school development plan be submitted to inspectors prior to inspection and recommendation that post-inspection action plan integrated with it	Headteachers

for staff. The priorities for later years are sketched in outline to provide the longer term programme.

The planning process was based on a yearly cycle consisting of four sequential processes or stages (p. 5):

- audit: a school reviews its strengths and weaknesses;
- plan construction: priorities for development are selected and then turned into specific targets;
- implementation: of the planned priorities and targets;
- evaluation: the success of implementation is checked.

Detailed plans are made for the year ahead, and for the next two in outline. At the end of the initial cycle, detailed plans for the following year are made with reference to the outline plans made previously. The development plan rolls forward at the beginning of each year, 'leaving room in the plan to meet future demands arising from national or local initiatives and the school's changing needs'. Planning therefore proceeds by annual increments, making some allowance for environmental turbulence through annual updating. Agreement on priorities and targets at the plan construction stage is to be followed by formulation of detailed action plans which include identifying 'success criteria' by which progress with implementation may be monitored.

The implementation and evaluation stages are regarded as 'interlaced, not as a period of implementation followed by a "big bang" evaluation at the end. If implementation and evaluation are linked, evaluation can help to shape and guide the action plan rather than being a post mortem upon it'. Through regular progress checks, formative evaluation enables adjustments to be made within the plan for any priority, in addition to the summative evaluation at the end of the cycle. This component of the model also allows for environmental turbulence (which might cause, say, delay in implementing a priority) but only within priorities agreed during the annual plan construction process.

Had lessons been learned from the false assumptions of the past? The assumption that sequential annual cycles could feasibly frame the suggested design was probably influenced by past experience and present demands: the advice built on what was already happening in the schools and LEAs visited by the development project staff. First, some school and LEA staff were familiar with the GRIDS cyclic approach to school self evaluation. GRIDS and other approaches were developed, however, at a time of greater stability than the turbulent world school and LEA staff were just starting to experience in 1989, when fieldwork for the development project was being carried out. The GRIDS and development planning process cycles have similarities, but the latter shifts the emphasis towards how to implement and evaluate action plans, perhaps reflecting awareness of difficulties experienced by school staff with many school self evaluation schemes. It gives greater prominence to external sources of innovations that were becoming such a prominent feature of the changing national context.

Second, annual planning cycles were being imposed on LEAs and schools by central government initiatives connected with the reforms: the financial year for the LMS budget and in-service training, and the academic year for phasing in the National Curriculum. The advice documents refrained from advising on the choice of annual cycle to adopt for development planning, although it was suggested (DES 1991) that a timetable should be built up of tasks relating to the various planning cycles.

Third, a bestselling guidebook, *The Self Managing School* (Caldwell & Spinks, 1988), advocating a yearly 'collaborative planning cycle', was widely read in schools and LEAs as staff sought to grasp the practical implications of the central government LMS initiative and, in some LEAs, was backed by training sessions led by one of the authors. Nevertheless, the book's advice was largely based on experience in one isolated Tasmanian school that apparently enjoyed a quite stable environment.

Meanwhile, things were hotting up as the central government reform agenda unfolded. Arguably, by the time many LEA development planning initiatives were reaching schools, their environment had become more turbulent than when the fieldwork was carried out for the development planning project which informed LEA schemes. Subsequent problems associated with the advocated design as adapted by LEA officials appear to have been due, at least in part, to the nature of change itself changing between the time of design and implementation.

PUTTING DEVELOPMENT PLANNING INTO PRACTICE

LEA officials were, on the one hand, change agents for and designers of the framework for development planning as introduced into schools, while on the other, users of the central government backed advice on development planning and the new system of bidding for in-service training grants and ensuring that there was a National Curriculum development plan in every school (Table 4). To a variable extent, headteachers were both users of the LEA innovation and change agents where they were able to shape the development planning process and documentation in their school. Room for mutual adaptation of the innovation across system levels meant that development planning as practised often diverged markedly from the vision expressed by the national development project leaders or central government ministers.

LEA development planning initiatives spread rapidly. According to a national survey to determine their prevalence for primary schools (MacGilchrist, Mortimore, Savage, & Beresford, 1995), the proportion of LEAs with a policy on development planning had increased from under 5% before 1988 to 83% in 1990/91, and the number continued to rise the following year. The influence of the national development project was evident in LEA advice documents, some of which were published and so available to any LEA (e.g. Sheffield Education Department, 1991; Warwickshire County Council, 1991; Bradford Education, 1992). This material was soon supplemented by published handbooks promoting a similar cyclic approach (Skelton, Reeves, & Playfoot, 1991; Davies & Ellison, 1992).

A picture of patterns of design may be built up from research which examined schemes in different LEAs (Wallace, 1991b; Constable, Norton, & Abbott, 1991; Weston et al., 1992; Wallace & McMahon 1994; MacGilchrist et al., 1995). Adoption of sequential annual cycles based on either the financial or academic year was a common feature, but there was variation in how far schemes advocated restricting identified priorities for development in any year (from no limit to just four priorities). Most schemes were mandatory, but compulsion applied in practice to the completion of the development plan document, rather than to the process of planning. There was considerable variation in contextual detail about the school and the priorities, targets and success criteria expected in the plan, but the prevailing assumption appeared to be that the school environment was stable enough for priorities (often limited in number) to be identified and updated only once a year.

Although they were designed to support school development, the plans also served the LEA interest in external accountability, under increased pressure from central government policy changes. Completed plans had to be submitted to most LEAs and were analysed in some way, primarily to meet the requirement that schools had a National Curriculum development plan and to inform LEA planning for provision of in-service training connected with central government reforms. In most LEAs, officials referred to development plans as part of the process of monitoring schools, including the conduct of formal inspections.

LEA implementation strategies differed in timing and level of intervention, but most relied on dissemination of written information and short preparatory training workshops for headteachers, sometimes extending to governors or other staff with management responsibility. Submission of completed plans to the LEA provided a means of monitoring implementation, though limited to presentation of the document as opposed to the process of planning supposedly surrounding it.

The impact of LEA initiatives on schools was soon felt. A survey of primary and secondary school headteachers (Arnott, Bullock, & Thomas, 1992), revealed that 99% of respondents were expected under LEA policy to prepare school development plans and two thirds found LEA guidelines helpful. Most research relating to early implementation restricted its focus to the process and intermediate outcomes of development planning, so neglecting to examine any relationship between this innovation and planning for other changes outside the priorities identified in the development plan. There was strong evidence that headteachers were able to act selectively on any external advice or demand in framing the consultation process leading to formulation of the plan, and their efforts as change agents (Table 4) had a major influence on the form taken by development planning at school level. Involvement of other staff, governors or parents was diverse, ranging from none (where the headteacher wrote the plan alone and submitted it to the LEA without anyone else having sight of it) to extensive consultation within and beyond the staff including, say, a questionnaire for parents.

One major study (MacGilchrist et al., 1995), entailing interviews and observation of classrooms in nine primary schools from three LEAs, sought to link identified priorities with intermediate outcomes in terms of pupils' educational experience (but not learning outcomes). A strong correlation was found between the quality of pupils' experience in areas identified for development in the plan and the form of planning process. In only two schools having a 'corporate plan', with a particularly strong focus on pupils' learning, did teachers feel a definite responsibility for outcomes and was their classwork in priority areas for development of high quality. Here headteachers enabled colleagues to be extensively involved in managing the development planning process and formulating the plan, and there was a sense of shared ownership. The written plan was a working document, including consideration of financial resources and staff development needs, and implementation was quite rigorously monitored and evaluated. Headteachers and other staff shared a professional culture valuing collaboration, consensus building and working towards improvement.

A generally consistent account of involvement and impact was given by Her Majesty's Inspectors (HMI) employed by central government. They singled out a primary, middle and secondary school for special praise (Ofsted, 1994), judging (according to inspections whose criteria for effectiveness were not entirely explicit) that recent improvement in practice was influenced by good practice in development planning.

On the strength of this evidence, it appears that development planning was both rapidly implemented and, under certain conditions, delivered its promise as a means of managing other innovations with an indirect but positive impact on quality of schooling. The innovation was subject to considerable mutual adaptation as change agents and users across system levels came up with a design and implementation strategy reflecting their circumstances. The extent to which headteachers were willing to involve others and share control of the process was an important variable explaining the success or otherwise of implementation. But in research the answers you get depend on the questions you ask. A question left unasked by most studies was: how far did the development planning framework provide a means of managing planning for the multiplicity of innovations and other changes that all school staff faced or wished to initiate (as implied in the national development plans project advice document)?

DESIGN FAULT OR IMPLEMENTATION PROBLEM?

My research (Wallace, 1991a, 1991b) moved towards investigating this question because of a surprise finding in the exploratory work on managing multiple innovations conducted at the time when the first central government advice document was published. The two primary and two secondary schools in this study came from an LEA whose officials had recommended them as particularly effective in managing change. Although LEA officials had just launched a mandatory development planning initiative and completed plans were submitted to the LEA from each school, they played a minor role in guiding planning for improvement. In one school, the plan document was lost and I never did see it; in another, the LEA initiative had overlaid a grass roots effort to develop a five year plan which staff continued, surreptitiously, to use.

The LEA development planning initiative became part of the planning headache for headteachers and other staff beset by a burgeoning profile of central government and related LEA innovations. The timetable for phasing in mandatory innovations like the National Curriculum and LMS was public knowledge and gave school staff no choice but to make them priorities. A development plan was certainly not necessary during the reform period for staff to identify more than enough priorities to keep them busy.

The environment was simply too unstable either for priorities to be realistically restricted to a given number, or to be firmly established at any one point for a whole year. Staff were forced repeatedly to respond to unpredictable changes in the implementation requirements of externally imposed innovations already on stocks, to take on new priorities, and to drop existing action plans. Detailed planning and action to achieve priorities for the following year began long before the end of the year in question, especially where appointment of teaching staff was involved. With a touch of irony, the design and implementation requirements of the LEA development planning initiative changed during the course of the fieldwork, adding to school level turbulence. What played the leading role in guide planning for development was a much more flexible and frequently incremental process led by the headteachers, more reminiscent of the evolutionary approach advocated by Louis and Miles (1990). Development planning and the informal approach coexisted in uneasy tension.

Three hypotheses emerged from this work (Wallace, 1992). First, two irreconcilable influences drive the process of planning for school improvement: planning based on annual cycles for long term coherence versus more or less continual, incremental planning for short term flexibility. On the one hand, a planning process based on annual cycles enables priorities to be established and a coherent direction for medium and long term development to be sustained. Yet in the often unpredictably changing circumstances encountered in the research schools, cyclic planning could lead to rigidity, with plans becoming increasingly irrelevant to current concerns. On the other hand, frequent incremental planning gives flexibility rapidly to modify existing plans and to create new ones whenever changing circumstances dictate the need. Yet loss of coherence and duplication of effort could result from plans which were not connected to long term aims. In extreme cases such an approach might amount to mere crisis management. There is no straightforward middle ground between longer term planning and short term flexibility.

Second, the origin of this tension lies in the shifting balance between environmental turbulence favouring an approach to planning that protects short term flexibility, and environmental stability which makes possible planning for long term coherence. Central government reforms and associated LEA initiatives (including development planning for schools) continued to shift the balance more heavily toward the turbulent.

Third, as the environmental balance shifts toward turbulence, the balance of cyclic and continual planning is forced to shift towards the continual although, even in the most extreme case, annual cycles must still be addressed. Conversely, if the balance shifts towards stability, school level planners have greater choice over whether to go for a single planning cycle, although some more frequent updating of plans is likely to be required during the cycle and planning for the next will probably begin before the present one ends.

According to these hypotheses the design of development planning looked hyper-rational: a logical but nevertheless rationalistic solution to the problem of managing planning for school improvement in the often chaotic world of reform. I therefore developed a speculative model of 'flexible planning' which acknowledges the limits to rationalistic planning in turbulent environments, but meets head on the endemic tension between the need (recognised in cyclic plans) to sustain a long term direction, and the need to respond rapidly to changing circumstances.

The core is a continual process of creation, monitoring and adjustment of plans for the short, medium and long term. These plans roll forward over time, medium term plans for the next few months being developed into more detailed plans for action. Plans may be updated whenever the spasmodic and often unpredictable arrival of new information about external innovations occurs, or when crises or other events happen. At the same time, planning takes into account the stage reached in the overlapping academic and financial year cycles. Management procedures consist of occasional consultative and strategic decision making exercises coupled with considerable day to day monitoring and adjustment. A routine procedure is established for calling a 'rapid response' review whenever information about a change in the environment suggests that present priorities and development activity may require tweaking. The regular consultative procedures may be cyclic: say, major reviews every year and minor, less extensive reviews every term. The 'rapid response' review may be inserted – and lead to adjustment of the cycle – whenever continual monitoring shows that it is required.

These hypotheses and the associated model were partially tested in a subsequent study which included six schools in three LEAs chosen for the probability that their environment would be the most turbulent anywhere in the UK (Wallace & McMahon, 1994). (The investigation did not, therefore, examine stable situations.) If development planning could work here, it could work anywhere. It did work where the timetable for innovations was announced well ahead and did not change later. It dealt less well with incremental updating following the incremental influx of information relating to working with financial and academic year cycles and making detailed plans during the year for the year beyond.

It did not work for the many shifts in information about externally initiated innovations and other events that could not be foreseen at school level. The implicit assumption of environmental stability proved false in so far as factors promoting turbulence – not least changes in central government reform policies – led to spasmodically shifting circumstances which, in turn, forced other priorities to arise, with consequent adjustment of priorities and targets set out in the development plan (usually without reference to the plan itself until the end of year review). Development planning did not allow for the evolutionary nature of some changes driving the planning process or for the inability to keep the number of innovations within predetermined limits, in contrast with the more comprehensive flexible planning model which did encompass nonrational interruptions to cyclic planning and alternative, more flexible procedures.

In the light of this and the other research discussed earlier, implementation of development planning was apparently subject to the factors and themes listed in Table 1. The limited knowledge base must be borne in mind: fieldwork was carried out several years ago, more work was done on primary than secondary schools, samples for in depth study were small, and implementation was tracked while it happened for no more than two years in any investigation.

The sense of need at LEA level was matched in schools whose headteachers shared a belief in this approach; elsewhere, perceptions of need seemed to be more about complying with the LEA mandate to submit a completed plan. Clarity about the design and implementation strategy of the innovation was difficult to retain at LEA and school levels because the surrounding policy context changed, with consequences for development planning. Full implementation of the interrelated managerial innovation of LMS in 1992 entailed a loss of LEA powers so that officials could no longer make submission of a completed plan mandatory, and led to the increasing necessity for plans for development to include consideration of their demands on the LMS budget.

Complexity varied with the degree of comprehensiveness of changes and budgeting issues that the development planning process was designed to encompass, the form of planning process adopted by headteachers, and response of other staff to it. The simpler the innovation, the less of planning for change it covered and the more was addressed outside the plan. Equally, the less consultation there was in school, the lower the level of staff commitment to achieving priorities identified in the plan. The environment in some schools was more turbulent than in others, although no teacher was enjoying a quiet life, and development planning guided practice more fully in the more stable situations. Quality and practicality of LEA initiatives also differed; where LEA officials rushed the introduction, knock on difficulties resulted in schools. The innovation did guide planning in relation to certain priorities, but the cyclic, rationalistic design put a ceiling on the utility of all approaches for more turbulent environments, however adapted at school level. Here much responsive and highly incremental planning for change took place outside the framework of development planning.

The vision for development planning that underpinned LEA initiatives was variably communicated to headteachers and other staff in schools, the more so where introduction was gradual, with substantial preparatory training and feedback. At school level, it appears that headteachers' vision was fully shared with staff and others in perhaps a minority of cases. There was little evidence of a consciously evolutionary approach to planning implementation, although both LEA officials and schools' staff did adapt the innovation with experience and responded as the policy context changed. Initiative taking and empowerment at LEA and school levels were possible within constraints posed by central government reforms. Many LEA officials shared the aspiration of the national development project leaders of enabling school staff and governors to gain greater control over the destiny of their school through development planning, yet the central and local government agendas for change severely restricted choice of priorities and, in most cases, the timing of plan construction and the written form it took. LEA officials had some room to manoeuvre, coming up with differences in detailed design, but central government pressure meant that development planning became an innovation that you dare not refuse and the option of refraining from launching an initiative was unlikely to be taken for long.

Staff development and resource assistance for LEA officials appeared non-existent beyond the national development planning project advice. Any networking between LEA staffs and the multiplicity of central government innovations for whose implementation officials were responsible, ensured that support for school staff and governors was generally restricted to short information-giving sessions for key individuals, especially headteachers. There was little LEA monitoring and evaluation of implementation in schools, partly because of the long tradition of light touch LEA monitoring, but also since LEA officials were too stretched with other reform related tasks.

Development planning did offer the promise of restructuring, but appeared to have made a real difference to staff roles, procedures and levels of participation in a minority of schools. Hargreaves and Hopkins (1991) claimed that development planning can change the professional culture of the school staff in the direction of collaboration towards mutually agreed goals for school improvement. The research evidence suggested, in contrast, that a collaborative, improvement orientated culture was a precondition of the participative development planning process they advocated being implemented in practice.

CONCLUSION

To summarise, the cyclic basis of LEA development planning initiatives and the advice that informed them may have proved hyper-rational for a world turned upside down by central government reforms. Those at the leading edge of innovations in planning for school improvement had learned lessons from the shortcomings of school self evaluation, but the legacy of the assumption of environmental stability was strong. The rug was pulled out from under their feet as central government ministers, with cavalier disregard for the complexity of the change process, imposed an unimplementable profile of innovations on LEA and school staff and pushed the turbulence level in the education system way beyond previous limits. The spasmodically evolving burden of mandatory central government innovations, often ill thought through and subject to policy reversals, was too heavy for a cyclic approach to planning for school improvement to shoulder, especially where the content, timing and resourcing of that improvement were so forcibly defined from the outside. LEA and school level implementation strategies led to problems associated with any other innovation, and to implementation which varied from superficial to profound.

There is a postscript to the story. I know of a school whose staff have survived years of extreme turbulence and made lasting school improvement efforts without a development plan until the time of writing, relying on a more flexible and informal approach to planning for change. Yet I can guarantee that a development plan will be produced before this chapter is published, to meet new central government external accountability demands. Since 1993 a revised centralised system of school inspection has been introduced, guaranteeing that every school in the country will be inspected inside a four year cycle. Documentation that inspectors require to see includes 'the school development plan (or equivalent)' (OFSTED, 1996a), and the inspection includes a focus on progress with priorities identified within it.

The school governing body is responsible for production of an action plan after the inspection, indicating how staff will address areas for improvement identified by inspectors. They are invited to consider whether to revise the development plan at this point in the light of the inspection report. There is a low chance that such a modification will be required conveniently when the development plan is undergoing its annual audit and reconstruction anyway. In the post-reform environment, just as central government ministers promise a period of stability (where development planning could flourish), another of their innovations promises a spasmodic requirement for incremental readjustment.

This extra push towards external accountability has probably ensured that at least a minimalist approach to development planning will be universally implemented prior to an inspection, but it will not guarantee institutionalisation. Already, moves are afoot to extend the length of the inspection cycle to six years (OFSTED, 1996b), implying that compliance could mean little more than completion of some kind of document before the rare event of a school inspection.

What lessons may we draw from the British experience of promoting innovations for managing planning for school improvement? Despite considerable learning among change agents from problems with school self evaluation – coming to focus guidance much more on process – school development planning was also not without problems. Their origin seems to lie deep: simple solutions within a paradigm for understanding change that led to a hyper-rational design constraining implementation. What may now be needed is the sort of paradigm shift for which Fullan (1993) has called, giving greater acknowledgement to the 'non-linear' and unpredictable nature of change in a context of iterative reform, where periods of post-reform stability are unlikely to last long before the next wave of reform arrives. In the spirit of such an enterprise I suggest that advice on how to manage planning for school improvement should embrace the intrinsically contradictory nature of the change process, rather than assume that a simple, logical procedure will get round it.

Three kinds of contradiction have been expressed throughout our story, the balance between each opposing factor varying over time and with the local context:

- contradictory environmental influences – the need for long term coherence versus short term flexibility;
- contradictory purposes – internal institutional development versus external accountability;
- contradictory cultural conditions – a staff professional culture conducive to a collaborative process focused on the continual search for improvement versus implementation of this process, in the hope of shifting a more individualistic and satisficing culture in the preferred direction.

Managing planning for school improvement need not be illogical but we require a more flexible logic, as is becoming clear from experience with strategic planning in the business sector (Mintzberg, 1994), allowing for environmental influences which are amenable to a lock-step cyclic approach alongside those which are not, and for variable interaction between the two. The flexible planning model offers a starting point for such a design. External interventions should allow for the likelihood of those involved pursuing incompatible purposes (as Hargreaves attempted to do in ILEA). They should be sensitive to varied local conditions: different planning procedures with varying levels of participation might be appropriate for staffs with different professional cultures, and could be designed to promote incremental change in values. Overall, a paradigm shift implies that we must seek more complex solutions to what must be understood as a complex problem if we are to make further progress in achieving the potential of innovations in planning to bring about school improvement.

REFERENCES

Arnott, M., Bullock, A., & Thomas, H. (1992). *The impact of local management on schools: A source book first report of the impact project*. Birmingham: University of Birmingham School of Education for the National Association of Headteachers.

Berman, P., & McLaughlin, M. (1978). *Federal programs supporting educational change: Implementing and sustaining innovations* (Vol VIII). Santa Monica, Ca: Rand Corporation.
Bolam, R. (1975). The management of educational change: Towards a conceptual framework. In V. Houghton, R. McHugh, & C. Morgan (Eds.), *Management in education*. London: Ward Lock.
Bolam, R. (1982a). *Strategies for school improvement report for the Organisation for Economic Cooperation and Development.* Bristol: University of Bristol School of Education.
Bolam, R. (Ed.). (1982b). *School focused in-service training.* London: Heinemann.
Bradford Education. (1992). *School development planning handbook.* Bradford: Bradford Education Committee.
Caldwell, B., & Spinks, J. (1988). *The self managing school.* London: Falmer.
Clift, P., Nuttall, D., & McCormick, R. (Eds). (1987). *Studies in school self evaluation.* London: Falmer Press.
Constable, H., Norton, J., & Abbott, I. (1991). Case studies in school development planning. Sunderland: Centre for Post Experience and Research, Sunderland Polytechnic School of Education.
Cuttance, P. (1994). The contribution of quality assurance reviews to development in school systems. In D. Hargreaves & D. Hopkins (Eds.), Development Planning for School Improvement. London: Cassell.
Davies, B., & Ellison, L. (1992). School development planning. Harlow: Longman.
Department of Education and Science. (1989). *Planning for school improvement.* London: DES.
Department of Education and Science. (1991). *Development planning: A practical guide.* London: DES.
Enfield. (1985). *Curriculum initiatives group: Supporting institutional development.* Mimeo: London Borough of Enfield.
Fullan, M. (1993). Change forces: Probing the depths of educational reform. London: Falmer.
Fullan, M. with Stiegelbauer, S. (1991). *The new meaning of educational change.* London: Cassell.
Fullan, M., Anderson, S., & Newton, E. (1986). *Support systems for implementing curriculum in school boards.* Toronto: OISE Press and Ontario Government Bookstore.
Hargreaves, D. (1990). Accountability and school improvement in the work of LEA inspectorates. *Journal of Education Policy,* 5(3), 230–239.
Hargreaves, D., & Hopkins, D. (1991). *The empowered school.* London: Cassell.
Hargreaves, D, Hopkins, D., & Leask, M. (1990). *The management of development planning – A paper for local education authorities.* London: DES.
Hopkins, D. (1985). *School based review for school improvement: A preliminary state of the art.* Leuven, Belgium: ACCO.
Hopkins, D. (1989). *Evaluation for school development.* Milton Keynes: Open University Press.
Inner London Education Authority. (1977). *Keeping the school under review.* London: ILEA.
Inner London Education Authority. (1984). *Improving secondary schools.* London: ILEA.
Inner London Education Authority. (1985). *Improving primary schools.* London: ILEA.
Keys, W., & Fernandes, C. (1990). *A survey of school governing bodies* (2 Vols.). Slough: National Foundation for Educational Research.
Louis, K., & Miles, M. (1990). Improving the urban high school: What works and why. Columbia, NY: Teachers College Press.
MacGilchrist, B., Mortimore, P., Savage, J., & Beresford, C. (1995). *Planning matters: The impact of development planning in primary schools.* London: Paul Chapman.
McDonnell, L., & Elmore, R. (1991). Getting the job done: Alternative policy instruments. In Odden, R. (Ed.), *Education policy implementation.* Albany, NY: State University of New York Press.
McMahon, A., Bolam, R., Abbott, R., & Holly, P. (1984a). *Guidelines for review and internal development in schools: Primary school handbook.* York: Longman for Schools Council.
McMahon, A., Bolam, R., Abbott, R., & Holly, P. (1984b). *Guidelines for review and internal development in schools: Secondary school handbook.* York: Longman for Schools Council.
Mintzberg, H. (1994). *The rise and fall of strategic planning.* London: Prentice Hall.
Nuttall, D. (1981). *School self evaluation: Accountability with a human face?* London: Schools Council.
Office for Standards in Education. (1994). *Improving schools.* London: HMSO.
Office for Standards in Education. (1996a). *Making the most of inspection: A Guide to inspection for schools and governors.* London: Ofsted.
Office for Standards in Education. (1996b). *Consultation on the arrangements for the inspection of maintained schools from September 1997.* London: Ofsted.
Patterson, J., Purkey, S., & Parker, J. (1986). *Productive school systems for a nonrational world.* Alexandria, VA: Association for Supervision and Curriculum Development.

Sheffield Education Department. (1991). *School development planning under LMS*. Sheffield: Sheffield City Council.

Skelton, M., Reeves, G., & Playfoot, D. (1991). *Development planning for primary schools*. Windsor: NFER-Nelson.

Solihull Education Committee. (1980). *Evaluating the primary school – A guide for primary schools in the Metropolitan Borough of Solihull*. Solihull: Solihull Education Committee.

Wallace, M. (1991a). Coping with multiple innovations in schools. *School Organisation*, **11**(2), 187–209.

Wallace, M. (1991b). Contradictory interests in policy implementation: The case of LEA development plans for schools. *Journal of Education Policy*, **6**(4), 385–399.

Wallace, M. (1992). Flexible planning: a key to the management of multiple innovations. In N. Bennett, M. Crawford, & C. Riches (Eds.), *Managing change in education: Individual and institutional perspectives*. London: Paul Chapman.

Wallace, M. (1996). Policy interaction and policy implementation. *Educational Management and Administration*, **24**(3), 263–275.

Wallace, M., & McMahon, A. (1994). *Planning for change in turbulent times: The case of multiracial primary schools*. London: Cassell.

Warwickshire County Council. (1991). *PRIDE (Process for the Review and Internal Development of Education) in our Schools: An Aid to Development Planning*. Warwick: WCC.

Weston, P., Barrett, E., & Jamison, J. (1992). *The quest for coherence: Managing the whole curriculum 5–16*. Slough: National Foundation for Educational Research.

Wise, A. (1983). Why education policies often fail: The huperrationalisation hypothesis. In V. Baldridge, & T. Deal, (Eds.), *The dynamics of organisational* change in education. Berkeley, Ca: McCutchan.

Curriculum Reform, Educational Change and School Improvement

GARY MCCULLOCH

University of Sheffield, UK

In many countries and throughout the modern era of educational change, curriculum innova-tion has been regarded as an essential strategy for educational reform. Yet, as Gary McCul-loch argues in this chapter, the positive impact of planned curriculum reform has been at best equivocal. In reflecting on the recent history of educational change in England and Wales he first considers curriculum reform in relation to the role of schools, and then the changing posi-tion of teachers. McCulloch focuses on the different strategies that have been devised to promote curriculum reform in this context and the tensions and contradictions that have developed as a result. In particular, he examines the strategies of 'independence' and 'absorption' in relation to specific curriculum initiatives in order to assess their relative impact both in terms of educational change and with respect to the more limited aim of school improvement. Later in the chapter he compares the espousal of teacher freedom' so characteristic of the reforms of the 1960s, with the emphasis on control and accountability in the reforms of the 1990s. McCul-loch concludes the chapter by assessing the relative importance of these issues for curriculum reform for school improvement.

Over the past forty years, in many different nations, reform of the school cur-riculum has been widely sought as a key instrument of educational change. Reform-ing the content and form of what is taught has often appeared to be even more important in this respect than other familiar approaches, such as reforming the organisation of the educational system. Since the 1950s, curriculum reform has been employed as a means towards a wide range of aims, often related explicitly to particular social and economic ends, but also to promote more specifically educational goals such as raising the standard of student achievement.

At various times, high hopes have been attached to the general strategy of planned curriculum reform. In the 1960s, for example, it was generally assumed that new curriculum ideas, if they were competently produced and thoroughly implemented, would be able to 'revolutionise' education (e.g. Kerr, 1968, p. 15). In spite of such hopes, however, over the longer term curriculum reform has gener-ally failed to generate educational change of a fundamental kind. In part, this failure reflects the nature of educational reform in general during the twentieth century. The structures and cultures of schooling have proven to be highly resilient to fundamental change, and what has appeared to be novel in principle or policy has commonly been interpreted in practice along familiar lines (see Fullan, 1991; McCulloch, 1994a; Tyack & Cuban, 1995). As Fullan remarks (1991, p. xiii), 'The forces reinforcing the status quo are systemic. The current system is held together in many different crosscutting ways. Confronting the isolationism and privatism

169

D. Hopkins (ed.), The Practice and Theory of School Improvement, 169-181.
© 2005 *Springer. Printed in the Netherlands.*

of educational systems is a tall order.' The problematic impact of educational reform on the practices and cultures of schools and education systems has been witnessed in the past generation in many different countries around the world (see e.g. Beare & Lowe Boyd, 1993; Carter & O'Neill, 1995).

Moreover, the school curriculum itself, for all the radical plans for change that have been attached to it, has been an especially conservative feature of schools and schooling, as it has embodied the cultural values inherited from the past much more than social and political aspirations for the future. In the United States, as Tyack and Cuban (1995, p. 7) have demonstrated, the curriculum has formed an ingrained part of the 'grammar of schooling', and has tended to encourage continuity rather than change. Similar characteristics have been evident in many other local and national contexts, for example in New Zealand, where the conservatism inherent in the curriculum has done much to thwart a number of reforming initiatives over the years (McCulloch, 1992). The historical experience of England and Wales is generally taken as an especially striking example of curricular continuity and inertia (e.g. Wiener, 1981; Goodson, 1982; Barnett, 1986; McCulloch, 1987a). Attempts in this particular context to modernise the school science curriculum and to discard its 'historical intellectual bric-a-brac' (Hailsham, 1963, p. 35) achieved only limited results over the longer term (see McCulloch, Jenkins, & Layton, 1985). So far as long-term educational change is concerned, therefore, the role of planned curriculum reform has been frustratingly elusive.

Within this more general framework of the problematic nature of educational and curricular change, the particular strategies devised for curriculum reform have also been highly influential in determining the structure and eventual impact of particular initiatives. Central to the debate over the kinds of strategy that should be adopted in this area has been an unresolved issue over what should be the role of schools and teachers. In an obvious sense, any reform of the curriculum would be dependent on the goodwill and ability of schools and teachers in carrying it out in practice, although even this basic point seems often to have been overlooked. More deeply, the issue revolves around the nature of the contribution to be made by schools and teachers in relation to the contribution of the State. Some initiatives towards curriculum reform have introduced new curricula within existing schools, while others have invented new kinds of schools with a particular kind of curriculum. So far as teachers are concerned, some initiatives have emphasised a leading role for teachers in curriculum development, while others have preferred to create a uniform national provision that minimises or undermines the active involvement of teachers beyond the implementation of decisions that have been arrived at elsewhere.

What are the implications of these strategic issues in curriculum reform for the nature of educational change and, in particular, for the potential role of curriculum reform in improving and changing the schools themselves? What are the advantages and the disadvantages of each of these strategies, and is it possible to draw any clear (even if interim) conclusions from the reforming experience of the

past forty years? The current chapter seeks to deal with these issues in depth, referring in particular to the curriculum reforms undertaken in England and Wales
since the 1950s.

INDEPENDENCE OR ABSORPTION?

The issue of whether to create new schools with a new or different curriculum or
to introduce new curriculum within existing schools is basically a choice between
'independence' and 'absorption'. This has become a familiar choice in the curriculum reforms that have taken place in England and Wales over the past forty
years. Both strategies offer some advantages, but each carries with it some notable
disadvantages when considered in terms of their potential for educational change
and school improvement. Initiatives that sought a measure of independence from
the constraints affecting the curriculum in existing schools have included the
development of secondary technical schools (STSs) in the 1940s and 1950s, and
the creation of city technology colleges (CTCs) and other specialist schools in the
educational reforms of the 1980s and 1990s. By contrast, an example of an initiative that has attempted to influence the curriculum of existing schools by being
introduced into them from outside would be the Technical and Vocational Education Initiative (TVEI) of the 1980s. These major initiatives may be taken together
to represent a paradigmatic example of a major tension in curriculum reform for
school improvement and educational change.

The STSs of the post-war years were intended to establish what was described
as an 'Alternative Road' to the academic and university-oriented curriculum of
the grammar schools. In the 'new secondary education' that developed following
the Education Act of 1944, they formed a key part of the strategy of the Ministry
of Education as it favoured three different kinds of secondary school for what
were seen to be three kinds of child. The grammar school would cater for the
academically able pupil who would go on to the sixth form and probably then into
university and the professions. The STSs were to be distinctive in 'selecting the
sphere of industry or commerce' as their 'particular link with the adult world'
(Ministry of Education, 1947, p. 48). The modern school would take the majority
of pupils at the age of eleven who had failed to be selected for either the grammar
school or the STS.

The Crowther Report, *15 To 18*, announced in 1959 that the secondary technical schools had encouraged a 'practical approach' to education, a real alternative
to 'the academic tradition which inspires and is embodied in our grammar schools
and universities' (Ministry of Education, 1959, p. 391). This 'practical approach',
it argued, was marked by a 'broad scientific curiosity' rather than by 'narrow
vocational interest' (Ministry of Education, 1959, p. 393). According to the
Crowther Report, it was especially important to promote this new kind of curriculum in order to encourage a larger proportion of boys and girls to stay on
longer at school and thus to allow the country 'to benefit fully from the intelligence of all its able boys and girls' (Ministry of Education, 1959, 391). The

independence of the STSs from grammar schools with their ingrained academic curriculum would make it possible to work out the details of this new curriculum with greater freedom.

In fact, however, this strategy of independence did not work out as well as had been hoped. Only a small minority of secondary school pupils ever went to an STS. By 1958 there were 279 STSs in England and Wales, with a total of 95,239 pupils, or 3.7 per cent of the total number of secondary school pupils. More than 40 per cent of local education authorities (LEAs) did not provide any STSs at all. In the 1960s they were swept away along with the grammar schools as comprehensive schools designed to cater for all abilities and aptitudes gained momentum (see McCulloch, 1989a, 1989b for detailed discussion of the STSs). The reasons for their disappointing impact are highly instructive towards a consideration of 'independence' as a curriculum strategy for educational change.

In spite of their lofty aspirations, the STSs were never fully understood by parents or even by the 'sphere of industry or commerce' that was supposed to be their 'particular link with the adult world'. On the one hand, they could not fully eradicate the image of the educationally inferior junior technical schools of earlier in the century, especially when they were often housed in the same premises, often with the same teachers. As *The Times Educational Supplement* pointed out (1960), 'Like everything else in technical education they were heirs to that long tradition of prejudice and suspicion by which the English have always supposed that technical studies mean dirty hands and the artisan.' This was a severe disadvantage to them when they were competing for pupils with well established grammar schools. On the other hand, if they attempted to become more 'respectable' by imitating the forms of curriculum that had been developed in the grammar schools they lost much of their distinctive rationale. A successful strategy of independence required a novel and clearly understood curriculum that would be attractive to the potential clientele of the schools, but in fact these remained elusive. What the STSs demonstrated in practice was that although they were separate institutions, they were far from independent of the ideals and assumptions that were widely held about different kinds of curriculum. In the end they were obliged either to conform to these received ideals, or to perish in obscurity.

Such problems meant that the STSs, which were in any case expensive to establish and maintain as separate institutions, were unable to gain widespread support. As an initiative in educational change, therefore, they were clearly a failure, and the 'grammar of schooling' emerged unscathed from their assault. They could not sustain an effective challenge to the dominance of the grammar school curriculum. On the other hand, where local circumstances permitted, there were a few STSs that were able to promote their own radical ideals. These schools, such as Gateway School in Leicester, Doncaster Technical High School, Leeds Central High School, and Cray Valley Technical High School for Boys in Kent, were each in their different ways successful and prominent 'pioneers' leading the way on the 'Alternative Road'. Even these schools, however, succeeded only at a local level and for a short period, and they did not persuade most grammar schools to imitate or incorporate aspects of their curriculum.

THE CASE OF THE TVEI

The Technical and Vocational Education Initiative of the 1980s adopted a different strategy towards the same goal of creating educational change through curriculum reform. Rather than establishing new schools with a different kind of
curriculum, it preferred the strategy of 'absorption', to promote technical and
vocational curricula within existing secondary schools. By the 1980s, the large
majority of state secondary schools in England and Wales were comprehensives,
but it was widely recognised that the academic, grammar school curriculum
continued to be dominant even within these changed organisational arrangements of schooling As Goodson (1988, p. 141) noted, 'As in the tripartite system,
so in the comprehensive system, academic subjects for able pupils are accorded
the highest status and resources. The triple alliance between academic subjects,
academic examinations and able pupils ensures that comprehensive schools provide
similar patterns of success and failure to previous school systems.' In the autumn
of 1976, the Labour Prime Minister, James Callaghan, had launched a self-styled
'Great Debate' on the need to relate education more fully to technology and
industry. This theme was taken up with increased vigour by the new Conservative
government after 1979, against a background of economic malaise and social and
industrial crisis. The TVEI was a major outcome of such concern.

The planned introduction of the TVEI was announced by the prime minister,
Margaret Thatcher, in November 1982. It was initially to constitute a pilot scheme
in technical and vocational education for fourteen to eighteen year olds, to be
organised not by the Department of Education and Science but by the Manpower
Services Commission, which was responsible to the Department of Employment.
The new scheme was unveiled amid high expectations of radical change that would
result in improved 'industrial strength' and 'economic prosperity' (Young, 1983).
On the other hand, it aroused strong suspicions among teachers and educators
that it would undermine educational interests and values. Such concerns were faithfully reflected by the *Times Educational Supplement* (1982) which, although it
acknowledged that 'something like this is a necessary counter-weight to the present
curricular domination exercised by O [Ordinary] and A [Advanced] level [examina-
tions]', nevertheless was strongly critical of the proposed use of the MSC 'to
intervene directly in the school curriculum and organization; that is in matters
which by statute are the responsibility of the local authorities'. Even so, the TVEI
was intended to develop through cooperation with LEAs and within the existing
comprehensive schools, and it was these aspects that proved to be of most
importance in determining the character of the initiative.

Pilot courses were started in September 1983 in fourteen local areas based on
projects put forward by interested LEAs and selected by the MSC. In subsequent
years more pilot projects were launched until in the summer of 1987 the TVEI
was extended from a pilot to a national scheme, involving every LEA in the country,
with a budget of £900 million over ten years (DOE / DES 1986). These major
developments entailed a broadening of the rationale of the programme in order
to make it more palatable for LEAs and schools. Although the extra resources

attached to the TVEI were themselves a powerful inducement to become involved, it was important also that the scheme itself was increasingly explained in terms of educational criteria rather than simply in vocational and economic terms (see e.g. McCulloch, 1987b on this process of consolidation). At the same time, in developing in the schools, the TVEI projects were influenced by the curricular constraints that operated within them. At times this led to more or less open resistance, and in some cases to sharp divisions between the TVEI 'enclave' and other less privileged sectors of the school (*TES*, 1988b). Although in some institutions the introduction of the TVEI was able to 'infiltrate and subvert' the academic and examinations-based nature of the curriculum (e.g. Nash, 1987), the TVEI was itself vulnerable to infiltration and subversion. In general, there was a high level of acceptance among teachers, who often, according to Helsby (1989, p. 78) 'found not only that they could accept the aims of TVEI, but also that they could become enthusiastic about developing them in practice'.

These processes of accommodation and consolidation within the schools underline the ambiguities underlying the strategy of 'absorption' as a means of educational change. On the one hand, involving the existing structures of established schools meant that the TVEI promised to influence the character of education for the mass of secondary school pupils around the country, as opposed to the small minority of pupils who had been directly involved in the STSs. On the other, it became exposed to resistance on the part of the schools and teachers, and also to more subtle forms of dilution or subversion. It should be observed that the strategy of 'independence' was also far from immune to such processes, as the STSs also illustrate. Moreover, the kinds of accommodation to the TVEI that were developed in the schools were certainly not always detrimental to the interests of the initiative, especially as it encouraged innovative practices on the part of the teachers involved, who found themselves 'manifestly in the vanguard of curriculum change' (Harland, 1987, p. 47). The extent to which these processes fostered overarching educational change of the kind that had been envisaged does, however, seem highly problematic. Again, as with the STSs, there is an important distinction to be drawn between the impact of curriculum reform on educational change at a systemic level, and its influence in improving, even galvanising, the practices of particular schools.

CTCS AND EDUCATIONAL CHANGE

The development of the city technology colleges (CTCs) after 1986 provide the third example that bears on these differing strategies in curriculum reform. Ignoring the earlier failure of the STSs, these were set up as specialist schools rather than as part of existing institutions. The new Secretary of State for Education, Kenneth Baker, announced that they would be government-funded, independent schools run by independent trusts, and that they would not be part of the LEA. It was hoped to establish, with the help of private sector sponsors, a network of about twenty such schools, each with 750 to 1,000 pupils, their prime purpose being 'to provide a broadly-based secondary education with a strong technological element thereby offering a wider choice of secondary school to parents in certain cities and a surer preparation for adult and working life to their children' (DES, 1986, p. 2). In his memoirs, Baker (1993, pp. 177–8) later made clear that he had been determined to avoid the CTCs being entrusted to what he regarded as 'reactionary' LEAs, especially those controlled by the Labour Party, and that the CTCs were intended to become 'beacons of excellence and exemplar models for what could be done in other state schools'.

As a curriculum initiative that was designed to encourage systemic educational change, however, the CTCs shared several problems in common with the STSs that had preceded them a generation before. The strategy of 'independence' on which they depended meant that they would only directly involve a very small proportion of secondary school and pupils. It also proved to be difficult to establish a clear and consistent public rationale for the CTCs as separate institutions. At the same time, it became clear that in most cases local industries were not as ready to invest in the new schools as had been assumed. Some of the colleges that were approved seemed to have little in common with the original technology-based notion of the enterprise. Indeed, in order to survive, the CTC initiative had to be revamped on a number of occasions, each change of tack effectively blurring the original concept (see McCulloch, 1994b for a detailed discussion of these developments).

Through their 'independent' positioning, the CTCs found themselves in conflict with the established schools in their areas, a conflict worsened because of the funding and resources that were allocated to them. Ninety million pounds of public money were earmarked to pay for up to 85 per cent of the capital cost of the colleges (Blackburne, 1988), with a few comprehensive schools being offered financial inducements in return for agreeing to become CTCs (e.g. *TES*, 1988a). The prospect of the CTCs effectively 'creaming off' the most able pupils and skilled teachers at the expense of neighbouring comprehensive schools also created strong concern, while many were critical of the CTC project for encouraging ideas of selection, choice, and competition between schools (e.g. Dale, 1989; Whitty, Edwards, & Gewirtz, 1993). At the same time, the CTCs cut across initiatives such as the TVEI which were operating in the comprehensive schools, often leading to a duplication of resources or even a deflection of potential support (Merson 1992, p. 13).

Despite these tensions in their relations with other schools and initiatives, moreover, the CTCs were also influenced by wider assumptions and values. Like the STSs before them, they failed to mount a coherent challenge to the academic nature of the secondary school curriculum, and again this was in part due to the fact that the CTCs were themselves influenced by liberal and academic values. Some began to develop as selective and 'elite' schools with a modified curriculum recognisably based on liberal and academic traditions. Parents of pupils at probably the best known of the CTCs, Kingshurst, seemed to regard them as 'the new grammar schools', providing opportunities for social mobility, rather than as radical assault on the curriculum usually associated with the grammar school (Walford & Miller 1991, p. 119; Gewirtz, Miller, & Walford, 1991, p. 183).

These contradictions in the CTC project were highlighted in disappointing results, in some cases in performance in examinations, and sometimes even in teaching in science and technology (Hughes, 1991; *TES* 1994b). Even so, there remained strong potential for at least some of the new colleges to establish themselves as pioneer schools in their right, and they continued to be given strong support by the Government in spite of widespread criticisms. Although only fifteen CTCs had been launched by 1992, the major White Paper *Choice And Diversity* (Department for Education, 1992, p. 45) declared the CTC programme to be 'an important means of stimulating innovation and excellence in education'. It also set out to establish similar programmes of 'technology schools' and 'technology colleges' in order to encourage specialisation and a greater diversity of provision. The tendency to encourage existing schools to change status and become technology schools and colleges continued in these initiatives, producing an interesting combination of the strategies of 'independence' and 'absorption', although criticisms of their exclusive and allegedly divisive character persisted (e.g. Hodges, 1996).

In general, then, each of the major initiatives recounted above, the STSs, the TVEI, and the CTCs reflect in their own different ways the highly problematic nature of curriculum reform as an instrument of system-wide educational change. They also suggest a wide range of possible effects of curriculum change when considered at the level of individual schools, whether the curriculum reform is being absorbed into the existing curriculum of established schools, or being developed independently in new purpose-built institutions. The character of the particular schools in generating particular kinds of curriculum change seems an important variable, and so also does the nature of the curriculum reform in affecting the character of the schools.

TEACHERS AND CURRICULUM REFORM

If the role of the schools has been important in helping to determine the impact of curriculum reforms, so too has been the role of teachers. Over the past forty years, however, strategies of curriculum reform have tended to develop from being 'teacher-led', as was most commonly the case in the 1960s, to being directed by the State, as has been the increasing tendency since the 1970s. This overall trend has had important implications for the character of curriculum reform as an instrument of educational change.

A tradition of teacher autonomy in the curriculum domain was celebrated in the 1960s as a distinctive characteristic of education in England and Wales. As had been accepted throughout the post-war years, it was not the role of the Ministry of Education, or of the State, to determine the curriculum, which was a matter to be left to the professionalism of teachers. This period has been described (Lawton, 1980, p. 22) as 'the Golden Age of teacher control (or non-control) of the curriculum'. It may be argued, as does Lawton, that teachers by and large failed to assert effective control over the curriculum, or to take responsibility for curriculum reform, when they had the opportunity to do so. The issue in this situation was how to make it possible to use curriculum reform as an instrument for educational change. The solution devised was to promote curriculum initiatives that would be 'teacher-led', but with the support and advice of other interested agencies. The problems involved in these initiatives again reflect the problematic nature of curriculum reform in relation to educational change.

The high hopes attached to teacher-led curriculum initiatives and projects in the 1960s were manifested particularly in the creation of the Schools Council for the Curriculum and Examinations, which was dedicated to the principle that 'schools should have the fullest possible responsibility for their own curriculum, which should be evolved by their own staff to meet the needs of their own pupils' (Jennings, 1985, p. 21). Attention was concentrated on the teacher as 'a professional who must be directly implicated in the business of curriculum renewal; not as a mere purveyor of other people's bright ideas, but as an innovator himself' (Schools Council, 1968, p. 10). Some civil servants and politicians were impatient with what Lord Hailsham, Minister for Science in the early 1960s, described (1961) as 'the traditional view held here that the content of curriculum and text books should not be a matter for the Ministry', but the orthodoxy remained that there was no alternative to 'the patient working out of syllabuses by teachers' (Weaver, 1961). As was pointed out by one leading official at the Ministry of Education in relation to the school science curriculum (Weaver, 1961),

> In our system there is no centre of power where differences can be resolved. In practice each science teacher bases his syllabus on a mixture of his own experience, the known views of the professional associations and of H.M. Inspectorate, and the examination syllabus chosen by the school. The points of change and growth are therefore likely to be found in the Science Panel of H.M. Inspectorate, in the Science Masters' Association, and in the Subject Panels of the several University examining bodies which in turn are subject to the influence of the SSEC [Secondary Schools Examinations Council]. It is not clear how the process is likely to be improved or accelerated by the intervention of outsiders, however powerful or distinguished.

This general outlook depended on the idea that where change was necessary, each school could 'work out its own scheme, depending on its own strengths and circumstances' (Porter, 1965).

In practice, however, it was soon found that the curriculum reforms of individual teachers and departments in particular schools would not by itself produce change throughout the education system. At the same time, support and advice for teacher-led curriculum reform, such as were produced by the Schools Council, tended often to have only a marginal influence. As one leading participant in these initiatives has confessed (Wrigley, 1985, p. 46), 'We were slow to see the abiding difficulty of effective innovation.' It was also true that despite the celebrations of teacher autonomy, there remained major constraints on curriculum reform and innovation such as the influence of teaching materials, teachers' own education and experiences, and often external examinations (Schools Council, 1973) which restricted teacher-led curriculum reform, in all but a few cases, to relatively minor interventions. Such problems meant that the hopes attached to teacher-led curriculum reform as a means of educational change failed to be realised. Once again, however, it is possible to draw a distinction between the failure of 'educational change' and the successes achieved in individual schools and specific circumstances by some of the teachers involved in these initiatives.

Since the 1970s, the dominant trend has been against teacher-led curriculum reform and in favour of increased control and prescription on the part of the State. Sir Keith Joseph, Secretary of State for Education in the early 1980s, dissolved the Schools Council and devised objectives for each main area of the curriculum, although he denied any intention of 'seeking to impose a centrally controlled curriculum, and to suppress the freedom to define the details of what is taught which had traditionally resided at local level' (Joseph, 1984, p. 147). The Education Reform Act of 1988, however, introduced a centrally prescribed National Curriculum. The key sponsor of this development, Kenneth Baker, was seeking thereby to promote 'radical change' in the education system in order for it to 'match the needs of twenty-first-century Britain' (Baker, 1993, p. 169) and to achieve higher pupil standards (Barber, 1996). In the context of the National Curriculum as it has developed in the 1990s, the key issue has become how far this systematic approach to curriculum reform can produce educational change of a kind that was not achieved by teacher-led initiatives, and what scope would remain for teachers to have an influence on the process.

The eventual impact of the National Curriculum remains to be seen, but it is already evident that its hopes for radical change are highly problematic. It is itself in some ways conservative in nature, based as it is on established school subjects in an arrangement reminiscent of the Secondary Regulations of 1904 (Aldrich, 1988; Goodson, 1988). It could also be read as a major initiative to rebuild the nation-state and to re-establish national identity and ideology, in response to fears of economic decline, cultural dissolution, and a loss of national power (Goodson, 1994, Ch. 7). At the same time, although all teachers in state schools were obliged to follow the prescriptions of the National Curriculum, at least in some cases they were able to do so in ways that allowed them to continue their existing practices (Helsby & McCulloch, 1996). There often appeared to be a mismatch between what the National Curriculum Orders intended and what was possible in the classroom, and indeed it has been suggested (Bowe & Ball, 1992, p. 102) that 'the substance of existing curriculum structures and the current institutional practices *may well not only remain in place but be reinforced by the way in which the National Curriculum is being introduced'.*

It was widely feared that the National Curriculum would destroy the capacity of teachers to contribute in their own ways towards curriculum reform. Some critics warned that the very notion of teacher professionalism was under direct threat (e.g. Gilroy, 1991), and that 'the national curriculum will take the place of local professional judgement of common provision, testing and schemes of work will confine pedagogy to what is conducive to publicly comparable performance, and the responsibility for curriculum experimentation, development, growth and change – the hallmark of educational professionalism – will no longer be the concern of teachers, schools and localities' (Simons, 1988, p. 80). However, at least to some extent it proved possible for teachers to retain scope for 'professional judgement', a notion that was defended in particular in a major review of the National Curriculum and its assessment under the chairman of the School Curriculum and Assessment Authority, Sir Ron Dearing (1994). It remains to be seen how far the National Curriculum was in fact 'back with the teachers' (*TES*, 1994a) and whether a more productive partnership between teachers and the State was becoming established (Barber, 1993), but the issue of how to promote educational change through curriculum reform is far from being settled.

CONCLUSIONS

The experience of the past thirty years, first from the Schools Council and the related initiatives of the 1960s, and presently in the context of the National Curriculum, indicate an unresolved debate over the respective roles of teachers and the State in relation to curriculum reform. The earlier emphasis on teacher-led initiatives seemed in practice too weak and unsystematic to produce fundamental educational change; the current reliance on State authority undermines the potential contribution of school-based curriculum innovation (see also e.g. Ribbins, 1993). Throughout the period, the hopes attached to curriculum reform as a means of radical educational change have been repeatedly disappointed although individual schools and teachers have exploited opportunities to improve and develop their own practices within this wider framework. Similar conclusions may be applied in relation to the successive curriculum initiatives involving secondary technical schools, the Technical and Vocational Education Initiative, and the city technology colleges over the past forty years.

The experiences of these differing strategies may suggest that the contradictions inherent in curriculum reform, the inbuilt conservatism of the 'grammar of schooling' and of inherited cultures, are too intractable to allow for radical educational change over the longer term. It may well be that hopes for 'educational change' through curriculum reform need to be tempered by a clearer focus on the problems and possibilities of this kind of reform as an instrument for the improvement of individual schools and teachers. As a prerequisite for such a reappraisal, however, it is unquestionably the case that there is an urgent need to review the hopes and expectations that are habitually attached to curriculum reform in the light of the historical experience that has been built up during the present century and especially during the recent, protracted, cycle of policy change.

REFERENCES

Aldrich, R. (1988). The National Curriculum: A historical perspective. In D. Lawton, & C. Chitty (Eds.), *The National Curriculum*, Papers 33 (pp. 21–33). Bedford Way, London: Institute of Education, University of London.

Baker, K. (1993). *The turbulent years: My life in politics*. London: Collins.

Barber, M. (1993). Teachers and the National Curriculum: Learning to love it? In M. Barber, D. Graham (Eds.), *Sense, nonsense and The National Curriculum* (pp. 10–25). London: Falmer.

Barber, M. (31 May, 1996). Why are you still smiling Kenneth, *TES*.

Barnett, C. (1986). *The audit of war*. London: Macmillan.

Beare, H., & Lowe Boyd, W. (Eds.). (1993). *Restructuring schools: An* international perspective on the movement to transform the control and performance of schools. London: Falmer.

Blackburne, L. (16 September, 1988). Newcomer worries the neighbours. *TES*.

Bowe, R., & Ball, S. (1992). *Reforming education and changing schools: Case studies in policy sociology*. London: Routledge.

Carter, D., & O'Neill, M. (Eds.). (1995). *Case studies in educational change: An international perspective*. London: Falmer.

Dale, R. (1989). The Thatcherite project in education: The case of the City Technology Colleges. *Critical Social Policy*, **27**, 4–19.

Dearing, R. (1994). *The National Curriculum and its assessment: Final report*. London: SCAA.

DES (Department of Education and Science). (1986). *A new choice of school: City Technology Colleges*. London: HMSO.

DOE / DES (Department of Employment / Department of Education and Science). (1986). *Working together – education and training*. London: HMSO.

Fullan, M. (1991). *The new meaning of educational change*. London: Cassell.

Gewirtz, S., Miller, H., & Walford, G. (1991). Parents' individualist and collectivist strategies at the City Technology College, Kingshurst. *International Studies in Sociology of Education*, **1**, 173–91.

Gilroy, P. (1991). The loss of professional autonomy. *Journal of Education for Teaching*, **17**(1), 1–5.

Goodson, I. (1982). *School subjects and curriculum change*. London: Croom Helm.

Goodson, I. (1988). *The Making of curriculum: Collected essays*. London: Falmer.

Goodson, I. (1994). *Studying curriculum*. London: Falmer.

Hailsham, Lord. (1961). *Letter to Sir David Eccles* (Minister of Education), 10 February, Ministry of Education papers, Public Record Office, ED.147/794.

Hailsham, Lord. (1963). *Science and politics*. London: Faber.

Harland, J. (1987). The TVEI experience: Issues of control, response and the professional role of teachers. In D. Gleeson (Ed.), *TVEI and secondary education: A critical appraisal* (pp. 38–54). Milton Keynes: Open University Press.

Helsby, G. (1989). Central control and grassroots creativity: The paradox at the heart of TVEI. In A. Harrison, S. Grettan (Eds.), *Education and training UK 1989: An economic, social and policy audit* (pp. 77–83). Newbury: Policy Journals.

Helsby, G. & McCulloch, G. (Eds.). (1996). *Teachers and the National Curriculum*. London: Cassell.

Hodges, L. (7 June, 1996). More special than all the rest? (Report). *TES*.

Hughes, C. (1991). CTCs technology teaching less than satisfactory (Report). *The Independent*, 18 October.

Jennings, A. (1985). Out of the secret garden. In M. Plaskow (Ed.), *Life and death of the schools council* (pp. 15–39). London: Falmer.

Joseph, Sir K. (1984). Postscript. *Oxford Review Of Education*, **10**(2), 147–8.

Kerr, J. F. (1968). *Changing the curriculum*. London: University of London Press.

Lawton, D. (1980). *The politics of the school curriculum*. London: Routledge and Kegan Paul.

McCulloch, G. (1987a). Curriculum history in England and New Zealand. In I. Goodson (Ed), *International perspectives in curriculum history* (pp. 297–327). London: Croom Helm.

McCulloch, G. (1987b). History and policy: The politics of the TVEI. In D. Gleeson (Ed.), *TVEI and secondary education: A critical appraisal* (pp. 13–37). Milton Keynes: Open University Press,

McCulloch, G. (1989a). *The secondary technical school: A usable past?* London: Falmer.

McCulloch, G. (1989b). City technology colleges: An old choice of school? *British Journal of Educational Studies*, **37**(1), 30–43.

McCulloch, G. (Ed.). (1992). *The school curriculum in New Zealand: History, theory, policy and practice*. Palmerston North: Dunmore Press.

McCulloch, G. (1994a). *Educational reconstruction: The 1944 Education Act and the 21st Century*. London: Woburn Press.

McCulloch, G. (1994b). *Technical fix? City Technology Colleges*. Leeds, University of Leeds School of Education, Education for Capability research group, occasional publication no. 7.

McCulloch, G., Jenkins, E., & Layton, D. (1985). *Technological revolution? The politics of school acience and technology in England And Wales since 1945*. London: Falmer.

Merson, M. (1992). The four ages of TVEI: A review of policy. *British Journal of Education and Work,* **5**(2), 5–18.

Ministry of Education. (1947). *The new secondary education* (Pamphlet No. 9). London: HMSO.

Ministry of Education. (1959). *15 To 18* (Crowther Report). London: HMSO

Nash, I. (1987). Taking the initiative to the most able students. *TES,* 4 September.

Porter, D. (1965). *Letter to C. Priestley,* 9 February, Department of Education and Science papers, Public Record Office, ED.147/896.

Ribbins, P. (1993). Telling tales of secondary heads: On educational reform and the National Curriculum. In C. Chitty (Ed.), *The National Curriculum: Is it working?* (pp. 24–79). London: Longman.

Schools Council. (1968). *Curriculum innovation in practice: A report by J. Stuart Maclure of the third international curriculum conference, 1967.* London: Schools Council.

Schools Council. (1973). *Pattern and variation in curriculum development projects.* London: Macmillan.

Simons, H. (1988). Teacher professionalism and the National Curriculum. In D. Lawton & C. Chitty (Eds.), *The National Curriculum* Papers 33 (pp. 78–90). Bedford Way, London: Institute of Education, University of London.

Threatened school. (26 February, 1960). *The Times Educational Supplement.* (TES), Leading article.

Bring back the DES. . . (19 November, 1982). *TES,* Leading article.

4m. offer to become CTCs. (5 August, 1988a). *TES,* Report.

Survey reveals classroom resentment and envy. (18 November, 1988b). *TES,* Report.

Back with the teachers. (11 November, 1994a). *TES,* Leading article.

High-cost CTCs fall short of excellence. (25 November, 1994b). *TES,* Lead report.

Tyack, D., &Cuban, L. (1995). *Tinkering toward utopia: A century of public school reform.* Cambridge Mass.: Harvard University Press.

Walford, G., & Miller, H. (1991). *City Technology College.* Milton Keynes, Open University Press.

Weaver, T. R. (20 February, 1961). *Note.* Ministry of Education papers, Public Record Office, ED.147/794.

Whitty, G., Edwards, T., & Gewirtz, S. (1993). *Specialisation and choice in urban education: The City Technology College experiment.* London: Routledge.

Wiener, M. (1981). *English culture and the decline of the industrial spirit, 1850–1980.* Cambridge: Cambridge University Press.

Wrigley, J. (1985). Confessions of a curriculum man. In M. Plaskow (Ed.), *Life and death of the schools council* (pp. 41–53). London: Falmer.

Young, D. (21 January, 1983). Equipping the young for the real world. *Times Higher Education Supplement.*

The Conduct of Inquiry on Teaching: The Search for Models more Effective than the Recitation

BRUCE JOYCE

EMILY CALHOUN
Booksend Laboratories, California, USA

During the past four decades Bruce Joyce has been inquiring into the impact of teaching on student learning. In particular he has been concerned to search out, research and describe those teaching strategies or models that accelerate the knowledge acquisition and learning potential of students. His exposition of the wide range of 'Models of Teaching' that do just that is well known. In this chapter Joyce together with Emily Calhoun summarise this long term and large scale enquiry by addressing four key issues. First, whether the research on teaching has produced knowledge on how to teach that is valid and generalisable. Second, they critique the role of recitation as the dominant mode of classroom transaction. Third, they describe a range of models that enhance the teacher's control of and impact on enhanced student learning. Finally, Joyce and Calhoun demonstrate that the self-conscious and strategic application of teaching models within the curriculum can compensate for the predictable disadvantages in terms of learning and achievement often associated with a student's gender, socioeconomic status and ethnicity. They conclude by calling for making the ongoing inquiry into teaching and learning the centrepiece of school improvement.

Let us start this essay with a quotation and an anecdote:

> The method of science, as stodgy and grumpy as it may seem, is far more important than the findings of science" (Carl Sagan – *The Demon-Haunted World*, p. 22).

Abraham Kaplan (1964) began his treatise on the conduct of inquiry in the social sciences by recounting the old story of a man who, on his way home one night, found a somewhat inebriated neighbor crawling around under a street lamp. Asking the neighbor what he was looking for, the answer came, "For my housekey. I dropped it." After some minutes of crawling around with his acquaintance without finding the key, our Good Samaritan thought to ask, "Where did you drop it?"

> The neighbor replied, pointing down a dark alley, "Down there."
> "Then why are we looking here?"
> "Cause there's light here, thass why."

Kaplan used his anecdote to characterize behavioral and social science research, maintaining gently that we look where we know how to look – in areas where we have a little light. The eventual critical questions may lie down the way in the

182

D. Hopkins (ed.), The Practice and Theory of School Improvement, 182-207.
© 2005 *Springer. Printed in the Netherlands.*

avenues that are still dark to us. Still, we have to look where we can, lighting, in the terms of the subtitle of Sagan's tract, the candles in the dark that come to hand.

Research on teaching is surely covered by Kaplan's analogy. For thousands of years philosophers, social scientists, and nearly every parent and teacher have conducted their inquiries under their own lampposts, crawling around and using the tools at hand. Some of our seekers have been equipped with broad philosophical systems and have searched for answers to massive and profound questions. A few exceptionally bold thinkers try to decide what will be the best kinds of teaching for entire societies – driven by the motivation to improve or even change the very society of which they themselves are a tiny part.

Others, armed with observational and experimental tools, have focused on efficiencies, asking what kind(s) of teaching will be the best to achieve a given, relatively narrow focus, such as the quickest way to teach children how to count or how to learn a foreign language.

Some have focused on defined populations of students, seeking methods for the quick or the slow, for the deaf or the blind, for females or males, the rich or the poor. A considerable number have concentrated on subject matters and curriculum areas: reading, writing, mathematics, science, social science, and the education of the body.

Practically everyone in the society conducts their own inquiries on teaching. They come to the task with the personal knowledge derived from trying to rear the young – the need to transmit the culture will get you, willy nilly, into teaching. Almost every adult has tried to learn how to rear their own children, coach the child next door, teach a Sunday School class, or help a child trying to learn to swim. In doing these things, nearly everyone either imitates people they have seen engaging in the same sort of activity, or they invent a teaching method on the spot. The informal inquiries of the general population are not usually reported in refereed journals, but popular magazines contain large quantities of advice about how you can raise children, change your own personality and capture members of the opposite sex – how you can teach yourself. Sometimes these home-grown methods become the stimulus for lines of formal inquiry. A case in point is the study of mnemonics, where a basketball players' book on memorizing (Lorayne & Lucas, 1974) included strategies that have been studied and elaborated by the great Pressley-Levin Team (Pressley, Levin & Delaney, 1982).

Taking stock of the yield of those of these inquiries that have been buttressed by empirical research to test their rationales and effectiveness, we can ask, at any given point in time, what we know. Have we discovered an array of ways of teaching that can be used for broad or narrow purpose with reasonable expectation that they will work?

(Substantive footnote – Work, in this context, means to work well in comparison with the culturally normative methods of teaching that everyone in the society "knows" – those methods that have been transmitted to all of us, whether laymen or professionals, because we are members of this society. More about that subject later as we consider what is culturally normative and how the assessment of innovative educational models relies on comparison with the normative approaches to teaching.)

DEBATE: IS THERE A SCIENCE-BASED KNOWLEDGE ABOUT TEACHING?

There would be little point in writing this essay were scholars generally agreed that there is or isn't a formal knowledge base about teaching, one developed through empirical research. But agreement there isn't.

Arguing that there is a knowledge base, Nate Gage (1982) has noted that the concern that we not accept hypotheses on inadequate evidence – the Type A error – has lead us to what he called "a massive Type B error", underestimating the size of the knowledge base and its firmness. Recently, addressing consistency of findings, he commented, "What these meta-analyses show is that many generalizations in education do hold up across many replications with high consistency. That high consistency across replications has occurred despite the fact that replications inevitably differ in the person studied, in the measurement methods used, in the social contexts involved and in other ways." (Gage, 1997)

To some, Gage and other scholars who favor empirical research have been persuasive, but to a large number of scholars they have not. To illustrate, just four years ago *American Educational Research Journal* was built around a large-scale meta-analysis by Wang, Haertel and Walberg (1993) who, also arguing the affirmative, contended directly that there is considerable knowledge about teaching and presented synopses of a number of lines of inquiry to buttress their argument. However, a dozen respondents claimed that those reviews were not persuasive, that there is not much on which we can rely. In fact, some reviewers of the Wang, Haertel and Walberg piece actually contended that the manuscript should not be published because the authors had not demonstrated, despite their citation of literally hundreds of studies, that there *is* a knowledge base. Some questioned whether scientific work *can* generate a knowledge base in education. These writers are not the only skeptics who are now active. Contemporary journals and presentations at the American Educational Research Association give considerable voice to epistemological positions that challenge classical paradigms of research.

CAN THERE BE A KNOWLEDGE BASE? OR, IS POSITIVISM DEAD?

The programmatic, experimental paradigm is challenged from a number of points of view.

A number of contemporary scholars question whether the nature of humankind doesn't actually preclude the development of prescriptive knowledge about teaching. As Bereiter (1994) and Phillips (1995) have pointed out, some of these argue that knowledge is so personal and ephemeral that the very search for common understanding is fruitless. In a different vein, some persons contend that the products of science are political constructions and represent the consensus of an elite and, further, a male, European elite, rather than unbiased representations of reality. They suggest that a rather different representation would occur were research conducted by persons of lesser status and education and by women and non-Europeans (see some of the essays in Hollingsworth & Sockett, 1994). This position turns out to be a political, as well as an epistemological one, as some of those same writers see the conduct of educational research from a class-war perspective and suggest that for university research personnel to conduct studies in schools is, as such, denigrating to school personnel.

Other skeptics suggest that the empirical paradigms that have served us so well in the "hard" sciences and engineering will be relatively useless in the social arenas, including education, because clinical experience is personal and unique. They argue for the abandonment of faith in classic research and ask for a "paradigm shift," toward the accumulation of accounts of personal knowledge of practitioners rather than the conduct of traditional programmatic research. In addition, some argue that the view of experimental science as sets of inductive programs is an inaccurate stereotype – that intuition and personal vision is far more a part of scientific advancement than are structured inquiries and, therefore, that the products of structured inquiry are not the place to look for knowledge, which is actually a product of insight rather than, say, fractional factorial designs. The extreme skeptics actually argue that the classic paradigm has run its course in the "hard" sciences.

A less extreme position, than those above, admits the possibility that empirical research can generate knowledge, but holds that individual learning styles, compounded by differences between cultures and genders, are so different that good teaching, should it be discovered, will be highly particularized – what is sauce for the goose will not be sauce for the gander. The most drastic implication is that what works for one person cannot be said to work for another because we all are so different from each other (Hollingsworth & Sockett, 1994). Thus, knowledge will be found situationally, in the interaction between individual teachers and individual students.

Similarly, some (Edelsky, 1990) argue, speaking primarily of the language arts, but with implications for all symbolic learning, that such variables as learning outcomes need to be seen in context, so that standard measures are invalid. Essentially, from this position, we could not use the same criteria of effectiveness in reading across studies.

A related argument is the rather ancient one about the relative value of qualitative and quantitative methodologies for carrying on research. We regularly meet the argument that the rich nature of human interaction is such that it cannot be captured in quantitative abstractions, and that only qualitative methodologies are worth pursuing. Again, at an extreme, some go so far as to argue that one cannot mix quantitative and qualitative methodologies, presumably even if they produced the same results.

So, as we assess formal, quantitative research on teaching, we do so in an environment that is far less settled as to the value of that research than we might like. Consider the arguments we have mentioned thus far:

- Knowledge is personal and time-bound specific – generalizable knowledge is not possible.
- Knowledge is situational – generalizable knowledge is unlikely.
- Knowledge is contextual – only qualitative methods can capture reality.
- Knowledge can be generated empirically and quantitatively, but the paradigms that have been used are wrong or are very limited.
- Knowledge can be generated empirically and quantitative methods can be used, but a social elite has been conducting the research and the findings would be different if non-Europeans and non-males conducted the research.
- Quantitative empirical paradigms of the classic sort can produce knowledge but have not – the findings to date are not persuasive.

Enough education professors take one or another of these positions, that it is small wonder, that the studies conducted by people who believe that the cranky old classic paradigm *has* produced replicable and useful knowledge, have not been disseminated thoroughly.

Thus, as we continue this essay, assessing the results of studies conducted by classic methods and which relied largely but not entirely on quantitative methods, we realize that we are speaking mainly to those who believe there is a scientific method, albeit imperfect, applicable to education.

OUR WORK AS PROFESSIONALS

Regardless of the debates over epistemology, education is carried on daily and teachers need to know whether they are on their own or whether something has been learned that they can rely on.

So, what should we do? Will we tell the novice teacher, or the experienced teacher for that matter, that we know nothing and that they must construct knowledge solely from their own experience and that what they learn is personal? Will we tell them that we know a little and that of limited applicability? Or will we tell them that, while much is to be done, we know some things that are seriously worthy of their consideration? Shall we go so far as to say that, if they are without some portions of knowledge they may disadvantage their students? In other words, can we build preservice or inservice knowledge on an admittedly partial but critical base?

For the last thirty-five years, we have been wrestling with this question, examining studies of teachers in action, reading philosophies and, most assiduously, digging into programmatic lines of research on specific ways of designing educational environments. We have limited capability and are humble by necessity. We agree both with Sagan's statement about the role of science and with Kaplan's conception of how it proceeds. We resist the notion that new and better paradigms will wipe out progress generated by the older ones. New paradigms may well generate new progress, which is the purpose of all serious sciencing, but to deny that the play of the intelligence of our predecessors has been worthwhile is quite another matter.

True, we are stuck with the lamps we have and the ideas that have been created under them. Research on teaching has been desperately underfunded for many years and important areas have been studied less than we would like. The research community has not yet developed a structured discipline for research on teaching, and many scholars have had to erect their own conceptual frameworks in order to proceed.

The lamps are not impossibly few or far between, however, and the more we search around under them the brighter they glow. For our part we believe that there *is* knowledge about teaching and that it *is* communicable. We have our candles in the darkness.

The current educational system in the United States leaves 30–40 percent of the students unable to read and write effectively enough to profit from secondary education. If we believe, and we do, that we have knowledge that can dramatically change this picture and greatly increase the efficiency of education, do we with- hold that knowledge until the epistemological positions and political arguments have been settled? We think not.

Throughout the rest of this essay we'll try to discuss how different bits of knowledge have been found as well as what they are.

Sequentially, we'll consider four topics, defined as questions:

- Do we know anything? Have the inquiries into teaching generated anything more effective than generally-accepted cultural knowledge about teaching? We'll begin with two field studies.
- What is the role of the recitation pattern in teaching both as a social norm and as a baseline against which ideas about teaching are tested?
- Have any reliable models of teaching emerged from the inquiries into teaching?
- In comparison with normative schooling, how effective are the developed models of teaching with respect to gender, socioeconomic status and ethnicity?

Caveats

These questions will be considered in terms of the social system of the United States only. There is important research on teaching in many societies and an international community is gradually developing.

However, we know only the social and educational system of the United States well enough to carry on meaningful discussions of teaching in a social context. Even when confining the essay to the social context of the United States and research carried out there, we cannot hope to cite all the research that is relevant to the questions that will be explored. We will attempt to provide bibliographic references that will enable anyone sufficiently motivated to track our path and assess our conclusions.

DO WE KNOW ANYTHING?: SOME WAKE-UP CALLS

Are there approaches to teaching that generate effects on student learning beyond those achieved by culturally-normative approaches to teaching? The lamppost under which we will scrabble around first are field studies where educational models are tested in the areas of reading and writing. Why begin with reading and writing? First, they are accepted as core areas of the American school. No one doubts their importance. All schools try to generate workmanlike reading and writing. Whatever may be the disagreements in other areas, the public has a deep interest in literacy. Second, teachers have considerable experience in the teaching of reading and writing and, thus, have had plenty of opportunity to develop skill in those areas. We can assume that they are as good as they can make themselves. Third, through preservice and inservice education and the efforts of commercial publishers, American teachers have been given more help in those areas than in any others.

We will begin with "field research" because it speaks more sharply to the existence of an applicable research base than do studies conducted in laboratory settings only or in classrooms that have been temporarily transformed into laboratories. Essentially, we will ask whether research-based school-improvement programs have been able to positively impact student learning of reading and writing in schools and school districts.

Field Studies in Inner-city Elementary Schools

In American society, the schools teach about two-thirds of the students to read and write effectively enough that they can manage the tasks of adult economic life, and about one-third are prepared to profit from some form of complex higher education. Many others attend post-secondary classes to learn vocation-related skills, as how to handle a large truck rig. In many inner-city schools only a small percentage of students learn to read well enough to extract meaning from the local newspaper.

The primary school years are critical, for very few students who have not learned to read competently by the end of grade three ever manage to do so later on. The American society has been so concerned about low achievement in the cities that it has provided resources to inner city schools in the form of programs to allow teachers to work intensively with small groups of children in what are called Title I (Chapter I) and Special Education programs. On the whole, these "categorical programs" have not changed the achievement picture materially.

Is there enough systematic knowledge about teaching to enable a larger percentage of children to learn to read better in those critical primary grades?

Consider the ten years of studies by Robert Slavin and his colleagues at Johns Hopkins University (Slavin & Madden, 1995). Drawing on research on the effects of tutoring and some aspects of research on the teaching of reading, Slavin and his colleagues developed a program named *Success for All*, after its objective, which was to ensure that all students had success in academic learning in the primary grades. Their early research was in inner-city schools of Baltimore, Maryland, schools considered unlikely settings for successful programs. Subsequently they have implemented the program and studied its effects in about 50 other schools, nearly all in inner-city settings. Slavin and his associates are assiduous, careful researchers, comparing student learning in schools using *Success for All* with student learning in comparable schools and even examining levels of intensity within the *Success for All* program for their effects.

While it would be too much to say that *Success for All* reaches every child and teaches him or her to be a powerful reader, the aspiration for the program has been largely fulfilled. Nearly all of the young students learn to read and most of them learn to read quite well. The achievement picture is not unlike that of schools in middle class suburbs, but better in that there are fewer really poor readers in *Success for All* schools than in most suburban schools.

We interpret the work of Slavin and his colleagues as evidence that there is knowledge about teaching that comes from research and enhances teaching beyond the effects of sheer teaching experience and non-technical cultural wisdom. Essentially, Slavin and his associates teach schools to behave differently than most do and the results are dramatic changes in the number of kids who learn to read.

A Field Study in High-achieving Suburban Elementary Schools

In recent years the study of learning to write has been submitted to exhaustive inquiry, and researchers for the National Assessment of Writing Progress (see NAEP, 1992) have conducted large-scale investigations of student progress in quality of writing with good-sized samples of students drawn from various types of school districts across the United States. These studies provide an increasingly accurate picture of the magnitude of year-to-year growth in students' ability to focus and organize pieces of writing, establish and support themes or story lines, and the complexity and correctness of the mechanics they use. Data are collected by providing the students with stimulus material, prompting them to write in several genre, and submitting the products to a content analysis. The grade four writing becomes a baseline against which the writing of the older students can be compared. When the writing of eighth grade students is compared with that of fourth grade students, the mean eighth grade score is about at the 62nd percentile of the fourth grade distribution and the variances of the grade four and grade eight writing are similar. The grade twelve mean is about at the 72nd percentile of the fourth grade distribution. Smaller studies making grade-to-grade comparisons (fifth with fourth, sixth to fifth, and so on) and studies following students for several years, confirm that the annual growth at the mean is about at a rate of three or three and a half percentile points. Even in traditionally "high achieving" suburban school districts, an annual gain of five percentile points at the mean is normal.

A growing community of researchers is attempting to generate models for the teaching of writing with the purpose of increasing several dimensions of quality.

In the nine elementary schools of a midwestern town, we will call University

Town (see Joyce & Calhoun, 1996), all the teachers studied an adaptation of an inductive model of teaching (for a description, see Joyce and Weil, 1996) to help students analyze the devices used by published writers and incorporate those devices into their writing.

For many years standard tests have indicated that this town is one of the highest-achieving in the nation, with means in all the curriculum area in the high sixtieth percentiles and even higher. About 60 percent of the graduates go to four-year colleges and nearly all the rest obtain some higher education. The teachers work in favorable conditions, supported by aides, rich instructional resources, even district-provided resources for their personal staff development, the resources of a major state university, and are accustomed to working with students who, in cultural terms, are relatively compliant and "easy to teach". Those teachers have had the opportunity to practice their skills in a setting where relatively high standards of achievement prevail.

What happened when they studied a research-based approach to the teaching of reading and writing and learned to use it?

Achievement prior to the intervention: Judging from the results of the analyses conducted during the 1991–92 school year over writing samples collected from all the fourth, sixth and eighth grade students (N = 1200), the children in the University Town schools were progressing at an effect-size rate of about .14, or almost half-again the national average. This translates to a gain, at the mean, of about five percentile points. Thus, in 1991–92 the average sixth grade student on the dimension "Focus and Organization" was at about the 60th percentile of the fourth grade distribution.

Achievement as a product of the inductive approaches to teaching and learning:

Grade Four Expository Writing. Table 1.0 compares the means for the two periods (Fall, 1992 and Spring, 1993) for the three dimensions for which quality was assessed (Focus/Organization, Support, and Grammar and Mechanics).

Effect sizes were computed for Fall and Spring scores: for Focus/Organization, 2.18; for Support, 1.53; and for Grammar/Mechanics, 1.37.

All these are several times the effect-sizes calculated for a year's gain for the national sample (0.10) and several times the annual baseline gains (ES = 0.14)

Table 1: Mean Grade Four Scores on Expository Writing for Fall, 1992 and Spring, 1993

	Dimensions		
Period	Focus/Org.	Support	Grammar/Mech.
Fall			
Mean	1.6	2.2	2.11
SD	0.55	0.65	0.65
Spring			
Mean	2.8	3.2	3.0
SD	0.94	0.96	0.97

estimated from the 1991–1992 study in University Town. For Focus and Organization, the differences are so great that, in the Spring, the average student reached the top of the Fall distribution, something that does not happen nationally during the entire time from grades four to twelve.

To illustrate the magnitude of the gain, Table 2.0 compares the mean results for the Spring fourth-grade assessment to the Fall sixth-grade results.

The fourth grade students ended their year substantially ahead of where the sixth grade students were at the beginning of the year. They also finished the year with higher scores than where the eighth grade students began the year on the Focus/Organization (Grade 8 mean = 2.32) and Support dimensions (Grade 8 mean = 2.95) and were close on the Grammar/Mechanics dimension (Grade 8 mean = 3.32).

Studies over the following years indicate that the district continues, annually, to generate gains in quality of writing several times their annual gain prior to the initiative in language arts.

Interpretation

The two cases lead us in the same direction. In Baltimore and subsequently, in other settings, Slavin and his colleagues took on an extremely tough problem and demonstrated that the knowledge exists to make it yield. In University Town, the effectiveness of a highly successful school district was enhanced substantially when the teachers studied a research-based model for the teaching of writing. Other, similar cases can be cited (Joyce & Calhoun, 1996; Joyce & Weil, 1996; Joyce & Showers, 1995), but the other questions we want to address beckon us.

THE RECITATION: CULTURAL WISDOM AND EDUCATION

Several times we have mentioned culturally-normative teaching and alluded to the role of normative practice in research on teaching and it is time to deal with it here.

Table 2: Mean Grade Four Spring, 1993, Scores on Expository Writing Compared with the Mean Grade Six Scores from Fall, 1992

	Dimensions		
	Focus/Org.	Support	Grammar/Mech.
Grade Four Spring Mean	2.8	3.2	3.0
Grade Six Fall Mean	2.11	2.90	2.87

Essentially, philosophers and empirical researchers have to face the fact that they are not the only seekers. Lots of people would like to generate high quality education. Undoubtedly many do so every day, but their efforts are not written down and do not become part of cumulative knowledge. As someone remarked the other day, one of the frustrating things about death is that each time someone passes on, we lose a living bibliography of life experience and have no way to retrieve it. In the world of teaching we lose teaching models we never knew we had.

Most relevant to us in present context, is that the entire society tries to learn to teach. Socialization is inseparable from culture itself. Long before there were written records, humankind gathered itself into little societies, learning essential and significant patterns of behavior just by figuring out how to live together in groups. Each little group proceeded to invent all sorts of things to enhance their quality of life, including ways of passing their cultural patterns along to the young. Those ways of teaching became an important part of the culture.

Over time, institutions devoted to aspects of socialization were developed and, thus, schools came into existence. Within them patterns of education were developed and became known to all of us in the society. Those patterns were (and are) how we teach. *Everybody* knows how to use those patterns. They are transmitted along with the rest of the culture and become part of us.

From the middle of the 20th century, researchers began increasingly formal ways of studying how teachers normally behave and, by the late 1980s, the research community had formal knowledge that the "recitation" was the normative teaching method in the United States. Essentially, students are presented with material through textbooks or another medium or through lectures, or laboratory or field experiences. The teacher then questions the students over the material they have been exposed to, clarifying points and providing the students with feedback about their responses. With the exception of a small percentage of teachers, questioning and then responding to student answers is the mode observed in American schools. In Bellack's terms, the teacher would solicit answers, the students would respond to the questions and the teacher would react to the student responses. In some studies, such as Bellack's (1962) investigation of secondary teachers of the social studies, *no* other pattern was observed. Hoetker & Ahlbrand (1969) and Sirotnik (1983), after analyzing dozens of studies of American classrooms, confirmed "the persistence of the recitation", and Goodlad and Klein (1970) reported that it persisted even in schools where considerable resources had been expended to disseminate very different approaches to teaching. Over the last fifty years, repeated studies of teachers' educational philosophies confirmed the position of most, that highly direct teaching, with consistent questioning and prompt feedback, was the best way to teach.

We have little doubt that the dominance of the recitation is a broadly cultural phenomenon, rather than an invention by a subculture of professional educators. Essentially, it is a major part of the process of socialization in American culture.

A mother asks her infant baby, "Who's that?"

"Da," replies the child.

"Oh, wonderful, sweetie. Yes, that's Da. Oh, George, she's so wonderful! She's *talking!*"

"Now, who's *that?*" chimes in Da, pointing to the dog.

"Da!" shouts the baby.

"No, dear, that's Rover, the Wonder Dog. Now, let's say 'Rover' together."

These good-hearted folks are winding up to spend innumerable hours quizzing their child. Most schools will provide them with many fine opportunities in the form of homework assignments requiring a little reading followed by a set of questions to be answered.

The recitation pattern is massively institutionalized in the conduct of schooling. An enormous testing industry questions children and lets the schools know whether their students can read, know science and so on. Testing by asking students to write is regarded suspiciously as "subjective". Most of the public, and many teachers, believe that qualities such as intelligence can be measured by brief quizzes and that the results are fixed; the quiz identifies a quality that cannot be improved.

The recitation appears in a surprising number of adult activities. We get driving licenses by answering questions and following directions. Our tax forms are questionnaires. The armed forces use a one-hour test to classify us for training.

The media loves the extension of the recitation into adult life. Televised "quiz shows" are enormously popular, as are talk shows, which are essentially public interviews filled with short-answer questions about, incidentally, what are often private matters. Sports commentators quote statistics (asking and answering their own questions in the manner of the skilled teacher) to the point where it's sometimes difficult to find out who's playing or winning the game being shown. Adults as well as children gain status by knowing the names of rock groups, singers and popular songs and demonstrating that knowledge in much the same way that they sang the ABC song in kindergarten.

In interaction, we are, to a substantial degree, a "recitation culture".

Seekers of innovative models of teaching generate two types of inquiry. The philosophical reflect on the culture and seek models that will change it in ways more healthy for both society and for children. The philosophers are trying to create new cultural processes which, put in place, will pull child development and societal interaction in new directions. They do not feel that the recitation is a good model for their purpose. The psychological, including therapists, seek models that will accomplish the tasks of teaching and learning more effectively than the recitation, used alone.

Both philosophical and psychological creators of innovative models of teaching have to deal with the cultural dominance of the recitation. Both philosophers and psychologists have to learn whether they have, in fact, created a model that will accomplish their purpose better than the recitation would.

The cultural norm of teaching is the massive control group against which all new models will be tested. We selected the two case studies in the previous section exactly because very few people will believe there is an educational knowledge base worth considering unless that knowledge, applied on a large scale, is demonstrated to make a difference in the critical assigned functions of the school – teaching reading and writing. Not just the psychologists, but the philosophers as well, will not be persuaded unless at least some of them develop ways to help students read and write better, whatever else of worth is accomplished.

As an aside, the recitation is so ingrained that much of the public is suspicious of any model of teaching that does not resemble the recitation. However powerful it may be, a model for teaching reading will arouse negative effect if it does not include provision for the children to be quizzed over the letters and their sounds. A mathematics curriculum that does not include the recitation of the "3 plus fives" will have hard going. Any alternative model has to be convincingly superior to have a chance of dissemination.

As we proceed to the next topic the recitation will be always present.

THE STUDY OF TEACHING: HAVE RELIABLE MODELS EMERGED?

Two empirical paradigms have been used in the attempt to generate and test teaching models that can be said to affect student learning either in new directions or to a greater degree than the dominant cultural model:

- Naturalistic studies of teachers and schools, particularly studies seeking to identify the characteristics of the most effective.
- Experimental studies where philosophical or psychological positions about the nature of humankind and how it learns have been operationalized and studied.

Although we have great respect for the creators of naturalistic research: what Gage called "process product" research, this knowledge base will not be assessed in this essay. We believe the yield has been substantial and is largely being ignored at present, which is a great mistake. We refer the reader to the handbooks of research on teaching, whose chapters have given considerable attention to the naturalistic studies. The chapters by Brophy and Good (1986) are useful, along with the synthesis by Medley (1977).

The product of the experimental paradigm will be the subject of this section of the paper.

Assessing experimental research on teaching involves taking into account a number of complexities. The sciences of education, as the other social sciences, are relatively immature and do not possess the conceptual frameworks that have been created through discourse in the more mature scientific communities and undergo revision as progress is made. Essentially, educational researchers work under their own lamposts, creating conceptual structures as they go. In the absence of a highly disciplined community, many educational theorists are often unaware of the frameworks being developed by their colleagues and, thus, cannot easily borrow from one another's ideas and findings. Currently, they also labor in an environment where some of the advocates of the multiple concepts of constructivism, socioculturalism and postmodernism have created an intellectual climate that is not always friendly to discourse with people who carry on experimental work. Nonetheless, from under the various lampposts various degrees of progress are being reported as the makers of educational models generate studies.

Scanning the research we have located, we have imposed a rough sort of conceptual structure by grouping the emerging models of teaching into four families: the social, personal, information processing and behavioral. The bases for the classification are the emphases put on particular dimensions of humans and how they learn. However, that a family has an emphasis does not mean that it eschews other dimensions that may be more central to another family. For example, scholars of cooperative learning place great emphasis on the social nature of humans and the effects of synergy on learning, but that does not mean that they are not interested in how students process academic content. Scholars of mnemonics are very much concerned with how students process information, but that emphasis does not prevent them from being interested in the self-esteem of students or whether they are self-actualizing, areas that are central in the thought of personalists.

To grasp the research one has also to deal with the wonderful variety in the purposes of the model builders. Some create methods that are directed at objectives that are hardly touched in today's schools, while others aim directly at objectives that have been accepted for thousands of years.

In common, despite their differences in emphasis, all these folks have to contend with our friend, the recitation. If they wish to test their model in classrooms, they have to teach teachers to use something (their model) other than the recitation. Weak implementation will kill a study. Also, inevitably, they have to compare the learning from their model with learning generated by the normative modes of rearing and educating children. The well-known complexities of conducting research in educational settings haunt all of them and affect the quality of their studies. Finally, when we assess the bodies of work they have produced, we have to try to understand the nature and magnitude of their progress. Their first tries may produce weak effects, but they may improve their model through their inquiry. Averaging the effects of all their studies may underestimate the strength they have developed later.

Here, we will look at just a few of the lines of research, asking the question, "Does it appear that a knowledge base is being created under some of those lampposts?" We'll look at several models that contrast sharply with one another.

Inquiry into information-processing models

Quite a number of models of teaching are designed to increase students' ability to process information more powerfully. These include methods for presenting information so that students can learn and retain it more effectively by operating on it more conceptually, systems that assist memorization and teach students how to organize information for mastery, models to teach students to collect and organize information conceptually and ones to teach students to use the methods of the disciplines, to engage in causal reasoning and to master concepts. We'll look at a line of inquiry designed to teach students to memorize more efficiently and one designed to teach students to think scientifically.

Mnemonics. Mnemonics is a good place to start, because the model-builders in mnemonics attempt to teach students learning skills that can be applied to a range of school subjects. In many of their studies they measure outcomes of the sort that make the recitation popular.

Although research on memorization and mnemonic strategies has been conducted for more than one hundred years, until a few years ago most of the yield for school practice offered few and very general guidelines, such as advice about when to mass and when to distribute practice. Little research had been conducted on the learning of school subjects. In the mid-1970s a productive line of work was begun by Atkinson (1975) at Stanford University – a line that has been greatly extended by Pressley and Levin at the Universities of Western Ontario and Wisconsin. They have developed a series of systems for organizing information to promote memory and have given particular, although not exclusive attention to one known as the "link-word" method. Atkinson applied the method during experiments with computer-assisted instruction in which he was attempting to increase students' learning of initial foreign-language vocabularies. He experimented with what he called "acoustic" and "imagery" links. The first was designed to make associations between foreign pronunciations and the sounds of known English words. The second was used to make the connection vivid (Atkinson, 1975). In one early study the link-word method produced as much learning in two trials as the conventional method did in three. The experimental group learned about half as many words more than the control group and maintained the advantage after several weeks. He also found that the method was enhanced when the students supplied their own imagery.

Further developmental work included experiments with children of various ages and across subjects. Using a link word system in Spanish vocabulary learning, second and fifth grade children learned about twice the words as did children using rote and rehearsal methods (Pressley, 1977). In later work with Levin & Miller (1981), Pressley employed a "pictured action" variant of the method with first and sixth grade children, who acquired three times as much vocabulary as did control groups. With Pressley and Dennis-Rounds (1980) he extended the strategy to social studies information (products and cities) and learned that students could transfer the method to other learning tasks with instruction. Pressley and Dennis-Rounds (1980) found that primary school students could generate sentences to enhance memorization. The results were three times as great as for students using their own methods. Similar results were found with kindergarten and preschool children (Pressley et al., 1982). With Levin and Miller (1981) the work was successfully extended to vocabulary with abstract meanings. Levin and his colleagues

(1993) have also extended the application to abstract prose and conceptual systems from the disciplines.

It was important to learn whether better "natural" memorizers, with practice, develop their own equivalent methods. Pressley, Levin, & Ghatala (1984) asked whether students, with age and practice, would spontaneously develop elaborated methods for memorizing material and found that very few did. The better performers had developed more elaborate methods than the majority, who used rote-rehearsal methods alone. However, the newly-developed mnemonic methods enhanced learning for the best memorizers, as well as for the others. Hence, it appears that the method or an equivalent one can be very beneficial for most students.

The consistency of the findings is impressive. The link-word method appears to have general applicability across subject matters and ages of children (Pressley, Levin, & Delaney, 1982) and can be used by teachers and taught to children. The effect sizes reached by many of the studies are quite high. The *average* for transfer tasks (where the material learned was to be applied in another setting), was 1.91. Recall of attributes of items (such as towns, cities, minerals) was 1.5. Foreign language acquisition was 1.3, with many studies reporting very high outcomes. Delayed recall generally maintained the gains, indicating that the mnemonics strategies have a lasting effect.

The community of scholars who are studying mnemonics have developed considerable interest in the area of metacognition and their work has given rise to the theory that helping students to inquire into themselves as learners and develop cognitive control over learning strategies can increase the capability of learners to learn.

Scientific inquiry. Models taken directly from the sciences have been the basis for curriculums for both elementary and high school children. The results of the research indicate that the scientific method can be taught and has positive effects on the acquisition of information, concepts and attitudes. More narrowly-defined studies have been made on inductive teaching and inquiry training. Beginning with Taba's (1966) exploration of an inductive social studies curriculum, periodic small-scale studies have probed the area. In 1968 Worthen provided evidence to support one of its central theses – that induced concepts would facilitate long-term recall. Feeley (1972) reviewed the social science studies and reported that differences in terminology hampered the accumulation of research, but that the inductive methods generally lived up to expectations, generating concept development and positive attitudes. Research on Suchman's (1981) model for teaching causal reasoning directly supported the proposition that inquiry training can be employed with both elementary and high school children. Schrenker (1976) reported that inquiry training resulted in increased understanding of science, greater productivity in critical thinking and skills for obtaining and analyzing information. He reported that it made little difference in the mastery of information, per se, but that it was as efficient as didactic methods or the didactic-cum-laboratory methods generally employed to teach science. Ivany (1969) and Collins (1969) examined variants in the kinds of confrontations and materials used and reported that the strength of the confrontation as a stimulus to inquiry was important and that richness in instructional materials was a significant factor. Elefant (1980) successfully carried out the strategy with deaf children in an intriguing study that has implications for work with all children. Voss' (1982) general review includes an annotation of a variety of studies that are generally supportive of the approach.

Currently the clearest evidence about the potential effects on students comes from the study of the academically-oriented curriculums in science and mathematics that were developed and used during the twenty-year period from 1955 to 1975 and from the experience with elementary curriculums in a variety of subject areas (Becker & Gersten, 1982; Rhine, 1981). The theory of the academic curriculums was relatively straightforward. The essence of the position was stated in *The Process of Education* (Bruner, 1961) and Schwab and Brandwein's *The Teaching of Science* (1962). The teaching of science should be as much as possible a simulation of the scientific process itself. The concepts of the disciplines should be studied rigorously in relation to their knowledge base. Thus science would be learned as inquiry. Further, the information thus learned would be retained well because it would be embedded in a meaningful framework and the student would possess the interrelated concepts that make up the structure of the disciplines.

In the academic reform movement of the 1950s and 1960s, entire curriculums in the sciences (e.g., BSCS Biology), social studies (e.g., Man, A Course of Study), mathematics (e.g., School Mathematics Study Group) and language (e.g., the linguistic approaches) were developed and introduced to the schools. These curriculums had in common their designers' beliefs that academic subjects should be studied with the tools of their respective disciplines. Most of these curriculums therefore required that students learn the modes of inquiry employed by the disciplines as well as factual material. Process was valued equally with content and many of these curriculums became characterized as "inquiry oriented".

Much curriculum research resembles the experimental studies of teaching, but the unit under study is a configuration of content, teaching methods, instructional materials and technologies and organizational forms. In the experiments any one of the elements of curriculum may be studied separately or in combination with the others, and the yield is expressed in terms of whether a curriculum produces predicted effects. Research on curriculum depends heavily on training in the content of the curriculum and the teaching strategies needed to implement it. Following training, implementation is monitored, either by classroom observation or interviews. Effects are determined by comparing student outcomes in experimental and control classrooms. In a few studies (e.g., Almy, 1970) combinations of curriculums are employed to determine effects on cognitive development and intelligence.

In reviewing the studies, El-Nemr (1979) concentrated on the teaching of biology as inquiry in high schools and colleges. He looked at the effects on achievement of information, on the development of process skills, and on attitudes toward science. The experimentally-oriented biology curriculums achieved positive effects on all three outcomes. The average effect sizes were largest for process skills (0.44 at the high school level and 0.62 at the college level). For achievement they were

0.27 and 0.11 respectively, and for attitudes, 0.22 and 0.51. Bredderman's (1983) analysis included a broader range of science programs and included the elementary grades. He also reported positive effects for information (0.10), creativity (0.13), science process (0.52), and, in addition, reported effects on intelligence tests where they were included (0.50). From these and other studies we can conclude that it is possible to develop curriculums that will achieve model-relevant effects and also will increase learning of information and concepts.

Also, vigorous curriculums in one area appear to stimulate growth in other, apparently unconnected areas. For example, Smith's (1980) analysis of aesthetics curriculums shows that the implementation of the arts-oriented curriculums was accompanied by gains in the basic skills areas. Possibly an active and effective curriculum in one area has energizing effects on the entire school program. Hillocks (1987) review of the teaching of writing produced similar effects. His conclusion indicated just how closely how we teach is connected with what we teach. Essentially, the inductive approaches to the teaching of reading and writing produced average effect-sizes of about .60 compared to treatments that covered the same material, but without the inductive approaches to the teaching/learning process.

Inquiry into cooperative learning models

There have been three lines of research on ways of helping students study and learn together, one lead by David and Roger Johnson at the University of Minnesota, a second by Robert Slavin at Johns Hopkins University and the third by Shlomo and Yael Sharan and Rachel Hertz-Lazarowitz in Israel. Grasping the research is difficult because the term, cooperative learning, is used to refer to a considerable variety of teaching strategies and there is a very large body of literature that is quite variable in quality. Further, various forms of cooperative learning are designed to accomplish quite different objectives. A model to teach students how to solve conflicts will be tested in relation to that objective whereas another model may approach academic learning directly.

Among other things, the Johnsons and their colleagues (1979, 1981, 1990) have studied the effects of cooperative task and reward structures on academic learning. The Johnsons' (1975, 1981) work on peers-teaching-peers has provided information about the effects of cooperative behavior on both traditional learning tasks and the effects on values and intergroup behavior and attitudes. Their models emphasize the development of what they call "positive interdependence", or cooperation where collective action also celebrates individual differences. Slavin's extensive 1983 review includes the study of a variety of approaches where he manipulates the complexity of the social tasks and experiments with various types of grouping. He reported success with the use of heterogeneous groups with tasks requiring coordination of group members both on academic learning and intergroup relations and has generated a variety of strategies that employ extrinsic and intrinsic reward structures. The Israeli team has concentrated on Group Investigation, the most complex of the social models of teaching.

What is the magnitude of effects that we can expect when we learn to use the cooperative learning strategies effectively? Rolheiser-Bennett's study (1986) compared the effects of the degrees of cooperative structure required by the several approaches (Joyce, Showers & Rolheiser-Bennett, 1989). On standardized tests in the basic curriculum areas (such as reading and mathematics) the highly-structured approaches to teaching students who work together generated effect sizes of an average 0.28 with some studies approaching half a standard deviation. On criterion-referenced tests the average was 0.48 with some of the best implementations reaching an effect of about one standard deviation. The more elaborate cooperative learning models generated an average effect size of somewhat more than one standard deviation, with some exceeding two standard deviations. (The average student above the 90th percentile student in the control group.) The effects on higher-order thinking were even greater, with an average effect of about 1.25 standard deviations and effects in some studies as high as three standard deviations.

Taken as a whole, research on cooperative learning is overwhelmingly positive – nearly every study has had from modest to very high effects, although some have had no effects on academic learning. The cooperative approaches are effective over a range of achievement measures. The more intensely cooperative the environment, the greater the effects: and the more complex the outcomes (higher-order processing of information, problem solving), the greater the effects.

The cooperative environment engendered by these models has had substantial effects on the cooperative behavior of the students, increasing feelings of empathy for others, reducing intergroup tensions and aggressive and antisocial behavior, improving moral judgment and building positive feelings toward others, including those of other ethnic groups. Many of these effect sizes are substantial – one or two standard deviations is not uncommon and one is as high as eight. Hertz-Lazarowitz (1993) recently used one of the models to create integrative interaction between Israeli and Arab students in the West Bank! Margarita Calderon has worked with Lazarowitz and Jusefina Tinajero to adapt a cooperative integrated reading and composition program for bilingual students with some very nice results (Calderon, Hertz-Lazarowitz, & Tinajero, 1991). An adaptation in higher education that organizes students into cooperative study groups reduced a dropout rate in engineering from 40 percent to about five percent (Bonsangue, 1993). Conflict-resolution strategies have taught students to develop integrative behavior and reduced social tension in some very divided environments in inner-city schools (Johnson & Johnson, 1994).

Probably the cooperative learning field is ready for a "shakeout" of some type, probably a clarification of the versions that accomplish various kinds of learning tasks most powerfully.

Interpretation

We believe there is a warrant under the models developed through these lines of inquiry (and a number of others not discussed here). Note, however, that because they appear to work, there is no guarantee that something else might work as well or better. They are not final solutions and, hopefully, further inquiry will generate more progress and these models will become historic or survive in barely recognizable form.

The question of why they work is a subject for another paper. Our working hypothesis is that the core of each of these models is their concentration on helping students develop effective modes of learning. Whereas the 'recitation mode' questions students about what they have learned on their own, including from "stand-and-deliver" forms of teaching, the processes developed by the researchers on scientific inquiry, mnemonics and cooperative learning have learned something about teaching the students to inquire. Essentially, they empower the learner, not in the political sense, but in the cognitive sense. In the rare cases where tests of intelligence and problem-solving ability have been employed, there have been gains. More work is needed in this area. For now, let's put the student into the picture.

THE STUDENT IN THE EQUATION: GENDER AND SOCIOECONOMIC FACTORS

The American School System plagues individual differences. Teachers using the recitation are driven nearly crazy because students simply will not all learn at the same rate, and the atomistic, bit-by-bit approach to subject matter that characterizes recitation teaching exacerbates differences. Many teachers and school officials regard individual differences as a plague *on them*. Myriads of plans have been developed for grouping students in an effort to narrow student variability in instructional settings. "Special" programs are developed to remove students from the "regular" classroom to give them special attention. Last year, we studied a large California school district where two-thirds of the students were in such programs. The "regular" classroom was becoming extinct in the effort to create homogenous settings! The futility of the effort was manifest in the fact that the "cure rate" of those special programs was almost zero.

Although it has been well-known that socioeconomic status is a phenomenal indicator of educational progress (for example, Coleman et al., 1966) and special programs have been developed for the children of the economically poor, those programs have mostly failed, but are continued unchanged. This is largely because it is very difficult for society to entertain the idea that its normative method of teaching might be a part of the problem.

Some negative effects of curriculum and instruction affect all social classes. Most Americans who were fairly successful in school regard foreign languages as very difficult to master, mathematics and science as both difficult and boring and high-quality writing as the province of a rare few. High school graduates' knowledge of history and geography is shocking. Curriculum and instruction gets some of the blame, but television and the properties of adolescence get more of it.

Less well known are the gender differences in achievement, or that each gender suffers in different ways. Many fewer boys learn to read adequately. Estimates differ, but the official estimate from the National Assessment of Reading Progress is that three out of four kids with "reading problems" are males. On scores indicating quality of writing, the average score of the males at the fourth, eighth and twelfth grade is about at the 30th percentile of the females. On the other hand, female self-esteem in mathematics and science drops dramatically between grades four and eight, despite the fact that gender differences in mathematics and science achievement are small. As a probable consequence of their loss of self-confidence many more females opt out of advanced courses.

Inevitably, thus, we might ask whether those models of teaching that appear to be emerging from educational science empower students regardless of gender and socioeconomic status, or at least narrow the gaps.

Many of the smaller laboratory studies do not report disaggregated data by gender, but quite a number do. Technically speaking, all should. The larger field studies are the most intriguing to us, because the sociocultural press cannot be controlled. To reduce the effects of demography, the model must be strong enough to overcome influences of parents, the textures of neighborhood life, and such.

We'll examine just a few cases, present a theory and suggest a line of inquiry.

Let's return to the work of Slavin and his colleagues described earlier. They have concentrated their efforts on inner-city schools populated by the economically poor and where neighborhood life can be chaotic and disturbing. In general, the kids in the *Success for All* schools are learning to read quite well. In addition, a smaller percentage of boys are failing to learn to read than is normal in suburban schools!

Similar results occurred in a Southeastern city where the teachers of a school district studied several inductive and concept-oriented models of teaching. In one middle school serving an economically poor, entirely Black community, only 30 percent of the children earned promotion each of several years before the effort. Within two years over 90 percent earned promotion by passing the same tests and standards used in the prior years. In schools serving middle-class neighborhoods, achievement measured by standard tests rose substantially. Gender differences in achievement narrowed substantially as both genders appeared to prosper (Showers, Murphy & Joyce, 1996).

In the University City study described earlier, where quality of writing increased as the teachers implemented inquiry-oriented models of learning, the gender differences narrowed as quality of writing improved for all students. The mean male score moved from the 30th to the 45th percentile of the female distribution.

In these and other studies where curricular and instructional models appear to reduce the effects of gender and socioeconomic status, the magnitude of acceleration of student learning has been considerable. A more detailed example will be useful in illustrating the point.

A group of secondary school teachers in Israel, led by Shlomo Sharan and Hana Shachar (1988), demonstrated the rapid acceleration in learning when they studied and first began to use the Group Investigation model, a very complex form of cooperative learning. They worked with classes in which the children of the poor (referred to as "Low SES", which is shorthand for "lower socioeconomic status") were mixed with the children of middle class parents (referred to as "High SES", for "higher socioeconomic status"). In a year long course on the social studies, the teachers gave pre-tests of knowledge to the students as well as final examinations, so that they could measure gains in academic learning and compare them with students taught by the "whole class" format most common in Israeli schools. Table 3.0 shows the results.

You can make several interesting comparisons as you read the table. First, in the pre-tests the Lower SES students scored significantly lower than their Higher SES counterparts. Typically, socioeconomic status is related to the knowledge students bring to the instructional situation and these students were no exception. Then, the Lower SES students taught by Group Investigation achieved average gains nearly two and a half times those of the Lower SES students taught by the whole-class method and exceeded the scores made by the Higher SES students taught with the "whole class" format. In other words, the "socially disadvantaged" students taught with group investigation learned at rates above those of the "socially advantaged" students taught by teachers who did not have the repertoire provided by group investigation. Finally, the "advantaged" students learned more also through group investigation. Their average gain was *twice* that of their whole-class counterparts. Thus, the model was effective by a large margin for students from both backgrounds.

Bloom's (1984) analysis of how effective tutoring can be (an effect size of 2.0 over direct instruction for certain kinds of learning) also illustrates the point about the magnitude of gain that is possible. Again, tutoring is effective for both genders.

Interpretation

We cannot draw an unshakeable conclusion from the literature, as many studies do not address either gender or socioeconomic status, but there appears to be a trend in the making. Whereas in normative American schools gender and socio-economic status are big factors with respect to academic progress, those models

Table 3: Effects of Complex Cooperative Learning in a History Course

	Cooperative Learning (Treatment)[1]		Whole Class Control	
	High SES[2]	Low SES	High SES	Low SES
Pre-Test				
M	20.99	14.01	21.73	12.31
SD	9.24	7.20	10.53	7.05
Post-Test				
M	62.60	50.17	42.78	27.23
SD	10.85	14.44	14.4	13.73
Main Gain	41.61	35.36	21.05	14.92

[1]The group investigation model of searching was used.
[2]SES refers to socioeconomic status.
Source: Sharan and Shachar 1989.

that consistently accelerate rates of learning appear to reduce gender and SES as factors. Put another way, they appear to help both sexes and kids from both rich and poor families. Much more work needs to be done in this particular area, but it is important that this trend runs counter to some contemporary thought about individual differences; thought leading in the direction of trying to develop models specifically tailored to gender characteristics, ethnicities and socioeconomic groups.

SUMMARY, AND FUTURE INQUIRY

Unless one chooses to disbelieve in social science, there is something of a knowledge base and, as the field studies demonstrate, one that is applicable to both the traditional and progressive missions of the school. A point not made above is that those models that were discussed here have been effective across a wide variety of subject areas and ages of children. The notion that effective teaching strategies inhere in subject matter does not hold up.

Partly because of the wide applicability, the knowledge base can enhance the substance of both preservice and inservice study by educators. Some powerful tools are available for teachers and, through them, for students. The existence of those tools might give persons designing curriculums and preservice and inservice programs some food for thought. The well-researched models provide a standard against which to judge the quality of program content. Essentially, we would hope that the teaching strategies embodied in curriculums and taught in programs for teachers would be at least as powerful as these ones seem to be.

Let's explore some notions that might lead to avenues for further inquiry as we try to expand the knowledge base.

First, a conclusion from our analysis:

The culturally normative mode of teaching is much less efficient than other models we can devise and is tremendously subject to demographic factors. Normative teaching does an effective job with only about 60 percent of students.

Now, a theory:

The models that will succeed will do so by teaching students more effective ways of constructing knowledge and building skills.

Another theory:

As students learn more about how to learn, demographic factors will be greatly reduced as barriers to learning.

A question:

Will learning styles and ethnic patterns be similarly reduced?

A thought:

Intelligence is problem-solving of which learning is a major component. If we learn how to learn better and how to teach others to learn better, can intelligence be seen as a major feasible outcome for education?

There are lifetimes of inquiry ahead of us. And, in the meantime, some important work to do in schools. While the debates about the nature of knowledge or what are the proper paradigms or methods go on, let us attack the problem of empowering learners by using the wonderful yield from the little places lighted by our imperfect candles.

REFERENCES

Almy, M. (1970). *Logical thinking in the second grade.* New York: Teachers College Press.

Atkinson, R. (1975). Nemotechnics in second language learning. *American Psychologist,* **30,** 821–828.

Becker, W., & Gersten, R. (1982). A followup of Follow Through: The later effects of the direct instruction model on children in the fifth and sixth grades. *American Educational Research Journal,* **19**(1), 75–92.

Bellack, A. (1962). *The Language of the classroom.* New York: Teachers College Press.

Bereiter, C. (1994, October). Constructivism, socioculturalism, and Popper's World 3. *Educational Researcher,* **23**(7), 21ñ23.

Bloom, B. S. (1984). The 2 sigma problem: The search for group instruction as effective as one-to-one tutoring. *Educational Researcher,* 13, 4–16.

Bonsangue, M. (1993). Long term effects of the Calculus Workshop Model. *Cooperative Learning,* **13**(3), 19–20.

Bredderman, T. (1983). Effects of activity-based elementary science on student outcomes: A quantitative synthesis. *Review of Educational Research,* 53(4), 499–518.

Brophy, J. E., & Good, T. (1986). Teacher behavior and student achievement. In M. Wittrock (Ed.), *Handbook of research on teaching* (3rd Edition, pp. 328–375). New York: Macmillan Publishing Co.

Bruner, J. (1961). *The Process of education.* Cambridge: Harvard University Press.

Calderon, M., Hertz-Lazarowitz, & Tinajero, J. (1991). Adapting CIRC to multi-ethnic and bilingual classrooms. *Cooperative Learning,* **12,** 17–20.

Coleman, J., Campbell, E., Hobson, C., McPortland, J., Mood, A., Weinfield, E., & York, R. (1966). *Equality of educational opportunity.* Washington, DC: Government Printing Office.

Collins, K. (1969). The importance of strong confrontation in an inquiry model of teaching. *School Science and Mathematics,* **69**,(7), 615–617.

Edelsky, C. (1990). Whose agenda is it anyway? *Educational Researcher,* **19**(8), 7–10.

Elefant, E. (1980). Deaf children in an inquiry training program. *The Volta Review,* **82,** 271–279.

El-Nemr, M. A. (1979). Meta-analysis of the outcomes of teaching biology as inquiry. Unpublished doctoral dissertation, University of Colorado, Boulder.

Feeley, T. (1972). *The concept of inquiry in the social studies.* Ph.D thesis, Stanford University.

Gage, N. L. (1997). Competing visions of what educational researchers should do. *Educational Researcher,* **26**(4).

Glass, G. V. (1982). Meta-analysis: An approach to the synthesis of research results. *Journal of Research in Science Teaching,* **19**(2), 93–112.

Goodlad, J., & Klein, F. (1970). *Looking behind the classroom door.* Worthington, Ohio: Charles Jones.

Hertz-Lazarowitz, R. (1993). Using group investigation to enhance Arab-Jewish relationships. *Cooperative Learning,* **11**(2), 13–14.

Hillocks, G. (1987). Synthesis of research on teaching writing. *Educational Leadership,* **44**(8), 71–82.

Hoetker, J., & Ahlbrand, W. (1969). The presistence of the recitation. *American Educational Research Journal,* 6, *145–167.*

Hopkins, D. (1987). *Improving the quality of schooling.* Lewes: Falmer.

Ivany, G. (1969). The Assessment of Verbal Inquiry in Elementary School Science. *Science Education,* 53(4), 287 93.

Johnson, D. W., & Johnson, R. T. (1979). Conflict in the classroom: Controversy in learning. *Review of Educational Research,* **49**(1), 51–70.

Johnson, D. W., & Johnson, R. T. (1981). Effects of cooperative and individualistic learning experiences on inter-ethnic interaction. *Journal of Educational Psychology,* **73**(3), 444–449.

Johnson, D. W., Maruyana, G., Johnson, R., Nelson, D., & Skon, L. (1981). Effects of cooperative, competitive, and individualistic goal structures on achievement: A meta-analysis. *Psychological Bulletin*, **89**(1), 47–62.

Johnson, D. W., & Johnson, R. T. (1975). *Learning together and alone*. Englewood Cliffs, N.J.: Prentice Hall, Inc.

Johnson, D. W., & Johnson, R. T. (1993). *Circles of learning*. Edina, Minn: Interaction Book Company

Johnson, D. W., & Johnson, R. T. (1994). *Leading the cooperative school*. Edina, Minn.: Interaction Book Company.

Johnson, D. W., & Johnson, R. T. (1990). *Cooperation and competition: Theory and research*. Edina, Minn.: Interaction Book Company.

Johnson, D. W., & Johnson, R. T. (1974). Instructional goal structure: Cooperative, competitive, or individualistic. *Review of Educational Research*, **44**, 213–240.

Johnson, D., & Johnson, R. (1996). Conflict resolution and peer mediated programs in elementary and secondary schools: a review of the research. *Review of Educational Research*, **66**(4), 459–506.

Joyce, B., & Calhoun, E. (Eds.). (1996). *Learning experiences in school renewal*. Eugene, Oregon: The ERIC Clearinghouse on Educational Management.

Joyce, B., & Calhoun, E. (1997). *Creating learning experiences*. Alexandria, VA: The Association for Supervision and Curriculum Development.

Joyce, B., & Weil, M. (1996). *Models of teaching*. Boston: Allyn Bacon.

Joyce, B., Calhoun, E., Halliburton, C., Simser, J., Rust, D., & Carran, N. (1996). University town. In B. Joyce & E. Calhoun (Eds.), *Learning experiences in school renewal*. Eugene, Oregon: ERIC Clearinghouse

Kaplan, A. (1964). *The conduct of inquiry*. San Francisco: Chandler.

Levin, M. & Levin, J. (1990). Scientific Mnemonics. *American Educational Research Journal*, **27**, 301–321.

Levin, J. R., McCormick, C., Miller, H., & Berry, J. (1993). Mnemonic versus nonmnemonic strategies for children. *American Educational Research Journal*, **19**(1), 121–136.

Lorayne, H., & Lucas, J. (1974). *The memory book*. Briercliff Manor, N.Y.: Memory Press.

Medley, D. (1977). *Teacher competence and teacher effectiveness*. Washington, D.C.: American Association of Colleges of Teacher Education.

National Assessment of Educational Progress (NAEP). (1992). *The reading report card*. Washington, D.C.: National Center for Educational Statistics, U.S. Department of Education.

Phillips, D. C. (1995). The good, the bad, and the ugly: the many faces of constructivism. *Educational Researcher*, 24(7), 5–12. *Educational Leadership*, **53**(1), September, 1995

Pressley, M. (1977). Children's use of the keyword method to learn simple Spanish vocabulary words. *Journal of Educational Psychology*, **69**(5), 465–472.

Pressley, M., & Dennis-Rounds, J. (1980). Transfer of a mnemonic keyword strategy at two age levels. *Journal of Educational Psychology*, **72**(4), 575–582.

Pressley, M., Levin, J. R., & Delaney, H. D. (1982). The mnemonic keyword method. *Review of Educational Research*, **52**(1), 61–91.

Pressley, M., Levin, J., & Ghatala, E. (1984). Memory strategy monitoring in adults and children. *Journal of Verbal Learning and Verbal Behavior*, **23**(2), 270–288.

Rolheiser-Bennett, C. (1986). *Four models of teaching: A meta-analysis of student outcomes*. Ph.D. thesis, University of Oregon.

Sagan, C. (1995). *The demon-haunted world: Science as a candle in the dark*. New York: Randon House.

Schrenker, G. (1976). *The effects of an inquiry-development program on elementary school children's science learning*. Ph.D. thesis, New York University.

Schwab, J., & Brandwein, P. (1962). *The teaching of science*. Cambridge, Mass.: Harvard University Press.

Sharan, S., & Shachar, H. (1988). *Language and learning in the cooperative classroom*. New York: Springer-Verlag.

Showers, B., Murphy, C., & Joyce, B. (1996). The river city program: Staff development becomes school improvement. In B. Joyce, & E. Calhoun (Eds.), *Learning experiences in school renewal*. Eugene, Oregon: The ERIC Clearinghouse on Educational Management.

Sirotnik, K. (1983). What you see is what you get. *Harvard Educational Review*, **53**(1), 16–31.

Slavin, R. E., & Madden, (1995). Success for all: creating schools and classrooms where all children can read. In J. Oakes, & K. Quartz (Eds.), *Creating new educational communities. The ninety-fourth yearbook of the National Society for the Study of Education* (pp. 70–86). Chicago: The University of Chicago Press.

Slavin, R. E. (1983). *Cooperative learning*. New York: Longman, Inc.

Smith, M. L. (1980). *Effects of aesthetics educations on basic skills learning*. Boulder, Colo.: Laboratory of Educational Research, University of Colorado.

Suchman, R. J. (1981). *Idea book for geological inquiry.* Trillium Press.

Voss, B. (1982). *Summary of research in science education.* Columbus, OH: ERIC Clearninghouse for Science, Mathematics and Environmental Education.

Wang, M., Haertel, G., & Walberg, H. (1993). Toward a knowledge base for school learning. *Review of Educational Research,* **63**(3), 249–294.

Three Rival Versions and a Critique of Teacher Staff Development

JOHN SMYTH

Flinders University of South Australia

John Smyth begins his critique of teacher staff development, by recalling Schwab's evocative phrase of some thirty years ago that "the field of curriculum is moribund". He claims that the same judgement applies to the field of staff development. Fortunately Smyth, like Schwab, on reflection sees that there are ways for staff development of teaching to emerge out of the 'unproductive cul-de-sac in which it had become lodged'. In pointing the way forward, Smyth suggests three conflicting conceptualisations of teachers' work through which staff development could critique itself. He uses metaphors as his starting point – teachers as technicians, teachers as artists / craftspersons / bricoleurs, teachers as intellectuals / political actors. For each metaphor or perspective, he draws out the implications for staff development. In concluding that "a major part of the disabling vision of staff development in schools, is because it is itself an incorrectly devised solution to a poorly understood problem", Smyth proposes a form of school improvement based around notions of staff development that are attentive to the 'politics of translation' rather than mindless implementation.

In setting out to find myself a possible framework within which to respond to the invitation to write this "critique of contemporary approaches to staff development" I could not help but make some comparisons. I was struck by what appeared to be some strong resemblances between the fields of curriculum and supervision in earlier times, and the area of staff development as it exists at the moment. The words of Joseph Schwab (1969) came flooding back to me in his pronouncement that "the field of curriculum is moribund". This provided me with at least the beginnings of a shorthand with which to describe my initial feelings of unease about the state of staff development. With first impressions still yet to be checked out, I had begun to have distinct feelings that staff development had many of the hallmarks alluded to by Schwab, even though I might have used a little more licence and been somewhat more colourful in the way I pegged them. From where I sat, staff development as conceived and enacted seemed to be: conceived within a predominantly individualist problematic; devoid of a sense of the political; structurally and systematically blind; discursively barren; educationally vacuous; epistemologically and paradigmatically bankrupt; intellectually poverty-stricken; conceptually amorphous; theoretically impoverished; practically, organisationally and pragmatically inept.

The more I came to think about it, the more it seemed as though delving into this area was likely to be an unproductive, frustrating and probably unrewarding task. As I began to turn the idea around and look at it from different angles, it seemed there

D. Hopkins (ed.), The Practice and Theory of School Improvement, 208-222.

might be a way forward, even in a field as riven as this one, for without my (and others) doing something, then there was little chance that staff development of teaching could ever emerge out of the unproductive cul-de-sac in which it had become lodged.

Thinking back to another occasion on which I had been (unwisely, perhaps) invited to write a similar piece, that time on the related topic of supervision (Smyth, 1987), I had this to say:

> The major problem with the study of supervision is that while there has been a plethora of research and much hortative literature on the practicalities of doing supervision, there has been virtually no attempt to stand back and look at the area of study itself (Smyth, 1984), what it purports to be, where it has come from, what it aspires to, where it is headed, and how it relates to discussion and debate in the broader area of philosophy of science. As Toulmin (1972, p. 84) argued, any field that hopes to make any conceptual advances must remain continually open to criticism and change if it is to move beyond being a mere pretender. It is, above all, this ability to develop an inquiring inner eye on itself, that represents the hallmark of a field of study (p. 567).

It seemed, therefore, that if what passes as staff development is to ultimately contribute to the creation of a credible field of study, at the same time as advancing our understanding of what is happening to changes in teachers' work, then it is imperative that what passes as scholarship should have a critical and problematic view of itself, and of its relationship to teaching (Smyth, 1984). If we are to be articulate about the merits, defects and appropriateness of the epistemologies, paradigms and methodologies of our work in the field of staff development, then there are several questions we need to ask ourselves:

- whether what passes as staff development is justified methodologically in relation to the problems and issues of the field ?
- whether the scholarship of staff development exhibits a critical awareness of the substantive issues of the field itself, especially a preparedness to criticise the foundations of the field, as well as questioning its technicalities ?
- whether the theory, policy and practices of staff development are clear about their own limitations and are able to demonstrate critical understanding of the outstanding issues and problems requiring resolution?

With these framing thoughts in mind, it seemed that my reading of Alasdair MacIntyre's (1990) *Three Rival Versions of Moral Inquiry* had the beginnings of some ideas that might advance my thinking on the topic. I could see interesting parallels in MacIntyre's struggles with notions of encyclopaedia, genealogy, and tradition as forms of knowledge – with the kind of tussles I was having with teacher staff development, where it had come from, what it represented, and where it might be headed. MacIntyre (1990) encapsulated it nicely for me when he described an encyclopaedia standpoint as one that rests upon authoritative pronouncements in which utterances are made in the expectation that they will not be disputed.

Genealogical forms, on the other hand, eschew such authoritative forms, preferring instead to see truth as residing in multiple perspectives of the world, and where utterances amount to moments in the development of one's position. The traditional standpoint, he contrasts with both of these, as having a much more sanguine view of history as permitting and enabling us to frame meaningful questions about what is worthwhile asking theoretically and practically, about the present, and how doing this enables a "reappropriation of the past" (p. 79) in a way that engages with "theoretical inquiry" as well as the "practical embodiment of such inquiry" (p. 79). The argument, then, is that individuals live lives (regardless of vocation or occupation), that "embody more or less adequately in those lives [a] key part to their own crafts, [and] what may often not be recognised as a theory, but which nevertheless is one" (p. 80).

What this means as we begin to move in on an issue like staff development in teaching, is that it is possible to read off what various approaches might embody within the wider context of knowledge and inquiry. For example, staff development for teachers is generally predicated on a set of views (held by governments and some sections of the community) that teachers are really little more than extended arms of industry, working in locations (that happen to be called schools but) which in reality amount to annexes of commerce, in that they ought primarily to be concerned with skills formation and producing acceptable forms of labour. This is what MacIntyre would term an encyclopaedia standpoint. Constructed in this way, staff development looks very much like another "iron cage" within which to encase teachers while requiring them to do a version of economic work for and on behalf of trans-national capital. Such instrumental forms of staff development are rarely blatantly promoted, although they do abound, and they generally have a public persona of schools being required by government to attain national standards, competence and performance to supposedly enhance international economic competitiveness.

Encyclopaedic knowledge is by now, of course, a largely flawed view of what constitutes education in the modern progressive world – as Kemmis (1995) notes, it is a view that has been roundly and thoroughly contested from interpretive/post-structuralist perspectives.

A genealogical perspective would regard knowledge about teaching as unfolding in a variety of ways depending upon values, preferences, location in history, and the like. From within this world view, the argument is that "teachers must make . . . judgements in a highly responsive way, and in making their judgements they must take into account that education is always a moral and a practical activity (as well as a technical one)" (p. 139). Criticism of teaching (as well as staff development) needs to move beyond the narrowness of exclusively technical interpretations. But, even these interpretivist views have been superseded now, by a second wave of more radical critics known as post-structuralists who regard interpretation as being distorted because perceptions depend on "who is doing the interpretation, when, where and from what perspective" (Kemmis, 1995, p. 139). The focus of post-structuralists shifts to critique based on the medium through which social constructions occur – namely, language, discourses, work, and power relations. For staff development, the discursive practices of teaching, the discourse communities within which it occurs, and the power relationships surrounding it, become the focus for discussion and debate.

Adopting Macintyre's (1990) third, or "traditional" moral standpoint, would be to regard what passes as staff development in teaching as being a basis upon which to debate the social and cultural life of schools, including consideration of the place of wider structures of society in schools, and vice versa. As MacIntyre (1990) put it, this is sometimes a set of perspectives labelled as utopian, which is to say more about the accusers than about the accused.

I want to proceed by developing a heuristic within which to explore a set of relationships, between what I am tentatively titling rival versions of staff development for teachers, and how these are embedded in and simultaneously sustain conflicting conceptions of teachers' work. To obtain a vantage point from which to analyse the notion of staff development, I shall adopt a broadly archaeological approach to teachers' work, where I take archaeology to mean "the history of the term in its uneven development within diverse theoretical fields" (Best & Kellner, 1991, p. 5). According to Best & Kellner (1991) this involves and invites "searching for sediments and layers of . . . discourses as they have accumulated historically" (p. 5), which is somewhat different from Foucault's technical sense of "an analysis that articulates rules which constitute and govern discourse" (p. 5). To that extent, it is possible to use this approach to discern "anticipations or precursors to ideas and terminology which [may] gain currency at a later date" (p. 5). To pursue the kind of genealogy being attempted here is to ask the obvious question, why are we having the kind of developments we are in staff development at the moment, and "what are the lines of descent that led to [this] event" (Labaree, 1992, p. 128):

> The genealogist . . . resists the tendency to search for the "timeless and essential secret" behind things . . . [preferring instead to identify] the preexisting components that constitute the historical event under consideration (Labaree, 1992, p. 128).

But maybe this is leaping ahead a little; first there is some excavation to be done in respect of teachers' work, for it is that which is ultimately the object (or subject, depending on your position) of staff development. Here the waters become a little muddier, but it is important to try and introduce some clarity before proceeding further with staff development.

CONFLICTING CONCEPTUALIZATIONS OF TEACHERS' WORK

There has been a lot of talk in recent times about teachers' work – what it is, who does it, how it might be restructured, how it might be more closely supervised, and how policy makers might change it so as to have schools better serve the needs of the economy. What is interesting about this discussion is that it is invariably located in some kind of metaphor; we have had a string of these over the years, and some of them are even beginning to be recycled. For example, there are: teachers as professionals (Hoyle & Megarry, 1980); teachers as researchers (Stenhouse, 1975); teachers as bricoleurs (or tinkerers) (Hatton, 1988); teachers as intellectuals (Giroux, 1988); teachers as reflective practitioners (Grimmett & Erickson, 1988); teachers as technicians (Scheffler, 1968); teachers as political actors (Carlson, 1987); teachers as artisans/craftspersons (Huberman, 1990); teachers as evaluators (Davis, 1980); teachers as executives (Berliner, 1983); teachers as collaborators (Smyth, 1991a); teachers as workers (Ginsburg, 1988); and more recently, teachers as scholars (Enns, 1991). It is worthwhile analysing a few of these in order to see a little more clearly the messages they hold for the mooted re-structuring of teachers' work that is occurring worldwide at the moment. The kind of internalized images teachers hold of themselves and their work, as well as the construals that others would like to impose upon them, are in a continual state of tension. How these tensions are resisted or accommodated need to be looked at in any attempt to understand how teachers' work is being (or might be) transformed. Egan (1988), for example, argues that we constantly "construct and recreate images of the world and of experience" (p. 63) in and around metaphors and analogies "as we try to tie them to the kinds of formal logical structures we can grasp more explicitly" (p. 64).

> Metaphors have become attractive organizers of education in times of increasingly strident calls for accountability – they provide reassurance that taxpayers' money is being spent prudently through the illusion that everything is under control. For example, when we use a factory or conduit metaphor (ie. a systems approach), we demonstrate that with a particular input of resources, that the schooling process is able to convert those resources into a measurable amount of output (ie. skills) of a specific kind, efficiently and effectively, so as to satisfy labour market requirements.
>
> The kind of metaphors we allow to be used to describe teaching, therefore, very powerfully shape not only the way we conceptualise teaching, but the manner in which we go about the professional development of teachers, too. Metaphors are not neutral or innocent; they are imbued with all manner of deliberate (but usually undeclared) political agenda. How we regard teaching has a profound impact on the kind of staff development we permit.

The downside of the use of metaphors about teachers' work is that we can often become trapped within them without even realizing it, and the language can become totalizing. We already know much about the power of language and the way it shapes thought and action. Once we become enamoured with the logic of a particular metaphor, it is hard to escape the language within which it is embodied, for to reject the language, is to jettison the metaphor.

(a)   *Teachers as technicians*

Over the years it has been fashionable to portray teachers (and indeed to treat them) as compliant workers. It was Scheffler (1968) who argued nearly 30 years ago that teachers' work was becoming construed as that of :

a minor technician within an industrial process, the overall goals of which are to be set in advance in terms of national needs, the curricular materials pre-packaged by disciplinary experts, the methods developed by educational engineers – and the teachers' job . . . just to supervise the last operational stage, the methodical insertion of ordered facts into the students mind (pp. 5–6).

This is still true today as we grapple with moves that reintroduce technical/rational ways of construing the work of teachers. Scheffler's (1968) argument is that to trivialize the work of teachers in this way is to deny its complexity. The teacher is more than a technician; he or she should be an active force shaping and determining the educational process. Scheffler's problem with the industrial analogy is that it flies in the face of what goes on in schools. Technicians do things to materials according to certain rules and procedures. These materials, in return, are shaped by what he/she does, but they are not responsive – there is no communication with them. Neither is there any questioning of "judgements . . . beliefs . . . perspectives and purposes [nor do] they present him [/her] with . . . new centres of personal experience [with] which his [/her] own meanings may be engaged or transformed" (p. 6). According to Scheffler (1968), teachers' work is vastly different on several counts: students *are not* inert materials to be worked on; teachers *do* enter into communications with their students and they *do* share varying degrees of a common culture; and, there *is* a dual process at work of refining the students' outlook while enabling the teacher to broaden his/her understanding. Students, on the other hand, are not passive, either – they "question", "explore", "doubt" and "evaluate" as they respond not only to the content of what they are taught, but also how it is taught, to the orientations and convictions thus reflected, and to the "larger rationale that underlies them" (p. 6). Teaching is thus a complex process of risk- taking in which disclosure is a key element in understanding the judgemental basis of the work of teaching. As Scheffler put it, it is only when teachers embrace this risk that they are "forced to a heightened self-awareness, and a more reflective attitude towards [their] own presuppositions . . ." (p. 6). The notion of reducing teachers' work to purely operational terms, is therefore, fallacious in the extreme. We can see this in the obvious and very public failure of several attempts over the years to treat teachers as if they were technicians. The reason why innovations like "competency-based instruction, mastery learning, teacher proof materials, performance contracting, accountability testing and programmed instruction" (Hlebowitsh, 1990, p. 147) have so demonstrably failed, is because of the way they have ignored the realities of teaching and tried to segment teachers' work in ways that make them operatives in somebody else's processes.

If teachers are not simply the purveyors of unproblematic received bodies of knowledge to compliant students, then their concerns and interests must go considerably beyond the classroom into the larger setting of the school involving an active responsibility for setting goals towards which they will work. Unless they do this, Hartnett and Naish (1980) argue, then teachers will develop a preoccupation with "means and [an] indifference to ends [that] is at best immoral" (p. 265). Specifying what teachers do through national curricula, statewide testing, curriculum guidelines and frameworks, is to force them into the educational cul-de-sac of being technical operatives. While this may appear to be an attractive administrative/bureaucratic solution to the relationship between schooling and the economy, and may seem to enable re-skilling to meet the new requirements for international competitiveness, it actually fails to acknowledge that educational ends are highly contentious, contested, negotiated, constructed and resisted.

IMPLICATIONS FOR STAFF DEVELOPMENT

The view of staff development that emerges from within this view of teaching is one that is created by a sense of "moral panic" (Goode & Ben-Yehuda, 1994) or "manufactured crisis" (Berliner & Biddle, 1995) that schools and teachers are responsible for the economic decline, that they are letting society down, and that there must be a restoration of values and competence in order to arrest the harm being caused. In other words, there is a view that teachers have deficits that have to be fixed, and that the way to do this is to bring in outside 'experts' to diagnose the problems and provide the remediation in the form of knowledge and information missing from teachers' repertoire of content. Many in-service and curriculum days operate along these lines with an applicative view of knowledge, and with teachers having an inert and passive role in what is usually an episodic or piecemeal encounter. The model is an ameliorative one in which judgements or success are made according to teachers' capacity to increase mastery of competencies against criteria.

(b)   *Teachers as artists/craftspersons/bricoleurs*

There is also a considerable and growing body of literature suggesting that the work of teaching is akin to that of a craftsperson or artisan. This is a view, broadly speaking, that says what counts about teaching is what is learned tacitly though practical experience and by following the lead of more experienced practitioners.

Huberman (1990) has written about the teacher as an independent artisan. He invites us to imagine the teacher:

> as a "tinkerer" or instructional "handyman", a do-it-yourself craftsperson who can put to use a host of materials lying around at various stages of a construction or repair job. Unlike, say, an engineer, he works seldom with pre-designed materials or tools, nor does he start with a blueprint. Rather, he reaches for some scrap or surplus material from previous jobs as his project takes shape. These materials meet the particular need he happens to have at

a specific point in his project, and he will fashion them to fit his particular purpose. Gradually, of course, he accumulates a workshop full of those materials most likely to be needed at some, still- unknown moment for the various kinds of things he builds or fixes (p. 3).

Elsewhere, Huberman (1990) invokes the image of:

> the teacher as creating or repairing learning activities of various kinds but with a distinctive style or "signature". She adapts on the spot those instructional materials she has bought, been given or has scavenged, as a function of the time of day, the degree of pupil attentiveness, the peculiar skill deficiency emerging in the course of the activity, the little, unexpected breakthrough on a grammatical rule, the apparent illogic to the children of mathematical bases other than 10. In doing this, she relies heavily on concrete bits of practice that have proved successful in the past, but which need to be reconfigured on the spot, as a function of the specific situation in the classroom, in order to make them work (p. 4).

The image conjured up here is clearly a metaphor designed to underscore the idiographic, non-generalizable and personal nature of the teaching act, which varies from situation to situation. What Huberman (1990) presents us with is an artisan model of teaching – one that is "highly individualistic and context sensitive, and that, as a result, implies the idiosyncratic accumulation of a requisite knowledge base . . ." (p. 11). It is, if you will, "an image of the schoolhouse as a community of artisans" and it has important ramifications for the "interplay between community and individuality" (Huberman, 1990, p. 3). The implications of this are really quite profound, for, what it means is that teachers who work alone also learn alone, and in the process derive their most important satisfactions from interactions with pupils rather then colleagues. The consequence is a certain "tool centredness" (Huberman, 1990, p. 16) in which teachers literally "squirrel" away strategies, devices and approaches for use on the appropriate occasion when it presents itself. This is a view supported by Ashenden (1990) who put it colourfully when he said: "Schooling is the last of the mass cottage industries" (p. 12). Herein, he says, lies the major paradox. While teachers:

> take justifiable pride in their finely-honed repertoire of tactics with which they tame the jungle life . . . [on] the other hand, most teachers are conscious of the endless frustration in their work, though they are not always conscious that it has to do with the situation within which their teaching is done (p. 13).

Ashenden (1990) argues that this tension between "situation" and "aspiration" is brought out in the long history of teachers experimenting, and in the ways they act like "backyard mechanics, always out in the shed tinkering, trying out new bits and pieces" (p. 14). He also claims that this particular model of the classroom has survived for so long "because teachers have protected it" (p. 15).

IMPLICATIONS FOR STAFF DEVELOPMENT

Here the emphasis is upon "fine tuning" forms of knowing and knowledge that are deeply entrenched in a set of broadly shared norms, values, and beliefs about teaching based on a practical understanding of the materials being worked with – children, curriculum artefacts, and accumulated wisdom. Staff development takes the form, at least initially, of induction and enculturation with neophytes being provided with the opportunity to see the work of more experienced teachers up-close. The focus, even among more mature teachers, is on forms of apprenticeship and mentoring that derive meaning from in situ forms of learning about teaching. There is still a strong tendency towards isolation and a certain degree of "tool centredness" that reinforces isolation and an idiographic view of teaching as work. The place of staff development is in promoting the kind of relationships in which teachers feel comfortable in sharing (as distinct from constructing) knowledge about teaching and learning with colleagues. There tends not to be much challenging of one another among teachers in this form of staff development, and collegiality can be for collegiality's sake.

(c)   *Teachers as Intellectuals/Political Actors*

Probably more than any other contemporary educator Henry Giroux (1988) has championed the cause of teachers as intellectuals. Giroux's prolific writings have occurred against a backdrop of "educational reforms" that have aimed at reducing teachers to "the status of low-level employees or civil servants whose main function seems to be to implement reforms decided by experts in the upper levels of state and educational bureaucracies" (Giroux, 1985a, p. 20). The consequence, Giroux argues, is that the search and the push for technical/administrative solutions (at least in the USA) to the complex economy/society/education linkage, has produced a growing gulf between those who decide on technical and methodological grounds what is best for schools, and the schools and teachers who deal with students, curricular and pedagogy on a daily basis. He argues that there is a process of subjugation of intellectual labour at work here that in may cases reduces teachers to the status of "high level clerks implementing the orders of others . . . or to the status of specialized technicians" (p. 21). This dominance of technocratic rationality has had the effect of producing a form of proletarianization of teachers' work, not dissimilar to what happened to factory workers in the nineteenth century, as the control of what had previously been highly independent craftsman, came increasingly under corporate and factory control.

In a similar vein teacher education (and by implication, staff development) has, Giroux says, all too often been reduced to questions of "what works", and issues to do with what counts as knowledge, what is worth teaching, and how one judges the purpose and nature of teaching become submerged (or even obliterated) in the press for routinization and standardization through "management pedagogies".

Giroux's claim is that one way of re-thinking and re-structuring teachers' work is to view teachers as intellectuals, and to see what teachers do as a form of intellectual labour. The argument here is that if we regard teachers in this light then we can begin to "illuminate and recover the rather general notion that all human activity involves some form of thinking [and] no activity, regardless of how routinized it might become, is abstracted from the functioning of the mind in some capacity" (Giroux, 1985a, p. 27). When applied to teaching, Kohl (1983) put it this way:

> I believe a teacher must be an intellectual as well as a practitioner . . . I don't mean an intellectual in the sense of being a university professor or having a PhD . . . I am talking about activities of the mind. We must think about children, and create many philosophies of life in the classroom . . . An intellectual is someone who knows about his or her field, has a wide breadth of knowledge about other aspects of the world, who uses experience to develop theory and questions theory on the basis of further experience. An intellectual is also someone who has the courage to question authority and who refuses to act counter to his/her experience and judgement (p. 30).

Equally important, Kohl (1983) argues that unless we as teachers :

> assume the responsibility for theory making and testing, then theories will be made for us by . . . the academic researchers and many other groups that are simply filling the vacuum that teachers have created by bargaining away their education power and giving up their responsibility as intellectuals (p. 30).

Viewed in this way, schooling becomes a project of helping students to see injustices, and assisting them to both locate themselves in relation to such issues, and to see how society is structured in ways that both sustain and maintain those inequities. This necessarily involves working with students in ways that enable them to see through their own pedagogical work in classrooms, that knowledge and power are inextricably linked and that students need to see themselves as "critical agents, problematizing knowledge, utilizing dialogue, and making knowledge meaningful so as to make it critical in order to make it emancipatory" (Giroux, 1985b, p. 87). The kinds of questions Giroux (1985b) suggests are necessary if teachers are to interrogate their work in the way he is suggesting so as to become intellectuals, include:

- What counts as school knowledge?
- How is such knowledge selected and organized ?
- What are the underlying interests that structure the form and content of school knowledge ?
- How is what counts as school knowledge transmitted ?
- How is access to such knowledge determined ?
- What cultural values and formations are legitimated by dominant forms of school knowledge?
- What cultural formations are disorganized and delegitimated by dominant forms of school knowledge? (p. 91).

Adopting a critical and political stance to one's work does not mean being partisan political; it involves what Popkewitz (1987) describes as "critical intellectual work", where:

> 'critical' means moving outside the assumptions and practices of the exist-ing order. It is a struggle . . . [to make] categories, assumptions, and practices of everyday life . . . problematic (p. 350).

But as Ginsburg (1988) argues, it is more than just problematizing the work of teaching because it involves "struggle to challenge and transform the structural and cultural features we . . . come to understand as oppressive and anti-democratic" (pp. 363–5). Ginsburg's point hinges around the need for teachers to see themselves as actively participating in progressive movements committed to bringing about fundamental social change. According to this view, the image of teachers as compliant, passive and easily moulded workers, is replaced by a view of the teacher "as an active agent, constructing perspectives and choosing actions" (Feiman-Nemser & Floden, 1986, p. 523).

IMPLICATIONS FOR STAFF DEVELOPMENT

There is quite a different tenor about the role of staff development here. The attempt is to challenge conventional habits, values, and beliefs and to produce indigenous forms of knowledge that connect with the lives, experiences and aspira-tions of students (Smyth, 1995). Extant categories about how teaching and learn-ing occurs are confronted, problematized, redefined and supplanted as new structures and processes are created through changed social relationships between teachers, students and parents. There is a focus on intellectualising and theorising about what is going on in classrooms and the influences of broader social and political structures. In this sense there is an emancipatory intent as teachers work with one another in staff development to use collective professional judgement as a way of connecting schools to society, with a view to changing the latter. Staff development of this kind is characterised by integration, diversity, uncertainty, ambiguity and excited confusion.

ENGAGING STAFF DEVELOPMENT WITH A 'POLITICS OF TRANSLATION' TOWARDS SCHOOL IMPROVEMENT

Against this kind of backdrop and despite these quite divergent construals of teach-ing, one thing that becomes clear about examining a concept like staff develop-ment in relation to teaching, is that despite recent attempts to construe it otherwise, and no matter what kind of twist or embroidery is put upon it (such as, it is an attempt to "professionalise teachers"), staff development is still generally conceived as basically an ameliorative and rehabilitative term.

Labaree (1992, 1995) captures this well in analyses of the various recent reports of the Holmes Group in the USA. He says, the tone of these documents is invariably a harsh one: "blanket condemnation" and "demonizing rhetoric", along with approaches that "admonish, hector, browbeat, ridicule, shame and punish" teachers who are basically regarded as being inefficient. This is, he says, "the way, in contemporary politics, that we talk about reforming criminals, welfare recipients and government bureaucrats" (Labaree, 1995, p. 179) – in short, it is "a disabling vision".

Earlier attempts at staff development were located within an unashamedly behaviouristic orientation. Discussion was (and in some cases still is) lodged within processes of intervention and treatment designed to "alter professional practices, beliefs and understanding of school persons, towards an articulated end" (Griffin, 1983, p. 2) – and, as Guskey (1986) notes, "In most cases, that end is the improvement of student learning" (p. 5). The predominant model of staff development, up until the mid-1980s, was typically one that aimed to "first initiate some form of change in the beliefs, attitudes and perceptions of teachers . . . [along with the presumption] that such change in teachers' beliefs and attitudes will lead to specific changes in their classroom behaviors and practices, and in turn, result in improved student learning" (Guskey, 1986, p. 6).

The difficulty, even with attempting to revise models of the type presented by Guskey, is that whichever way they are re-configured they still amount to fundamentally flawed engineering models. While I have argued elsewhere (Smyth, 1995) they may appear to have a certain degree of populist appeal, they fail to adequately grasp or take account of the substantial advances that have been made recently in the understanding of teaching, outside of what were once dominant process-product paradigms. Put simply, the study of research on (sic) teaching has moved "well beyond its recent roots in process-product research" (Labaree, 1995, p. 142) and its unsuccessful attempt to produce a "science of teaching" (Gage, 1978). Dialogue has begun to open-up from within a number of alternative approaches – ones that represent more genuinely radical approaches. Three of these tendencies are particularly noteworthy:

One trend is the rise of various forms of interpretive qualitative analysis of classroom interaction based on observation. Another is the emergence of the case study, which represents a shift in emphasis from a positivist concern about generalizability to a focus on texture and context. A third trend is the effort to examine the ways in which teachers understand and guide their own practice, as an example of reflective and contextualized knowledge that is practical rather than theoretical. As a result the field appears to have outgrown its early stress on law-seeking, abstraction from context, and prescription from practice . . . (p. 142).

The kind of disabling visions Labaree (1995) speaks about are by no means extinct – they live on and are sustained and maintained by populist images that as long as staff development can somehow be "focussed on children and teaching", then all else can be "subordinated to school improvement efforts".

The difficulty with such natural and apparently logical and commonsense "solutions" to the alleged problem of inefficient and ineffective schools, is that they fail to adequately grapple with the deeper and more complex issues – in this instance, a widespread loss of public confidence in publicly provided education, and not a lack of competence as sometimes suggested on the part of teachers. In other words, a major part of the disabling vision of staff development in schools, inheres within an incorrectly devised solution to a poorly (or even mis)understood problem.

The kind of images for school improvement that flow from this third version of staff development and that I want to invoke, incorporates a "language of probability" (Deever, 1996) in the way it gives prominence to the following:

- it listens to teachers' voices more, and less to those of distant researchers, administrators and educational policy makers;
- it adopts a more trusting stance to teachers in terms of acknowledging that they understand the complexity of the contemporary contexts within which they work;
- it pursues processes that actively encourage and permit schools to re-define themselves as sites of democracy, community, diversity and social justice (Deever, 1996, p. 174);
- curriculum, pedagogy and evaluation are not regarded as definitive, prescriptive or established, but rather as capable of being constructed around the lived experiences of children and teachers;
- teachers in the school place a great deal of importance on staying up-to-date with the latest theoretical developments in their field, and what is known by one person in the school is shared with all;
- new policies, ideas and practices are not adopted quickly, but after extensive debate and discussion, and even then, only after carefully trialing and monitoring;
- ideas, preferences, directives and edicts emanating from hierarchical and bureaucratic sources are neither rejected nor adopted, but subjected to rigorous scrutiny by teachers in terms of how they might advantage *all* students in the school;
- a "critical mass" of teachers are involved in formulating and articulating goals and changes in the school; and, above all
- the school is committed to engaging students with the "big questions" that fire the "imagination", the "spirit", the "feelings" and the "intellect" (Clifford & Friesen, 1993).

In Deever's (1996) terms, this is a form of school improvement based around notions of staff development that are attentive to the "politics of translation", rather than mindless implementation, and where there is a clear understanding of what it means to develop a "radical economy of utility" (p. 177) – new and challenging perspectives are articulated in a context where compromises are known to be inevitable, but also where original intentions are capable of restoration in the longer term. School improvement thus conceived, emphasizes the need to continually work at creating better collaborative ways of restoring the notion of genuine community in schools, and putting the educative back into prominence in all facets of the work of the school.

REFERENCES

Ashenden, D. (1990). Award re-structuring and productivity in the future of schooling. *Victorian Institute for Educational Research Bulletin*, **64**, 3–32.

Berliner, D. (1983). Executive functions of teaching. *Instructor*, **43**, 28–40.

Berliner, D., & Biddle, B. (1995). *The manufactured crisis*. Reading, MA: Addison-Wesley.

Best, S., & Kellner, D. (1991). *Postmodern theory: Critical interrogations*. London: Macmillan.

Carlson, D. (1987). Teachers as political actors. *Harvard Educational Review*, **57**(3), 283–306.

Clifford, P., & Friesen, S. (1993). A curious plan: Managing on the twelfth. *Harvard Educational Review*, **63**(3), 339–54.

Davis, E. (1980). *Teachers as curriculum evaluators*. Sydney: Allen & Unwin.

Deever, B. (1996). If not now, when? Radical theory and systematic curriculum reform. *Journal of Curriculum Studies*, **28** (2), 171–191.

Egan, K. (1988). Metaphors in collision: Objectives, assembly lines and stories. *Curriculum Inquiry*, **18**(1), 63–86.

Enns, R. (1991). *The teacher as scholar: Extending professionalism*. Winnipeg, Manitoba: Seven Oaks Symposium Series.

Feiman-Nemser, S., & Floden, R. (1986). The cultures of teaching. In M. Wittrock (Ed.), *Third handbook of research on teaching*. New York: Collier-Macmillan.

Gage, N. L. (1978). *The scientific basis of the art of teaching*. New York: Teachers College Press.

Ginsburg, M. (1988). Educators as workers and political actors in Britain and North America. *British Journal of Sociology of Education*, **9**(3), 359–67.

Giroux, H. (1985a). Intellectual labour and pedagogical work: re-thinking the role of the teacher as intellectual. *Phenomenology and Pedagogy*, **3**(1), 20–32.

Giroux, H. (1985b). Critical pedagogy and the resisting intellectual. *Phenomenology and Pedagogy*, **3**(2), 84–97.

Giroux, H. (1988). *Teachers-as-intellectuals: Toward a critical pedagogy of learning*. Sough Hadley, MA: Bergin & Garvey.

Goode, E., & Ben-Yehuda, N. (1994). *Moral panics and the construction of deviance*. Cambridge, MA: Blackwell.

Griffin, G. (1983). *Staff Development, Eighty Second Yearbook for the National Society for the Study of Education Part II*. Chicago: University of Chicago Press.

Grimmett, P., & Erickson, G. (Eds.). (1988 *Reflection in teacher education*. New York: Teachers College Press.

Guskey, T. (1986). Staff development and the process of teacher change. *Educational Researcher*, **15**(5), 5–12.

Hartnett, A., & Naish, M. (1980). Technicians or social bandits? Some moral and political issues in the education of teachers. In P. Woods (Ed.), *Teacher strategies: Explorations in the sociology of the school*, (pp. 254–74). London: Croom Helm.

Hatton, E. (1988). Teachers' work as bricolage: Implications for teacher education. *British Journal of Sociology of Education*, **9**(3), 337–57.

Hlebowitsh, P. (1990). The teacher technician: Causes and consequences. *Journal of Educational Thought*, **24**(3), 147–60.

Hoyle, E., & Megarry, J. (1980). *Professional development of teachers*. London: Kogan Page.

Huberman, M. (1990). *The social context of instruction in schools*. Paper to Annual Meeting of American Education Research Association. Boston.

Kemmis, S. (1995). Emancipatory aspirations in a postmodern era. *Curriculum Studies*, **3**(2), 133–67.

Kohl, H. (1983). Examining closely what we do. *Learning*, **12**(1), 28–30.

Labaree, D. (1992). Power, knowledge and the rationalization of teaching: a geneaology of the movement to professionalize teaching. *Harvard Educational Review*, **62**(2), 123–54.

Labaree, D. (1995). A disabling vision: Rhetoric and reality in "Tomorrow's Schools of Education". *Teachers College Record*, **97**(2), 166–205.

MacIntyre, A. (1990). *Three rival versions of moral enquiry: Encyclopaedia, geneaology and tradition*. London: Duckworth.

Popkewitz, T. (1987). *Critical studies in teacher education: Its folklore, theory and practice*. London & Philadelphia: Falmer Press.

Scheffler, I. (1968). University scholarship and the education of teachers. *Teachers College Record*, **70**(1), 1–12.

Schwab, J. (1969). The practical: a language for curriculum. *School Review*, **78**(1), 1–24.

Smyth, J. (1984). Toward a 'critical consciousness' in the instructional supervision of experienced teachers. *Curriculum Inquiry*, **14**(4), 425–36.

Smyth, J. (1987). Cinderella syndrome: a philosophical view of supervision as a field of study. *Teachers College Record*, **88**(4), 567–88.

Smyth, J. (1991). *Teachers as collaborative learners: challenging dominant forms of supervision.* London: Open University Press.

Smyth, J. (Ed.). (1995a). *Critical discourses on teacher development.* London: Cassell.

Smyth, J. (1995). Teachers' work and the labour process of teaching: central problematics in professional development. In T. Guskey & M. Huberman (Eds.), *Professional development in education: New paradigms and practices*, (pp. 69–91). New York: Teachers College Press.

Stenhouse, L. (1975). *An introduction to curriculum research and development.* London: Heinemann.

Toulmin, S. (1972). *Human understanding: The collective use and evolution of concepts.* Princeton: Princeton University Press.

Why Teachers need their Colleagues: A Developmental Perspective

JENNIFER NIAS

University of Plymouth, UK

In this chapter, Jennifer Nias presents a humanistic view of teacher development in which the individuals' continuing concern is the preservation of a stable sense of personal and professional identity, that is realised in different ways at varying times during their careers. Drawing on two decades of research in English primary schools, Nias argues that a teacher's colleagues play a central role in this development, meeting (or failing to meet) the need, in turn, for: practical and emotional assistance; referential support; professional stimulation and extension; and the opportunity to influence others. Because compatibility in beliefs and values is the key to productive collegial relationships, Nias concludes by arguing that individual development often depends upon sub-group support and this may in turn impede school-wide development.

This chapter is deliberately constrained in four ways. First, it is based on the view that teachers' professional development cannot be separated from their personal growth. Second, it emphasises the relationship between teachers and their colleagues, taking the view that the school is a workplace for adults, not simply a venue in which teachers daily interact with young people. This is not to argue that teachers' dealings with their students do not affect their development; in this chapter however students are the backdrop against which teachers live out their adult-adult relationships. Third, no account is taken of teachers who are not full-time, permanent members of staff. As far as I know, there has been no detailed research into the professional development needs and patterns of part-time, temporary or substitute teachers, even though these constitute a significant and growing proportion of the teaching profession in many countries. I have made reference to the career difficulties and feelings of such teachers in Nias (1989a, 1989c) and Nias and Aspinwall (1995), but the whole topic urgently merits further study. Fourth, this chapter focuses upon teachers in elementary (primary) schools. Although reference is made to schools outside England and Wales, most of the evidence on which is draws most heavily comes from ethnographic studies of English primary and middle schools, undertaken over two decades. (It should be noted that primary schools in the UK are for children from 5–11 years old; middle schools from 5–12 or 13, or from 8–11 or 9–13 years old. These schools range in size from 1 or 2 teachers to 18–20 teachers; but about half have teaching staffs of 5–10.)

These studies are reported in detail in Nias (1989a); Nias et al., (1989); Nias et al., (1992). Here, reference is also made to related papers and to an unpublished

D. Hopkins (ed.), The Practice and Theory of School Improvement, 223-237.
© 2005 *Springer. Printed in the Netherlands.*

study (Nias, 1994). All the research except Nias (1994) was long-scale (minimum, one academic year), and ethnographic. Nias (1989a) draws very heavily on in-depth interviews, repeated after 10 years with about half the original 99 respondents. Nias et al., (1989), Nias et al., (1992), Nias (1994) used a mixture of participant observation, interviews and documentary sources, with a heavy reliance on observation, cross-referenced to subsequent interviews.

I did not acquire most of the evidence on which this chapter is based by directly looking for it, though as my understanding of teachers' adult relationships increased, so did my capacity to enquire and perceive. In Nias (1989a) my focus was upon the subjective reality of being a primary school teacher; I came to realise only as I listened to practitioners how important to them their colleagues were, and in what ways. Partly as a result of this work, Nias et al., (1989, 1992) sought to understand how and why the way a school functions affects teachers' ability to work well together and to learn from one another. Nias (1994) looked at staff relationships alongside other factors affecting school-wide development. In other words, it was only slowly that I came to understand the subtle interrelationships between collegial relationships and professional growth.

For this chapter, I have re-visited these research projects. What emerges is a developmental view of teachers' inter-adult relationships which should be seen as complementary rather than alternative to other perspectives, notably those which emphasise issues of power, politics and micropolitics. Moreover, this view is not firmly sited within any specific theory of development (e.g. cognitive, life-age; life-stage) since none of these makes sufficient room for interaction between the practitioner and the person. Rather, I suggest that throughout their careers teachers have one over-riding concern – the preservation of a stable sense of personal and professional identity (a "substantial self", Ball, 1972) – but that this identity is realised in varying ways at different times through the developing concerns of different 'situational selves'. This paradoxical view of professional development also offers further insights into teachers' subjective careers (Nias, 1989c; Nias & Aspinwall, 1995), and helps to explain why teachers may appear not to grow: their sense of self is not satisfied by their workplace conditions or by the job itself and is not therefore fully engaged. Such a view is consistent with but goes beyond Fuller's notion of the development of personal concerns (Fuller, 1969; Fuller & Bown, 1975).

SURVIVAL: HELP AND SUPPORT

When the teachers I studied entered or re-entered the profession, or when they started teaching students markedly different from those of whom they already had experience, they often had massive doubts about their professional adequacy, about their capacity to help individuals learn, to be satisfactory disciplinarians, to fulfil the amorphous yet heavy responsibilities which they felt pressing upon them. In addition, to meet the demands of the job, they worked very hard. Anxious, exhausted and guilty, they felt themselves becoming narrow-minded and petty, self-conceptions which compounded their lack of technical self-confidence.

Although they usually turned for reassurance to trusted friends and family outside their schools, it was to their colleagues that they most often looked for immediate assistance. They desired to be, as soon as possible, competent and skilled practitioners. So, they wanted to see examples in action of craft skill, to observe models of good practice in order to learn how "(in this school) successful teachers behave". They also wanted practical help – materials, constructive advice, relief with paperwork, administration or out-of-class chores, tactful intervention by someone who would occasionally take over the class or remove recalcitrant children from it. As one teacher said, "If someone had been there to help me, I might not have made such a mess of my first year"; she felt that she would, in consequence, have developed faster and more surely into an effective teacher.

In very few schools was it possible to observe the classroom practice of other teachers, since the conditions under which most primary teachers work meant that "you never see anyone teaching". Exceptions to this were the schools which took the professional learning of teachers seriously and which, in consequence, built into their daily and weekly programmes opportunities for teachers to see one another in action, to work alongside one another, to discuss curriculum materials or examples of children's work (see in particular, Nias et al., 1992). The optimum conditions for such developmental support were pairs or small groups. When pressures on staff and resources made help of this kind a luxury, much was achieved by whole school meetings in which children shared current work with one another and with all the teachers in the school (Nias, 1989b, 1993). Staff constantly paid tribute to the amount and quality of professional help that they received from such "sharing assemblies". Individuals also found it easy to ask for help from teachers in nearby rooms or, more generally, in the staffroom, because of the value attached to learning by the culture of these schools.

In other schools teachers' felt-need for technical assistance, support and reassurance was often met by an older or more experienced staff member (not always a teacher: I have evidence of caretakers (janitors), secretaries, ancillary and even cleaning staff fulfilling this role). Whatever their formal status, such "rescuers" tended to be perceived as "middle-aged", "experienced", "capable". Sometimes they were explicitly described as "motherly" or "fatherly". They were remembered with affection for their kindness, interest, readiness to listen, and for their generosity with time, materials and ideas. Sikes et al., (1985) found older colleagues of this kind fulfilling a similar role in secondary schools. In Nias (1987a) I explored in greater detail the part played by such "professional parents"; and in Nias and Aspinwall (1995) I argued that some older women have created a satisfying 'horizontal' career for themselves by using their energy, talent and enthusiasm to help and influence their less experienced colleagues. There is little evidence that such teachers were officially designated as "mentors". Accessibility, willingness and kindness were more important than organised systems. Whatever their origins, the presence of such teachers in a school served two developmental purposes: the induction and support of neophytes and the career extension of capable women frustrated by conventional, vertical promotion systems (see Nias 1987b for a case study of such a woman).

When inexperienced teachers failed to find in their schools the kind of practical help which they craved, it was almost always because the school culture was individualised or Balkanised (Fullan & Hargreaves, 1991) rather than collaborative (Nias et al., 1989). In other words teachers felt isolated or restricted to their own resources or those of a staff sub-group and could not turn for assistance to the staff as a whole. There was little feeling that individuals' problems were "ours" rather than "yours". Their comments reflected a sense of enforced and unwelcome independence (e.g. "There's no one here to fall back on"), or of inter-adult competition and their own resulting insecurity (e.g. "They think you can't cope, if you ask for help").

Another effect of individualistic or divided staffrooms was to deepen individuals' territorialism, often making them suspicious of proffered support and defensive or selective in their use of it. In addition, as the confidence and felt-autonomy of inexperienced teachers grew, they needed to establish boundaries between themselves and others, in order fully to establish their own professional identities. So, whatever the culture of the school, it was common for teachers to talk of a period during which they had seen the assistance of their colleagues as "pushing ideas on me" or "not giving me the chance to develop my own ways". There is evidently a fine line, perhaps analogous to that required in parenting and certainly familiar in teaching, between giving the inexperienced enough help to ensure self-confidence and healthy risk-taking and giving so much that it encourages dependence or fosters resentment.

Teachers experience disturbing emotions as well as practical difficulties. Among the most common are fear, anxiety, guilt, anger and frustration (Drummond, 1996). Behind them all lies a felt-need to be responsible for and in control of all aspects of learning in the classroom and, frequently, a moral imperative to adopt a compassionate, caring stance towards students. The difficulty of meeting these socially-prescribed but individually internalised goals means that teachers often suffer loss of self-esteem, a sense of failure and of depressive guilt (Hargreaves, 1994). We found that teachers wanted their colleagues to be sensitive to their emotional needs, to respond with empathy, sympathy, and, occasionally, wise counselling. They were deeply appreciative of opportunities to talk, to share their sense of worthlessness and failure, to relax and above all to laugh.

By the same token, they wanted opportunities to share the moments of excitement, fulfilment and extreme happiness which were as much part of their experience as were terror, anxiety and rage. Yet often they found it even more difficult to share their successes than their failures, encountering in their schools an expectation that neither joy nor anguish would be publicly shared; the professional privacy of the classroom helped to create a related climate of emotional isolationism. As teachers sometimes said, "In this school, we all keep in our rooms".

The schools in which all teachers, not just the insecure, felt happiest and most confident were those in which adults "shared" – equipment, students, space, time, ideas, authority, expertise, feelings. The use of this phrase indicated the existence within a staff group of a sense of mutual dependence and collective responsibility, encouraged by reciprocal openness and by a respect for others' need for self-confidence and emotional security. In all these senses "sharing" strongly resembles the "culture of collaboration" which we later identified (Nias et al., 1989) as the hallmark of schools in which staff members work productively and harmoniously together, whatever their personal differences. However, to be fully effective, such collaboration must not be "contrived" or "comfortable" (Fullan & Hargreaves, 1991). When it is achieved, "You never feel on your own", as one teacher said, explaining why she had turned down opportunities for promotion to stay in the same school for eight years.

Central to "sharing", that is, to collaborative cultures, were talking and listening, laughter and praise. I noted two decades ago (Nias, 1980) that the most powerful contribution which principals could make to the development of new teachers was to be readily available for discussion with them. All our subsequent evidence has confirmed this finding and in addition, the professional value of frequent and unfettered discussion among colleagues. Teachers learn a great deal from talking with and listening to those whom they respect for their craft skills and high standards, but whom they also see as accessible and non-judgmental. Nias et al. (1992) identified forms of organisation which bring teachers together (e.g. meetings; leadership structures) as one of the factors facilitating "whole school" curriculum development; collegial talk is seen as such an essential aspect of professional learning that it cannot be left to chance. Yet without a culture which values such learning and promotes a supportively open context for it, forms of organisation by themselves achieve little.

Humour and laughter were highly valued because they served a number of purposes: reducing tension, inducing relaxation, promoting and maintaining a sense of social cohesion, symbolising resistance to unpopular policies or intrusive agencies (e.g. inspectors). The importance of humour in maintaining staff morale and promoting individual confidence is a continuing theme in the literature (see for example Nias, 1989a; Nias et al., 1989; Acker, 1991; Jeffrey & Woods, 1996). But the interpersonal attribute both most valued and most noticeable for its absence was a readiness to give praise and recognition. Schools in which a 'culture of collaboration' existed were characterised by a great deal of mutual appreciation and encouragement. I also noted a great deal of laughter and of praise among a primary school staff struggling together with the practical and ideological problems of "mainstreaming" children with learning difficulties (Nias, 1994).

In all of these schools, much was due to the example set by leaders (e.g. principals, deputies, curriculum coordinators) who themselves modelled the capacity to discuss, listen, laugh and give recognition to others. Even they, however, found it difficult to recognise adequately the previous achievements and experiences of late entrants to teaching and of women who had taken a career break for child rearing. Such teachers, especially if they were women, often felt profoundly unappreciated and in consequence resentful (Nias & Aspinwall, 1995).

Schools where "sharing" is the norm are probably not in the majority in England

and Wales, though their number may be growing, paradoxically in response to a centrally imposed National Curriculum (Acker, 1991; Woods, 1995; Croll, 1996). However, there are still "tensions in the staffroom" (Nias, 1989a) which make it hard for teachers to relax with their colleagues and prepare themselves emotionally for their next encounter with children. In my research, there were four main causes of such tension, all tending to promote micro-political activity. The first was differences in beliefs and values about, for example, the social and moral purposes of education, the nature of knowledge, how children learn. In an extreme form such differences polarised teachers into the Balkanised cultures identified by Fullan and Hargreaves (1991). The second was a spirit of competition among the staff, itself nearly always a manifestation of unresolved historical rivalries (e.g. over promotion, control of resources). Related to this was unequally distributed power which enabled some staff to bully, dominate or intimidate others. Lastly, a very close relationship between the principal or other senior manager and one other staff member inhibited general communication, especially when this relationship was known to extend into their private lives.

Many teachers saw clearly that workplace conditions characterised by these kinds of tensions did not nourish them or their colleagues. To be sure, the purpose of the school was to care for and educate children. Nevertheless, the welfare of the children was intimately bound up with the well-being of the adults who worked with them. If the latter did not feel accepted as people in the staffroom, they would not be fully at ease in the classroom. Besides, it was philosophically inconsistent to treat children as 'whole' and 'individual' but to ignore the personhood of their teachers. One principal put it forcefully:

> Teaching isn't just working with children, it's enjoying the staffroom and the laughing that goes on there. This needs to be built up if it doesn't exist. If you find other teachers boring then you shouldn't be in teaching. They probably are narrow and boring and conformist, but then so are most accountants and most plumbers. If you feel that way about your colleagues then you are better out of the profession. Schools need their staffrooms.

IDENTIFICATION: REFERENCE GROUPS

The fact that practitioners know they can cope, even cope well, with the job does not mean that they therefore see themselves as teachers. In Nias (1985; 1989a) individuals' willingness to identify as teachers depended in large measure on their ability to find an educational context which "felt right for me" or "let me be myself". They actively searched, within their schools and by seeking new positions, for an in-school reference group whose members shared their social, moral or educational beliefs and confirmed them in their self-defining values. If they failed to find such a group, they often left teaching or marginalised its importance in their lives. When they found referential support, they felt more confident in their choice of career and could "become" teachers. Such a group might consist of "just one other"; its salience lay not in its size but in its capacity for mutual self-confirmation. It was particularly influential when it had a social or, even more powerfully, an affective dimension; and when individuals could also see other teachers as negative reference groups, i.e. as examples of what "I do not want to be like".

In-school reference groups affected not only the kind and level of self-investment that individuals chose to make in their work, but also the nature and direction of their commitment. Membership could deepen satisfactions, fuel discontents and provide mutual support in innovation and retrenchment. Such groups sometimes formed "niches" for their members (i.e. places where people, shared values (culture) and institutional resources came together, Little, 1996), and enabled their members to secure their educational interests by "subversion" (Pollard, 1985) or "strategic compliance" (Sikes, Measor, & Woods, 1985). However, they did not always work in the direction of professional improvement. Indeed, some teachers advanced strong in-school referential pressure as the reason why "I'm a worse teacher than I was three years ago".

Despite teachers' strong felt-need for referential support from their colleagues, they often found themselves in schools where they felt "I'm the only one who . . . (for example, believes in competition/encourages children to think independently/ does not rely on the maths textbook)". Under these circumstances, they were faced with a conflict between their need for practical and emotional support and their desire to avoid the cognitive dissonance induced by over-close contact with colleagues whose behaviour exemplified values they did not share. If they could not move to another school, they adopted one of two sets of self-protective strategies. They became adept at impression management and other forms of strategic compliance, thus assuring themselves of essential support without compromising their freedom to behave in the classroom as they believed best. Alternatively, they avoided interaction with their colleagues. (Recently I was in a school where a teacher, requested not to isolate herself so much in her classroom but to join the rest of the staff at break times, duly appeared in the staffroom – but wearing a personal stereo.) Such behaviour safeguarded the individual's sense of professional identity, but reduced the likelihood that staff members would be able to work wholeheartedly together on the formation or execution of common policies.

In other words, school-based reference groups have a two-edged development potential. Within cohesive sub-groups, individuals find an identity. Their members often collaborate closely and strengthen one another's practice. Moreover, as Kelchtermans (1996) suggests, teachers may need the defence provided by such groups if their definition of self-as-teacher is challenged by influential others. In this sense, professional growth and the "politics of identity" (Calhoun, 1994) are closely related. But a price is paid in terms of whole-school development for the sense of belonging and potency that individuals gain from group membership. The stronger their identification with particular educational, social or moral perspectives, the less easy it is for them to consider alternatives, to compromise, to work with others towards the implementation of whole-school programmes. It is the continuing existence of conflicting reference groups, even within small schools, that gives the micropolitical view of schools (e.g. Ball, 1987, 1994; Hoyle, 1986; Blase, 1991) a particular salience. Whole-school development can seldom be achieved without negotiation, compromise and mutual manipulation, because of the extreme difficulty of creating and sustaining a complete staff group which is also, and on all relevant matters, an educational or moral reference group. Even in the schools whose staffs were identified for us as "working well together" (Nias et al., 1989) or "trying to develop a whole-school curriculum" (in relation to one or more issues) (Nias et al., 1992; Nias, 1994), we found disagreements, differences in policy or practice, matters on which individuals found it hard to compromise and in relation to which principals were therefore forced to exercise their authority. Collegially-based professional development at any level other than that of the individual or sub-group will always be impeded by the basic assumptions and value-orientations of different teachers and of the reference groups which grow up round them.

"GETTING BETTER" AND "MAKING A MARK": LEARNING FROM AND INFLUENCING OTHERS

Teachers need their colleagues to help them survive their early encounters with the job or settle into it with a sense of personal fit. Yet, perhaps surprisingly, collegial relationships seem to become even more salient as individuals become older and more experienced. This may be because, with greater confidence, teachers' concerns move outwards from their own survival, first towards accomplished craft performance and then to their impact on others. Their preoccupation is still with themselves, but as increasingly skilled practitioners who look to other teachers both for new ideas, stimulation and challenge and as the potential recipients of their own knowledge and expertise.

Nias (1989a) suggested that many mid-career teachers actively searched for professional extension, viewing their colleagues as one means of achieving this. They found successful peer learning rewarding and exciting. Those who had at some point worked, however fleetingly, with people who had "stretched" or "recharged" them, recalled these encounters with animated faces and their language was full of metaphors of energy and movement. This sense of dynamism, enthusiasm and growth was a hallmark of all the schools we studied in Nias et al., (1992). So too were the job-satisfaction and enthusiasm of all the staff members, despite their long hours of work and resulting fatigue (see also Woods, 1995).

Some teachers also wanted "challenge" from their colleagues, using harsher, more confrontational verbs such as "hammer", "thrash" or "hack". Few found it. As many other studies have noted, open debate and disagreement are not the norm among primary teachers. Teachers themselves suggested a number of reasons, other than traditions of isolationism and individualism, why this might be so. Influenced through their training and that of their colleagues by the legacies of Rousseau and Froebel, they felt constrained by the need to preserve "good relations" in schools which aimed to present children with a model of adult harmony. They were aware that they and their colleagues had invested their beliefs and values in their work and it was therefore hard to offer an intellectual challenge which was not also perceived as a personal one. They had little training in the discussion of ideas and worked in a profession which tended to be hierarchical and authority-dependent. To these reasons, I would add the perpetual and increasing pressure upon teachers' time (Campbell & Neill, 1994), their tendency to spend any time they have for interaction in the company of those who reinforce rather than challenge their perspectives, and to the divided and bureaucratic management structures of many schools which make it difficult for teachers to meet one another in an atmosphere which invites challenge rather than consensus.

Notwithstanding, teachers continue to look to other members of their staff group to help them grow professionally, to keep them alive in the job and excited with it. Despite the move towards a centralised curriculum in England and Wales, teachers still have scope and incentive to develop their practice by working together in creative ways (Nias et al., 1992; Pollard et al., 1994; Woods, 1995; Croll, 1996). Provided that time and enthusiasm are not further eroded by the growing burden of paperwork and administration imposed upon practitioners by recent government policies, they have a continuing potential to help one another grow. Whether the need for collegial "challenge" felt by a minority of practitioners will be fully met is more doubtful; neither the education of teachers nor their present workplace conditions encourage them in the belief that confrontation is developmentally productive. As one teacher ruefully claimed, "No one ever says 'You're wrong'".

To argue that over time a change takes place in many teachers' personal concerns is not to suggest a view of professional development with phases which are normative, mutually exclusive or irreversible. This is particularly the case when individuals move into what Fuller (1969) calls a concern for their "impact' upon children and which I have construed as a desire also for influence over other teachers and more generally, upon some aspect of the educational system. Some individuals sought promotion to leadership or management positions and others found ways of exercising influence, even power, over their colleagues without taking on formal roles. However, a desire for "impact" developed over very different time spans. Moreover, not all the experienced teachers involved in our research projects wanted to make a mark upon other adults. Some seemed content to retain the classroom as their centre of gravity and interest for all of their working lives. To complicate matters, some kinds of activities, notably working in teams or cohesive whole staff groups, satisfied the need both to learn from and to influence others. To be a member of a successful team enhanced individuals' sense of accomplishment. At the same time, it increased their influence over one another. Similarly, teachers who stimulated or extended one another's thinking were sometimes interested in their own professional growth, sometimes in that of others. Generalisations about the pace and sequence of teachers' developmental concerns must always be open to modification and subject to qualification. This has been recently demonstrated in England and Wales where the introduction in the past decade of a National Curriculum and centralised assessment has thrust curricular responsibilities upon all staff members and, in some instances (e.g. testing, information technology) has given younger teachers an influence which they have enthusiastically accepted. Similarly, the introduction of compulsory teacher appraisal has opened up a fresh area in which teachers with different levels of experience and developmental concerns can interact, exercise mutual influence and learn from one another (Bollington, Hopkins, & West, 1990).

That said, in all our research projects there were teachers who decided to seek promotion to senior management posts, or to assume unpaid positions of responsibility, in order to have a more direct influence over their colleagues than they currently had. In different ways they came to realize that they could "affect all the children, through my colleagues" (e.g. by leading curriculum development, through involvement in financial and curricular decision-making). Alternatively, their desire to act upon their educational ideals led them into principalships (through which they hoped "to make my mark" or "fulfil my educational vision") (Hayes, 1996), union affairs, teacher education, advisory or inspectorial posts. However, in the UK many of the routes for self-extension, other than principalships, have been blocked or made less professionally attractive by changes imposed since 1992. It is not clear what paths primary teachers who do not want to become managers will now take, if they wish to have a wider influence within their profession.

Those who chose to stay in school as teachers rather than principals often tried to shape their colleagues' practice or thinking by working closely with or alongside them. However, this could become a potentially self-defeating activity. Teachers found it hard to share the intimacy of their classrooms with those who did not have similar frames of reference in relation to, for example, learning, teaching, discipline and control. They could "pull together", as they commonly expressed it, with colleagues who "saw things the same way", but only with very great difficulty and mutual tolerance could they undertake joint activities with those outside their reference groups. But because there were affective, social and professional development rewards to be gained from working in cohesive groups or teams, individuals continued to search for opportunities to work collaboratively. All too often the result was the development within a school of "camps" or "factions", each enriching to their members, but an obstacle to whole-staff discussion and decision-making.

The more senior teachers were, the more destructive to the school community they felt such groups to be. Often, they dedicated a good deal of time and effort to "building bridges", as they often described their efforts to bring sub-groups constructively together. Their most common frustrations were teachers' allegiance to their own beliefs, the physical isolation of most classrooms, lack of talking time, absence of back-up from principals and lack of shared assumptions among the staff about the nature and purposes of the school. Nias et al., (1989, 1992) and Nias (1994) all make it clear that it took skilled principals, who had an unshakeable vision of what could ultimately be achieved, years of perseverance and untiring work successfully to create a "whole school".

Such principals were greatly aided in this task by the presence of one or more teachers who took a whole-school rather than a sub-group perspective. Such teachers were often, but not always, older women with a keen sense of their own need for professional extension and a great willingness to achieve this by helping the development of others. In some senses they were "extended professionals" (Hoyle, 1974). Frequently, they had undertaken advanced professional studies, they perceived classroom events in relation to school policies and goals, valued collaboration, compared their methods with those of their colleagues, derived satisfaction from problem-solving and from having control over their work situation. But they acted as they did in large measure in order to become better "restricted professionals", that is they had an atheoretical, pragmatic concern for the effectiveness of their practice, but saw that this would be enhanced if it were consistent with or complementary to that of others. In Nias (1989a) I have called such teachers "bounded professionals". They had whole-school perspectives and worked to improve collegial relationships, but they were school-bounded in their approach to other educational issues.

"Bounded professionals" of this kind often felt frustrated by the "restricted" views of their colleagues and by the career structure of teaching which increasingly seemed to deny them vertical promotion without also removing them from teaching. They were ready to take on responsibilities, eager to share their expertise with others, anxious to improve practice throughout the school, but often felt their workplace conditions did not encourage these activities. Anecdotal evidence suggests that the introduction into the UK of teacher appraisal and of school "mentors" for education students and newly qualified teachers has provided much-needed lateral career extensions for teachers of this kind. What we do not yet know is whether they will suffer a similar frustration to that experienced by teachers who in the past two decades have taken on curriculum or policy leadership, only to find themselves unable, for all the reasons suggested earlier, significantly to influence their colleagues' practice (see also Huberman, 1993; Little, 1996). As one such teacher wearily said of her fellow-teachers as she applied for early retirement, "It doesn't matter what you do. They go their own way anyway".

THE PERSON AT WORK

A central assumption of this chapter is that primary teachers make little distinction between their personal and professional identities. They invest a great deal of their self-defining values, aspirations, personality, talents, interests, emotions in the job; and, all too often for the comfort of their friends and families, take their work into their private lives, literally, mentally and emotionally. Three things follow from this merging of identities: individuals' personal development influences the work that they do in school and may even in part account for it; private problems and preoccupations (e.g. health, domestic anxieties, bereavement, financial commitments) are not left at the school gate; and for both these reasons individuals may therefore look, consciously or unconsciously, to their colleagues for the satisfaction of personal needs through work. For example, the lonely hope for friendship and a sense of belonging at work, sometimes too for a social life outside school. Those who feel unloved at home often turn to their colleagues for acceptance, tolerance, even affection. Lacking success and self-esteem outside work, they look for recognition and praise within it, and are grateful for opportunities to display and use their talents with adults as well as students. When their private lives seem to go out of control, they restore the balance in school, taking or making opportunities to be effective and in charge. School, or sub-groups within it, can also provide individuals with a chance to learn and grow and a sense of shared purpose, of self-fulfilment through active corporate membership.

Repeatedly, during twenty years of ethnographic research into English primary schools I have been struck by the extent to which cognitive, life-age or life-stage developments, individual problems and pastoral needs are all brought into school. Even more remarkable is the extent to which these are met by the demands of the job and through interaction with colleagues. However, this is not always the case. To take a humanistic perspective on teacher development is to accept the limitations as well as the strengths of schools as workplaces for adults. Not all schools have cultures or even "niches" which accept, let alone value, the individual as a 'whole person' nor which provide opportunities for self-expression and fulfilment. Schools can frustrate and constrain the adults who work in them while genuinely attempting to develop students.

BRINGING IT ALL TOGETHER

Finally we should note the potentially conflictual nature of the varied expectations which teachers have of their colleagues. For example, at different times they may want emotional support and technical help, but also autonomy; collaborative work towards common ends but the challenge of new ideas. Are these needs compatible? Can a staff which is affectively supportive also be professionally alive? How far can teachers encourage dependence on one another by giving help and guidance while also fostering interdependence through dispersed leadership? Is it possible for any collegial context to satisfy individuals' personal needs while also extending each of them professionally in appropriate ways?

In Nias (1987c, 1989a) I attempted to give tentative answers to these questions by drawing upon the detailed accounts given me by four teachers of what one described as "the best experience of all". These four accounts, two from men, two from women, all well-established in career terms, but each describing a different situation, describe working groups which were seldom larger than six in number and which arose in part spontaneously. Relationships within them were non-competitive and relatively egalitarian. Each group had a leader, in the sense that someone took the initiative in starting discussions, but he/she then became a member of the group, encouraging leadership to move as appropriate between them all. Despite their differences in age, background and experience, members had enough in common to start talking, and once the habit of talking had been formed, they found it so valuable that they made time for it whenever they could.

In discussion they felt valued and secure, so they talked openly. Topics for discussion arose spontaneously and reflected individual preoccupations, both personal and professional. Differences of opinion were welcomed, often invited, and individuals were willing to learn from one another. Over time, the groups developed a life of their own, enriching the thinking and behaviour of their members who felt they had achieved "a new kind of stability based on the recognition and acceptance of ambiguity, uncertainty and open choice" (Abercrombie, 1969).

These characteristics are also to be found, though not so uniformly or in such a pronounced fashion, in the staffs observed in Nias et al., (1989, 1992) and Nias, (1994). In particular, as the groups were larger (up to 16), their members tended to talk together in overlapping twos and threes, coming together less frequently as a whole group. Evidently situations can exist in which colleagues assist one another's daily work, confirm yet extend one another's basic assumptions about education and its purposes, widen one another's professional horizons and responsibilities, provide for one another an experience of independence within interdependence, and offer one another attention, esteem and affection (even love). At their best, such groups were reminiscent of the "peak experience" described by Maslow (1973). This state, he argues, earns its description because through it we transcend the contradictions and conflicting urges of our human natures and discover who and what we are. In a similar fashion, teachers in these collegial groups were able to transcend the contradictory requirements that they had of one another, discovering in the process a fuller sense of personal identity as part of a whole.

CONCLUSION

I have argued that teacher development depends upon the growth of the person in the role and that the teacher-as-person is simultaneously stable and changing: stable in the sense that individuals continually seek to preserve their 'substantial self'; changing in that this sense of self is realised in different ways at different phases in teachers' professional lives. As a means of understanding this contradiction I have used the notion of developing personal concerns, building on Fuller's seminal work. Teachers enter the profession preoccupied first with survival and then with a sense of fit between self and choice of occupation. If both of these concerns are satisfied, they look for ways of becoming better practitioners. Some then move into a phase where they want to exercise a wider or more lasting influence upon others, to leave their footprints in the sands of time. Throughout, however, their concerns are self-referential.

Such a development is not teleological. It depends not just upon successful and rewarding interactions with students, but also upon appropriate collegial relationships. Initially teachers need their colleagues for practical and emotional support, though they are selective in the help that they accept, rejecting ways of teaching or relating to children which run counter to their view of themselves as people as well as practitioners. They are therefore happiest in a social setting where 'sharing' and collaboration are the norm, allowing them to preserve their self-esteem by avoiding a one-sided sense of dependence. Individuals also need an in-school reference group to reinforce and sustain their view of themselves. If they do not find it, they adopt self-preserving strategies which often reduce the likelihood of further professional growth. Those who do receive referential support for "the sort of teacher I want to be" usually then look to their colleagues for professional stimulation. Some find further extension in an ability to teach or otherwise influence those with whom they work.

Throughout, the key to collegially-assisted development is compatibility in teachers' moral and educational beliefs and values. So, different sub-cultures within a school may enhance their members' growth, but may in the process obstruct or stalemate that of others. Put another way, the professional development of some individuals may be achieved only by inhibiting the development of the school as a whole. Resolving this dilemma is a formidable task. Under the 'soft-centred', humanistic view of teacher development presented here, lies a hard-edged awareness of the power of individual values and of the need for political and micropolitical processes which may help to reconcile them.

REFERENCES

Abercrombie, M. L. J. (1969). *The anatomy of judgement* . Harmondsworth: Penguin.
Acker, S. (1990). Teachers' culture in an English primary school: Continuity and change. *British Journal of Sociology of Education*, **11**, 257–273.
Acker, S. (1991). Teacher relationships and educational reform in England and Wales. *Curriculum Journal*, **2**, 301–316.
Ball, S. (1972). Self and identity in the context of deviance: the case of criminal abortion. In R. Scott & J. Douglas (Eds.), *Theoretical perspectives in deviance* . New York: Basic Books.
Ball, S. (1987). *The micropolitics of schools: Towards a theory of school organizations*, London: Routledge.
Ball, S. (1994). Micropolitics of schools. In T. Husen & J. Postlethwaite (Eds.), *The international encyclopaedia of education*, 2nd Edition. Oxford: Pergamon.
Blase, J. (Ed.). (1991). *The politics of life in schools: Power, conflict and cooperation*. London: Sage.
Bollington, R., Hopkins, D., & West, M. (1990). *Introduction to teacher appraisal*. London: Cassell.
Calhoun, C. (Ed.). (1994). *Social theory and the politics of identity* . Oxford: Blackwell.
Campbell, R. J., & Neill, S. (1994). *Primary Teachers at Work*, London: Routledge.
Croll, P. (Ed.). (1996). *Teachers, pupils and primary schooling: Continuity and change* . London: Cassell.
Drummond, M. J. (1996). The pain must go on. Essay review. *Cambridge Journal of Education*, **26**(3).
Fullan, M., & Hargreaves, A. (1991). *What's worth fighting for? Working Together for your school* . Milton Keynes: Open University Press.
Fuller, F. (1969). Concerns of teachers: A developmental characterisation. *American Educational Research Journal*, **6**, 207–226.
Fuller, F., & Bown, P. (1975). Becoming a teacher. In K. Ryan (Ed.), *Teacher Education*, 74th Yearbook of the National Society for the Study of Education. Chicago: University of Chicago Press.
Hargreaves, A. (1994). *Changing teachers, changing times: Teachers' work and culture in the postmodern age* . London: Cassell.
Hayes, D. (1996). Aspiration, perspiration and reputation: Idealism and self-preservation in small school primary headship. *Cambridge Journal of Education*, **26**(3).
Hoyle, E. (1974). Professionality, professionalism and control in teaching, *London Educational Review*, **3**, 13–19.
Hoyle, E. (1986). *The politics of school management*. London: Hodder & Stoughton.

Huberman, M. (1993/1989). *The lives of teachers*, translated by Jonathan Neufeld. New York: Teachers' College Press.

Jeffrey, R., & Woods, P. (1996). Feeling deprofessionalized: The social construction of emotions during an OFSTED inspection. *Cambridge Journal of Education,* **26**(3).

Kelchtermans, G. (1996). Teacher vulnerability: Understanding its moral and political roots. *Cambridge Journal of Education,* **26**(3).

Little, J. W. (1996). The emotional contours and career trajectories of (disappointed) reform enthusiasts. *Cambridge Journal of Education,* **26**(3).

Maslow, A. (1973). *Further reaches of human nature.* Harmondsworth: Penguin.

Nias, J. (1980). Leadership styles, and job satisfaction in primary schools. In T. Bush, R. Glatter, & C. Riches (Eds.), *Approaches to school management* . London: Harper & Row.

Nias, J. (1985). Reference groups in primary teaching: Talking, listening and identity. In S. J. Ball & I. F. Goodson (Eds.), *Teachers' lives and careers.* London: Falmer Press.

Nias, J. (1987a). Learning the job while playing a part: Staff development in the early years of teaching. In G. Southworth (Ed.), *Readings in primary school management* . London: Falmer Press.

Nias, J. (1987b). One finger, one thumb: A case study of the deputy head's part in the leadership of a nursery/infant school. In G. Southworth (Ed.), *Readings in primary school management.* London: Falmer Press.

Nias, J. (1987c). Learning from difference: A collegial approach to change. In W. J. Smyth (Ed.), *Changing the nature of pedagogical knowledge* London: Falmer Press.

Nias, J. (1989a). *Primary teachers talking: A study of teaching as work* London: Routledge.

Nias, J. (1989b). *Meeting together, the symbolic and pedagogic importance of school assemblies within a collaborative culture.* Paper presented to the Annual Conference of the American Educational Research Association, San Francisco.

Nias, J. (1989c). Subjectively speaking: English primary teachers' careers, *International Journal of Educational Research,* **13**(4), 391–401.

Nias J., Southworth, G., & Yeomans, R. (1989). *Primary school staff relationships: A study of organizational cultures* . London: Cassell.

Nias, J., Southworth, G., & Campbell, P. (1992). *Whole school curriculum development in the primary school* . London: Falmer Press.

Nias, J. (1993). *Primary headteachers' use of school assemblies to promote whole school curriculum development.* Paper presented at the Annual Conference of the British Educational Research Association, Liverpool.

Nias, J. (1994). *Review of integration at Drybrook Lower School.* unpublished report, University of Plymouth.

Nias, J., & Aspinwall, K. (1995). Composing a life: Women's stories of their careers. In D. Thomas (Ed.), *Teachers' stories.* Milton Keynes: Open University Press.

Pollard, A. (1985). *The social world of the primary school* . London: Cassell.

Pollard, A., Broadfoot, P., Croll, P., Osborn, M., & Abbott, D. (1994). *Changing English primary schools?* London: Cassell.

Sikes, P., Measor, L. & Woods, P. (1985). *Teachers' concerns: Crises and continuities* . London: Falmer Press.

Woods, P. (1995). *Creative Teachers in Primary Schools.* Milton Keynes: Open University Press.

IV: The Effectiveness of School Improvement Strategies

"World Class" School Improvement: An Analysis of the Implications of Recent International School Effectiveness and School Improvement Research for Improvement Practice

DAVID REYNOLDS

Unversity of Newcastle upon Tyne, UK

In this chapter David Reynolds presents an analysis of the implications of recent international school effectiveness and school improvement research for improvement practice. In so doing he transcends the somewhat artificial boundaries that grew up in the eighties and early nineties between school effectiveness researchers and school improvement practitioners. Such distinctions are, as Reynolds argues, a thing of the past, as those who are at the "cutting edge" of 'managing educational change' transcend both disciplines. Reynolds describes the contribution both fields of activity have made to a new merged paradigm. His analysis of the new paradigm leads to a series of policy recommendations for 'world class' school improvement i.e. importance of school context; avoidance of re-inventing the wheel; increase in international orientation; and the necessity to intervene at 'levels below that of the school'. In concluding Reynolds suggests a number of other directions that the new school improvement paradigm could embrace in the future.

The contexts in which educational systems are situated are now changing rapidly as the international economic, social and political systems change. In virtually all societies there are pressures upon educational systems to increase their outcomes, such as from the 'America 2000' goals adopted in the United States (Stringfield, Ross & Smith, 1996) and from the programme of simultaneous 'pressure and support' adopted by the incoming Labour government in Britain (Department for Education and Employment, 1997).

In virtually all societies there are pressures to expand the range of outcomes that educational systems produce, with for example the British system being urged to improve its achievement levels of basic skills and at the same time adopt new more work-related outcomes (Barber, 1996). By contrast some of the countries of the Pacific Rim are attempting to add new, more social outcomes at the same time as maintaining their very high levels of basic academic skill achievements (Reynolds, 1997).

However, the resources that educational systems currently possess, to combat their problems and surmount the pressures upon them by increasing their level of outcomes, are now more substantial than ever before. Firstly, we now possess a body of knowledge about 'what works' in the field of school effectiveness that simply did not exist two decades ago (Teddlie & Reynolds, 1997) and which relates to issues such as the size of school effects, their consistency/stability and crucially

241

D. Hopkins (ed.), The Practice and Theory of School Improvement, 241-251.
© 2005 *Springer. Printed in the Netherlands.*

to the processes at school level that are associated with effectiveness (see reviews in Reynolds et al., 1994; Mortimore, 1991; Bosker & Scheerens, 1997).

Secondly, we now possess a rigorous body of knowledge in the area of teacher or instructional effectiveness that has recently been cemented by the addition of much useful Dutch work (e.g. Creemers, 1994) to that already existing within the American research tradition established in the 1980's by Brophy and Good (1986). Crucially, the mechanisms of ensuring professional development by means of this knowledge base have been reliably developed through the work of Joyce and associates (see this volume), and the possibilities of individual teachers being able to access this information and utilise it within their schools, have been facilitated by the growing availability of methods of classroom/teacher observation that are of established reliability and validity (Schaffer, 1994).

Thirdly, the development of systems of performance indicators for undertaking school evaluation has meant that schools possess the capacity for 'data richness' (Stringfield, 1995) that has been argued to be essential for reliable organisational functioning. Through systems such as ALIS ('A' Level Information System), YELLIS (Year Eleven Information System) and PIPS (Performance Indicators in Primary Schools), it is now possible for schools to have their internal variation in effectiveness exposed, to aid the benchmarking of their less able or effective departments and individuals against their more effective (Fitz-Gibbon, 1996).

Fourthly, school improvement itself has emerged with a quite robust knowledge base concerning those processes that are needed to improve both individual schools and entire educational systems (see reviews in Fullan, 1991; Hopkins, Ainscow, & West, 1994). Four phases seem to have been in evidence in the improvement discipline over time:

- a focus upon the adoption of curriculum material that characterised the 1960's and 1970's, and which had such disappointing results in terms of take up (Reynolds, 1988);
- a focus upon the explanation of failure that took up the early 1980's, in which the differences between implementation and institutionalisation became a focus of study and ultimately of understanding (Miles, 1983);
- a focus upon the processes of school improvement of the mid to late 1980's, in which major large scale study was undertaken in the United States (Crandall et al., 1982; Rosenholtz, 1989; Louis & Miles, 1990) and in Europe through The International School Improvement Project (ISIP) (Hopkins, 1987);
- a contemporary focus upon the management of change, in which researchers and practitioners actually participate in school development and generate accounts as they bring school change about (Fullan, 1993).

THE SCHOOL EFFECTIVENESS/SCHOOL IMPROVEMENT INTERFACE

All the above considerable resources that educational systems now possess, both in terms of knowledge and in terms of valid programmes, are of course potentiated by the increasing ease with which the knowledge travels between countries. The school improvement 'paradigm' is international, with recent accounts of the literature routinely referring to scholarship from a dozen or more countries (Fullan, 1991; Hopkins et al., 1994). School effectiveness research too, after a period of heavy ethnocentrism in which researchers stopped the search for good practice at their own geographical boundaries (see reviews in Reynolds & Cuttance, 1992), has now become internationalised. The effectiveness field consequently now exhibits an internationalised knowledge base in which references within studies are usually to multiple countries rather than merely to the 'home' country of the authors (see Teddlie & Reynolds, 1997) and in which an increasing number of research groups are forming which combine scholars from multiple countries (as in the International School Effectiveness Research Project team of Reynolds, Creemers, Stringfield and Teddlie), the collaborative work of Joyce and Hopkins, and the close links between those school effectiveness researchers with methodological interests, such as Goldstein, Bosker, Hill, Sammons, Thomas, Rowe and Scheerens (see the co-operative material in Bosker and Scheerens, 1997).

However, it is only comparatively recently that school improvement programmes in their basic conceptualisation and design have reflected the influences of these multiple constituencies and bodies of knowledge, because of the past major differences between the paradigms or belief systems of the 'school improvers' and of the school 'effectiveness research community'. The detail of this is explored elsewhere (Reynolds, 1993; Reynolds, Hopkins & Stoll, 1993; Reynolds, 1996) but, briefly, school improvement historically celebrated:

- a 'bottom up' orientation in which improvement was owned by the individual school and its staff;
- a qualitative orientation to research methodology;
- a concern with changing organisational processes rather than the outcomes of the school (the much lauded concern with the 'journey');
- a concern to treat educational outcomes as not 'given' but problematic;
- a concern to see schools as dynamic institutions requiring extended study more than 'snapshot' cross sectional studies.

These core assumptions clashed with those of school effectiveness, generating an absence until recently of any 'synergy' or 'confluence' of perspectives and programmes in the two fields. Effectiveness research by contrast evidenced historically:

- a commitment to quantitative methods;
- a focus upon outcomes which were accepted as being a 'good' that was not to be questioned;
- a concern with the formal organisation of schools rather than with their more informal processes;
- a focus upon description of schools as static, steady state organisations generated by brief research study.

THE NEW, MERGED PARADIGM

After the clearly fragmented intellectual communities of the 1980's what is now emerging is a group of individuals who might be called pragmatists, rather than being either the 'scientists' of the school effectiveness paradigm, or the 'humanists' of the school improvement community. This new group avoids being either one thing or the other by combining elements of both traditions into a new paradigm, in which mixed methods rather than either quantitative or qualitative ones are utilised for description and explanation, and in which the improvement of schools is to be through 'pulling levers' selected from both former traditions.

In part, the contexts that have led to this new group have been the emergence of international organisations such as ICSEI (The International Congress for School Effectiveness and Improvement) that have permitted individuals to 'mix' across paradigms as well as across countries. Much of this 'synergy' has also resulted from the influence of practitioners and policy makers, who have not been willing to confine either their thinking or their methods into the pattern of existing disciplinary restrictions, given their needs to generate rapid improvement in educational quality and outcomes within their localities (see Chapter Four of Reynolds, 1996 for a further elaboration of this point).

Whatever the precise explanations for the emergence of this 'new paradigm', it represents a new way of thinking about school improvement and development whose full ramifications have yet to be felt. What are the key characteristics of the 'new wave' of thinking?

Firstly, there is an enhanced focus upon the importance of pupil outcomes. Such concerns are shown in the data collected within the justifiably well known Halton improvement programme in Canada (Stoll & Fink, 1992) and in the 'Improving the Quality of Education For All (IQEA)' project in the United Kingdom (Hopkins et al., 1996). Instead of the earlier emphasis upon changing the processes of schools, the focus is now upon seeing if these changes are powerful enough to affect pupil outcomes.

Secondly, many more projects than before are adopting a 'mixed' methodological orientation, in which bodies of quantitative data plus qualitative data are used to measure programme quality, programme effects and programme deficiencies as appropriate. Rather than taking a philosophical stance as to the form of data that fits with the supposed philosophical orientation of the field, qualitative for improvement and quantitative for effectiveness, the new paradigm adopts the belief of 'fitness for purpose' and uses whichever methods are appropriate to the problem under study. Quantitative methods are therefore often used to measure the outcomes of schools, and both quantitative methods (questionnaires, interview schedules) and qualitative methods (informal/unstructured observation, ethos indicators, use of historical documents, life histories of key informants) are utilised. The 'Halton' project noted above, and the IQEA project noted above all use mixed methods, as do the High Reliability School Project (Reynolds & Stringfield, 1996; Stringfield, 1995), the Dutch School Improvement Project (Houtveen & Osinga, 1995) and the Barclay/Calvert Project (Stringfield, Bedinger, & Herman, 1995).

Thirdly, the new paradigm utilises knowledge from both the school effectiveness and school improvement traditions in its programmes, utilising the same 'problem centred' rather than 'philosophical' orientation that has determined the blend of methodologies outlined above. The Halton Project, for example, began as an attempt to bring effectiveness knowledge into schools utilising a conventional dissemination strategy, and then later added the traditions of school improvement and school development to take account of the internal school conditions that the effectiveness knowledge was being brought to. The Dutch School Improvement Project involves utilisation of multiple knowledge bases also, and is particularly interesting in that it combines teacher or instructional effectiveness together with school effectiveness and school development knowledge. The High Reliability School Project adds further knowledge bases concerning departmental effectiveness (Harris, Jamieson & Russ, 1995) to those utilised in the Dutch School Improvement Project, and the IQEA Project appears to utilise insights from group-work theory and the human relations tradition in some of its attempts to change internal school and teacher conditions.

Fourthly, the learning level, the instructional behaviours of teachers and the classroom level are increasingly being targeted for explicit programme attention as well as the school level, a marked contrast with school improvement work from the 1980's where 'the school' was often the sole focus. The ISIP noted above itself had reflected this focus (Hopkins, 1987).

It is easy to understand why the "lever" of the school level had historically been pulled so frequently, since of course school improvement and school effectiveness personnel have had close relationships with senior school level personnel, since these level personnel have gone on the courses run by school effectiveness and school improvement persons. The policy discourse in most societies has concerned the school level, not the classroom level. In some societies, as the United Kingdom, there has been until recently no knowledge base or literature about teacher effectiveness or on practices at classroom level which can potentiate student achievement which would lead to any possibility of obtaining balance rather than the maintenance of the past obsession with the school level.

It is now widely agreed, though, that the neglect of a coherent focus upon learning in classrooms has been very costly indeed. Firstly, it is clear that the greatest variation is within schools by department and by individual teacher, rather than between schools. Put simply, the classroom learning level has maybe two or three times the influence on student achievement than the school level does (Creemers, 1994). Secondly, the historical reluctance to focus upon classrooms directly or to turn interventions at school level 'downwards' in schools until they impact on classrooms has hindered the development of successful programmes, because teacher focal concerns within all schools are likely to be much more related to those variables that are located at the classroom level, such as teaching, pedagogy and curriculum, than they are related to those activities at the school level, like management and organisation. This is probably particularly important in ineffective schools, where there may well exist a majority of staff who define the role of the teacher very narrowly as being related to curriculum and instruction, rather than being more broadly related to school level management and organisational factors (Reynolds, 1996). It is clear that the neglect of the classroom level and the celebration of the school level may have historically cost us valuable teacher commitment in these schools in particular, and in all schools in general.

Virtually all the programmes mentioned above from within the 'new paradigm' by contrast share a focus upon the classroom. In the High Reliability School Project, the provision of teacher effectiveness literature to schools is followed by sessions in which teachers in the school meet in departments and consider the implications for their particular subject of the knowledge base. Instruments for individual teachers to observe each other's teaching in their classrooms are then introduced and distributed to staff, and staff then attempt to observe the characteristics of the methods of teachers that are more successful than their own, involving the matching together or 'buddying' of 'less effective' teachers with 'average' ones and 'average' with 'very effective' ones (details of the observation systems are in Schaffer, 1994).

Fifthly, the new paradigm stresses the importance of ensuring reliability or 'fidelity' in the programme implementation across all the organisational members within schools, a marked contrast with the past when improvement programmes did not have to be organisationally 'tight'.

Whilst the High Reliability Schools Project is perhaps the most explicit in terms of attempting to both reduce within school organisational variation by bringing all teachers up to the level of the best and by requiring schools and teachers to participate in a common 'core' of activities, it is clear that the need for reliable implementation and institutionalisation is a concern that features in all the programmes mentioned before. Interestingly, the report in this volume of Stringfield and associates also picks out inadequate or variable implementation, even of the outside school developed programmes that schools utilised 'off the shelf', as a key factor that affected the quality of the programme and the effect of the programme upon student outcomes.

Because of the fact that most improvement programmes have been voluntaristic, because they have usually been linked to existing ongoing school level and individual level continuing professional development, there seems to have been a huge differential within schools in the extent to which the programmes have been taken up. Reading between the lines, it is clear that there has been a tendency for programmes to impact most on the competent "leading edge" of teachers and it is also clear that a more or less significant "trailing edge" may not have participated in the programmes, or at least may not have participated fully. It is therefore likely that there has been, within schools participating in the programmes, therefore, a substantial variation in the extent to which they have permeated within schools and in the extent to which organisational innovations have moved through to implementation from the initiation phase, and ultimately to the institutionalisation phase. Given that there is increasing evidence within school effectiveness of the importance of organisational cohesion, consistency and constancy (Reynolds & Cuttance, 1992), the situation in which there is greater variation between members of staff in a school because of their differential take-up of improvement activities may well have been adversely affecting the quality of student outcomes.

TOWARDS WORLD CLASS SCHOOL IMPROVEMENT

The new paradigm whose characteristics we have outlined above is currently being outlined and celebrated in a number of different ways. At the national policy level, there is evidence of a significant influence of a 'pressure and support' orientation in the recent policy proposals for British schools, with knowledge from school effectiveness, educational evaluation and school improvement being used to resource change (Department for Education and Employment, 1997). At State level in Australia, the 'merged' paradigm appears to be axiomatic (Hill, 1997) and in the United Kingdom the activities of certain local authorities like Birmingham appear to be taken from a wide variety of bodies of scholarship (Barber, 1996). At school level, the popularity of the networks of school/Higher Education collaboration such as the International School Effectiveness and Improvement Centre at the Institute of Education in London, and the activities of the other centres at Bath, Keele, Nottingham and Newcastle is clearly in part linked to their transcendence of the old divisions and their celebration of the 'merged' paradigm that is shown in the contents of three recent British collections (Gray et al., 1996; Reynolds et al., 1996; Stoll & Fink, 1996). The contribution of Stringfield and associates in this volume also shows programmes that are, as we would expect from everything that has gone before, characterised by borrowing from multiple disciplinary, an outcomes orientation, a mixed methodological orientation, a concern to impact on the learning environment (even if this is more rarely realised) and a concern to ensure reliability and consistency in programme implementation.

However, there are a number of further 'cutting edge' directions in which development needs to take place to deliver further intellectual and practical advance in the new paradigm. These include the following, which are outlined below as a series of recommendations of a tentative kind:

(1) *Improvement programmes must be tailored to the individual school context.* What is required by individual schools to improve their organisational functioning and their individual outcomes will vary with the characteristics of that school. An ineffective school with serious weaknesses or problems is unlikely to be in a position to self generate the knowledge needed for its improvement (Reynolds, 1996) whereas a very effective school may need nothing more than a very 'light touch' through the introduction of a performance indicator system in order to increase its effectiveness level further (Fitz-Gibbon, 1996). Contextual factors of importance are likely to be:

- age phase;
- socio economic context of the school's catchment area (Hallinger & Murphy, 1986);
- denominational status (Coleman, Hoffer, & Kilgore, 1981);

- improvement trajectory over time;
- school culture/ethos (Rutter et al., 1979);
- urban/rural context (Teddlie & Reynolds, 1997).

(2) *Improvement programmes must avoid the re-invention of the wheel.* In contrast to a past perspective that emphasised a need for schools to 'own' the particular characteristics of school improvement, even if this meant them individually inventing at school level what could have been told to them from outside agencies or persons, it is important to consider the advantages of 'external to school' knowledge in improving schools. Whereas expecting schools to invent their own 'good practice' generates variation between schools in the extent to which schools *can* generate their needed knowledge, provision of intellectual and practical foundations will reduce the range between individuals and schools that 'self discovery' magnifies.

It is interesting in this context that Stringfield and associates in this volume report the higher levels of achievement gained over time in the 'Special Strategies' schools that adopted externally generated improvement designs (such as the 'Success For All' and Comer products) by comparison with schools that relied on locally developed programmes.

It is also interesting that countries which achieve high scores in international achievement surveys, also rely on the provision of 'good practice' rather than simply let the system invent its own at local level. In Taiwan, for example, teacher training combines a craft orientation of 'teacher apprenticeship' in which good practice is absorbed from former teachers, with exposure to the 'rational empirical paradigm' that is reflected in the world's most valid teacher effectiveness knowledge that students are given. The aim is to ensure that all can reliably practice a 'common core' of effective activities that will provide a foundation for their future development, whilst not constraining that development completely (see Reynolds & Farrell, 1996 for speculations on this theme).

(3) *Improvement programmes must be internationally orientated in their identification of useful improvement technologies.* Whilst it is important not to simply 'pick and mix' factors from the educational practice of different countries in ways that violate the importance of cultural context in determining 'what works', it is equally important that improvement programmes bring *all* available knowledge to the solution of continuing problems such as underachievement. As an example, the effect sizes achieved by intensive interventions such as 'Success For All' (Slavin, 1996) are amongst the highest ever achieved by programmes in education, but only recently has the technology of Slavin's intervention been utilised in the United Kingdom. As a further example, 'whole class interactive teaching' has been noted as of potential use in achieving high gain scores in subjects like mathematics in countries like Switzerland and Taiwan (Bierhoff, 1996; Reynolds & Farrell, 1996), but the practice seems to be comparatively rare in the United Kingdom.

As a final example, the traditional emphasis in the United Kingdom upon use of high quality performance data to facilitate long term professional development

(Fitz-Gibbon, 1996) is a discourse of school improvement relatively underexplored in the United States.

(4) *Improvement programmes must intervene at levels below that of the school.* We noted in our survey of the characteristics of the 'new paradigm' above that there is an increased focus currently upon affecting the learning level or classroom level. This trend, though, has not yet gone far enough to ensure that the internal world of schools and the variation in competence that exists there is utilised itself to facilitate improvement. In particular, the departmental or faculty level provides a valuable source of improvement data because of the considerable variation in effectiveness that exists at this level, and can be a valuable building block of improvement since the department can relate 'upwards' to the school level and 'downwards' to the classroom level.

However, the existing performance indicator systems that explore this variation do not build in activities and strategies that can be utilised to further professional development, because their architects believe this is best left undefined (e.g. Fitz-Gibbon, 1996).

CONCLUSIONS

The new paradigm we have outlined above is still of course in the early stages of its development. Whilst the four 'cutting edge' areas outlined are those where there is the beginning of the emergence of disciplinary agreement, it is clear that other interesting areas for development include possibilities in the following directions:

- the necessity of school improvement paying particular attention to fine grained detail in teacher behaviours and classroom organisation, since it is those details that are experienced and consumed by children;
- the importance of school improvement paying attention to the relational patterns of schools, since this third dimension of schooling additional to those of organisation and culture may severely limit improvement if unattended (Reynolds & Packer, 1992);
- the importance of school improvement blending together the provision of 'foundations' of knowledge in the areas of effectiveness and improvement research, with the systems involving self evaluation and review that are necessary for schools as they advance, to erect 'superstructures' of quality;
- the importance of school improvement focusing upon dysfunctional, poorly performing, 'sick' and ineffective schools, since many disciplines such as medicine have built their knowledge bases on the back of the attempts to make the 'sick' 'well'. Improvement, even in contemporary times, studies the 'well' rather more than the 'sick', and simply assumes that the 'sick' schools lack merely the characteristics of the 'well schools'.
- All the above are merely conjectures about the next useful areas for the new, merged paradigm to focus on. All we can say with certainty is that, judging by the intellectual progress made over the last few years, the future of school

improvement, in alliance with school effectiveness, looks brighter than at any time over the last thirty years.

REFERENCES

Barber, M. (1996). *The learning game.* London: Victor Gollancz.

Bierhoff, H. (1996) *Laying the foundations of numeracy: A comparison of primary school textbooks in Britain, Germany and Switzerland.* London: National Institute for Economic and Social Research.

Bosker, R., & Scheerens, J. (1997). *The foundations of school effectiveness.* Oxford: Pergamon Press.

Brophy, J., & Good, T. (1986). Teacher behaviour and student attainment. In M. Wittrock (Ed.), *Handbook of research on teaching* (3rd edition). New York: Macmillan.

Coleman, J., Hoffer, T., & Kilgore, (1981). *Public and private schools.* Chicago, IL: University of Chicago.

Crandall, D., et al. (1982). *People, policies and practice: Examining the chain of school improvement* (Vols. 1–10). Andover, MA: The Network.

Creemers, B. (1994). *The effective classroom.* London: Cassell.

Department for Education and Employment. (1997). *Excellence in education.* London: HMSO.

Fitz-Gibbon, C. (1996). *Monitoring education.* London: Cassell.

Fullan, M. (1991). *The new meaning of educational change.* London: Cassell.

Fullan, M. (1993). *Change forces.* Lewes: Falmer Press.

Gray, J., Reynolds, D., Fitz-Gibbon, C., & Jesson, D. (1996). *Merging traditions: The future of research on school effectiveness and school improvement.* London: Cassell.

Hallinger, P., & Murphy, J. (1986). The social context of effective schools. *American Journal of Education,* **94**, 328–355.

Harris, A., Jamieson, I., & Russ, J. (1995). A study of effective departments in secondary schools. *School Organisation,* **15**(3), 283–299.

Hill, P. (1997). *Shaking the foundations: Research driven school reform.* Plenary address to ICSEI, Memphis.

Hopkins, D. (Ed.). (1987). *Improving the quality of schooling.* Lewes: Falmer Press.

Hopkins, D., Ainscow, M., & West, M. (1994). *School Improvement in an era of change.* London: Cassell.

Hopkins, D., Ainscow, M., & West, M. (1996). *Improving the quality of education for all.* Cambridge: David Fulton Publishers.

Houtveen, A. A. M., & Osinga, N. (1995). *A case of school effectiveness: Organisation, programme procedure and evaluation results of the Dutch national school improvement project.* Paper presented to ICSEI, Leeuwarden.

Louis, K. S., & Miles, M. B. (1990). *Improving the urban high school: What works and why?* London: Cassell.

Miles, M. (1983). Unravelling the mysteries of institutionalisation. *Educational Leadership,* **41**(3), 14–19.

Mortimore, P. (1991). 'School effectiveness research: Which way at the crossroads'. *School Effectiveness and School Improvement,* **2**(3), 213–229.

Reynolds, D. (1988). British school improvement research: The contribution of qualitative studies. *International Journal of Qualitative Studies in Education,* **1**(2), 143–154.

Reynolds, D. (1993). Linking school effectiveness knowledge and school improvement practice. In C. Dimmock (Ed.). *Leadership, school based decision making and school effectiveness.* London: Routledge and Kegan Paul.

Reynolds, D. (1996). Turning around ineffective schools: Some evidence and some speculations. In J. Gray, D. Reynolds, C. Fitz-Gibbon, & D. Jesson (Eds.), *Merging traditions.* London: Cassell.

Reynolds, D. (1997, June 27). East west trade off. *Times Educational Supplement,* p. 21.

Reynolds, D., Creemers, B., Hopkins, D., Stoll, L., & Bollen, R. (1996). *Making good schools.* London: Routledge.

Reynolds, D., Creemers, B. P. M., Stringfield, S., Teddlie, C., Schaffer, E., & Nesselrodt, P. (1994). *Advances in school effectiveness research and practice.* Oxford: Pergamon Press.

Reynolds, D., & Cuttance, P. (1992). *School effectiveness: Research, policy and practice.* London: Cassell.

Reynolds, D., & Farrell, S. (1996). *Worlds apart? – A review of international studies of educational achievement involving England.* London: HMSO for OSFTED.

Reynolds, D., Hopkins, D., & Stoll, L. (1993). Linking school effectiveness knowledge and school improvement practice: Towards a synergy. *School Effectiveness and School Improvement*, **4**(1), 37–58.

Reynolds, D., & Stringfield, S. (1996, January 19th). Failure free school is ready for take off. *Times Educational Supplement*, p.10.

Reynolds, D., & Packer, A. (1992). School effectiveness and school improvement in the 1990's. In D. Reynolds & P. Cuttance, (Eds.), *School effectiveness*. London: Cassell.

Reynolds, D., Sullivan, M., & Murgatroyd, S. J. (1987). *The comprehensive experiment*. Lewes: Falmer Press.

Rosenholtz, S. (1989). *Teachers workplace*. New York: Longman.

Rutter, M., Maughan, B., Mortimore, P., & Ouston, J. (1979). *Fifteen thousand hours: Secondary schools and their effects on children*. London: Open Books.

Schaffer, G. (1994). The contributions of classroom observation to school effectiveness research. In D. Reynolds, B. P. M. Creemers, P. Nesselrodt, G. Schaffer, S. Stringfield, & C. Teddlie (Eds.), *Advances in school effectiveness research and practice*. Oxford: Pergamon.

Slavin, R. E. (1996). *Education for all*. Lisse: Swets and Zeitlinger.

Stoll, L., & Fink, D. (1992). Effecting school change: The Halton approach. *School Effectiveness and School Improvement*, **3**(1), 19–41.

Stoll, L., & Fink, D. (1996). *Changing our schools*. Buckingham: Open University Press.

Stringfield, S. (1995). Attempting to improve students' learning through innovative programs – The case for schools evolving into high reliability organisations. *School Effectiveness and School Improvement*, **6**(1), 67–96.

Stringfield, S., Bedinger, S., & Herman, R. (1995). *Implementing a private school program in an inner city public school*. Paper presented to ICSEI, Leeuwarden.

Stringfield, S., Ross, S., & Smith, L. (Eds). (1996). *Bold plans for school restructuring*. Malwah, N. J.: Lawrence Erlbaum.

Teddlie, C., & Stringfield, S. (1993). *Schools make a difference: Lessons learned from a ten year study of school effects*. New York: Teachers College Press.

Teddlie, C., & Reynolds, D. (1997). *The international handbook of school effectiveness research*. Lewes: Falmer Press.

"Inside-Out" and "Outside-In": Learning from Past and Present School Improvement Paradigms

EMILY CALHOUN
Booksend Laboratories, California, USA

BRUCE JOYCE
Booksend Laboratories, California, USA

In this chapter, Emily Calhoun and Bruce Joyce compare two major school reform paradigms: the R & D, externally-driven Research and Development approach most prominent from the late 50s through the early 70s, and the site-based school improvement approach most prominent today. Their analysis of both approaches suggests that neither have worked as well as they might. Although in some respects different, both paradigms require for successful implementation substantive curriculum and instructional innovation. This in itself is dependent on the establishing of sustainable staff development in the work place and school wide action research enquiry on teaching and learning. Calhoun and Joyce conclude that both paradigms can be successful if these conditions are integrated with a focus on the centrality of student learning.

School improvement is still an uncertain practice. Our continuing challenge is to enhance knowledge to, eventually, provide schools with methods that will have a high probability of success.

Fortunately, the last forty years have brought us an unprecedented flow of information about approaches to school improvement. The Progressive movement[1] was followed with the large-scale national curriculum reform efforts that were fueled by Sputnik. Since then, we have seen wave after wave of reform efforts, many funded by federal and state governments and foundations, and many generated by local school districts, school faculties and local community groups with few resources. Many of these efforts have been studied intensively. With the struggles, successes, and failures increasingly well-documented, we are now much more able to outline the characteristics of the successful efforts and build on them than we have ever been before.

In this chapter the focus is on two major strategies for curricular and school renewal: the classic "external R&D" approach and the "school-based, faculty-centered" approach. The evolution of each approach is instructive on its own terms; taken together, they yield information that can enable us to tackle the problems of school improvement more effectively.

D. Hopkins (ed.), The Practice and Theory of School Improvement, 252-264.
© 2005 *Springer. Printed in the Netherlands.*

THE CLASSIC R&D APPROACH (RESEARCH/DEVELOP/IMPLEMENT/ DISSEMINATE)

For many years, the most visible approach to school improvement was the generation of programs by research and development centers beyond the school district which was then followed by their implementation in schools. Funding was by agencies external to the schools or school districts. Commonly, the R&D approach included:

- using scholars and experts within a curriculum area or field of study to design the programs;
- using in-school practitioners to think about and review materials and to field-test documents, procedures, specific strategies, and the program as a whole but not using them as major program designers;
- building an indepth, carefully-rationalized curriculum;
- studying the knowledge base in and out of education for information, instructional strategies, and materials to support student interaction with this curriculum;
- maintaining a high level of quality in program materials, with an emphasis on accuracy of content and instructional strategies that lead students to engage with the curriculum as young scholars of the field;
- careful field-testing of the developed program curriculum materials and instructional strategies;
- disseminating only programs that had documented positive effects on students.

A critical characteristic – infrequently remembered today, but probably the most critical – is that the sole purpose of the R&D centers was the development of programs to improve student learning and capability. Many of these programs were funded and conducted with the objective of ensuring the future of our country, and the world, by educating our youth more fully and powerfully. Funders and developers were convinced that the curriculums of the school and the teaching methods most used were out of date and they were passionate about the need for improvement. (See, for example, Bruner, 1961; Elam, 1964).

Government and foundation funding sources established the "Academic Reform Movement," as the collection of R&D efforts came to be called. Between 1957 and 1967, the products were extensive. Among others, the Physical Science Study Committee (PSSC) developed a course in physics; the School Mathematics Study Group (SMSG) aimed at introducing modern mathematics; the Biological Sciences Curriculum Study (BSCS) developed textbooks and laboratory manuals; the Chemical Bonds Approach Project (CHEM BONDS) prepared textbooks, laboratory guides, and achievement examinations; the High School Geography Project worked to develop a course on tape with accompanying materials; Man: A Course of Study (MACOS) provided a one-year course for the upper elementary designed to have students engage in an almost pure form of scientific inquiry; and Science-A Process Approach (S-APA) provided curriculum and teacher's guides and materials kits for grades kindergarten through six.[2]

Following closely in time these primarily secondary level mathematics and science programs came programs for early enrichment and/or intervention, such as Head-Start (Osborn, 1965) and Follow Through (Bereiter & Kurland, 1981; Rhine, 1981; Stallings, 1979) to help disadvantaged children with a better "start" than they were otherwise getting. Technological applications such as Sesame Street (Ball & Bogatz, 1970) and other products of the Children's Television Workshop and other communications and media agencies were also developed to provide environmental enrichment for preschool and in-school students. The federal government moved to establish twenty "Centers" for research and development and twenty "Laboratories" for disseminating the information and supporting its utilization. In time, the distinction between the Centers and Laboratories became blurred.

The R&D paradigm evolved as it did for two major reasons. One is that time for research and development is not built into the workplace of teachers and school administrators; therefore, special "development" groups were believed to be necessary to build high-quality approaches to curriculum, instruction, and technology. The other reason is that high-level development and curricular thought requires technical knowledge not ordinarily resident in school districts. "School people" could play important roles, but not the only roles. The effort attempted to involve the most advanced thinking about academic subjects and, to do that, involved scholars not ordinarily involved in curriculum design.

Program and curriculum developers working within the R&D paradigm outside the school district are generally combinations of academicians and technical experts in mathematics, science, language, and program design; however, even in these external development projects, teachers and school administrators were/are often participants. It is little known or acknowledged today that the major projects in the Academic Reform Movement involved large numbers of teachers who helped develop materials, tested them in their classrooms, and conducted field studies with other teachers.

The primary curriculum and instruction questions were ever-present in program design: what knowledge/process is of most worth in an area of study and what strategies/interactions will cause students to use this knowledge in school and in the future, while simultaneously providing general intellectual development. A pervasive curriculum emphasis across all projects/programs was to design the materials so that students would learn to inquire in much the same way as scholars within the discipline. Once a curriculum "package" had been developed, tested, revised, tested, and shown to have positive results with students, it was disseminated through publicity and training.

To assess the effectiveness of the R&D approach to school improvement, we need to consider separately the results of the research and development component and the results of the dissemination/implementation component.

In the area of program development, this paradigm has contributed a large number of curricular, instructional, and technological models that demonstrated effects on student learning in the field-test sites. The magnitude of the effects of some of those models has been greatly underestimated in recent years. In various combinations they not only enabled children to acquire information, complex concepts, skills, and ways of thinking and solving problems effectively, but also increased their capacity to learn. (For brief, general reviews, see Bredderman, 1981,

1983; El Nemr, 1979; Joyce & Weil, 1996; Wang, Haertel, & Walberg, 1993). Perhaps the outstanding achievements have been in improving logical thinking and aptitude to learn in primary school children (Almy, 1970; Spaulding, 1970).

With few exceptions, the R&D paradigm's implementation efforts however have been as unsuccessful as the development phases were successful. By the early 1970s, it was apparent that the implementation strategy of providing summer workshops to teachers had not affected more than a small percentage of classrooms (Goodlad & Klein, 1970). Additionally, the response to the intense effort to improve for example mathematics, and problem-solving in mathematics, was a strong negative attitude by the public (and by many teachers and administrators) toward the "New Math" and its companion efforts.

Lessons Learned from the R&D Approach. There has been a tendency to attribute the failures of the R&D approach to the fact that the products were developed outside of the schools where faculty members were attempting to implement them. That explanation places the blame on the funding agencies and the developers; it does not explain why a faculty would reject an alternative to present practice that promises dramatic improvements in student learning. Common current explanations are that implementation failed because the school faculties did not "think of it" themselves or because each faculty was not broadly and integrally involved in the creation and development phases. While there is probably some truth in both explanations, they sound naive when so many non-education enterprises in contemporary society depend on the work of R&D personnel inside and outside of an organization together with implementation by local practitioners. Engineering, medicine, electronics, and media and communications are obvious examples. However, it is commonly believed in educational circles that external development is doomed to failure because it is inherently "top-down." Essentially, it is argued that the social situation in America and elsewhere is such that communities of scholars who create educational approaches are inevitably in conflict with the "truths of the workplace" and the professional dignity and competence of teachers.

The study of school change during the last twenty-five years has provided alternative explanations about why these models and projects that yielded so much in field-test sites failed to achieve implementation in most public schools. One explanation is that the developers greatly underestimated the amount and type of training necessary for those who would adopt the model or use the process developed. Partially as a result of studying what happened in the R&D efforts, researchers on change have attempted to improve training paradigms and have produced considerable evidence to support this explanation. Training designs have now been developed that greatly enhance the rates of implementation of curricular and instructional packages and that connect the implementation of these packages to considerable gains in student learning (Joyce & Showers, 1995; Slavin, Dolan, & Madden, 1996; Joyce, Wolf, & Calhoun, 1993; Joyce & Calhoun, 1996). Knowledge about how to support teachers in learning new teaching practices has now reached the point where implementation designs can virtually assure use and subsequent positive effects on students.

In one recent study directed at improving the quality of writing, a combination of curricular and instructional models enabled students in all elementary and middle schools in a high-achieving district to increase quality of writing several times more than the average annual gains in previous years (Joyce & Calhoun, 1996). In a number of other recent studies, students thought to have low ability increased both achievement and learning capability in large-scale implementations (Sharan & Shachar, 1988; Slavin, Dolan, & Madden, 1996; Pinnell, 1989). In these successful efforts, the workplace of teaching was changed considerably by the addition of substantial amounts of time for embedded staff development.

Another explanation of why these R&D products fared so poorly when they encountered the schools is that successful implementation depended on the self-renewing condition of the schools into which they were introduced. For example, many of the R and D "products" were intensively used in those few schools that were also adopting other innovations. Some support also derives from the research in training and implementation. For example, successful training designs make many changes in the workplace and, as a result, collegiality is increased through collaborative teams working on implementation. Slavin (1996) argues persuasively that a large percentage of schools are in a professional/social condition such that very extensive staff development on R&D models is virtually their *only* option for school improvement at this time. He also argues that only a small percentage of schools can "pick up an innovation" and make it their own without considerable external assistance.

As we examine the history of the R&D approach, the documentation of development and effects and the dissemination of these programs, two points stand out:

- A number of programs were developed that had very substantial effects on student learning in a large number of areas when they were field-tested; and
- these programs encountered great difficulties in dissemination.

The common explanation for failure is that the problem in dissemination was socio-political: i.e., that external R&D is inherently doomed to failure because externally-developed programs will be rejected because they violate the conditions of professional life in education. It is difficult to accept this explanation as inevitable. This is because of the body of research evidence that suggests the thesis that substantial well-designed staff development will enable externally-developed programs to be implemented strongly and generate the effects on student learning that were achieved in the pilot studies.

THE SCHOOL-BASED, FACULTY-CENTERED APPROACH

The currently most-visible approach to school improvement is "school-based, faculty-centered school improvement" or "site-based management" (SBM). Other than denoting that the school is the center for action, these phrases have many meanings, and several characteristics are present to minimal or great degrees:

- There is some degree of shared decision-making between teachers and administrators within a school. The parameters of this shared decision-making range from areas such as planning staff development at the school level to full participation in the allocation of the school budget and the hiring of staff. The breadth of participation ranges from all teachers being involved, to all staff (clerical, custodial, and paraprofessional), to parents, and to students. (See Glickman, 1993, for the rationale for the broadest levels of inclusion.)

- Frequently there is a representative decision-making council, such as a school Leadership Team or Executive Council, whose members are recruited, nominated, or elected. Sometimes the faculty acts as a whole without a leadership team.
- Schools using the site-based approach must have district/school board approval for site-based management, and in most cases they must have approval for faculty-centered school improvement that uses shared decision-making between teachers and administrators. In some districts, a school-based approach has been "mandated" for all schools; in other districts, schools try this approach on a voluntary basis. Today, approval of a site-based plan by a district is almost *pro forma.*
- In some districts, school staff and Councils have control of the full school budget; in other districts, schools have control of specific budget allocations, such as curriculum funds, staff development funds, materials funds.
- A school improvement program or plan is generally developed by the school Council or a task force group. Most often, the focus of these plans are on student discipline and organizational changes (e.g., communications, scheduling, grouping patterns, climate). Frequently, the school improvement program or action plan is a smorgasbord of activities related to scheduling, discipline, curriculum, administration, evaluation, or some combination of these. Occasionally, the plans or programs are curriculum modifications in a specific area (e.g., adding more problem-solving objectives to the mathematics curriculum; allowing and communicating with parents about invented spelling at the primary grades; providing a course in word processing to middle school students) or they focus on the adoption of a particular innovation or approach (e.g., whole language, integrated language arts, Dimensions of Learning, Cognitive Instructional Strategies in Writing, Cognitively Guided Instruction). (See David, 1995, 1996 or Calhoun, 1994, for summaries of common practices.)
- Schools often belong to a network or group, composed of schools within and/or beyond the school district, in which members of the school Council and other staff members can share their experiences and support each other.

The theory underlying the approach, not often addressed directly, but implicit in many of the writings advocating site-based approaches, is a trust that local control will automatically yield school improvement. At least four arguments underlie this trust:

- One – School faculties have the capability to engage in site-based research and development.
- Two – Organizational constraints have previously prevented faculties from exercising their capability to solve problems.

- Three – External R&D is linked to those organizational constraints and implicitly or explicitly denigrates teacher capability and dignity. (See Hollingsworth & Sockett, 1994)
- Four – Individual school sites have unique problems that require unique solutions. Thus, attempts to develop a common storehouse of effective approaches and programs is inherently misdirected.

Several variants on the site-based paradigm have developed. Organizational development specialists have worked to build, first, faculty collegiality, and second, initiatives for innovation (Schmuck and Runkel, 1985). A more rigorous variant, schoolwide action research, emphasizes the development of democracy and collegiality, but also involves the faculty in vigorous data collection and cycles of study in which initiatives are generated and modified and others are made (Calhoun, 1994; Glickman, 1993). Stemming from the work of industrial social-psychologists (Lewin, 1948), action research is enjoying a resurgence in education, partly as such and partly in the variants spawned by Deming (1986) and his colleagues, currently popularized as Total Quality Management (Bonstingl, 1993).

Another boost to the school-based approach is that many states and foundations, providing grants directly to schools, have generated programs that require the involvement of all faculty, increased community involvement, and various degrees of data-based study. The approaches taken by the California School Improvement Program-SIP (Berman and Gjelten, 1983) and the 1274 Program[3] are examples.

For at least twelve years, the site-based movement has been studied. Researchers have studied urban schools (Louis & Miles, 1990); teams from schools (Huberman & Miles, 1984); well-funded and lightly-funded school-based improvement programs, state-mandated site-based management (David, 1995, 1996); California's massive School Improvement Program-SIP (Berman & Gjelten, 1983); groups of schools seeking improvement through shared governance and action research (Calhoun & Allen, 1996); and networks of academically-oriented high schools (Muncey & McQuillan, 1993).

In terms of creating a workplace in which teachers and site-based administrators are more involved in decision-making beyond the classroom level, site-based approaches have been successful. Adults in the school do participate in decisions that they did not participate in before and they do have choices they did not have before; therefore, many of them feel better about what is happening, even if nothing about the business of education has changed and they are making identical decisions to those made earlier by the administration. But, on the other hand, the approach rarely yields productive changes in curriculum and instruction. In schools using this approach for as much as five years, very few changes have occurred in instruction, in the teacher/learner interaction, or in student learning/achievement. (See Calhoun & Glickman, 1993; Calhoun & Allen, 1996; David & Peterson, 1984; David, 1995, 1996; Louis & Miles, 1990; Muncey & McQuillan, 1993.)

The story throughout the site-based literature is about the same as that reported in the studies of the R&D programs. *Essentially, only about ten percent of the schools have been able to generate initiatives that substantively changed the curricular, instructional, or technological dimensions of the school.*

Lessons Learned from the Site-Based Approach. Several hypotheses have been raised about why the site-based approach generally fails to make significant changes in curriculum, instruction, or technology.

One hypothesis is that a process orientation is not enough: in studies of successful schools, nearly all of the faculties secured for themselves the intensive services of a facilitator who offered, in addition to organizational development expertise, in-depth competence in curriculum and instruction (Calhoun & Allen, 1996). Sometimes this facilitator was from within the school; sometimes from the district office; but more often it was someone from outside the school district.

The hypothesis that faculties need sustained assistance over several years by "experts" in the approach or innovation they have selected is also supported by research on assessment and instructional changes at the classroom level (Shepard, 1995) and by the research on the implementation of Success for All, a schoolwide program for students in grades pre-K to five that organizes resources to ensure that every child will read by the end of grade three and have basic skills to build on throughout the elementary grades (Slavin, Madden, Dolan, Wasik, Ross, Smith, & Dianda, 1996).

A second hypothesis, also based on the study of successful schools, is that few schools have the colleagueship to overcome the idiosyncratic normative structure of most American schools and become "stuck" (to use Rosenholtz' 1989 term) very quickly. This is unless they adopt an innovation (borrow from the R&D products) within the first year or year and a half of their initial commitment to improve (Calhoun & Allen, 1996; Louis & Miles, 1990).

Few faculties pursue schoolwide efforts in curriculum, instruction, or technology as part of their school improvement process (David & Peterson, 1984; Louis & Miles, 1990; Fullan & Miles, 1992; Calhoun & Glickman, 1993; Calhoun & Allen, 1994). Faculties and teams tend to focus on changing working conditions or speculate about what would be possible with "different students, parents, and home environments" unless they have help, internal or external, that draws them to their own instructional and curricular environment. Even in those schools where norms are strong enough to support common goals focused on student learning through curriculum and instruction, two other impediments to progress are common: no substantive staff development and no follow-up support for implementation.

Apparently many districts that have "mandated" site-based management and many schools that have entered into it voluntarily have not recognized from the outset either that changes in curriculum and instruction would be necessary or that very substantial amounts of staff development would be necessary if such changes were to be implemented. In many settings, the adoption of the site-based alternatives appears to have been made almost as an end in itself, rather than as a means to the improvement of the education of the students.

LEARNING FROM THE R&D AND THE SITE-BASED APPROACHES

Both paradigms have not quite worked, although they might if they were modified. *They seem sensible on the surface. They have good rationales.* In many settings, they both have been pursued with great energy and backed with massive funds.

On first examination, the school-based paradigms appear to be almost in opposition to the research and development paradigms. And, in fact, the popularity of site-based school improvement is partially due to a widespread disenchantment with the R&D approach. In one way, they *are* really *different*: for the school-based approaches depend on developing local faculty energy to generate school-improvement, on the premise that faculties have or can develop the knowledge necessary to build innovations that conform to the needs of the local community. In another way, they *are similar*: because curricular, instructional, or technological innovation is essential to school improvement, and thus, either intra-school R&D or the adoption of externally-developed approaches is necessary if site-based programs are to be successful.

From Both Paradigms: A Hypothesis about Results. As Goodlad reminded us in his 1994 treatise on "better teachers, better schools": "The renewal of schools depends heavily on viewing schools as cultures, but this appears to be an idea whose time is not yet come." Such evidence leads to the following hypothesis that applies to both of the school improvement paradigms discussed above: unless a school operates with a self-renewing modality, the number (percent) of our approximately 80,000 U.S. schools that will be able to improve the education their students experience schoolwide under the currently popular site-based paradigm will be no larger than it was under the R&D paradigm.

From Both Paradigms: Characteristics of Successful Schools. There is a similar consistency to the characteristics of schools that were successful under either paradigm:

- All focused their development energies directly on benefits for students.
- All used the knowledge base for ideas or actual innovations.
- All generated formative evaluation processes in which they studied the implementation and its effects on students.
- Most generated broad-based staff involvement schemes, and many included parents and community/local institutions from both the public and private sectors.
- Most provided time for collegial activity that would sustain innovations. For the most successful sites, the amount of time was equal to approximately 1/10 of the work week and occurred on a weekly schedule.

From Comparing Both Paradigms and the Knowledge Base. As we sift through the structures and results of the R&D approach, the school based school improvement approach, and through the general knowledge base, what can we find that will help us create more powerful centers of learning for our students and for ourselves. The large number of failures under both approaches appear to share several features:

- In most schools, the approach, program, or innovation selected is not supported with adequate staff development to enable implementation. This lack of support places unreasonable expectations on adults as learners and on the staff as a community, while automatically limiting results and decreasing staff efficacy.
- In most schools, the redesign of the workplace to sustain implementation of the approach, program, or innovation selected does not occur. For example: 1) Restructuring of the school day or week to provide time for the staff to work and study together as a community does not occur. 2) Restructuring of staff time and deployment to provide time for all faculty members to work regularly in their study groups/peer coaching teams does not occur. 3) Providing for sustained technical assistance, generally needed for at least three years, does not occur.
- Comparing the operational focus of the R&D approach to the operational focus of the school-based approach: the R&D approach focused its design, actions, and resources specifically on curriculum and instructional changes to support student learning; the school based approach has a more general focus in which goals, actions, and resources are aimed at any aspect of schooling that participants want to work on. Rarely in the school-based approach is there attention to designing actions and materials to support the staff-generated goals.

However, student benefits are more likely to occur schoolwide if we combine aspects from both foci. For example, in schoolwide action research, staff are asked to focus the goal(s) they select around student learning and the action plans they develop around instructional and curricular changes that will support the attainment of these goals (Calhoun, 1994). In this way, participants select the areas they wish to explore and the actions they want to implement within a structure that requires a direct focus on students and on teaching.

This focus on teaching and learning is far more difficult to establish than it sounds. Even in school-based approaches such as the Coalition of Essential Schools (Sizer, 1985), a school reform effort that focuses on improving classroom teaching and learning, what is developed and implemented in schools is a far cry from the potential reflected in the Coalition principles (Muncey & McQuillan, 1993). The same difficulty is evident in school-based approaches such as The League of Professional Schools, a school improvement program whose premises include shared decision-making between teachers and administrators, a focus on enhanced education for students, and a commitment to study the learning environment of the school and it effects on students. The focus on student learning and on teaching and instruction does not simply occur on school action plans because a school staff voluntarily affiliates with the League (Calhoun & Glickman, 1993). Even in the most successful schools, the School Facilitation Team or Leadership Team must keep a continuous eye on whether at least some of their goals focus on student learning and some of their actions focus on instructional strategies and curriculum approaches that would support these goals (Calhoun & Allen, 1996).

COMMON MISTAKES, COMMON SOLUTIONS: INQUIRY, INQUIRY, INQUIRY!

The difficult history of school reform has led some observers, such as Sarason (1990) and Cuban (1990), to a pessimism we do not share.

We believe that the advocates of both of the major paradigms made essentially the same, reasonable, mistake: *they believed they had a sure-fire strategy, that they were unlikely to fail and, thus, didn't conduct school improvement as an inquiry, making modifications as they went.* Beliefs are very important. In both cases, the advocates were *sure* their strategy would work. When it didn't, they failed to strengthen the support systems but, rather, lengthened the time line for success. We see that today, where reports indicate that some heavily-funded site-based programs are failing to achieve student learning gains in most schools and the advocates and organizers are taking the position that success may take ten years, rather than providing the level of support that would ensure success in the first or second year, which occurs when adequate assistance is available (Calhoun & Allen, 1996).

Hindsight about both is now plentiful. We believe it would be a terrible mistake to discard either approach. However, to make either work will require changes in the structural organization of the school of a far greater magnitude than either assumed, particularly in the provision of time and assistance in the development of collegial structures and well-designed and extensive staff development. The recent successful disseminations of Success for All (Slavin, Madden, & Dolan, 1996) indicate how effective the R&D approach can be. Several other large-scale successful efforts (See Joyce & Calhoun, Eds., 1996) demonstrate that with the careful tending of the faculty culture, the provision of adequate staff development, and a focus on the centrality of student learning, there is a very high probability of success,whichever paradigm is selected.

ENDNOTES

[1] The Progressive Movement in American education lasted for approximately 80 years (around 1880 to 1960). The first 40 years focused on pluralism, using public schools and education to increase the participation of all members of society in economic, political, and cultural developments. The second forty years, building heavily on the ideas of John Dewey (1916, 1938), continued the emphasis on expansion of access to education, but focused more on the role of schools and education in fostering individual growth and democratic social competence. See Cremin (1961) *The Transformation of the School: Progressivism in American Education,* for a thorough discussion of this movement.

[2] For an overview of the national projects developed during this time, their originators, and major purposes see Doll (1978), pages 140–146; for an excellent historical perspective on curriculum reform in the United States in the fifties and sixties see McClure (1971); to have an idea of the nature of education being promoted by the major academicians during this time see Bruner (1961, 1966); for an indepth analysis of the effects of these reform efforts on classrooms and teaching see Goodlad and Klein (1970).

[3] The AB 1274 Program is a State of California Restructuring grant designed to stimulate and support school improvement in California. School staff must agree to pursue their school improvement initiative through shared decision making, focusing on instructional changes, and focusing on student achievement. If the proposal describing their goals and how the staff will pursue them is accepted, the funding (generally $125,000 to $250,000 per year) will be from one to five years.

REFERENCES

Almy, M. (1970). *Logical thinking in the second grade.* New York: Teachers College Press.

Ball, S., & Bogatz, G. A. (1970). *The first year of Sesame Street.* Princeton, NJ: Educational Testing Service.

Bereiter, C., & Kurland, M. (1981). A constructive look at follow through results. *Interchange,* **12**(1), 1–21.

Berman, P. & Gjelten, T. (1983). *Improving school improvement.* Berkeley, CA: Weiler Associates.

Bonstingl, J. (1993). *Schools of quality: An introduction to quality management in education.* Alexandria, VA: Association for Supervision and Curriculum Development.

Bredderman, T. (1981). *Elementary school process curricula: A meta-analysis.* ERIC Document Reproduction Service. ED 170 333.

Bredderman, T. (1983). Effects of activity-based elementary science on student outcomes: A quantitative synthesis. *Review of Educational Research,* **53**(4), 499–518.

Bruner, J. S. (1961). *The process of education.* Cambridge, MA: Harvard University Press.

Bruner, J. S. (1966). *Toward a theory of instruction.* Cambridge, MA: Harvard University Press.

Calhoun, E. (1994). *Action research in the self-renewing school.* Alexandria: Association for Supervision and Curriculum Development.

Calhoun, E., & Allen, L. (1996). The action network: Action research on action research. In B. Joyce, & E. Calhoun (Eds.), *Learning experiences in school renewal.* Eugene, OR: The ERIC Center for Educational Management. University of Oregon.

Calhoun, E. & Allen, L. (1994). *Results of schoolwide action research in the League of Professional Schools.* Paper presented at the Annual Meeting of the American Educational Research Association. New Orleans.

Calhoun, E., & Glickman, C. (1993 *Issues and dilemmas of action research in the League of Professional Schools.* Paper presented at the annual meeting of the American Educational Research Association. Atlanta.

Cremin, L. A. (1961, 1964). *The transformation of the school: Progressivism in American education.* New York: Vintage Books.

Cuban, L. (1990). Reforming again, again, and again. *Educational Researcher,* **19**(1), 3–13

David, J. (1995, 1996). The who, what, and why of site-based management. *Educational Leadership,* **53**(4),4–9.

David, J. L. & Peterson, S. M. (1984). *Can schools improve themselves? A study of school based improvement programs.* Palo Alto, California: Bay Area Research Group.

Deming, E. (1982). *Out of the crisis.* Cambridge: Massachusetts Institute of Technology Center for Advanced Engineering Study.

Dewey, J. (1916). *Democracy or education.* New York: Macmillan.

Dewey, J. (1938). *Experience and education.* New York: Macmillan.

Doll, R. C. (1978). *Curriculum improvement: Decision making and process* (4th edition). Boston: Allyn and Bacon.

El-Nemr, M. (1979). *Meta-analysis of the outcomes of teaching biology as inquiry.* Doctoral thesis. Boulder: University of Colorado.

Elam, S. (Ed.). (1964). *Education and the structure of knowledge.* Chicago: Rand McNally.

Fullan, M., & Miles, M. (1992). Getting reform right: What works and what doesn't. *Phi Delta Kappan,* **73**(10), 744–52.

Glickman, C. (1993). *Renewing America's schools.* San Francisco: Jossey-Bass.

Goodlad, J. (1994). *Better teachers, better schools.* San Francisco: Jossey-Bass.

Goodlad, J., & Klein, F. (1970). *Looking behind the classroom door.* Ohio: Charles Jones.

Hollingsworth, S. & Sockett, H. (Eds.). (1994). *Teacher research and educational reform.* Chicago: University of Chicago Press.

Huberman, M., & Miles, M. (1984). *Innovation up close: How school improvement works.* New York: Praeger.

Joyce, B., Wolf, J., & Calhoun, E. (1993). *The self-renewing school.* Alexandria, VA: Association for Supervision and Curriculum Development.

Joyce, B., & Calhoun, E. (Eds.). (1996). *Learning experiences in school renewal.* Eugene, Oregon: The ERIC Clearinghouse for Educational Management, University of Oregon.

Joyce, B., & Showers, B. (1995). *Student achievement through staff development* (2nd edition). White Plains: Longman, Inc.

Joyce, B., & Weil, M. (1996). *Models of teaching* (5th edition). Needham, MA: Allyn & Bacon.

Lewin, K. (1948). *Resolving social conflicts.* New York: Harper and Row.

Louis, K., & Miles, M. (1990). *Improving the urban high school.* New York: Teachers College Press.

McClure, R. M. (1971). The reforms of the fifties and sixties: A historical look at the near past. In R. M. McClure (Ed.), *The curriculum: Retrospect and prospect – The seventieth yearbook of the National Society for the Study of Education, Part I.* Chicago: University of Chicago Press.

Muncey, D. & McQuillan, P. (1993). Preliminary findings from a five-year study of The Coalition of Essential Schools. *Phi Delta Kappan,* **74**(6), 486–489.

Osborn, K. (1965). Project Head Start – An assessment. *Educational Leadership,* **23**, 98–103.

Pinnell, G. (1989). Reading recovery: Helping at-risk students learn to read. *Elementary School Journal,* **90**(2), 161–183.

Rhine, R. (1981). *Making schools more effective: New directions from Follow Through.* New York: Academic Press.

Rosenholtz, S. (1989). *Teachers' workplace.* White Plains: Longman, Inc.

Sarason, S. (1990). *The predictable failure of educational reform.* San Francisco: Jossey Bass.

Sharan, S., & Shachar, H. (1988). *Language and learning in the cooperative classroom.* New York: Springer-Verlag.

Shepard, L. (1995). Using assessment to improve learning. *Educational Leadership,* 52(5), 38–43.

Schmuck, R., & Runkel, P. (1985). *The handbook of organization development in schools* (3rd edition). Palo Alto, California: Mayfield Publishing Company.

Sizer, T. (1985). *Horace's compromise.* Boston: Houghton Mifflin.

Slavin, R., Dolan, L., & Madden, N. (1996). *Scaling up: Lessons learned in the dissemination of Success for All.* Baltimore: Center for Research on the Education of Students Placed at Risk, Johns Hopkins University.

Slavin, R., Madden, N., Dolan, L., Wasik, B., Ross, S., Smith, L., & Dianda, M. (1996). Success for All: A summary of research. *Journal of Education for Students Placed at Risk,* 1(1), 41–76.

Spaulding, R. (1970). *The early intervention program.* Durham, N.C.: Duke University Press.

Stalling, J. (1979). Follow Through: A model for inservice-teacher training. *Curriculum Inquiry,* 9(2), 163–181.

Wang, M. C., Haertel, G. D., & Walberg, H. J. (1993). Toward a knowledge base for school learning. *Review of Educational Research,* **63**(3), 249–294.

Sand, Bricks, and Seeds: School Change Strategies and Readiness for Reform

ROBERT E. SLAVIN

Johns Hopkins University, Baltimore, USA

In this chapter Robert Slavin argues against a prevailing orthodoxy by maintaining that differences between schools in terms of "effectiveness" are less important than what and how a school teaches. Slavin contends that there are fewer highly effective, in his terms "seed" schools than others suppose, and by the same token a similary fewer number of "sand" or highly ineffective schools. Most schools he claims are "brick" schools, in so far as they are amenable to reform by the introduction of prepared curriculum and instructional packages. In a similar vein Slavin argues that of the three main types of innovation – organisation development, single curricular innovations or comprehensive reform models – it is only the latter that holds any promise for positively affecting student achievement in a majority of schools. Slavin concludes by proposing a series of policy implications that involve the funding and implementation of well-specified ("brick") models of school improvement.

Over the past fifteen years, there has been a growing recognition of the need for fundamental change in the practices of elementary and secondary schools. In the U.S., the poor performance of students in international comparisons and persistent gaps between the performance of poor and minority students and that of white students have led to a perpetual climate of crisis. At the political level, calls for parental choice of schools, vouchers to allow children to attend any public or private school, and legislation facilitating the creation of independent "charter" schools amount to an admission that public schools have failed and must at least be challenged by external competitors and perhaps must be replaced with a completely new system.

The quest for fundamental change in schooling practices immediately faces a dilemma, which could be called the problem of scale (see Elmore, 1996). Any educator or school reformer knows that important changes in student performance only come about if teachers use markedly better methods and materials every day, and that this requires large amounts of high-quality professional development and a process of school change unfolding over a period of years (Fullan, 1991). The change process is not only difficult and expensive, but it is also uncertain; key changes in personnel, funding, district, state, or national policies, and other threats can and do disrupt and often terminate even the most successful reforms, and many reforms are never successful in the first place (Stringfield, Herman, Millsap, & Scott, 1996). Individual schools and pilot projects have always shown compelling examples of what schools could be (see Levine & Lezotte, 1990), but these

265

D. Hopkins (ed.), The Practice and Theory of School Improvement, 265-279.
© 2005 *Springer. Printed in the Netherlands.*

"lighthouse" schools are rarely replicated even in their own districts, much less on a broad scale.

In recognition of these difficulties, two quite different streams of reform have sprung up over the past decade. One, typically called "systemic reform" (see Smith & O'Day, 1991), is frankly pessimistic about school-by-school reform. Its proponents argue that broad-scale change is most likely to occur as a result of changes in assessment, accountability, standards, and governance. The idea is that if government establishes broadly accepted standards of student performance, and then rewards schools whose students are progressing on those standards (and punishes those whose students are not progressing), teachers and administrators will be motivated to change their practices, seek more effective methods and materials, invest in professional development, and so on. Similarly, such policies as allowing parental choice or facilitating charter schools are expected to change teachers' practices by threatening ineffective schools with closure if they cannot compete in the marketplace. In the U.S., an emphasis on systemic reform has characterized the policies of the Bush and Clinton administrations and of Republican as well as Democratic governors. In fact, in the Clinton administration, two of the three top education officials were formerly governors of states deeply involved in systemic reform (as was President Clinton himself as Governor of Arkansas); the third is Marshall Smith, one of the key academic proponents of systemic reform before entering government. Systemic reform of this kind has been equally dominant in the education policies of many other countries, including Britain, Australia, New Zealand, and Israel.

The principal alternative to systemic governance reform attacks the problem of scale from the opposite direction, designing ambitious models for school reform and then building networks of technical assistance and school-to-school support to serve ever-expanding numbers of schools that freely choose to implement the model. These models deal with the problem of scale by creating plausibly replicable models and then developing national or international training capacity, regional training sites, and mechanisms for local and national sharing of information and technical assistance. They may only start with a few schools but are intended from the outset to ultimately serve hundreds or thousands. The models fall into three categories: organizational development models, comprehensive reform models, and single-subject innovations. These are discussed in the following sections.

Organizational Development Models. Perhaps the dominant approach to school-by-school reform is models built around well-established principles of organizational development, in which school staffs are engaged in an extended process of formulating a vision, creating work groups to move toward implementation of that vision, identifying resources (such as external assistance, professional development, and instructional materials) to help the school toward its vision, and often locating "critical friends" to help the school evaluate and continually refine its approaches. In the U.S., the largest networks of this kind are Sizer's (1992) Coalition of Essential Schools, currently approaching a thousand middle and high schools, and Levin's (1987) Accelerated Schools network, with more than 800 mostly elementary and middle schools. Another widespread model of this kind is the National Alliance for Reforming Education, closely affiliated with the New Standards Project, which is an important organization in the promotion of state and district systemic reforms around standards, assessments, and accountability (Rothman, 1996). Comer's (1988) School Development Project has more specific guidelines for activities relating to parent participation and integrated approaches to mental health and self-esteem, but in the instructional arena it also asks each school to create its own approaches to curriculum, instruction, and professional development. The National Alliance and Comer projects also serve hundreds of schools throughout the U.S. Dozens of smaller networks of reforming schools also exist, including the Carnegie Corporation's Middle Grade School State Policy Initiative, the Paideaia Network built around the work of Mortimore Adler (1982), the Foxfire network, Carl Glickman's School Improvement League, and the ATLAS project, which incorporates elements of Sizer's and Comer's programs (Orell, 1996). This approach to educational reform is also common outside of the U.S. In Canada, the Learning Consortium is a network of schools influenced by the work of Michael Fullan (1991). In Britain, IQEA (Improving the Quality of Education for All) promotes a dual focus on the internal conditions of schools and the enhancement of classroom practice (Hopkins, Ainscow, & West, 1994). The National Schools Network in Australia and the Thousand Schools Project in South Africa are additional examples. These projects have in common a philosophy of change emphasizing teachers and administrators finding their own way to reform with some guidance from the national project but few if any student materials, teachers' guides, or specific approaches to instruction.

Comprehensive Reform Models. A markedly different approach to whole-school reform is taken by comprehensive reform models that provide schools with specific student materials, teachers' manuals, focused professional development, and relatively prescribed patterns of staffing, school governance, internal and external assessment, and other features of school organization. Our own Success for All and Roots and Wings programs provide the most elaborate examples of this approach (Slavin, Madden, Dolan, & Wasik, 1996; Slavin, Madden, Dolan, Wasik, Ross, Smith, & Dianda, 1996). Success for All, in use in more than 450 U.S. elementary schools in 31 states and adapted in four other countries, provides specific curriculum materials for prekindergarten, kindergarten, and grades 1–6 reading, writing, and language arts. Roots and Wings adds to this materials in mathematics, social studies, and science. Both programs provide one-to-one tutoring to primary-grade students who are struggling in reading, family support teams to build positive home-school relations and deal with such issues as attendance, behavior, health, and mental health, and a building facilitator to help teachers implement and coordinate all program elements. The Core Knowledge project (Hirsch, 1993; Mentzert & Shaughnessy, 1996) and the Modern Red Schoolhouse (Kilgore, Doyle, & Linkowsky, 1996), which uses Core Knowledge materials, are two additional approaches that also have relatively well-specified approaches to curriculum, instruction, and school organization, and are increasing in use in the U.S.

Single-Subject Models. A third category of school reform networks is made up of programs focusing on a single subject and, often, a limited grade span. In recent years, the most extraordinary example of this type of reform is Reading Recovery, a one-to-one tutoring program originally developed by Marie Clay (1985) in New Zealand and now used in thousands of schools throughout the English-speaking world (see Pinnell, 1989). However, there are hundreds of curriculum-specific programs in existence, serving tens of thousands of schools. The U.S. Department of Education's National Diffusion Network (NDN) identified more than 500 projects that met a minimal standard of effectiveness and replicablity, and some of these are in widespread use (the NDN has also certified some whole-school reform models). A much smaller set of single subject (as well as schoolwide) programs with more convincing evidence of effectiveness was reviewed by Fashola & Slavin (1996).

Of course, school reform approaches can and do cross categories. Some school change models, especially the National Alliance, are closely associated with systemic change strategies. Any approach to school change may be motivated by such systemic policy consequences as accountability threat or adoption of state or local standards. Curriculum-specific reforms may be adopted by schools engaged in organizational development strategies. The California State Department of Education, for example, is currently promoting a "do it yourself" approach to school reform in which school staffs are engaged in identifying and adopting strategies in five areas (e.g., curriculum/instruction, parent involvement, early intervention) that together approximate the main elements of such comprehensive designs as Success for All/Roots and Wings. Yet it is still useful to make distinctions among these strategies, as they have profoundly different implications for broad scale school reform.

READINESS FOR REFORM

Which type of approach to reform is most likely to result in change in teachers' practices and improvement in student achievement? The answer to this, I would argue, depends on certain characteristics of individual schools. Some of these characteristics relate to such factors as funding available for reform and available local capacity to support the reform process. However, at least as important as these issues is the school staff's readiness for change. Of course, schools can be characterized as being more or less ready for change, but in addition, schools must be seen as differentially ready for different *kinds* of change. For example, Hopkins (1994) suggests that change strategies for some schools should emphasize organizational development while others should emphasize innovations in curriculum and instruction, depending on the developmental readiness of the school to take on each type of change.

Building on this idea, I would propose three different categories of readiness based more on the capabilities, relationships, and immediate past history of a given school than on effectiveness alone. I'd call the strategies appropriate to these categories of schools "seeds," "bricks," and "sand."

"Seeds" schools are ones that have extraordinary capacity to translate a vision into reality. Such schools are ones in which staff is cohesive, excited about teaching, led by a visionary leader willing to involve the entire staff in decisions, and broadly aware of research trends and ideas being implemented elsewhere. In such schools a reformer need only introduce a vision and a set of principles, connect the school staff with other staffs undergoing reform, expose the staff to new ideas, and try to protect the staff from external pressures opposing the reform process. The "seeds" analogy refers to the idea that the soil is fertile and the seed has within it the capacity to grow and bear fruit; it only needs time, nurturing, and protection. This is the ideal situation envisioned by the organizational development models. However, recognizing that such staffs are rare, organizational development models often spend years trying to change the organizational climate in the school to one that is ready for the transformation process.

In contrast, "bricks" schools are ones in which school staffs would like to do a better job and are willing and able to engage in a reform process if they are convinced it would work, but are unlikely to create their own path to reform, even with external assistance. These are schools with good relations among staff and leadership, a positive orientation toward change, and some degree of stability in the school and its district. Yet the teachers in the school do not perceive the need or the capability to develop new curricula, instructional methods, or organizational forms. Introducing reforms in such schools is like building a structure out of bricks. The bricks must be brought to the building site, and detailed, comprehensive blueprints are needed to put them together into a viable, functional structure. The structure may be modified and is certainly furnished by its users, and a great deal of effort is still needed to build it. However, once built, the structure may stand for many years with moderate efforts at maintenance. This is the situation envisioned by developers of both comprehensive reform models, such as our Success for All and Roots and Wings programs, and most subject-specific reforms, such as Reading Recovery. These models are not expected to work in all schools, but are expected to work in nearly all schools that make an informed, uncoerced decision to implement them and have adequate resources to do so. For example, in Success for All and Roots and Wings, teachers must vote by secret ballot to take on the program, with a majority of at least 80%. Almost any school that can muster this level of support should be able to implement the program.

Finally, there are schools in which even the most heroic attempts at reform are doomed to failure. Trying to implement change in such schools is like trying to build a structure out of sand. Even if something recognizable can be built, the least wave, windstorm, or even passage of time will reduce it to nothingness. There are several reasons that schools may fall into this category. Perhaps the largest number of such schools are complacent schools in which the school staff feels as though it is doing and always has done a good job. Many schools serving high-socioeconomic status areas fall into this category, even if, in fact, the schools may not be tapping the full potential of their students. For example, Teddlie & Stringfield (1993) studied "negative outlier" schools, some of which were complacent, middle class schools doing adequately by state standards but poorly after controlling for input characteristics. Other "sand" schools, however, are ones that are in turmoil or transition. They have recently experienced changes of principals or other key staff, are in districts undergoing major change, have lost funding, have poor relationships among staff and principals, or have conservative, fearful, or incompetent leadership. Sand schools require fundamental changes before they can support any type of school change.

Note that these categories are not the same as a rating of the school's current effectiveness. It is entirely possible for schools to be doing a terrible job of educating students and still be ready for "bricks," well-organized and comprehensive reform. "Sand" schools are not necessarily ones that are failing. Complacent "sand" schools are almost by definition succeeding with many students, and many have islands of real excellence. "Seeds" schools may have the potential for extraordinary change, but this in no way implies that they are already successful.

HOW MANY SCHOOLS ARE IN EACH CATEGORY?

Schools are certainly not equally distributed among the "seeds," "bricks," and "sand" categories. I would guess, based on our experience with several hundred schools, that as many as 90% of elementary schools could, if they had the resources and assistance and made an affirmative and informed choice to do so, implement a comprehensive well-specified reform model like Success for All or Roots and Wings. If there were a range of such programs with evidence of effectiveness, supportive networks, and a variety of curricular and philosophical approaches, my guess is that a large portion of elementary school staffs motivated to see better outcomes and adequately funded for this purpose would choose to implement one of these or one or more equally well-specified subject-specific models (such as Reading Recovery). The proportion of secondary schools willing and able to implement comprehensive models is unknown, as such models do not currently exist at the secondary level. However, because of the greater size, complexity, and subject-matter focus of secondary schools it seems that achieving a common mission and whole-staff cohesion around that mission would be more difficult in secondary schools. It may be that there would be "bricks" or even "seeds" departments or "houses" within large secondary schools not ready for change across the board.

All told, I would expect that fewer than 5% of elementary or secondary schools would fall into the "seeds" category. I base this pessimistic assessment on the growing body of observational studies that have examined exemplars of organizational development models *selected as outstanding by their developers* in which observers could see only limited and partial evidence of change in actual teacher's practices. Such studies have focused in particular on Sizer's Coalition of Essential Schools (e.g., Muncey & McQuillan, 1993; Prestine, 1993; Stapleford, 1994; Stringfield, Herman, Millsap, & Scott, 1996); but also on some of the New American Schools models (Bodilly et al., 1996) and other exemplary reform models (Newmann et al., 1996). Perhaps the best-known counterexample, New York's Central Park East (Meier, 1995), is an exception that proves the rule. Central Park East is a magnet school that draws a diverse but generally high-achieving (and self-selected) student body from all over Manhattan, and more importantly is able to select teachers who are deeply committed to the specific reform under way.

These studies aside, there are certainly some schools that are ready and able to develop and implement very ambitious reforms. In a national study of 24 exemplary reforming schools, Newmann et al., (1996) found a few, and Levin's Accelerated Schools Network has described some outstanding implementations (Hopfenberg & Levin, 1993). Yet such schools appear to be a minority of a minority.

MISMATCHES BETWEEN REFORM STRATEGIES AND REFORM READINESS

A key problem of school reform, I would argue, is when the wrong strategies are applied to the wrong settings. When any reform model is applied to a "sand" school, of course, it is doomed, and the attempt drains the energy and enthusiasm of all concerned, not least the developer/disseminators.

Of course, there is a serious problem in determining in advance what kinds of reform, if any, a school is capable of implementing. However, with a modest investigation, it should be possible to determine this. For example, requiring an informed vote by secret ballot with a supermajority (we specify 80%) is one way to identify schools that are at least willing to engage in a specific reform; we find that school staffs riven with factionalism, distrustful of the principal, or seriously demoralized, are rarely able to achieve this degree of consensus. Discriminating "seeds" from "bricks" schools may be more difficult, but a "seeds" school should be able to point to one or more creative programs it devised and implemented in more than one or two classes.

The probability and consequences of attempting the wrong kind of reform in a given school vary for the different categories. Innovators can often avoid "sand" schools by refusing to work with schools that do not overwhelmingly vote to implement their design, with schools that were apparently coerced into participating, and with schools that give evidence of dissension and turmoil. More problematic, however, and probably far more common, are situations in which "seeds" strategies are applied to schools ready for "bricks" solutions. If such schools are unable to create their own curricular and instructional reforms, this of course wastes time, energy, and money, as well as creating disillusionment with the whole reform process. However, there is a less obvious but perhaps more important cost. Schools are often rewarded for appearing to be involved in reform rather than actually changing their practices. They often want the banner on their school that identifies them as a member of a given network of reforming schools. However, banners are cheap and easy to erect, while real change is expensive and difficult. Some schools may subscribe to a given network because it brings them status or recognition, and in some cases they may do so because it in a sense protects them from having to participate in other, more demanding reforms. Some of the most widely used "bricks" strategies with strong research bases, such as Reading Recovery and our own Success for All/Roots and Wings, have very high standards (including financial commitments) that schools must meet to enter or remain in the network. In contrast, many organizational development ("seeds") strategies involve schools in a planning process that may last for years, giving schools a chance to say they are a part of a reform network without actually having to spend much money or engage in serious change for a long time. To the degree that schools use participating in a network with a long planning period as a means to avoid serious reform, real reform is both set back in the individual schools involved and written off by many educators as too expensive or difficult.

"Seeds" methods introduced to schools that are able to construct their own comprehensive reforms can provide a benefit that goes beyond the education of the students involved. They can also contribute new ideas, new conceptions of what schools could be (see, for example, Meier, 1995). However, the dangers of introducing "bricks" solutions to schools capable of succeeding in "seeds" models do not seem serious. Assuming that school staffs have freely chosen a well-specified model, they should be able to apply their creative powers to improving their practices from a high baseline rather than having to invent everything from scratch. Few schools have the time, resources, and skills to develop outstanding approaches in every subject and grade level; even schools willing and able to build, for example, an outstanding science program might well adopt "bricks" models in reading and mathematics, for example.

REFORMING "SAND" SCHOOLS

The foregoing discussion leaves aside the question of how to reform schools whose staffs are neither ready nor willing to be reformed. An old joke maintains that it only takes one organizational development expert to change a light bulb, but the light bulb has to want to change.

Of course, there are many reasons a school may not be ready for reform, and these require different solutions. Schools that are complacent either because they are serving low-risk populations or because they are actually succeeding may perhaps be left alone; well-crafted assessment/accountability systems may provide an adequate incentive for such schools to examine and gradually improve their practices. Other "sand" schools are only in this category for reasons that are temporary, as with schools undergoing changes in principals or serious funding cutbacks or districts experiencing teacher strikes or work-to-rule actions. The job of reform is enormous and the human and financial resources to do it are limited, so it makes sense to focus on schools that are ready for change with an expectation that many, perhaps most schools not ready for change this year may in the normal course of events become ready within a few years. Again, well-crafted accountability systems, consistent district-level support for reform, and the growing availability of technical assistance over time (as, for example, more reform-ready schools in the same district become expert at a given reform) make it likely that schools that sat out one opportunity due to temporary reasons will adopt or create a reform plan in later years.

In some cases, schools not otherwise willing to adopt a reform (but in need of major change) might be offered substantial inducements to do so, but the element of choice is still critical to maintain. In other cases, it may be possible for schools to work with organizational development experts or other advisors to help them become ready for reform. For example, if interpersonal problems, factionalism, or inadequate leadership are inhibiting a school's ability to reach an informed consensus on a direction of reform, an organizational consultant might help the school's staff recognize and solve the problem. Another supportive role might be played by "brokers," individuals aware of a broad range of innovations who can help students assess their needs and resources to make a rational choice among promising alternatives. This assistance may also help a "sand" school move toward readiness for reform.

The most difficult situation is "sand" schools that are deeply dysfunctional. At the extreme, these schools may be actively harming children; more often, an incompetent principal or factionally riven staff are running an ineffective school incapable of developing a common vision or plan. Working with such schools to try to create a climate for reform is extremely difficult and unlikely to succeed. These schools are prime candidates for principal changes and, in some situations, reconstitution. Reconstitution, an increasingly popular negative sanction in the U.S., is applied to schools that are low and declining on accountability measures. It usually means transferring out all staff except those who apply to remain and are accepted by a new principal. For example, reconstitutions have actually been carried out in the State of Maryland and in the San Francisco school district and are part of policies going into effect in many others. Hargreaves (1990) describes a reconstitution strategy in London in which inspectors were moved into schools to support a change process. The reconstitution process can provide an opportunity to introduce "bricks" reforms. A principal experienced or knowledgeable about the reform may interview potential staff and require that applicants make an informed choice to implement the new program if they wish to teach in the school. Resources to implement the program might be provided as part of the reconstitution plan.

POLICY IMPLICATIONS

The most critical implication of the foregoing discussion is that while co-constructed ("seeds") models focusing on organizational development can play an important role in the broader school reform movement, primarily allowing for the development of outstanding examples of what is possible in school reform, they should focus on the relatively small percentage of schools that are ready and able to make the best of them; a far larger set of schools, I have argued, need and can implement well-specified ("bricks") models. Some "sand" schools that could not readily implement either type of strategy may be left alone if they are neverthe-less doing an adequate job. However, schools in turmoil with low and falling test scores might be reconstituted, possibly to emerge with a new staff committed in advance to implementing a comprehensive, well-specified design.

Additional policy elements that would be necessary to create an infrastructure for progressive reform would be as follows.

1. Implement state-level reforms around standards and accountability

An important first step in any broad scale reform plan is to come to an agreement about what children should be learning and then hold schools accountable for moving their students toward ever-higher performance on broadly focused measures tied to these standards. I am pessimistic about standards, assessment, and accountability making a substantial difference in student achievement by themselves, but if tied to an array of practical, attractive, proven options for school and classroom reform they can help motivate school staffs to do the hard work necessary to implement more effective practices. They can also help identify schools that are doing a terrible job with students so that these schools can receive special assistance and, if assistance is ineffective, reconstitution.

2. Fund development and evaluations of well-specified ("bricks") models

The greatest flaw in the argument made here is that there may be too small a pool of comprehensive, well-specified, well-evaluated models. Building a school reform system around such models requires that there be many of them, so that school staffs can make meaningful choices among them. There are several subject-specific methods (such as Reading Recovery and various writing process models) that are well-validated and replicable (see Fashola & Slavin, 1996), but Success for All/Roots and Wing is the only well-specified, comprehensive model up and run-ning today with independently verified evidence of effectiveness and replicablity. However, there are a number of additional developments on the horizon that could change this situation. First, New American Schools (formerly the New American Schools Development Corporation) has funded the development of seven whole-school reform designs (including Roots and Wings). In addition to Roots and Wings, two or three of these have enough structure and materials to be con-sidered "bricks" designs. Second, a group led by Anthony Bryk at the University of Chicago is working on building a comprehensive elementary reform model around Reading Recovery. Third, the Core Knowledge program has the potential to serve as a "bricks" model, and is currently being evaluated by Sam Stringfield at Johns Hopkins University. An experiment in Baltimore established positive effects of a comprehensive elementary school plan built around a private school's (Calvert School) well-developed curriculum (Stringfield, 1995). There are serious political problems in making this model replicable, as Calvert has little interest in replicating its design broadly, but if this problem can be overcome it could contribute another promising "bricks" design. The Edison Project is establishing a network of for-profit schools in districts around the U.S. Their design uses Success for All materials for elementary reading, writing, language arts, tutoring, and family support, and the University of Chicago Mathematics Program; other program elements, including a comprehensive technology plan, longer school days and years, and internal organization, are unique to the model. A comprehensive model called the Early Literacy Research Project (ELRP) based on Success for All but incorporating different curricular elements (including Reading Recovery as its tutorial approach) is currently being implemented and evaluated in that state of Victoria, Australia (Hill, 1996), and a separate project in New South Wales (Sydney), led by Yola Center, is developing and evaluating another adaptation of Success for All. In Israel, comprehensive approaches related to Success for All are being implemented and evaluated by Joseph Bashi and his colleagues, and in a separate project led by Rachel Lazarowitz. Any of these international adaptations could become a separate design that could ultimately enrich the range of options available in the U.S. and elsewhere.

Beyond these, it would be relatively straightforward for developers to weave together subject-specific components into whole-school designs. Some of the existing designs already do this, as in the case of the Edison Project using Success for All for All materials and the Modern Red Schoolhouse using Core Knowledge materials. Not everyone needs to reinvent the wheel.

Still, there are two critical needs in this area. One is for funding and encouragement for developers to create new comprehensive and subject-specific designs in areas where few models exist (such as middle and high schools) and in areas of enormous importance (such as beginning reading and school-to-work programs). The second is for third-party evaluations of replicable designs. A key assumption in the idea of focusing on "bricks" reforms is that if school staffs select a given design and implement it well, it will have an important impact on student achievement. Only third-party evaluations conducted by independent investigators can give school staffs confidence that a well implemented model will work. Elsewhere, I have argued for a system of "design competitions" that would fund the production of a range of replicable, attractive models for various levels of schooling and subject areas and ultimately carry out such independent assessments, comparing innovative models to control groups (Slavin, 1996).

3. Help schools make informed choices among a variety of models.

One general problem of innovation is that school staffs choose a model of reform because it happens to be available at the point when the school is ready and able to make a change. Rarely do schools make considered choices among a set of attractive options to find a match between the model's characteristics and the school's needs and capabilities (see Stringfield & Herman, 1995). This results in frequent mismatches between innovative models and implementing schools.

To change this situation, two system-level reforms are needed. First, schools in a given district should be presented several contrasting models ("seeds" as well as "bricks") at the same time. New American Schools (NAS) is currently organizing such opportunities to enable schools in ten U.S. jurisdictions (states or large cities) to make an informed choice among the seven NAS designs plus others of equal comprehensiveness. This process often includes "design fairs" in which school teams, after reviewing preliminary information, can hear about several designs over the course of one to two days. Other states and districts have also held design fairs of various kinds. This approach gives the school teams comparable information about the designs, of course, but also more subtly changes the conversation about reform from "what can we make up to solve our problems" to "what can we select and adapt to meet our needs." Following design fairs school teams may visit schools using a given design, may have representatives from the design come to talk to the school staff, and may engage in extended discussions within the school and district to arrive at a satisfactory and widely supported choice.

The second reform implied by an "informed choice" approach is to have local brokers knowledgeable about the available models able to meet with school staffs to help them analyze their needs, strengths, and limitations, and then select a strategy for change. Competent brokers can help identify schools able to implement "seeds" strategies, those ready for "bricks," and those not currently ready for major change.

4.   *Target funding to adoption of proven practices*

Almost all school reform models can be implemented in the long run more or less within the current financial structure of schools, but many require significant additional investments in the early years (for extensive professional development, materials, technology, and so on). Further, additional funding may be necessary to motivate schools to invest their own resources in the reform process. For example, the Ohio State Department of Education makes "Venture Capital" grants of $25,000 to schools that write proposals showing how (among other things) they will use their own resources, such as Title I, to support schoolwide change. A number of Success for All/Roots and Wings schools in Ohio have come into the program through this route.

The problem of funding for schoolwide reform is serious. Even when schools have control of very large proportions of their funding, and even when their resources are substantial, it is difficult to pry loose adequate resources for professional development and innovation, because existing untargeted resources are usually absorbed in higher teachers' salaries, lower class sizes, aides, and other expenditures that are hard to reverse. Schoolwide reform in the U.S. has largely been funded by Title I formula allocations to high-poverty schools. Title I has a specific purpose (raising the achievement of students in poverty), and cannot be used for many purposes (such as raising teachers' salaries). Further, even though the amounts of money they receive do not depend on proposal writing, schools do have to submit a Title I plan each year, forcing them to rethink their uses of these funds. Traditionally, Title I funds have been used primarily for pullout remedial programs or classroom aides, two uses long found to be ineffective (see Slavin, 1994; Puma, Jones, Rock, & Fernandez, 1993).

To promote the use of schoolwide reform models on a broad scale, a stable, predictable source of funds needs to be earmarked just for this purpose. There was a proposal for a 20% set- aside of Title I funds for this purpose that was never enacted (Commission on Chapter I, 1992), but even encouragement for this use by federal, state, and local Title I officials has been very helpful. One interesting approach is being implemented in Israel where the government allocated substantial funds for various agencies (including for-profit companies) to work with schools in 30 high-poverty communities to implement promising practices. Even in the U.S., and certainly in other countries with no analog to Title I, dedicated funding for schoolwide reform is essential, regardless of the level of funds available to schools for other purposes.

CONCLUSION

The school reform movement is now entering a new phase. Both systemic reforms (such as changes in standards, assessments, and accountability) and school-by-school reforms have made a great deal of progress in recent years, but both have also run into significant obstacles. It is now time to become more sophisticated and selective about how reforms are applied to schools at different stages of readiness for reform. This paper proposes one conceptual scheme to describe schools ready for co-constructed "seeds" models based on organizational development principles, those ready for structured, comprehensive "bricks" models that provide student materials, teacher's materials, and other supports, and "sand" schools not ready for reform. As the school reform movement progresses we must learn how to identify the different needs of schools and provide for these needs, so that the efforts of dedicated reformers are exerted where they will do the greatest good for children.

REFERENCES

Adler, M. J. (1982). *The Paideia proposal: An educational manifesto*. New York: Macmillan.
Bodily, S.J., Purnell, S., Ramsey, K., & Keith, S. (1996). *Lessons from New American Schools Development Corporation's development phase*. Washington, DC: RAND.
Clay, M. M (1985). *The early detection of reading difficulties*. Exeter, NH: Heinemann.
Comer, J. (1988). Educating poor minority children. *Scientific American, 259*, 42–48.
Commission on Chapter 1. (1992). *Making schools work for children in poverty*. Washington, DC: American Association for Higher Education.
Elmore, R. F. (1996). Getting to scale with good educational practice. *Harvard Educational Review, 66*, 1–26.
Fashola, O. S., & Slavin, R. E. (1996). *Effective and replicable programs for students placed at risk in*

elementary and middle schools. Baltimore, MD: Johns Hopkins University, Center for Research on the Education of Students Placed at Risk.

Fullan, M. (1991). *The new meaning of educational change.* New York: Teacher's College Press.

Goodlad, J. I. (1993). *A place called school.* New York: McGraw-Hill.

Hargreaves, D. H. (1990). Accountability and school improvement in the work of LEA inspectorates: The rhetoric and beyond. *Journal of Education Policy, 5* (3), 230–239.

Hill, P. 1996). *Early Literacy Research Project (ELRP): Project brief.* Melbourne, Australia: University of Melbourne

Hirsch, E. D. (1993). The Core Knowledge curriculum: What's behind its success? *Educational Leadership, 50*(8), 23–30.

Hopfenberg, W. S., & Levin, H. M. (1993). *The Accelerated Schools resource guide.* San Francisco: Jossey-Bass.

Hopkins, D. (1994). Towards a theory for school improvement. In J. Gray et al. (Eds.), *Merging traditions.* London: Cassell.

Hopkins, D., Ainscow, M., & West, M. (1994). *School improvement in an era of change.* London: Cassell.

Kilgore, S., Doyle, D., & Linkowsky, L. (1996). The Modern red schoolhouse. In S. Stringfield, S., Ross, & L. Smith (Eds.), *Bold plans for school restructuring: The New American Schools Development Corporation designs.* Mahwah, NJ: Erlbaum.

Levin, H. M. (1987). Accelerated schools for disadvantaged students. *Educational Leadership, 44*(6), 19–21.

Levine, D., & Lezotte, L. (1990). *Unusually effective schools.* Madison, WI: National Center for Effective Schools Research and Development.

Meier, D. (1995). How our schools could be. *Phi Delta Kappan, 76*(5), 369–373.

Mentzer, D., & Shaughnessy, G. (1996). Hawthorne elementary school: The teachers' perspective. *Journal of Education of Students Placed at Risk, 1*(1) 13–34.

Muncey, D. E., & McQuillan, P. J. (1993). Preliminary findings from a five-year study of the Coalition of Essential Schools. *Phi Delta Kappan, 74*(6), 486–489.

Newmann, F. M., et al. (1996). *School restructuring and student learning.* San Francisco: Jossey-Bass.

Newmann, F. M. & Wehlage, G. G. (1995). *Successful school restructuring.* Madison: University of Wisconsin, Center on Organization and Restructuring of Schools.

Orell, C. (1996). ATLAS Communities: Authentic teaching, learning, and assessment for all students. In S. Stringfield, S. Ross, & L. Smith (Eds.), *Bold plans for school restructuring: The New American Schools Development Corporation designs.* Mahwah, NJ: Erlbaum.

Pinnell, G. S. (1989). Reading Recovery: Helping at-risk children learn to read. *Elementary School Journal, 90*, 161–182.

Prestine, N. A. (1993). Feelings the ripples, riding the waves: Making an Essential School. In J. Murphy & P. Hallinger (Eds.), *Restructuring Schooling: Learning from ongoing efforts.* Newbury Park, CA: Corwin.

Puma, M. J., Jones, C. C., Rock, D., & Fernandez, R. (1993). *Prospects: The congressionally mandated study of educational growth and opportunity.* Interim report. Bethesda, MD: Abt Associates.

Rothman, R. (1996). Reform at all levels: National Alliance for Restructuring Education. In S. Stringfield, S., Ross, & L. Smith (Eds.), *Bold plans for school restructuring: The New American Schools Development Corporation designs.* Mahwah, NJ: Erlbaum.

Slavin, R. E. (1994). School and classroom organization in beginning reading: Class size, aides, and instructional grouping. In R. E. Slavin, N. L. Karweit, B. A. Wasik, & N. A. Madden (Eds.), *Preventing early school failure: Research on effective strategies.* Boston: Allyn & Bacon.

Slavin, R. E. (1996). *Design competitions: A proposal for a new federal role in educational research and development.* Baltimore, MD: Johns Hopkins University, Center for Research on the Education of Students Placed at Risk.

Slavin, R. E., Madden, N. A., Dolan, L. J., & Wasik, B. A. (1996a). *Every child, every school: Success for All.* Newbury Park, CA: Corwin.

Slavin, R. E., Madden, N. A., Dolan, L. J., Wasik, B. A., Ross, S., Smith, L. & Dianda, M. (1996b). Success for All: A summary of research. *Journal of Education for Students Placed at Risk, 1*, 41–76.

Sizer, T. (1992). *Horace's school.* New York: Houghton Mifflin.

Smith, M., & O'Day, J. (1991). Systemic school reform. In S. Fuhrman & B. Malen (Eds.), *The politics of curriculum and testing* (pp. 233–267). Bristol, PA: Falmer.

Stapleford, T. A. (1994, April). *The power of coalition: A comparative study of two school reform projects.*

Paper presented at the annual meetings of the American Educational Research Association, New Orleans.

Stringfield, S. (1995). *Fourth year evaluation of the Calvert School program at Barclay School.* Baltimore, MD: Johns Hopkins University, Center for Research on the Education of Students Placed at Risk.

Stringfield, S., & Herman, B. (1994). *Observation of partial implementations of the Coalition of Essential Schools: The need for higher reliability organizational methods.* Baltimore: Johns Hopkins University, Center for Research on the Education of Students Placed at Risk.

Stringfield, S, & Herman, B. (1995, April). *The effects of promising programs on students: Results from the special strategies study.* Paper presented at the annual meeting of the American Educational Research Association, San Francisco.

Stringfield, S., Herman, R., Millsap, M., & Scott, E. (1996, April). *The three year effects of ten "Promising Programs" on the academic achievements of students placed at risk.* Paper presented at the meeting of the American Educational Research Association, New York.

Teddlie, C., & Stringfield, S. (1993). *School matters: Lessons learned from a 10-year study of school effects.* New York: Teachers College Press.

Using "Promising Programs" to Improve Educational Processes and Student Outcomes[1]

SAM STRINGFIELD
Johns Hopkins University, Baltimore, USA

MARY ANN MILLSAP
Johns Hopkins University, Baltimore, USA

REBECCA HERMAN
Johns Hopkins University, Baltimore, USA

In this chapter Sam Stringfield, Mary Ann Millsap and Rebecca Herman examine a 1990s study of 10 "promising programs" for improving the academic achievements of students whose families' life circumstances have placed them in danger of failing to thrive academically. These are children born to poverty, members of racial or cultural minorities, and/or children in whose homes a language other than English is spoken the majority of the time. The percentage of U.S. students that will be in one of those risk-indicating conditions will exceed 50% in the early 21st century. The structure of the chapter is as follows: a brief history of research on the use of specific programs to affect student achievement is followed by a description of the U.S. federal compensatory education program. Next is a description of the design of the Special Strategies studies. Each of the 10 designs are briefly described, followed by an overview of findings. In concluding the chapter Stringfield and his colleagues conclude with a discussion of the implications of those findings for additional research and practice.

The history of the huge advances in the material well being of much of humanity over the centuries is largely a history of the development and spread of powerful, practical technologies (Burke, 1995). The evolution of the scratch plow and then the mouldboard plow, and more recently the tractor, chemical fertilizers and hybrid seed have brought agriculture through a series of "revolutions" that have resulted in unprecedented numbers of humans eating more nearly healthy diets. While there were often very intelligent, wise, and moral people practicing medicine before the 1930s, it was the evolution of sulfa drugs, penicillin, and an ever-more-rapidly exploding cornucopia of other "miracle drugs" and treatments over the last 60 years that has lead to the doubling of our life expectancies over those of citizens of our countries at the turn of the 20th century (Thomas, 1979).

Throughout the 20th Century, researchers studying school improvement in the United States have designed reforms aimed at expanding students' knowledge bases and improving their abilities to seek and integrate information. Not unlike the histories of medicine or aviation (Yenne, 1996), this process in education has resulted in some fervently-advocated but impractical designs. As in other fields,

D. Hopkins (ed.), The Practice and Theory of School Improvement, 280-304.
© 2005 *Springer. Printed in the Netherlands.*

the evolution of a science producing practical, widely usable improvements has taken decades. In the mean time, historians of 20th century U.S. education have frequently noted a pattern of reform characterized by a great deal of surface turmoil and an equal level of stability and fundamental non-change in the core technologies of teaching (e.g., Cuban, 1993). Having started formal, scientifically based experimentation much later, educational researchers are similarly later in producing practical results for school improvement designs. The knowledge base needed for fundamental school improvement is still being developed.

Reviews of prior proactive studies of promising school reform efforts are reviewed by Hopkins (this volume) and Stringfield, Nunnery & Datnow (in process); therefore, they are reviewed very briefly here. The progressivist period (roughly 1910 – 1940) produced the "Eight Year Study" (Aikin, 1942). In the 1960s, the Federal government initiated diverse Research, Development and Dissemination efforts, the most discussed of which was *Follow Through* (for review, see Kennedy, 1978). A large, national study of several of the *Follow Through* designs was conducted by Stallings & Kaskowitz (1974).

The next major study of the 1960s – 1970s period became known as "The Rand Change Agent Study" (Berman & McLaughlin, 1977).

Collectively, these studies could be interpreted as indicating the following:

- Most reform efforts, however elegant in academic theory, have typically failed in practical implementation.
- Programs that have been more successful at producing pre-specified student outcomes have tended to focus more specifically on academic content.
- Implementation dominates outcome.
- Targeted use of task-specific external consultants often improves implementation level (see also Crandall et al., 1982).

In the years since the *Follow Through* and Rand studies, the U.S. government had not actively supported the development of diverse designs, but through a program known as the National Diffusion Network (NDN, National Diffusion Study Group, 1992) the U.S. Department of Education had sponsored the identification and "diffusion" of "Educational Programs That Work." These tended to be locally developed reading programs, math programs, and other targeted-but-not-whole-school efforts. Evidence that the programs actually "worked" was generally anecdotal, and, partially as a result, NDN came under increasing criticism, eventually losing all federal funding.

FEDERAL INVOLVEMENT IN COMPENSATORY EDUCATION

The United States Constitution does not provide a specific role of the federal government in education, and education has traditionally been viewed as one of the responsibilities devolved to the individual states. However, in the 20th century, the U.S. courts, the Presidents, and the Congress have slowly become more involved in issues regarding education[2]. The Elementary and Secondary Education Act

(ESEA) of 1965 marked the first formal federal funding of a wide-spread elementary and secondary schooling program. Title I of ESEA provided one billion federal dollars in its first year, all of which was targeted to assist schools serving large numbers of economically disadvantaged students. Title I (from 1981 through 1994 called Chapter 1) has continued to receive funding for over 30 years, and has grown to over $7,000,000,000 per year. Title I now serves over 5.5 million students per year.

During the first 25 years of federal funding for compensatory education, the majority of uses of the program tended to be "pull-out" services. These proliferated, in part, out of a federal concern that the Title I funds be used to "supplement, not supplant" previously existing services. That is, the federal government did not want Title I funds to provide basic services in schools serving poor children, only to have local savings from those schools used to create ever-more-attractive schools for more affluent communities. Schools that could not clearly demonstrate that the services were a supplement to traditional levels of service provided to disadvantaged students were penalized with audit exceptions (e.g., very unattractive pay-back requirements), so schools increasingly used Title I money to fund observably separate personnel and services. In effect, Title I came to resemble some components of Special Education.

This trend was reversed in the 1988 and 1994 reauthorizations of the federal compensatory education laws. These specifically provided schools serving large numbers of disadvantaged students with greater flexibility in their use of federal funds.

Title I was the first major piece of social legislation to require ongoing local and national evaluation. Even with the liberalization present in the 1988 and 1994 laws, all Title I schools are subject to local outcome evaluations. These data are then aggregated to the district, state, and national levels.

A second level of national evaluation of the effects of Title I has been mandated with every five year authorization. In preparation for and in responding to the 1988 Congressional mandate for a large-scale, longitudinal study of the effects of compensatory education, two panels of researchers were able to argue that some of the funds for the larger study (which they feared would yield modest useful information) should be diverted to studies of "promising programs" (Williams, Richmond & Mason, 1986, Abt Associates, et al., 1988). The *Special Strategies* studies (Stringfield et al., 1993, 1996) were funded under this national evaluation of compensatory education mandate. The *Special Strategies* studies were funded in conjunction with a much larger study of Title I/Chapter I services which was known as *Prospects* (Puma, Jones, Rock, & Fernandez, 1993). *Prospects* researchers gathered longitudinal data on nationally representative samples of first, third, and seventh grade students over several years.

THE *SPECIAL STRATEGIES* STUDIES FOR EDUCATING DISADVANTAGED CHILDREN

The next section of this chapter presents the major purposes of the Urban and Suburban/Rural *Special Strategies* Studies for Educating Disadvantaged Children, describes the studies' methods, provides findings from the full three years of data gathering, and explores policy implications of the studies. The *Special Strategies* studies were developed to accomplish three goals:

- Describe promising alternatives for Chapter 1 practices.
- Compare the characteristics of promising alternatives to more traditional practices.
- Assess the replicability of programs that appear most successful.

DESCRIPTIONS OF THE TEN SPECIAL STRATEGIES

The researchers gathered *qualitative* and *quantitative* data at sites representing six urban program types and six suburban/rural program types. Some categories, such as Chapter 1 schoolwide projects[3], were required by the initial Federal request for proposals to be in both the urban and the suburban/rural contracts, so the total number of strategy types investigated was ten.

A multi-criterion sampling scheme for programs brought together a final sample of programs that had unusually promising histories of effectiveness, and programs that figured prominently in national school reform efforts. For example, Chapter 1 schoolwide projects were relatively new in 1990 and had not developed a research track record. Yet clearly they were important given the 1988 funding re-authorization that encouraged the development of such efforts. Similarly, the research base on the Coalition of Essential Schools was not well developed, but as the major high school restructuring initiative in the country, it justified study. After all criteria were met, the strategy types discussed below were selected for longitudinal study.

These diverse strategies differ along several dimensions. For this and the Final Report we have chosen to present the various programs or designs as they differ within a two-dimensional space[4]. The first dimension has to do with the intended scope of the strategy reform. Several of the strategies are intended to change entire schools. These include the Comer School Development Program, Success for All, the Paideia program, the Coalition of Essential Schools, Chapter 1 schoolwide projects, and extended year schoolwide projects. By contrast, Reading Recovery, METRA/peer tutoring, computer-assisted-instruction (CAI) laboratories, and Chapter 1 after-school and summer programs leave the majority of the traditional school day intact and provide services that are physically or temporally separate from the regular classroom.

The second dimension is concerned with the original source of program development. Chapter 1 schoolwide projects, most summer programs, and peer-tutoring programs are developed locally, often at the specific school. By contrast, the Comer School Development Program, Success for All, Paideia, the Coalition of Essential Schools, Reading Recovery and the hardware, software, and integrated designs of computer-assisted-instruction laboratories are developed externally to the local school by program researchers and developers. All of the external programs offer or require levels of expert technical assistance, typically in the form of visiting consultants. Both of the METRA/Peer Tutoring schools in *Special Strategies* experimented with externally developed components integrated into locally developed programs.

In practice, both dimensions often become fuzzy. Reading Recovery is now experimenting with schoolwide formats, and many forms of CAI are delivered not in special laboratories but in regular classrooms. Similarly, externally developed reform efforts typically strive to develop local expertise and invariably make some adaptations to local constraints. Locally developed schoolwide projects often use an amalgam of externally developed components.

Each program is briefly described below.

EXTERNALLY DEVELOPED SCHOOL RESTRUCTURING STRATEGIES

The *Comer School Development Program (SDP)* (1988) is rooted in the developer's experiences in community psychiatry and child development at the Yale Child Study Center. Over several years, Dr. James Comer and the staff of the School Development Program have developed a program that replaces traditional school

TWO KEY DIMENSIONS ALONG WHICH *SPECIAL STRATEGIES* PROGRAMS DIFFERED

FOCUS OF PROGRAM/STRATEGY		SOURCE OF PROGRAM/STRATEGY	
		External	Local
	Whole School Restructuring	Comer SDP Success for All Paideia Coalition of Essential Schools	Schoolwide Projects* Extended Year SWPs*
	Targeted Sub-population	Reading Recovery CCC	Extended Time METRA/Peer Tutoring*

* Each contained several components, some of which were externally developed.

Figure 1

organization and management with a collaborative school governance and management team, integrates the school's social service programs, and enhances parent participation in all aspects of school life. The purpose of the program is to improve academic achievement and to enhance the social, psychological, and emotional development of the students. The SDP does not provide separate curricula or instructional methods to schools.

Success for All (Slavin, Madden, Karweit, Dolan, & Wasik, 1992, 1996) is an extensively articulated, intensive school restructuring program designed to be implemented in schools serving large numbers of highly disadvantaged students. The goals of the program are to have all students reading on grade level by the end of third grade and to sustain those gains through the elementary years. Student reading skills are developed in small group and tutoring sessions, supported by a host of recommended teaching practices and materials.

Mortimer Adler's (1983) *The Paideia Proposal: An Educational Manifesto* served as a clarion call for improved quality of schooling for all children. Adler stated that all children are entitled to academic "cream," rather than some being given cream while others receive "skim milk." Through the reading of challenging material, didactic instruction, coaching, and weekly "Socratic seminars," students in Paideia Schools are encouraged in the "development of [higher order] intellectual skills."

The *Coalition of Essential Schools (CES)* was developed by Brown University's Theodore Sizer (1984; 1996). CES is a school restructuring design that outlines broad directions and leaves the construction of specific curricula and instructional methods in the hands of local educators. Re:Learning is a support and dissemination mechanism for CES developed by the Education Commission of the States. The goal of Re:Learning is to provide support for the nine CES principles "from the statehouse to the schoolhouse."

LOCALLY DEVELOPED WHOLE SCHOOL RESTRUCTURING PROJECTS

A variety of projects can be implemented under Chapter 1/Title I's *Schoolwide Project* option (Pechman & Fiester, 1996). In the *Special Strategies* suburban/rural sites, the schoolwide project schools virtually eliminated pullout programs, reduced class sizes in the primary grades, and greatly increased staff development activities. Urban sites mixed reduced class size and other advantages of the schoolwide option with the availability of additional instructional specialists, such as program support teachers and mathematics specialists.

Two of the urban schoolwide projects were selected because they also chose to offer *Extended School Year* services to students. Both schools offered 19 days per year of additional schooling to students during years one and two and more than two additional weeks per year of planning and staff development time to teachers. The extended-year services to students were discontinued after the second year of the *Special Strategies* studies, though the extended planning and staff development time components were continued and expanded.

EXTERNALLY DEVELOPED PROGRAMS TARGETED TO SPECIFIC GROUPS

Reading Recovery is an intensive, first-grade, one-to-one tutoring program (Pinnell, 1989; Swartz & Klein, 1997) developed in New Zealand by Marie Clay. In Reading Recovery, first grade students who are having difficulties learning to read spend a half hour per day for up to 16 weeks with a highly trained reading specialist. The time is spent reading several books with known difficulty levels, and in writing activities. Two assumptions of Reading Recovery are that students who are having difficulty learning to read can be taught to read in 12–16 weeks, and that once they have learned a set of reading skills, the students can progress for several years without needing further remedial assistance. Members of Ohio State University's Reading Recovery team are now working with a University of Chicago team on a grade and/or schoolwide version of Reading Recovery.

The *Computer Curriculum Corporation (CCC)* offers one of the more widely implemented integrated computer-assisted-instruction (CAI) packages. In CCC, students spend 12–25 minutes each day in interactive, computer-driven instruction. A file server records each student's pattern of answers, and selects new activities for each child for the following day. The particular commercial program was chosen not as a commercial endorsement, but because it has a longer and more often independently documented evaluation history. "Release 14" of CCC was studied in *Special Strategies*. The summer 1995 release was "Release 16."

Most commercially developed computer-assisted instruction products such as CCC, Jostens, and IBM's Write to Read can be offered to all students or targeted to compensatory education students only; most can be offered in a separate laboratory or in classrooms. In *Special Strategies*, one school used CCC for all students and one for compensatory education only. Each used a separate computer laboratory.

LOCALLY DEVELOPED, TARGETED PROGRAMS

Both of the local tutoring programs studied in *Special Strategies* used an amalgam of tutoring approaches during the study's three years of field work. *METRA* was one component of larger, locally developed tutoring programs. Therefore, although METRA is a commercial product, it is described here.

METRA is a highly structured reading tutorial program that has been found to produce significant gains in achievement (Levin, Glass, & Meister, 1984). METRA can be implemented either in a cross-age peer tutoring format, or as a paraprofessionally delivered program. In its typical implementation, METRA is a relatively low-cost program.

Locally developed, targeted programs included a cross-age and same-age *peer tutoring program* that was examined as a companion to METRA. Over time, the schools chose to incorporate several components of METRA into their scheme.

The logic of *extended-day* and *extended-year programs* is straightforward: if students aren't able to progress at the rate of their peers, provide them with more, perhaps varied, instructional activities during extended-time periods. It is often argued that American students don't perform as well on international comparative studies because students in the U.S. go to school for fewer hours per day and fewer days per year than students in other first-world countries. In the *Special Strategies* studies, both an after-school program for Chapter 1 students and a summer school for migrant students were examined. The latter served both migrating and "settled out" migrant students.

SELECTION OF SITES

The site selection process was necessarily purposeful. Sites were selected because they were purported to be exemplars of the chosen strategies. Although the routes through which sites were identified varied, the common theme was nomination by persons regarded as *experts within the program type*, often the program's developer or a well-known disseminator. In most cases, after a program specialist had nominated a school, both the state and local Chapter 1 directors were asked to verify the exemplary status of the school's program. In the rare instances where state Chapter 1 coordinators expressed doubt as to the exemplary status of a nominated school's program, the sites were dropped and other sites identified. In 23 of 25 instances, selected schools received multiple nominations.

Our design proposals called for three-year studies of cohorts of students in two schools of each type. In one case the longitudinal sample was expanded to three schools out of a concern, never realized, that a district desegregation settlement might eliminate the program during year one of the study. This resulted in a 25-school core sample.

The grade of the cohort identified for each program is shown in Figure 2. Each school's cohort was followed over a three-year period beginning in the fall of 1990. For example, in the case of first graders, *Special Strategies* followed the majority of the students through the spring of their third-grade experience. A few students were retained in a grade for one year, and a smaller number "skipped" a grade and moved ahead. So long as students remained at their *Special Strategies* school, they were considered to be in their cohort, regardless of their academic progress over the three years.

In addition to the longitudinal sample, the design called for visiting multiple replication sites for each of the programs. The replicates provided valuable data on diverse contextual variables that may facilitate or impede implementation for

DISTRIBUTION OF SAMPLE SCHOOLS BY PROGRAM TYPE AND GRADE OF PRIMARY FOCUS			
URBAN PROGRAMS	INITIAL-CONCLUDING GRADE*	SUBURBAN/RURAL PROGRAMS	INITIAL-CONCLUDING GRADE*
Comer SDP	1-3	Reading Recovery	1-3
Success for All	1-3	METRA/Peer Tutoring	1-3
Extended Year Schoolwide	1-3	Extended Day/ Extended Year	1-3 3-5
Schoolwide	3-5	Schoolwide	3-5
Paideia	3-5	Computer Assisted Instruction (CCC)	3-5
Coalition of Essential Schools (CES)	9-11	Re:Learning/Coalition of Essential Schools	9-11

* The *Special Strategies* studies followed cohorts over three school years, so at study's end the majority of first graders were in third grade, third graders in fifth grade, and ninth graders in eleventh grade.

Figure 2

specific strategy types. The result of the sampling scheme was four to six sites (longitudinal plus replication) for each of the major program types, with sites in over 15 states.

METHODS

At each of the 25 longitudinal-study schools, *Special Strategies* research teams spent a minimum of three days on site for each of five semesters from fall of 1990 through fall of 1992. This resulted in a total of at least 30 person days of on-site data gathering at each longitudinal site. During those visits, researchers interviewed administrators, teachers, parents, and students. During the site visit, detailed observational data on classroom processes were collected. At each school, three students were identified during year one for extended observation. Those students were followed through detailed "whole school day" observations at each subsequent school visit. Based on their Fall 1990 pretests, augmented by principal and teacher judgments, students generally were chosen in three categories: students with reading comprehension pretests in the bottom 17 percent nationally, in the 18–35 percentile range, and between the 36th and 50th percentiles. In the case of a student transferring or dropping out of school in years one or two, back-up students were identified and, to the extent practical, followed. These detailed records often provided remarkable windows into the longitudinal impact of programs on schooling, including the organization, curriculum, and instruction students received.

A unique feature of *Special Strategies* was its link to the nationally representative *Prospects* data set. (Puma, Jones, Rock, & Fernandez, 1993). *Prospects* quantitative data gathered at each site included norm-referenced achievement test scores[5], archival data from student records, and questionnaires given to administrators, teachers, parents and students. Student questionnaire data were gathered at the third grade and above. *Prospects* data permit comparisons between *Special Strategies* outcomes and those achieved at more nationally representative sites.

FINDINGS

Eight broad findings are discussed here and in more detail in the *Special Strategies Final Report* (Stringfield et al., 1994).

Finding #1: America's students who have been placed at risk of academic failure are capable of achieving at levels that meet and perhaps exceed current national averages. The ability of disadvantaged students to achieve academically was clearly demonstrated at some of the Special Strategies sites.

Recently, some have raised the troubling hypothesis that children of poverty do not merely not achieve, but that they are genetically incapable of achieving at high levels (Hernstein & Murray, 1994). Predating the current debates by 15 years, Ron Edmonds (1979) reasoned that to counter a genetic-limitation hypothesis, one would only have to identify one school in which large numbers of urban poor children were achieving at high levels.

Disadvantaged students in several *Special Strategies* schools began the study far below the national average, yet made academic gains toward or exceeding national means. In some schools the gains were dramatic. Figure 3 (p. 1324) presents three-year data from initially low-achieving students in two *Special Strategies* schools, and contrasts those data with data from the *Prospects* (Puma et al., 1993) nationally-weighted findings.

The *Special Strategies* schools are Success for All-A (SFA-A) and Comer School Development Program-A (Comer SDP-A). Both schools served inner-city communities, both served 90+% minority student populations, and in both schools 70+% of the students received free lunches, indicating that both schools served communities that were economically very disadvantaged. SFA-A served a community that included a significant number of first-generation immigrants in whose homes the primary language was other than English.

Because *Special Strategies* was designed to focus on students who potentially could have received Chapter 1 services, Figure 3 presents data only on students whose CTBS Reading Comprehension scores in the fall of first grade were below the 50th percentile (e.g. students who would have been eligible for traditional

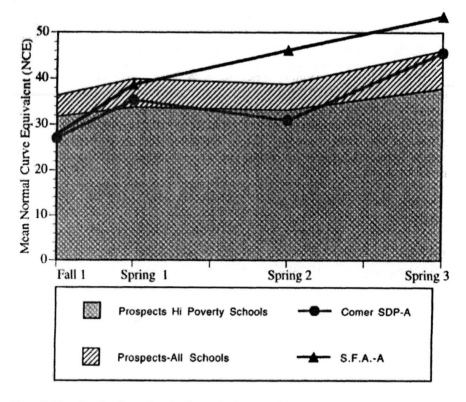

Figure 3: Mean Reading Comprehension Scores for Students with Pretest <50%: Comer Schol Development Program and Success for All at Strong Implementation Sites.

Chapter 1 services). As a practical matter, this eliminated very few students from SFA-A or Comer SDP-A. Virtually all students in these two schools began first grade at well below the national average.

Figure 3 presents three years of data for four groups of students in a compact form, so a brief explanation may aid in interpretation[6]. The figure presents data from four groups, including two study groups and two comparison groups:

- the first grade cohort at SFA-A, represented by triangles (Special Strategy);
- the first-grade cohorts at Comer SDP-A, represented by circles (Special Strategy);
- the nationally weighted sample of *Prospects* students who initially scored below the 50th percentile (e.g., were potentially available for Chapter 1 services), represented by the line across the striped area (comparison group); and
- the nationally weighted sample of *Prospects* students who initially scored below the 50th percentile and who attended high poverty schools (e.g., schools in which 75+% of students received free or reduced price lunches), represented by the line across the shaded area (comparison group).

Each group was tested four times: fall of first grade, and springs of first, second, and third grades. The data are presented on the Normal Curve Equivalent (NCE) scale[7].

The first comparison group, initially low achieving first grade students in the nationally weighted sample, averaged a NCE score of 36.3 (26th percentile) in the fall of first grade and rose slightly over time to a mean score in the spring of third grade NCE of 40 (32nd percentile). Mean test scores for the second comparison group, initially low achieving first grade students in high-poverty schools, rose only slightly over time, and remained substantially below the achievement of the first comparison group. *Prospects* data indicated that schools serving more disadvantaged students were, in general, having more difficulty helping low-achieving students catch up to national averages than were schools serving fewer disadvantaged students.

Progress made by students in the two *Special Strategies* schools in Figure 3 was particularly encouraging. The initially low-achieving students in Comer SDP-A and SFA-A began the study with reading comprehension levels below even the average for low-achieving students in high-poverty schools. Yet over their first three years in school, students in Comer SDP-A and SFA-A produced reading achieve-ment scores that substantially exceeded both those of other students in high-poverty schools, and equalled or exceeded those of initially low-achieving students in typical schools. Initially low-achieving students at Comer SDP-A approached the national average score by the end of grade three (NCE=45.5, or the 42nd percentile on the CTBS Reading Comprehension subscale; N of students with test data at all data points=21). Initially low-achieving students at SFA-A surpassed the 50th percentile (NCE=53.4, or the 56th percentile on the CTBS; N=38).

Given that the predominantly poor, overwhelmingly minority, initially low-achieving students in these schools demonstrated reading comprehension levels near or above the national average by the end of grade three, there is good reason to believe that most children of poverty, when well educated, can achieve at similar levels. The current national average can be viewed as an achievable benchmark for schools serving America's children of poverty, when programs that have proven to be effective are well implemented.

Finding #2: Each of the programs studied in Special Strategies offered clear strengths, yet even when visiting sites that were multiply nominated as exemplars, we often found great variance in both implementation levels and effects.

The strengths of the various *Special Strategies* have been described by their vari-ous developers and in the *Special Strategies First Year* and *Final Reports* (String-field et. al., 1993, 1996). While some programs offer complementary components, in no sense could the programs be measured on a simple "effectiveness" scale. For example, Reading Recovery is intended to ensure initial reading and writing skills for targeted groups of first graders, while the Coalition of Essential Schools strives to instill higher levels of thoughtful knowledge and skills to teens.

By analogy, aspirin, penicillin, and chemotherapy all represent extraordinary advances in modern medicine's ability to treat human suffering. But no common scale for determining which drug is "better" or "more effective" makes sense. Penicillin provides no relief to a headache, chemotherapy would not assist a patient with pneumonia, and aspirin cures no form of cancer. Each of the three is a "miracle drug" at treating a specific problem[8].

A quick examination of the 25 longitudinal sites in *Special Strategies* makes some of the context issues clear. Within *Special Strategies* there were schools in which under 25% of students received free or reduced price lunches (a common measure of poverty), and schools in which 99% of all students received free or reduced price lunch. There were schools in which over 80% of all students were of European extraction, schools in which over 90% of students were Hispanic, schools in which 100% of students were African American, and a school in which 100% of the students were Native American. It is implausible that, even under the best of implementation conditions, one single reform type would be the "best" solution for each of these schools.

The Comer School Development Program, Success for All, Reading Recovery, and the other designs may each prove valuable in helping some schools improve, but none of the developers claim that their program can "fix" all schools or students. Some of the nominated-as-exemplary schools in *Special Strategies* were clearly losing their race to educate all children.

Figure 4 makes this point clearly. The *Prospects* background data and the programs being implemented are the same as in Figure 3. Again, the *Special Strategies* schools have student populations among which 80+% of students receive free lunch, and 90+% are members of minority groups. However, the School Development Program was never embraced by the principal at Comer SDP-B, and the district did not actively intervene to ensure that the components of the program were working as intended. As a result, major components of the School Development Program existed in name only. Similarly, at Success for All-B, the district's support for the program was at best lukewarm. The principal who had brought the program to the school became a district administrator, and the new principal was selected without being informed that SFA-B was a Success-for-All school. When district-administered test scores for the entire school did not rise in her first year at the school, the principal dismantled the program during year two of *Special Strategies*. Replacement ideas proved ineffective and reading comprehension scores fell. The school partially re-implemented Success for All during year three.

Students in both schools increased their academic achievement gains marginally more than the *Prospects* averages for students attending similarly high-poverty schools. These gains are respectable but far from the very large gains in Comer SDP-A and SFA-A. At no point did these groups of students surpass the high poverty comparison group, much less the national average.

Finding #3: The Special Strategies schools obtaining the greatest academic gains for their at-risk students paid a great deal of attention to issues of initial and long-term implementation, and to institutionalizing the reforms. Several

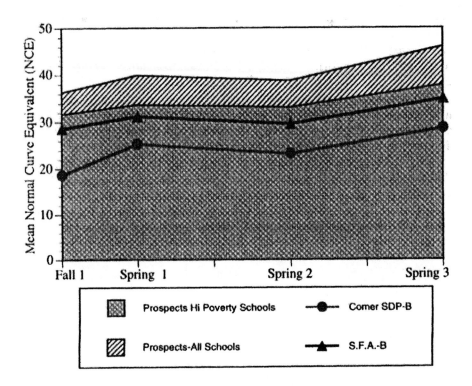

Figure 4: Mean Reading Comprehension Scores for Students with Pretest <Pretest50%: Comer School Development Program and Success for All at Uneven or Interrupted Implementation Sites.

general and a great many program-specific implementation issues, if not successfully addressed, permanently crippled otherwise promising programs.

A realistic perception of local strengths and areas in need of improvement was key in the most successful schools in *Special Strategies*. What were the specific problems facing students at risk in the school? In the most successful schools the answer was derived in advance of program selection and was much more detailed than just "low test scores." Was the principal willing to lead the faculty through the challenges of successfully implementing a particular innovation? What percentage of the faculty was willing to consider various magnitudes of meaningful changes in their teaching and in the organization of their work? If a particular administrator or teacher was unwilling to consider any practical changes to a clearly less than optimal educational program, how willing was the district or the principal or the faculty to provide further inducements for change? What community, district, and state supports could be counted on? To greater or lesser degrees in various sites, all of the above issues mattered during program implementations.

Initial choices among diverse program or design improvement options are many. In *Special Strategies* we studied ten promising options, and perhaps a hundred others are discussed nationally. Countless other "programs" are developed annually in America's 16,000+ school districts. During the late 1980s and early 1990s, schools had at least theoretical access to the National Diffusion Network, Regional Educational Laboratories, Chapter 1 Technical Assistance Centers, and the resources of state Chapter 1 offices and state departments of education. In addition, schools had at least theoretical access to information from diverse professional associations at the state and national levels. Given that wide band of options, several *Special Strategies* researchers were struck with the relatively small number of options most schools examined before choosing a specific program.

Several of the schools had no option at all: They were simply told by central administrators that their school would be receiving a particular computer-assisted-instruction program, or would be implementing a particular type of school reform.

By contrast, the principal in SFA-A had gone with a district team to examine several different school reform options before considering Success for All, and several members of her staff visited a Success-for-All site before the full faculty voted on that particular reform. In two of the schoolwide projects, the principals and the full faculties considered at least four different routes to reform before selecting their somewhat site-tailored paths.

Full and active district, school administration, and faculty commitment to the final choice of reforms was not always sought. Yet there was always a price paid when the commitment of one of the three groups was not achieved. In *Special Strategies*, regardless of the abstract strengths of a reform, the fact that a principal and faculty had considered diverse options and voted to follow a particular path increased the probability of successful implementation.

On the other hand, the Coalition of Essential Schools was only partially implemented in the five high school sites due in part to consistently scattered commitment. No whole faculty fully embraced reorganizing high school curricula away from their traditional scope and sequence, school support lagged for scheduling joint teacher preparation periods and multi-period classes, and only one of the five high schools studied produced a stable, multi-grade, multi-year program of assessment through performance.

Allowing "transfer with dignity" for any faculty member unwilling to undertake a reform that had been voted by the great majority of a faculty and the principal was often helpful. Program implementation at several *Special Strategies* schools was permanently hampered by steps taken by one or a few faculty who did not wish to participate in the effort. At successful sites, administrators occasionally spoke of district policies that allowed any faculty member in any school attempting reform to "transfer with dignity" (without negative repercussions and with all seniority) at her or his own initiative. Similarly, schools that were allowed to hand-pick new administrators and faculty based on the applicants' awareness of and commitment to the school's particular reform were much more likely to sustain the reform. "Transfer with dignity" was policy in the district supporting SFA-A and two of the more successful schoolwide projects.

Acquiring and productively using long-term, targeted technical assistance was often key to program implementation. Becoming a Reading Recovery teacher requires a full year of focused training, followed by permanent cycles of focused staff development, classroom observation, and feedback. In the extended-year schoolwide projects, all staff received almost three weeks of coordinated staff development each year for five years. Schools involved in Success for All are expected to continue a relationship with a regional support team. By contrast, at several locations central administrators assumed that once a school had experienced initial training in a new program, they "had done" that program. In site after site, *Special Strategies* observers noted that new teachers and administrators were not taught the specifics of a particular program or design as they entered, and that these new hires often did not buy into the design.

A few characteristics were common to sites at which programs were discontinued during or shortly after the three years of *Special Strategies* observations. In a few cases there was a school and/or district perception that the program was not living up to its goals, and was discontinued for this reason. Others were victims of what appeared to be political decisions or shifts to "the latest thing".

Each Special Strategy had program-specific requirements for full implementation. Typically, those specifics were not fully spelled out by developers before a school began implementation. Principals and faculty members who had visited at least one other school involved in their particular reform were often less surprised by and better prepared to address program-specific implementation issues when those issues inevitably arose.

> *Finding #4: While the research literature on most programs was promising, norm-referenced achievement measures of effects within the limited Special Strategies samples were more mixed. In general, promising programs that concentrated their efforts in the early grades tended to obtain larger achievement gains from students placed at risk than did programs spreading resources more evenly over the elementary grades or in secondary schools. Within the schools observed during first through third grades, students in schools using externally developed designs tended to achieve greater academic gains than did students in locally developed programs. Students in schools working with whole school reform tended to achieve greater gains than did students in schools attempting various pull-out programs. None of the secondary schools achieved stable implementation across the full school, and, perhaps as a result, none produced a pattern of achievement gains.*

The literature reviews conducted on each of the ten promising programs provided statements, and in most instances, quantitative studies, suggesting that each of the programs could work under some circumstances. (See *Special Strategies Final Report, Stringfield et al, 1996*.) Given that the sites followed through three years by *Special Strategies* researchers were nominated as exemplars of their program or design types, the research team's initial expectation was that academic achievement gains would be nearly universally positive. This expectation was not realized.

The background characteristics of the longitudinal *Special Strategies* schools varied greatly. Variables beyond the control of the school and program, such as regional recessions affecting several communities, city-wide riots affecting two others, and levels of drug infestation in the communities surrounding the schools, all had impact on schools' abilities to implement programs and to obtain desired effects on students' achievements. Given that *Special Strategies* research teams gathered longitudinal data in only two schools per program type, that programs had diverse goals, and that there were often powerful contextual variables affecting outcomes, the following data should be examined with caution.

While three of the six elementary-level whole-school reform programs studied in *Special Strategies* clearly exhibited multi-year reading comprehension gains for initially low-achieving students; on average, the other schools involved in elementary grades targeted (pull out) programs did not produce long term reading comprehension gains for their students. Initially low achieving students in the high school reform did not obtain mean reading gains.

Three years of *Special Strategies* observations produced dozens of stories of individuals and whole schools struggling valiantly to improve the academic lives of students living in poverty. Yet by the end of *Special Strategies*, some of the considerable efforts made by educational professionals seemed to be reaping greater rates of academic growth than others. Effects of strong vs. weak or inconsistent implementations were discussed in Finding #2. Three additional achievement-related findings are discussed in the following paragraphs.

Within *Special Strategies* it appeared that programs concentrating scarce resources early in students' careers, before a pattern of failure could set in, were more successful than schools at which the intervention began later[9]. The mean achievement gains of all students participating in *Special Strategies* schools from the fall of first grade (age six) through spring of third grade (age nine to ten) was 8.6 NCEs, or about 14 percentiles.

All of the secondary schools participating in *Special Strategies* were involved in the Coalition of Essential Schools. As noted earlier, none was able to sustain whole school implementation of CES. While qualitative data noted many examples of individual teachers' instructional efforts and student's declarations of the value of the program, none of the schools was able to produce a pattern of academic gain on the CTBS Reading Comprehension or Mathematics tests. It should be remembered that Theodore Sizer, founder of the Coalition, has repeatedly expressed the view that demonstration of knowledge rather than norm-referenced test scores are the desirable measures of the impact of the Coalition of Essential Schools.

Given limited numbers of schools implementing any specific program type and the small number of *Special Strategies* programs and schools in the third- and ninth-grade samples, further achievement outcome analyses in this overview are limited to the first-grade cohort and its 11 schools[10]. The interventions concentrated in the primary grades tended to produce positive effects for whole schools, and large positive effects for students whose pre-tests were lowest. Among those schools, students attending schools that were attempting whole school reforms tended to receive a greater three year academic benefit. Analyses of mathematics' gains produced similarly large gain scores, again with differences favoring whole school reforms (as opposed to targeted "pull-out" programs).

It was also possible to examine mean gains in reading comprehension for first-through third-grade students attending *Special Strategies* schools that were experimenting with locally vs. externally developed designs. While most of these students experienced academic gains through third grade, schools using externally developed designs were generally achieving greater academic gains for their students. Schools often drew unifying strength and focus from their associations with external, reform-focused organizations. It was often the case that the tighter the connection, the greater the school's ability to sustain the reform. Both Comer SDP-A and SFA-A in Figure 3 had strong histories of connections to the respective program development teams.

In retrospect, it does not seem surprising that the two schools in Figure 7 produced unusually large gains in reading. Each involved a relatively strong implementation, began early, involved virtually the whole faculty, and sustained connections over many years to a focused national reform effort.

Finding #5: A series of findings regarding classroom activities across virtually all of the programs was, in one sense, distressing. Extensive observations of class periods and students' whole school days provided a picture of instruction driven by management issues, of very uneven access to subjects beyond reading/ language arts and mathematics, and of reforms often stifled by seemingly straightforward issues, such as scheduling.

Over the three years of *Special Strategies*, we conducted nearly 1,000 hours of detailed classroom observations, and gathered nearly 200 detailed descriptions from observations of students' whole school days. These observations provided a particularly valuable window through which to view programs and their impacts. They are described in detail in the *Special Strategies First Year, Second Year, and Final Reports.* However, a few generalizations from those data follow:

There were often considerable differences between the program as described and the program as observed in the lives of students. For every program, we observed examples of "it" being received by students almost exactly as intended, and of "it" being highly compromised. Design components, however elegant, are irrelevant if they don't affect students' days.

Elementary students had widespread access to reading/language arts and mathematics, but access to curricula in science, social studies, computers and writing was very uneven. This replicates a series of earlier, similar findings (e.g., Brown, 1991; Means, Chelemer, & Knapp, 1991; for review, see Brophy & Good, 1986). The good news was that virtually all students were receiving daily instruction in a few core subjects. However, on many days many students simply received no instruction in the sciences or in writing. Further, it was unclear where most teachers were to find the necessary planning time for diverse subjects, given five hours per day of teaching time, a press to focus on reading and math, and limited support or accountability for science and writing.

Special Strategies elementary schools used a wide variety of approaches to literacy instruction; however, the predominant modes observed were teacher-led and discrete skills instruction. Few of the observed sites consistently provided instruction emphasizing student inquiry across the three years. Few of the whole school day observations recorded sustained periods of student reading or applying what they were learning.

At the high school level, recurring, multi-year scheduling problems-particularly, but not exclusively, in mathematics and the sciences-often hindered implementation. Limited faculty understanding of and commitment to CES principles, and a scarcity of time reserved for teachers to work together, were also obstacles.

Finding #6: The challenges faced by Special Strategies schools attempting to educate large numbers of students at risk were often enormous, and resources with which to address those challenges were often in short supply.

In three years of fieldwork we visited several nominated-as-exemplary schools where instructional materials were too often scarce and instruction far from optimal, where paint was peeling in classrooms and halls, where teachers told us that on Mondays some students devour their federally subsidized free breakfast because it is the first regular meal they have had since their Friday free lunch, where teachers' cars were parked surrounded by barbed wire, where armed guards met visitors at the door, and in one case, where people had been found dead in the elementary school stairwells between *Special Strategies* visits. It was easy for us to understand why Kozol (1991) wrote *Savage Inequalities* and Kotlowitz (1991), *There Are No Children Here.*

Finding #7: Schools used federal compensatory education funds to create or adopt, and then sustain, new programs they often could not have considered otherwise. In the hands of instructionally focused, creative educational administrators and teachers, Chapter 1 became the primary engine for reform in otherwise distressed schools.

A school's ability to obtain and sustain sufficient fiscal support was often critical to implementation success. While a few schools obtained a few years of support from private foundations or businesses, and others received special district funding to improve low-achieving schools, the importance of Chapter 1 funds for facilitating reform in schools serving high numbers of financially disadvantaged families could hardly be overstated. In particular, the Chapter 1 schoolwide project option often created an environment in which administrators and teachers firmly believed that long-term support would be provided for their reform efforts[11]. The belief that adequate fiscal support would be available was often crucial during the initial choice and implementation phases, and the presence of actual support was often crucial during advanced implementation and refinement.

When funding was for a finite period, even for as long as five years, that was often effectively used by opponents of the reform as "proof" that the reform would not last. In one memorable school, a veteran teacher opined that "all of these reforms are alike: Mastery Learning, Madeline Hunter, the Coalition of Essential Schools". Asked how such seemingly diverse changes resembled each other, the teacher explained, "I was here before the first one [Mastery Learning] arrived, and I'll be here after the last [CES] is gone." Even five years of Re:Learning funding did not dissuade him and several colleagues from believing they could outlast this latest reform effort. In the absence of strong administrative commitment to Coalition principles, and in the presence of "short-term" (e.g., five-year!) funding, CES was effectively "outlived" by the naysayers. By contrast, less-potentially-coherent Chapter 1 schoolwide projects were often sustained, in part because the teachers believed Chapter 1 was permanent.

Fullan and Miles (1992) observed that "Change is resource-hungry" (p. 750). In *Special Strategies*, when resources were removed as a result of local fiscal problems, or even when resources were repeatedly threatened over several years, the effect was always to permanently hobble or kill the reform effort.

> *Finding #8: Most of the programs studied in Special Strategies are continuing to evolve and expand. These systematic self-improvements bode well for the future of school reform.*

Reading Recovery is exploring methods of connecting its reading program to whole school reform. The version of Computer Curriculum Corporation's software studied in *Special Strategies* was "Release 14," running on Intel 80286 processor computers. The current version of CCC is "Release 16," running on 80486, Pentium, and Power Macintosh equipment. Other CAI programs have made similar advances. Dr. James Comer, founder of the Comer School Development Program, and Dr. Theodore Sizer, founder of the Coalition of Essential Schools, are both participating in one of the New American Schools (NAS) designs. Their hybrid NAS design is called Authentic Teaching, Learning, and Assessment for all Students, or ATLAS Schools (Orrell, 1996). Similarly, the Success for All staff are involved in a NAS sponsored Success for All extension, Roots and Wings (Slavin, Madden, & Wasik, 1996). The distributors of the METRA program now market their materials as part of a schoolwide paired-reading project. By law, all Chapter 1/Title I schoolwide projects re-examine their progress every three years and undertake program refinements based on that self-study.

It is possible that the developments described above are leading to the gradual evolution of better schooling systems for the U.S. If so, that evolution may be the most important trend chronicled in *Special Strategies*.

DISCUSSION

Combined with the larger *Prospects* study, three years of *Special Strategies* data have provided an unusual glimpse into the practical, day-to-day and year-to-year workings of "promising programs" in the lives of at-risk students and their schools. The picture that emerges simultaneously provides cause for hope and cause for worry.

The troubling news was that many of the schools serving America's most disadvantaged students were and remain, as Kozol (1991) and Natriello, McDill, and Pallas (1990) pointed out, in the situation of needing to succeed in environments that are not conducive to students' success. Even when *Special Strategies* researchers visited schools nominated as providing exemplary implementations of some of America's most promising educational programs, research teams often saw very uneven implementation of programs.

Clearly, the good news was that at some schools, often located in very disadvantaged contexts, educators were using "promising programs" to significantly improve the academic lives and performances of many students placed at risk. Where the faculty and administration had considered diverse options and chosen a program matched to local needs, where principals and central administrators sustained a focus on full implementation plus intelligent local adaptation, where technical assistance and staff development were continuing and targeted to specific issues and problems, and where the curriculum was demanding, the effects on students' achievements were dramatic.

In some regards, *Special Strategies* replicated several previous studies. The *Follow Through* studies (Stallings & Kaskowitz, 1974), Crandell et al (1982), and *Innovations Up Close* (Huberman & Miles, 1984) indicated that some programs, well implemented, can make a positive difference in students' lives. Aiken (1942) and Goodlad (1970) found much the same variation in implementation levels within and among schools implementing "promising programs" that was found in *Special Strategies*, though with less evidence of positive effect. Much evidence of conditions positively affecting implementation similar to those found in *Special Strategies* can also be found in Fullan's *The New Meaning of Educational Change* (1991). What was new in *Special Strategies* was the strength of evidence that some programs, well implemented, appear to help students make dramatic academic progress; that pursuing schoolwide change may well be worth the effort; that intensive early intervention may yet be the best bet; and that after a third of a century of research on school change, we still have not provided adequate human and fiscal resources, appropriately targeted, to make large-scale program improvements a reliably consistent reality in schools serving students placed at risk.

While the future holds ample reasons for deep concern, we choose to end this overview of *Special Strategies* on a positive note. We now know a great deal about the necessary conditions for positive school change. We know that some programs, well implemented, can make dramatic differences in students' academic achievement. We know that programs have emerged during the 1980s and 1990s that may offer additional, valid options to schools serving large numbers of students placed at risk. We know that many of these programs are continuing to evaluate and develop themselves in ways that should further improve their impacts. Assuming that funding for long-term examination of the processes and effects of these and other programs comes forward, the 21st century can dawn with all students having the potential and the programmatic support to succeed in school.

Implications for Practice:

- There remains no substitute for a school conducting a thorough and fully candid self-audit, and setting multi-year goals based on that audit.
- It is important to work to achieve whole-school participation in any change effort. There are fewer and fewer reasons for trying locally to invent all aspects of a school improvement effort.
- It is important and rewarding to join with like-minded other schools and professionals.

Stay the course.

Implications for Research:

The current state of the field of school improvement research is such that many, many studies are needed. Among our suggestions are the following:

- Studies of how and why schools decide to become involved in school improvement/school restructuring efforts, and studies of the different effects of those diverse reasons for beginning.
- Studies of the implementability of various reforms and sub-reform packages.
- Assuming virtually full implementation of a design, what are the typical effects in areas deemed important to the designers/disseminators?
- Assuming a norm of "mutual adaptation," more studies are needed of the contextual effectiveness of diverse reforms.
- What are the policy environments that foster, and/or hinder, full implementation, mutual adaptation, or non-implementation of each design? Of all designs?

SUMMARY

This chapter began with a series of analogies to larger areas of progress in the material well-being of people and civilizations. Fundamentally, those advances have followed the development and dissemination of new, powerful technologies.

In this chapter data were presented from a study of 10 promising programs for improving the academic achievements of students who are at risk of falling far behind in school. These designs may be thought of as attempts at improved technologies. The findings of the *Special Strategies* studies offer some hope that the U.S. may be evolving some beginning technologies for helping schools improve.

It is important to frame conclusions about these programs within a moment in time. It would make no more sense to claim that the Comer School Development Program or Success for All was (or, together, are) "the answer," than it would to say that the sulfa drugs of the 1930s (the first "miracle drugs"), were "the answer." Rather, the reforms studied in *Special Strategies* can be (and, in the cases of the sulfa drugs, were), a next quite valuable step along a long and continuing road. As with the "miracle drugs", the developers themselves continue to modify the existing treatments, and others continue the search for ever-more-promising interventions. Note, for example, that several of the developers involved in the *Special Strategies* designs are now involved in several of the New American Schools Designs (Stringfield, Ross, & Smith, 1996). As in other areas, many of those efforts may prove fruitless, in and of themselves. This would not make them failures. What is important is to gather enough data on each effort so that the next generation of researchers and practitioners will not have to repeat those efforts, and can build on our successes.

Ours is a very young field. Medicine required hundreds of years to reach its current advanced and rapidly advancing state. Although modern cultures have found ways to reduce the "cycle time" of research, development and dissemination of finding and practice, inevitably there is a required element of restless patience.

Evolving better designs is a process that takes years. Evaluations of those modified designs, if they are to be of any value, will be longitudinal, adding more years to the process. Our field had a great deal of important work in front of it. We need to refine our skills at working very hard, patiently.

ENDNOTES

[1] The conduct of the Special Strategies studies and the preparation of the related reports were sponsored by the U.S. Department of Education, Office of Policy and Planning, under Contracts Nos. LC90010001 and LC90010002 (Dr. Elois Scott, Project Officer). The preparation of this chapter was supported by a grant from the Office of Educational Research and Improvement, U.S. Department of Education, to the Center for Research on the Education of Students Placed at Risk at Johns Hopkins and Howard Universities (Grant No. R117D-40005). However, any opinions expressed by the authors are their own, and do not represent the policies or positions of the U.S. Department of Education.

[2] A new high point of presidential interest in education may have been reached in President Clinton's 1997 State of the Union Address, in which he outlined a 10 point plan to improve the education of all American children.

[3] The 1988 reauthorization of Chapter 1 had allowed schools serving 75+% highly disadvantaged students to stop targeting services, and instead use federal compensatory education funds to improve the entire school. These were known as "schoolwide projects."

[4] We are indebted to Matthew Miles for providing this classification scheme.

[5] The norm-referenced test chosen for Prospects, and hence used in Special Strategies, was the Comprehensive Test of Basic Skills, Fourth Edition (CTBS-4, CTB/McGraw-Hill, 1989).

[6] A full description of the relevant Special Strategies and Prospects data sets can be found in the Special Strategies Final Report, Chapters 16–18, and Technical Appendix I.

[7] An NCE is a normalized standard score matching the percentile distribution at values of 1, 50, and 99 with a mean of 50 and a standard deviation of 21.06 (Tallmadge & Wood, 1981). A student with an NCE score below 50 on a particular test would have scored below the national average on that test. A student with an NCE score of 1 would have scored at the first percentile, with 99% of all students having a higher score.

[8] In this analogy it does not follow that all educational improvement designs are equal and merely different. Chemotherapy can successfully treat some forms of cancer. Laetrile, though once a widely-discussed fad, never demonstrated that ability. Given a specific problem, some reforms are almost certainly superior to others. However, the diversity of challenges facing schools serving large numbers of students placed at risk is considerable, and a variety of programs or program components may be required to address any one of those challenges at a specific school. To pursue the medical analogy somewhat further, some "drugs" (e.g., vaccinations) prevent diseases and the need for more drugs. Similarly, successful early interventions may help reduce or eliminate the need for more expensive later interventions.

[9] Other studies, involving programs not studied in Special Strategies, provide evidence of positive effects in the middle school years, e.g., Pogrow, 1990; Stevens & Durkin, 1992; MacIver & Plank, 1996. However, the general trend favoring early intervention found in Special Strategies appears to be reflective of the larger field (Slavin, Karweit, & Wasik, 1994).

[10] Analyses including individual programs and schools are available in the Special Strategies Final Report, Chapters 15–18.
[11] For an example of a school currently suffering from the removal of Chapter 1/Title I funding, see Hirshman (1996).

REFERENCES

Abt Associates, Johns Hopkins University, Educational Testing Service, & WESTAT. (1988). *Design of the Chapter 1 longitudinal study*. Chicago: Abt Associates.

Adler, M. (1983). *The Paideia proposal: An educational manifesto*. NY: Macmillan.

Aikin, W. M. (1942). *The story of The Eight Year Study*. New York: Harper.

Berman, P., & McLaughlin, M. (1977). *Federal programs supporting educational change (Vol. VII), Factors affecting implementation and continuation*. Santa Monica, CA: Rand.

Brophy, J. E., & Good, T. (1986). Teacher behavior and student achievement. In M. Wittrock (Ed.), *Handbook of research on teaching* (3rd ed.). New York: Macmillan.

Burke, J. (1995). *Connections*. London: Little, Brown, & Co.

Comer, J. P. (1988). Educating poor minority children. *Scientific American*, **259** (5), 42–48.

Crandall, D. and associates. (1982). *People, policies and practices: Examining the chain of school improvement* (Vols. 1–10). Andover, MA: The NETWORK.

CTB/McGraw-Hill. (1989). *The comprehensive tests of basic skills*. Monterey, CA: CTB/McGraw-Hill.

Cuban, L. (1993). *How teachers taught* (2nd ed.). New York: Teachers College Press.

Edmonds, R. (1979). Effective schools for the urban poor. *Educational Leadership, 37*, 15–27.

Fullan, M. (1991). *The new meaning of educational change*. New York: Teachers College Press.

Fullan, M., & Miles, M. (1992). Getting reform right: What works and what doesn't. *Phi Delta Kappan, 73*(10), 744–752.

Goodlad, J., & Klein, M. F. (1970). *Behind the classroom door*. Worthington, OH: Charles A. Jones.

Hernstein, R. J., & Murray, C. (1994). *The Bell curve: Intelligence and class structure in American life*. New York: Free Press.

Hiebert, E. H. (1994). Reading recovery in the United States: What difference does it make to an age cohort? *Educational Researcher, 23*(9), 15–25.

Hirshman, J. (1996). Lingelbach Elementary School: A case study of a Chapter 1 schoolwide project. *Journal of Education for Students Placed at Risk, 1*(2), 135–146

Huberman, M., & Miles, M. (1984). *Innovation up close*. New York: Plenum.

Kennedy, M. (1978). Findings from the Follow Through Planned Variation Study. *Educational Researcher 7*(6), 3 – 11.

Kotlowitz, A. (1991). *There are no children here*. New York: Doubleday.

Kozol, J. (1991). *Savage inequalities*. New York: Crown, Harper Perennial.

Levin, H. M., Glass, G. V., & Meister, G. R. (1984). *Cost effectiveness of four educational interventions* (Project No. 84-A11). Washington, DC: National Institute of Education.

MacIver, D., & Plank, S. (1996). *Creating a motivational climate conducive to Talent Development in middle schools: Implementation and effects of Student Team Reading*. Technical Report #4, Center for Research on the Education of Students Placed At Risk. Baltimore: Johns Hopkins University.

Means, B., Chelemer, C., & Knapp, M. (1991). *Teaching advanced skills to at-risk students*. San Francisco: Jossey-Bass.

National Diffusion Study Group. (1992). *Educational programs that work* (18th ed.). Longmont, CO: Sopris West.

Natriello, G., McDill, E. L., & Pallas, A. M. (1990). *Schooling disadvantaged children: Racing against catastrophe*. New York: Teachers College Press.

Orrell, C. (1996). ATLAS Communities: Authentic teaching, learning, and assessment for all students. In S. Stringfield, S. Ross, & L. Smith (Eds.), *Bold plans for school restructuring: The New American Schools designs*. Mahwah, NJ: Lawrence Erlbaum Associates.

Pechman, E., & Fiester, L. (1996). Creating good schools for children in poverty through Title I schoolwide programs. *Journal of Education for Students Placed at Risk, 1*(2), 173–194.

Pinnell, G. S. (1989). Reading Recovery: Helping at-risk children learn to read. *The Elementary School Journal, 90*(2), 161–183.

Pogrow, S. (1990). Challenging at-risk students: Findings from the HOTS program. *Phi Delta Kappan, 71*, 389–397.

Puma, M. J., Jones, C., Rock, D., & Fernandez, R. (1993). *Prospects The Congressionally mandated study of educational growth and opportunity, Interim report.* Bethesda, MD: Abt Associates.

Sizer, T. R. (1984). *Horace's compromise: The dilemma of the American high school.* Boston: Houghton Mifflin.

Sizer, T. R. (1996). *Horace's hope.* New York: Houghton Mifflin.

Slavin, R. E. (1989). The PET and the pendulum. *Phi Delta Kappan,* 70(10), 752–758.

Slavin, R. E., Karweit, N. L., & Wasik, B. A. (1994). *Preventing early school failure: Research, policy, and practice.* Boston: Allyn and Bacon.

Slavin, R. E., Madden, N. A., Dolan, L. J., & Wasik, B. A. (1996). Roots and Wings: Universal excellence in elementary education. In S. Stringfield, S. Ross, & L. Smith (Eds.), *Bold plans for school restructuring: The New American Schools designs.* Mahwah, NJ: Lawrence Erlbaum Associates.

Slavin, R. E., Madden, N. A., Dolan, L. J., Wasik, B. A., Ross, S., Smith, L., & Dianda, M. (1996). Success for All: A summary of research. *Journal of Education for Students Placed At Risk,* 1(1), 41–76.

Slavin, R. E., Madden, N.A., Karweit, N. L., & Wasik, B. A. (1992). *Success for All: A relentless approach to prevention and early intervention in elementary schools.* Arlington, VA: Educational Research Service.

Slavin, R. E., Stringfield, S., & Winfield, L. F. (1990). *Effective alternatives to traditional Chapter 1 programs.* Baltimore, MD: Johns Hopkins University, Center for Research on Effective Schooling for Disadvantaged Students.

Stallings, J., & Kaskowitz, D. (1974). *Follow through classroom observation evaluation (1972–1973)* (SRI Project RU-7370). Menlo Park, CA: Stanford Research Institute.

Stevens, R., & Durkin, S. (1992). *Using Student Team Reading and Student Team Writing in middle schools: Two evaluations.* Technical Report #36, Center for Research on Effective Schooling for Disadvantaged Students. Baltimore: Johns Hopkins University.

Stringfield, S., Millsap, M. A., Winfield, L., Brigham, N., Yoder, N., Moss, M., Nesselrodt, P., Schaffer, E., Bedinger, S., & Gamse, B. (1993). *Urban and suburban/rural Special Strategies for educating disadvantaged children: Second year report.* Washington, DC: U.S. Department of Education, Office of Policy and Planning.

Stringfield, S., Millsap, M. A., Herman, R., Yoder, N., Brigham, N., Nesselrodt, P., Schaffer, E., Karweit, N., Levin, M., Smith, L., Gamse, B., Puma, M., Rosenblum, S., Randall, B., & Stevens, R. (1996). *Urban and suburban/rural special strategies for educating disadvantaged children: Final report.* Washington, DC: U.S. Department of Education.

Stringfield, S., Datnow, A. & Nunnery, J. (in progress). Reconceptualizing research on school change. In K.S. Louis & J. Murphy (Eds.), *Second Handbook of Research on Educational Administration.* Washington, D.C.: American Educational Research Association.

Stringfield, S., Ross, S., & Smith, L. (1996). *Bold plans for school restructuring.* Mahwah, NJ: Lawrence Erlbaum Associates.

Stringfield, S., Winfield, L., Millsap, M.A., Puma, M., Gamse, B., & Randall, B. (1994). *Special strategies for educating disadvantaged children: First year report.* Washington, DC: U.S. Department of Education.

Swartz, S., & Klein, A. (1997). *Research in reading recovery.* Portsmouth, NH: Heinemann.

Tallmadge, G. K., & Wood, C. T. (1981). *User's Guide: ESEA Inc. Title I evaluation and reporting system.* Mountain View, CA: RMC Research.

Thomas, L. (1979). Medical lessons from history. In L. Thomas (Ed.), *The medusa and the snail.* New York: Viking.

Williams, B. I., Richmond, P. A., & Mason, B. J. (Eds.). (1986). *Designs for compensatory education: Conference proceedings and papers.* Washington, DC: Research and Evaluation Associates, Inc.

Yenne, B. (1996). *The world's worst aircraft.* New York: Barnes & Noble.

International Handbook of Educational Change - Table of Contents

ANDY HARGREAVES. ANN LIEBERMAN, MICHAEL FULLAN AND DAVID HOPKINS
International Handbook of Educational Change - Introduction

THE ROOTS OF EDUCATIONAL CHANGE
Ann Lieberman, Editor
Preface

Introduction: The Growth of Educational Change as a Field Study:
Understanding its Roots and Branches

I. The Roots

SEYMOUR SARASON
World War II and Schools

MATTHEW MILES
Finding Keys to School Change: A 40-Year Odyssey

MILBREY W. MCLAUGHLIN
Listening and Learning From the Field: Tales of Policy Implementation and Situated Practice

PETER MORTIMORE
The Vital Hours: Reflecting on Research on Schools and their Effects

LOUIS M. SMITH
A Kind of Educational Idealism: Integrating Realism and Reform

MALCOLM SKILBECK
School-Based Curriculum Development

DAN LORTIE
Unfinished Work: Reflections on Schoolteacher

JOSEPH GIACQUINTA
Seduced and Abandoned: Some Lasting Conclusions about Planned
Change from the Cambire School Study

KENNETH SIROTNIK
Ecological Images of Change: Limits and Possibilities

ERNEST HOUSE AND PATRICK MCQUILLAN
Three Perspectives on School Reform

MICHAEL FULLAN
The Meaning of Educational Change: A Quarter of a Century of
Learning

II. Expanding the Dialogue

IVOR GOODSON
Patterns of Curriculum Change

MARK HOLMES
Change and Tradition in Education: The Loss of Community

CLEO H. CHERRYHOLMES
Educational Reform, Modernity and Pragmatism

EXTENDING EDUCATIONAL CHANGE
Andy Hargreaves, Editor

Introduction: Pushing the Boundaries of Educational Change

I. Contexts

DEAN FINK AND LOUISE STOLL
Educational Change: Easier Said than Done

AMY STUART WELLS, SIBYLL CARNOCHAN, JULIE SLAYTON, RICKY LEE ALLEN
AND ASH VASUDEVA
Globalization and Educational Change

WILLIAM BOYD
Markets, Choices and Educational Change

CHRIS BIGUM AND JANE KENWAY
New Information Technologies and the Ambiguous Future of
Schooling - Some Possible Scenarios

HEATHER-JANE ROBERTSON
Public Education in a Corporate-Dominated Culture

SONIA NIETO
Cultural Difference and Educational Change in a Sociopolitical
   Context

JIM CUMMINS
Language Issues and Educational Change

JILL BLACKMORE
The Politics of Gender and Educational Change: Managing Gender
   or Changing Gender Relations?

MAVIS G. SANDERS AND JOYCE L. EPSTEIN
School-Family-Community Partnerships and Educational Change:
   International Perspectives

II. Challenges

LEW ALLEN AND CARL D. GLICKMAN
Restructuring and Renewal: Capturing the Power of Democracy

LYNNE MILLER
Redefining Teachers, Reculturing Schools: Connections, Commitments
   and Challenges

JOSEPH BLASE
The Micropolitics of Educational Change

ANDY HARGREAVES
The Emotions of Teaching and Educational Change

THOMAS J. SERGIOVANNI
Organization, Market and Community as Strategies for Change:
   What Works Best for Deep Changes in Schools

DEBORAH MEIER
Authenticity and Educational Change

WILLIAM MULFORD
Organizational Learning and Educational Change

LINDA DARLING-HAMMOND
Policy and Change: Getting Beyond Bureaucracy

FUNDAMENTAL CHANGE
Michael Fullan, Editor

Introduction: Scaling Up the Educational Change Process

I. Macro Change

CARL BEREITER AND MARLENE SCARDAMALIA
Beyond Bloom's *Taxonomy:* Rethinking Knowledge for the Knowledge
   Age

DAN KEATING
A Framework for Educational Change: Human Development in the
   Learning Society

ANN LIEBERMAN AND MAUREEN GROLNICK
Educational Reform Networks: Changes in the Forms of Reform

NOBUO KEN SHIMAHARA
Educational Change in Japan: School Reforms

MICHAEL BARBER
National Strategies for Educational Reform: Lessons from the British
   Experience Since 1988

MEL WEST
Quality in Schools: Developing a Model for School Improvement

DALE MANN AND VLADIMIR BRILLER
School Administration in Russia: Centralization Versus
   Decentralization

II. Large Scale Strategies for School Change

HENRY LEVIN
Accelerated Schools: A Decade of Evolution

MAX ANGUS AND WILLIAM LOUDEN
Systemic Reform in a Federal System: The National Schools Project

EDWARD JOYNER
Large-Scale Change: The Comer Perspective

ROBERT CROWSON AND WILLIAM BOYD
New Roles for Community Services in Educational Reform

III. Professional Development for Reform

NINA BASCIA
Teacher Unions and Educational Reform

MARILYN COCHRAN-SMITH
Teaching for Social Change: Towards a Grounded Theory of Teacher
  Education

JEANNIE OAKES, KEVIN WELNER, SUSAN YONEZAWA AND RICKY LEE ALLEN
Norms and Politics of Equity-Minded Change: Researching the "Zone
  of Mediation"

MARK SMYLIE AND GEORGE S. PERRY
Restructuring Schools for Improving Teaching

LAWRENCEINGVARSON
Teaching Standards: Foundations for Professional Development
  Reform

THE PRACTICE AND THEORY OF SCHOOL IMPROVEMENT
David Hopkins, Editor

Introduction: Tensions in and Prospects for School Improvement

I. Towards a Theory of School Development

PER DALIN
Developing the Twenty-First Century School: A Challenge to
  Reformers

KAREN SEASHORE LOUIS
Reconnecting Knowledge Utilization and School Improvement:
  Two Steps Forward, One Step Back

JAAP SCHEERENS
The School Effectiveness Knowledge Base as a Guide for School
  Improvement

II. The Contemporary Context of School Improvement

ROLF LANDER AND MATS EKHOLM
School Evaluation and Improvement: A Scandinavian View

PETER CUTTANCE
Quality Assurance Reviews as a Catalyst for School Improvement in
  Australia

BETTY LOU WHITFORD AND KEN JONES
Assessment and Accountability in Kentucky: How High Stakes Affects
  Teaching and Learning

III. Tensions and Contrasts in School Improvement Strategies

MIKE WALLACE
Innovations in Planning for School Improvement: Problems and
  Potential

GARY MCCULLOCH
Curriculum Reform, Educational Change, and School Improvement

BRUCE JOYCE AND EMILY CALHOUN
The Conduct of Inquiry on Teaching: The Search for Models more
  Effective than the Recitation

JOHN SMYTH
Three Rival Versions and a Critique of Teacher Staff Development

JENNIFER NIAS
Why Teachers Need their Colleagues: A Developmental Perspective

IV The Effectiveness of School Improvement Strategies

DAVID REYNOLDS
"World Class" School Improvement: An Analysis of the Implications
  of Recent International School Effectiveness and School
  Improvement Research for Improvement Practice

EMILY CALHOUN AND BRUCE JOYCE
"Inside-Out" and "Outside-In": Learning from Past and Present
  School Improvement Paradigms

ROBERT SLAVIN
Sands, Bricks, and Seeds: School Change Strategies and Readiness for
  Reform

SAM STRINGFIELD, MARY ANN MILLSAP, AND REBECCA HERMAN
Using "Promising Programs" to Improve Educational Processes and
  Student Outcomes